LIBRARY OF NEW TESTAMENT STUDIES

671

Formerly Journal for the Study of the New Testament Supplement Series

Editor
Chris Keith

Editorial Board
Dale C. Allison, Lynn H. Cohick, R. Alan Culpepper, Craig A. Evans,
Jennifer Eyl, Robert Fowler, Simon J. Gathercole, Juan Hernández Jr.,
John S. Kloppenborg, Michael Labahn, Matthew V. Novenson,
Love L. Sechrest, Robert Wall, Catrin H. Williams, Brittany E. Wilson

ENCOUNTERING THE PARABLES IN CONTEXTS OLD AND NEW

Edited by

T. E. Goud, J. R. C. Cousland, and John Harrison

LONDON • NEW YORK • OXFORD • NEW DELHI • SYDNEY

T&T CLARK

Bloomsbury Publishing Plc

50 Bedford Square, London, WC1B 3DP, UK
1385 Broadway, New York, NY 10018, USA
29 Earlsfort Terrace, Dublin 2, Ireland

BLOOMSBURY, T&T CLARK and the T&T Clark logo
are trademarks of Bloomsbury Publishing Plc

First published in Great Britain 2023
Paperback edition published 2024

Copyright © T. E. Goud, J. R. C. Cousland, John Harrison, and contributors, 2023, 2024

T. E. Goud, J. R. C. Cousland, and John Harrison have asserted their right under the Copyright, Designs and Patents Act, 1988, to be identified as Editors of this work.

All rights reserved. No part of this publication may be reproduced or transmitted in any form or by any means, electronic or mechanical, including photocopying, recording, or any information storage or retrieval system, without prior permission in writing from the publishers.

Bloomsbury Publishing Plc does not have any control over, or responsibility for, any third-party websites referred to or in this book. All internet addresses given in this book were correct at the time of going to press. The author and publisher regret any inconvenience caused if addresses have changed or sites have ceased to exist, but can accept no responsibility for any such changes.

A catalogue record for this book is available from the British Library.

Library of Congress Cataloging-in-Publication Data

Names: Goud, Thomas E., editor; Cousland, J.R.C., editor; Harrison, John, editor.
Title: Encountering the parables in contexts old and new /
edited by T.E. Goud, J.R.C. Cousland, and John Harrison.
Description: London ; New York : T&T Clark, 2022. | Series: The library of New Testament studies, 2513-8790 ; 671 | Includes bibliographical references and index. |
Summary: "This volume examines the material elements and mundane aspects of daily life in the first century that underlie Jesus's Synoptic parables"-- Provided by publisher.
Identifiers: LCCN 2022009485 (print) | LCCN 2022009486 (ebook) |
ISBN 9780567706133 (hb) | ISBN 9780567706171 (paperback) | ISBN 9780567706140 (epdf) |
ISBN 9780567706164 (epub)
Subjects: LCSH: Jesus Christ--Parables.
Classification: LCC BT375.3 .E55 2022 (print) | LCC BT375.3 (ebook) |
DDC 226.8/06--dc23/eng/20220321
LC record available at https://lccn.loc.gov/2022009485
LC ebook record available at https://lccn.loc.gov/2022009486

ISBN:	HB:	978-0-5677-0613-3
	PB:	978-0-5677-0617-1
	ePDF:	978-0-5677-0614-0
	ePUB:	978-0-5677-0616-4

Series: Library of New Testament Studies, volume 671
ISSN 2513-8790

Typeset by: Trans.form.ed SAS

To find out more about our authors and books visit www.bloomsbury.com
and sign up for our newsletters.

Contents

Preface	vii
Abbreviations	ix
INTRODUCTION: ENCOUNTERING THE PARABLES	1
MANY-FOLD YIELDS BY POLYVALENT INTERPRETATION: THE PARABLE OF THE MUSTARD SEED IN SYNOPTIC TRADITION	
Ruben Zimmermann	5
HARVEST IMAGERY IN Q PARABLES	
Dieter T. Roth	31
WRITTEN AND UNWRITTEN OBLIGATIONS: DEPENDENCY RELATIONS IN EARLY ROMAN GALILEE	
Douglas E. Oakman	49
A REALISTIC READING OF THE PARABLE OF THE LOST COIN IN Q: GAINING OR LOSING EVEN MORE?	
Ernest van Eck	64
IN FERMENT: IS JESUS'S PARABLE OF THE LEAVEN HYPERBOLIC OR TRUE TO LIFE?	
J. R. C. Cousland	82
TELLING STORIES IN A VIOLENT WORLD	
Thomas E. Goud	105
οἰκοδεσπότης, κύριος, AND βασιλεύς: IDENTIFYING THOSE WITH SLAVES IN MATTHEAN PARABLES IN LIGHT OF THE LITERARY EVIDENCE AND *REALIA* OF ROMAN PALESTINE IN THE FIRST CENTURY	
John Harrison	129

WHOSE VOICES MATTER?
A PERSISTENT WIDOW IN A POLYPHONIC PARABLE (LUKE 18:1–8)
    Ellen Aasland Reinertsen   150

MIRRORING AND ECHOING:
REALISM AND FIGURATION IN JESUS'S PARABLES
    Stephen I. Wright   170

MATTHEW 20:1–15:
THE PARABLE OF THE WORKERS IN THE VINEYARD
OR OF A MANAGER-DISCIPLE?
    Deborah R. Storie   195

TWENTY YEARS OF EXPERIENCING THE PARABLES IN AFRICA
    Glenna S. Jackson   222

ENCOUNTERING THE PARABLES:
APPRECIATION AND CRITIQUE
    Mary Ann Beavis   240

List of Contributors   257
Index of Parables   259
Index of Sources   261
Index of Authors   271
Index of Subjects   276

Preface

This book had its origins in a meeting of the steering committee of the Synoptic Gospels section of the International Society of Biblical Literature. Sakari Häkkinen graciously hosted that meeting in Kuopio in the days before the conference at Helsinki in July 2018. Glenna Jackson, long-serving chair of the Synoptic Gospels section, Rob Cousland, co-chair with Sakari, John Harrison, who was about to take over for Sakari, and two new people at the table, Tom Goud and Daniel Ayuch, met to discuss the future administration and goals. From our discussions the proposal emerged to focus on the parables in the Synoptic Gospels in the next two to three years. Of particular interest to us was to find ways to connect the parables to their contexts in terms of the realia of the parables and in terms of how those parables might have been seen and heard.

For our meeting in Rome in 2019 we were delighted to have the earlier versions of the papers by Ruben Zimmermann, Dieter Roth, Ernest van Eck, and Ellen Aasland Reinertsen. Of course, as with almost everything in the past two years, our plans were hampered by the rise of the Covid-19 pandemic. The meeting scheduled for 2020 in Adelaide, Australia was cancelled and with that meeting went the opportunity for other papers to get a first presentation in the presence of colleagues. With our optimism still not crushed, we looked forward to 2021 and the meeting at the University of Kent in Canterbury, England. Alas, that too was cancelled. Our wonderfully patient contributors—from Australia, Canada, England, Germany, Norway, and the United Sates—graciously stuck by the project and we carried on; as we look forward to meeting in person again in Salzburg in July 2022, we hope that the completion of this book may also coincide with an end to the pandemic.

We want to thank Dominic Mattos and Chris Keith for their support of this project from the beginning. We are pleased that this book will join the long line of fine volumes of the Library of New Testament Studies under their oversight. We also want to thank Sarah Blake for her role in moving the production forward and the whole team at Bloomsbury. Thanks are also due to Thomas Ellison for his sharp-eyed attention in preparing the indexes and we would be remiss not to give a special thanks to Duncan Burns for his skill, care, and patience.

Finally, our deepest gratitude to our contributors and to our friends and colleagues of the International Meetings of the Society of Biblical Literature.

T. E. Goud
J. R. C. Cousland
John Harrison

Abbreviations

AASOR	*Annual of the American Schools of Oriental Research*
AB	Anchor Bible
ABD	*Anchor Bible Dictionary*
ANE	Ancient Near East
ANRW	*Aufstieg und Niedergang der römischen Welt*
BAR	*Biblical Archaeology Review*
BASOR	*Bulletin of the American Schools of Oriental Research*
BBB	Bonner biblische Beitrage
BBR	*Bulletin for Biblical Research*
BDAG	Bauer, W., F. W. Danker, W. F. Arndt, and F. W. Gingrich, *Greek-English Lexicon of the New Testament and Other Early Christian Literature*
BECNT	Baker Exegetical Commentary on the New Testament
BETL	Bibliotheca Ephemeridum Theologicarum Lovaniensium
BibInt	Biblical Interpretation Series
BTB	*Biblical Theology Bulletin*
BTS	Biblical Tools and Studies
BWANT	Beiträge zur Wissenschaft vom Alten und Neuen Testament
BZ	*Biblische Zeitschrift*
CBQ	*Catholic Biblical Quarterly*
CBQMS	Catholic Biblical Quarterly Monograph Series
CQ	*Classical Quarterly*
CRINT	Compendia rerum iudaicarum ad Novum Testamentum
DJD	Discoveries in the Judaean Desert
EDNT	*Exegetical Dictionary of the New Testament*
EKKNT	Evangelisch-katholischer Kommentar zum Neuen Testament
ETL	*Ephemerides Theologicae Lovanienses*
ExpTim	*Expository Times*
FB	Forschung zur Bibel
FRLANT	Forschungen zur Religion und Literatur des Alten und Neuen Testaments
GNB	Good News Bible
HB	Hebrew Bible
HNT	Handbuch zum Neuen Testament
HTR	*Harvard Theological Review*
ICC	International Critical Commentary

IEJ	*Israel Exploration Journal.*
Int	*Interpretation*
JBL	*Journal of Biblical Literature*
JJS	*Journal of Jewish Studies*
JQR	*Jewish Quarterly Review*
JRS	*Journal of Roman Studies*
JSHJ	*Journal for the Study of the Historical Jesus*
JSJ	*Journal for the Study of Judaism in the Persian, Hellenistic, and Roman Period*
JSNTSup	Journal for the Study of the New Testament Supplement Series
JSPSup	Journal for the Study of the Pseudepigrapha Supplement Series
JTS	*Journal of Theological Studies*
KJV	King James version of the Bible
LCL	Loeb Classical Library
LNTS	Library of New Testament Studies
LSJ	Liddell, H. G., R. Scott, and H. S. Jones, *A Greek English Lexicon*. New ed. Oxford, 1983
LXX	Septuagint
MT	Masoretic Text
NCBC	New Cambridge Bible Commentary
NICNT	New International Commentary on the New Testament
NIDNTT	*New International Dictionary of New Testament Theology*
NIGTC	New International Greek Testament Commentary
NLT	New Living Translation of the Bible
NovT	*Novum Testamentum*
NovTSup	Novum Testamentum Supplement Series
NRSV	New Revised Standard Version of the Bible
NTAbh	Neutestamentliche Abhandlungen
NTS	*New Testament Studies*
NTTS	New Testament Tools and Studies
ÖBS	Österreichische biblische Studien
OCD	Oxford Classical Dictionary
OED	Oxford English Dictionary
PW	*Paulys Real-Encyclopädie der classischen Altertumswissenschaft*
SAC	Studies in Antiquity and Christianity
SBB	Stuttgarter biblische Beiträge
SBLSP	Society of Biblical Literature Seminar Papers
SBLTT	Society of Biblical Literature Texts and Translations
SBS	Stuttgarter Bibelstudien
SNTSMS	Society for New Testament Studies Monograph Series
STAC	Studies and Texts in Antiquity and Christianity
STDJ	Studies on the Texts of the Desert of Judah
SWBA	Social World of Biblical Antiquity
TANZ	Texte und Arbeiten zum neutestamentlichen Zeitalter
TAPA	*Transactions and Proceedings of the American Philological Association*

TDNT	*Theological Dictionary of the New Testament*
TENTS	Texts and Editions for New Testament Study
VC	*Vigiliae Christianae*
WBC	Word Biblical Commentary
WMANT	Wissenschaftliche Monographien zum Alten und Neuen Testament
WUNT	Wissenschaftliche Untersuchungen zum Neuen Testament
ZPE	*Zeitschrift für Papyrologie und Epigraphik*

Introduction:
Encountering the Parables*

And he was teaching them many things in parables,
and in his teaching he said to them: "Listen! Behold...."

Mark 4:2–3

And he said to them, "Therefore every scribe who has
been trained for the kingdom of heaven is like the master
of a household who brings out of his treasure
what is new and what is old."

Matt 13:52

1. Encounters, Contexts, Responses

In Mark 4, Jesus begins his parable of the Sower with the double command to listen and see. Similarly, throughout the gospels, those who have ears are urged to hear the parables. The second command, and its various meanings—to "look" or "see"—is not as common in the gospels, but it, too, draws attention to Jesus's urging his original audience to open their eyes and pay close attention to the parables.[1] In the context of the parable of the Sower, all three synoptic evangelists cite a passage from Isaiah that, at least for Mark and Matthew, forms a sort of parable methodology: "that seeing they may see but not perceive, and hearing they may hear but not understand…" (Isa 6:9). As has been emphasized by much recent scholarship on the parables, Jesus's audiences were presented with narratives that drew on material from a familiar world and, at the same time, were sufficiently enigmatic to invite, and sometimes frustrate, further understanding. Those who first encountered the parables in the contexts of their real and lived experience will have had an immediate grasp of those realities. But, the invitation and frustration inherent in the parables will have been as much a part of their experience as they are for those who encounter those same parables nearly two

---

* The core of this volume originated in the Synoptic Gospels sessions at the international meetings of the Society of Biblical Literature in Helsinki (2018), Rome (2019), and what would have been the meeting in Adelaide (2020) that was cancelled on account of the Covid-19 pandemic.

[1] Luise Schottroff, *The Parables of Jesus*, trans. Linda M. Maloney (Minneapolis: Fortress Press, 2006), is notable for her focus on "seeing" the parables. Part 1 of her book is titled "Learning to See."

thousand years later. Furthermore, the limited capacity to see and hear in contemporary contexts is further compounded by distance in time and space from the realia that informed the ancient encounters. And, of course, one must also reckon with the ways that new contexts impinge on making meaning.

Three important lines of enquiry in parable study have been formative for this work and are woven throughout the following chapters. One is best represented in the work of the Parable Group at Mainz under the direction of Ruben Zimmermann and manifested in a wide range of publications, especially in the monumental *Kompendium der Gleichnisse Jesu*.[2] Zimmermann and his colleagues draw into their work not only careful consideration of the historical and material world of the first century, but also the conceptual and especially the metaphorical contexts of the parables. In addition, they are always attentive to the responses that hearers of the parables may have had and continue to have. The second line of inquiry that informs this collection of papers is the "material turn," as it has been called by John Kloppenborg, and as seen in the work of B. B. Scott, John Dominic Crossan, William Herzog, Richard Rohrbaugh, Luise Schottroff, Douglas Oakman, and Ernest van Eck—to name but a few. The focus on the social, political, economic, and material realia of the first century has been very fruitful and attention must be paid if we are to answer questions like: What does it mean to engage with the world of Jesus and those who heard him in Galilee, on the road, and in Jerusalem? What does it mean to tell stories that draw on the realia of the world in which they are told? What were the sights and sounds, the smells and tastes and, in short, the contexts of that world? The third line of inquiry seeks to connect how the parables may have been seen and heard in ancient contexts with how they have been and continue to be seen and heard. Such inquiry seeks analogues in material contexts, cross-cultural perspectives, and efforts to (re)imagine experiencing these stories.

2. Overview

Ruben Zimmermann's paper sets the tone for exploration of contexts, especially the contexts of original and early audiences. He lays out the key elements of his method of reading parables in a hermeneutical triangle that both constrains and opens the field of interpretation that lies in the space between the narrative features, the socio-economic-historical elements, and the stock metaphors and images that inform the reader/hearer of the parable. He then turns to the specifics of the parable of the Mustard Seed and shows how attention to the horticultural realia, coupled with a consideration of the metaphoric field and the religious/cultural context allows for a range of interpretation and for what he calls a "bounded openness."

---

[2] Ruben Zimmermann et al., eds., *Kompendium der Gleichnisse Jesu* (Gütersloh: Gütersloher Verlagshaus, 2007).

Dieter Roth's contribution, which draws on his work as part of the group at Mainz and especially on his recent book on parables in Q, is clearly complementary to Zimmermann's. In a discussion of harvest imagery in Q parables, Roth focuses on the metaphors and images that form the cultural-religious-imaginative contexts. Although Doug Oakman's paper is not overtly connected to the work of Zimmermann and Roth, it is complementary in that it concentrates on a particular aspect of socio-economic realities, namely dependency relations in Roman Galilee. Unlike most of the papers in this volume which tend to start from the parables and work outward, Oakman begins with the issue of dependency relations and then looks to the ways in which the parables inform and illumine those relations. When juxtaposed, the papers of Roth and Oakman address two of the key fields of inquiry that are fundamental to making sense of the parables.

Oakman's paper also provides clear links with the socio-realistic approach to the parables that Ernest van Eck employs. It is well known that van Eck has important differences with Zimmermann, especially over the matter of metaphor, but his reading of the parable of the Lost Coin, approached through a close study of details of monetary value, the social standing of the woman, the cost of lighting a lamp, and other matters, seeks meaning in expanding the understanding of those very realia. While eschewing metaphor and "theological" interpretations, van Eck does not exclude "something beyond," as noted by Stephen Wright in his paper. In a similar manner J. R. C. Cousland examines the material realia of aspects of breadmaking—from grinding grain through to the use of leaven—in his discussion of the parable of the Leaven. Cousland raises the interpretive questions of hyperbole or "ordinariness" of the realities reflected in this parable and argues that the parable is not hyperbolic, but is nonetheless remarkable; just like the kingdom of heaven.

Tom Goud's and John Harrison's papers are largely descriptive of two aspects of the ancient contexts for the parables: violence and slave ownership. Rather than focus on an effort to "solve" problems of violence in parables such as the Tenants in the Vineyard, Goud seeks to lay a historical and literary foundation for such discussions. He examines the evidence for the persistence, ubiquity, and diversity of violence, as well as the language used in the parables. He then discusses the actors and victims in the parables and insists that the very real violence must not be ignored. Harrison's focus is on six parables in Matthew that include slaveowners. He explores the literary and physical evidence from first-century Palestine to suggest a context for and identity of those slaveowners as part of an elite class. As importantly, he seeks to understand how Matthew's early audiences would have understood slaveowners in contrast to how they might be perceived in contemporary contexts.

Ellen Aasland Reinertsen's paper brings the discussion back to "hearing" in a nuanced and imaginative way. Her focus on the voices in the parable of the Persistent Widow forces careful consideration of who is heard or not heard as well as who is doing the hearing. As Zimmermann pursued *polyvalent readings*, Aasland Reinertsen insists on *polyphonic hearings* in which the voices of the parable itself as well as the reverberations for those who hear are taken into account. Her reminder that even the question of how we construct an imagined "original" hearer is essential. Complementary to Aasland Reinertsen's insights is Stephen Wright's use of "mirroring" and "echoing" as images of the ways in which the parables reflect the real historical contexts as well as reverberate with hearers. He reviews the ways in which the "realistic turn" has engaged with fraught literary problems of allegory, metaphor, synecdoche, metonymy, and narrative, and then turns to an interpretation of the parable of the Sower.

For both Deborah Storie and Glenna Jackson understanding the parables was profoundly and irreversibly affected by their personal experiences in Afghanistan and Africa respectively. Storie examines the parable of the Workers in the Vineyard in light of coming to see it entirely differently after living and working in rural Afghanistan. To that experiential reaction she adds discussion of the theoretical approach that she takes to reading the parables; an approach heavily influenced by the work of Paulo Freire and having much in common with Herzog, Schottroff, or van Eck. Finally, she considers two specific details of the parable of the Workers in the Vineyard that are often overlooked: the manager and the use of denarii for payment.

Glenna Jackson's twenty years of reading the parables with, and hearing the stories from, students and colleagues in Africa has led her to reflect on what she calls "experiential reading." Her approach has similarities to reader-response, but for her the experience of actually engaging with new hearers and tellers is indispensable. These are cross-cultural, contextually sensitive, and experiential encounters with the parables. Jackson has been regularly humbled and enlightened by her encounters with voices and perspectives that she is only too aware are not common, if even present, in her own lived context in America. She begins with the premise that the material context of Jesus's original audience was agrarian, peasant, village life. While fully aware that other factors are important, she notes that, at least in those respects, the people she has met in Africa share important conditions with a Galilean peasant of the first century. She also asks Aasland Reinertsen's question "Whose voices matter?" and the related question, "Who tells the story?"

There are tensions and divergences in these papers, just as surely as there are agreements and through-lines that bind them together. It is for that reason that we speak of contexts, of encounters, of responses; all in the plural and all either explicitly or implicitly seeking to link those very real ancient contexts with our own varied modern contexts. By attending to such matters, we seek to indicate how the parables can continue to be "heard" and "seen" today. In all of this we hope to be good scribes bringing forth from the treasure of the parables at least something of what is new and what is old.

Many-fold Yields by Polyvalent Interpretation: The Parable of the Mustard Seed in Synoptic Tradition

Ruben Zimmermann

1. Basic Hermeneutical and Methodological Aspects

Parables are not easy to understand. The difficulties in comprehending these texts did not only arise with modern readers. The disciples themselves apparently had their difficulties, following Jesus's rhetorical question in Mark 4:13: "Do you not understand this parable? How then will you understand all the parables?" Indeed, incomprehensibility seems to be a constitutive element of parable speech.

1.1. Incomprehensibility Leads to Comprehension

Yet, the ambiguity of the parables is not created in order to annoy or frustrate the readers. In fact, parables are actually found in communication contexts that require clarity of meaning and straightforwardness as they are intended to fulfill a certain communicative function.[1] They are meant, for example, to help settle arguments about the Torah, to expose the problems of family roles or to denounce social injustices. Parables actually should be understood and become meaningful for one's life. But how can the parables' expectation of calling for comprehension be reconciled with their enigmatic character and mysteriousness?

The seemingly paradoxical inner logic of this apparent contradiction is that parables are meant to create understanding through their mysteriousness. *Parables are incomprehensible in order to lead to comprehension.* That is to say, there is a calculated potential for misunderstanding in order to create a deeper understanding.

---

[1] I disagree on that point with Charles Hedrick, *Many Things in Parables: Jesus and His Modern Critics* (Louisville, KY: Westminster John Knox, 2004), 103: "They raise questions and issues but provide no answers." See Ruben Zimmermann, *Puzzling the Parables of Jesus: Methods and Interpretation* (Minneapolis: Fortress Press, 2015), 6.

This process of understanding cannot be restricted to one single meaning. Even though comprehension is the ultimate goal of the hermeneutical process, this goal cannot be equated with finding the solution to a mathematical problem. Parables are not equations. There may be different meanings, and they can even contradict each other. The meaning of a parable will differ according to time and context, a reality which is unequivocally demonstrated in the history of parable interpretation. Different readings of one and the same parable may also occur at different points in one individual's lifetime. It is precisely the many divergent interpretations and the resultant controversy and debate that create an enticement for communication and stimulate a collective search for meaning.

1.2. The Hermeneutical Triangle of Understanding the Parables

The hermeneutics of Jesus's parables remain linked to the fundamental issues of biblical hermeneutics, which themselves are closely interwoven with the hermeneutic discourse of related disciplines such as philosophy, historical studies or literary studies.[2] Within this wide framing I will focus, in a heuristic sense, upon three aspects that have defined the (biblical) discourse on hermeneutics throughout the centuries, namely, the (historical) author, the text, and the readers.

Following Dannhauer's definition of general hermeneutics as employing methodological rules that serve the general interpretation of texts,[3] hermeneutics were considered for a long time to be the methodologically governed *art of interpretation* of a written work. The goal of the process of understanding was therefore to grasp the inherent meaning of the text by means of the correct application of certain interpretive rules. This meaning had to be identical with the original intention of the author. Within this framework, understanding was regarded entirely as a *reconstructive process* through which, for example, deficits in understanding that arose due to the chronological distance from the author and to ignorance concerning the origins and provenance of a text had to be compensated for. The text and its author were clearly in the forefront of the search for meaning. It was Schleiermacher, then, who emphasized *two poles in the process of understanding* and thus assigned a value in the construction of meaning not only to the text and its author, but also to the reader or interpreters. Thus hermeneutics must be described both as "grammatical-historical" and "psychological" interpretation.[4] According to Schleiermacher, the interpreter enters into an inter-

---

[2] See the textbook with sources, Susanne Luther and Ruben Zimmermann, eds., *Studienbuch Hermeneutik: Bibelauslegung durch die Jahrhunderte als Lernfeld der Textinterpretation: Portraits—Modelle—Quellentexte* (Gütersloh: Gütersloher Verlagshaus, 2014).

[3] See Johann C. Dannhauer, *Idea boni interpretis et malitiosi calumniatoris*, 4th ed. (Strassburg: Argentorati, 1652); see excerpts of this text with German translation in Luther and Zimmermann, *Studienbuch Hermeneutik*, CD-Rom and the introduction by Walter Sparn, "Johann Conrad Dannhauer (1603–1666), Allgemeine und Biblische Hermeneutik," in Luther and Zimmermann, eds., *Studienbuch Hermeneutik*, 187–97.

[4] Schleiermacher came to this insight by retrospectively retracing the origins of a speech; thus understanding is the reconstruction of the language and thought in a speech. See Friedrich D. E.

action with the text and its author in which the art of interpretation is described as a (post-)creative process.

In the wake of Schleiermacher and Dilthey, the phenomenological hermeneutics of the twentieth century challenged the concept of understanding as an "object-related process of decoding" and instead concentrated on the subjective process of perception or reception. As Gadamer wrote: "interpreter and text each have their own 'horizon' and…every act of understanding constitutes a fusion of horizons."[5]

In (post-)structuralist and reader-response hermeneutics, focusing on the reader even led to an explicit displacement of the text from its author and its original setting, which Barthes cast in the well-known dictum: the "death of the author."[6] The text was regarded as an autonomous work of art that unfolds its meaning only in the productive "act of reading"[7] and interpretation. "The meaning of the text no longer coincides with what the author wanted to say."[8] Thus, hermeneutics is no longer restricted to the interpretation of a text and is expanded to a *general consideration of understanding* and of the world in which interpretation takes place. As such, the goal of the hermeneutical process is no longer the decoding of textual meaning but the comprehensive interpretation of the self and of the world that is initiated through the engagment with a text.

Although differentiating the various perspectives appears helpful, it would be wrong to separate and isolate the individual aspects. With regard to deconstructionist approaches, U. Eco pressed for a balance between the *intentio lectoris*, the *intentio auctoris* and even an *intentio operis*.[9] Meaning and significance cannot be made merely one-sided by limiting it to only one of the three aspects. In agreement with this perspective, my parable hermeneutics is marked by the conviction that historical author, text, and recipient all belong together and that meaning is constituted in and through their reciprocal engagement with each other.

1.3. The Four-step Method in Interpreting the Parables

The question of understanding parables is closely connected to methodology. A particular question calls for a particular method in order to arrive at an answer. Seen in this way, *methods are hermeneutical keys*, each of which opens a different

---

Schleiermacher, *Hermeneutik und Kritik*, Suhrkamp Taschenbush Wissenschaft 211, ed. and introduction M. Frank, 7th ed. (Frankfurt a. M.: Suhrkamp, 1999), 93–4.

[5] Hans-Georg Gadamer, "Klassische und Philosophische Hermeneutik," in *Wahrheit und Methode: Ergänzungen und Register*, Gesammelte Werke 2.2 (Tübingen: Mohr Siebeck, 1993), 109.

[6] See Roland Barthes, "La mort de l'auteur," in *Oeuvres Complètes*, ed. É. Marty (Paris: Le Seuil, 1994), 491.

[7] See Wolfgang Iser, *Der Akt des Lesens: Theorie ästhetischer Wirkung*, Uni-Taschenbücher 636, 4th ed. (Munich: Fink, 1994).

[8] Paul Ricœur, "Philosophische und Theologische Hermeneutik," in *Metapher: Zur Hermeneutik religiöser Sprache*, ed. P. Ricœur and E. Jüngel (Munich: Kaiser, 1974), 28.

[9] See Umberto Eco et al., *Interpretation and Overinterpretation*, ed. S. Collini (Cambridge: Cambridge University Press, 1992); Umberto Eco, *The Limits of Interpretation* (Bloomington: Indiana University Press, 1990).

lock in order to achieve understanding. In other words, one particular key can unlock only one particular understanding. Each method provides opportunities but each also has its limits. Some methods of analysis open up possibilities of understanding that require connections to be made with other dimensions before they can collectively contribute to the understanding of the text.

In the following I will suggest an integrative and open model for the analysis of parables that can be used for all parable texts. According to my definition of the parable genre,[10] parables are defined as reader-oriented, metaphoric, narrative texts that are found in communicative contexts. Accordingly, the fourfold sequence of the interpretation distinguishes between various key aspects that support this definition: (1) linguistic, narrative analysis, (2) socio-historical analysis, (3) identification of stock metaphors and symbols, (4) summarizing interpretation.

In order to observe the often artistic, literary form of these fictional texts, the interpretation begins with an exact *linguistic, narrative analysis* that identifies narrativity and metaphoricity as the basic criteria of the parable. With regard to the narrative perspective we must examine the literary devices concerning the discourse, the manner of recounting the story (e.g. focalization, implied narrator and reader, time and space matters) and the characters developed (e.g. constellations of characters, classification of characters, traits, activities).

The parables of Jesus acquire their power from the transfer of real experiences and concrete, real life contexts into the religious domain. In order to understand this process of transformation, it is necessary to know the "actual" meaning of the concepts used and the processes described. The parables primarily reflect the environment and life of the people in Palestine, or at least in the Mediterranean world, in the first century CE. If we want to understand the parables, we need to try to enter this world. The research into the geography, clothing and food, objects, work forms and so on is just as interesting as the political and socio-cultural conditions. Thus, *socio-historical analysis* in a broader sense refers to the question of the real requirements for understanding.

The analysis of real experiences and daily life as the source of a metaphor is only one necessary element within the process of the discovery of meaning. Another element is the *identification of stock metaphors and symbols* that were common within Jewish, Greco-Roman, and/or Early Christian communities and that could have had a definitive influence on the understanding of parable texts. Although Jülicher, Schottroff, and Thurén repudiated such concepts as the allegorizing "overforming" (*Überformung*) of the parables, I consider it to be absolutely necessary to investigate the embedding of transferal phenomena in linguistic conventions and traditions. It is not possible to read the parables "unplugged" as

---

[10] See Zimmermann, *Puzzling the Parables of Jesus*, 137–8: I named a bundle of six characteristics, four are core criteria, two are supplemental criteria: "The parable is 1. narratival, and 2. fictional, and 3. realistic, and 4. metaphoric, and/or 5. active in appeal, and/or 6. contextually related."

Thurén more recently has suggested.[11] Language does not start from scratch or with a *tabula rasa* since it is always already culturally conditioned. Semantics, the theory of meaning, has demonstrated that the meaning of a word or text is not only linked to a certain phonetic sound or a certain combination of linguistic characters. Meaning is, in fact, closely bound to the use of a word in an historical and cultural context. So-called historical semantics has investigated, in particular, how the meaning of a word is shaped by the cultural context, formed within traditional use, and transformed in the process of tradition.[12]

Drawing on the theory of Harald Weinrich, I speak here of a "Bildfeldtradition"[13] (the tradition of this imagery) in which we see a traditional coupling of metaphorical domains.[14] A linguistic community can repeatedly connect certain semantic domains so that new metaphors become immediately obvious and understandable within this frame of reference. A metaphor is constructed in order to explain something new and unknown. However, the metaphoric text requires a traditional fixed meaning to be used within a new communication situation. Therefore, within the metaphor the interaction of tradition and innovation can obviously be seen. As Buntfuß states: "Metaphors remind in order to say something new and they renew in order to retain the old."[15]

In the *summarizing interpretation*, the lines of reasoning from the previous analytical steps are brought together in order to arrive at several different coherent interpretation(s). Many exegetes perceive their task to be the production of unambiguous, compelling interpretations. In many cases, these interpretations are put forth as the only possible path of understanding based on linguistic or historical argumentation. I take a different methodological approach. From an epistemological and hermeneutical perspective, historically unambiguous interpretation remains an impossible ideal and it is incorrect to believe that there could be one *interpretatio sancta* for the figurative texts dealt with here. Suggesting one single interpretation even amounts to a conscious disregard of the form of the text set forth in the parables. Furthermore, such a narrowing down of possible meanings would also contradict the hermeneutics and even the theology of the parables. The final step in parable interpretation should actually open up horizons of interpretations, not restrict them.

---

[11] See Lauri Thurén, *Parables Unplugged: Reading the Lukan Parables in Their Rhetorical Context* (Minneapolis: Fortress Press, 2014).
[12] See Dirk Geeraerts, *Diachronic Prototype Semantics: A Contribution to Historical Lexicology* (Oxford: Clarendon Press, 1997); Gerd Fritz, *Historische Semantik*, Sammlung Metzler 313, 2nd ed. (Stuttgart: Metzler, 2006).
[13] Concerning this term, see Harald Weinrich, "Münze und Wort: Untersuchungen an einem Bildfeld," in *Sprache in Texten* (Stuttgart: Klett, 1976), 276–90.
[14] Weinrich, "Münze und Wort"; also Ruben Zimmermann, *Geschlechtermetaphorik und Gottesverhältnis: Traditionsgeschichte und Theologie eines Bildfelds in Urchristentum und antiker Umwelt*, WUNT 2/122 (Tübingen: Mohr Siebeck, 2001), 41–4.
[15] See Markus Buntfuß, *Tradition und Innovation: Die Funktion der Metapher in der theologischen Theoriesprache*, Theologische Bibliothek Töpelmann 84 (Berlin: de Gruyter, 1997), 227.

The reader-oriented hermeneutics of the parables must lead to a polyvalent interpretation. Years ago Tolbert reflected on the affirmation of polyvalence in the interpretation of parables in her work *Perspectives on the Parables: An Approach to Multiple Interpretations*.[16] The multiplicity of interpretation has been positively evaluated particularly in English language exegesis.[17] Nevertheless, this interpretive openness must not be confused with arbitrariness or the postmodern loss of understanding. Straus introduced an accurate image for the tension between openness and limitation with the metaphor of *Spielfeld* (field of play).[18] It is possible to identify clear boundaries for the playing field outside of which the game is no longer possible, where the ball is "out." With regard to our subject, this means that there are clear limitations of understanding that are marked by unambiguous philological elements or set by the limits of historical plausibility, outside of which one must speak of a "misunderstanding."[19]

On a literary-linguistic level there might be philological misinterpretation, for instance, if the term λαμπάδες is translated with "lamps." Such a translation contradicts all other uses of the term in ancient Greek, where it means "torches." A misleading interpretation on the historical level would be that the Samaritan is a temple employee, following the line of the priest and the Levite, because it is obvious that the term Σαμαρίτης refers to an ethnic-geographic origin of a person and not to a certain religious official, or that the innkeeper runs a hospital, because the Christian *hospites* caring for the ill and poor cannot be shown to have existed before the fourth century CE. In the same manner an anti-Jewish reading of Mark 12:1–12, which misunderstands the rhetoric of the parable in an antisemitic way cannot be tolerated on the level of reader-orientated perspective.[20] In other words, there are limits to the variety of interpretations which must be named, though, of course, also debated.

Within these boundaries, however, there is considerable leeway for interpretive possibilities. Interpretation and the creation of meaning do not arise along monocausal routes of explanation. Therefore, at least two or three different interpretations shall be provided within the exegesis of parables next to each other. The different steps finally lead to the following structure of interpretation:

---

[16] Mary A. Tolbert, *Perspectives on the Parables: An Approach to Multiple Interpretations* (Philadelphia: Fortress Press, 1979).

[17] See John D. Crossan, "Polyvalence in Parable Interpretation," in *Cliffs of Fall: Paradox and Polyvalence in the Parables of Jesus* (New York: Seabury Press, 1980), 102; V. George Shillington, ed., *Jesus and His Parables: Interpreting the Parables of Jesus Today* (Edinburgh: T. & T. Clark, 1997), 17–18; see for details Chapter 5.

[18] Erwin Straus, *Vom Sinn der Sinne: Ein Beitrag zur Grundlegung der Psychologie*, 2nd ed. (Berlin: Springer, 1978), 274–80; also Ruben Zimmermann, "Bildersprache verstehen oder die offene Sinndynamik der Sprachbilder: Einführung," in *Bildersprache verstehen: Zur Hermeneutik der Metapher und anderer bildlicher Sprachformen: Mit einem Geleitwort von H.-G. Gadamer*, ed. R. Zimmermann, Übergänge 38 (Munich: Fink, 2000), 25–6.

[19] Forms of misinterpretations can arise from the different perspectives which I have dealt with within the first part of my book *Puzzling the Parables*.

[20] See the history of anti-Jewish reading of Mark 12:1–12 in Tania Oldenhage, *Parables for Our Time: Rereading New Testament Scholarship after the Holocaust* (Oxford: Oxford University Press, 2002).

1. Text: Analyzing Narrative Elements and Context
2. Reality: Mapping the Socio-Historical Background
3. Tradition: Exploring Stock Metaphors and Symbols
4. Meaning: Opening up Horizons of Interpretation

2. The Parable of the Mustard Seed in the Synoptic Tradition (Q 13,18f./Mark 4.30–32/Matthew 13.31–32/Luke 13.18–19)

The tradition of the parable of the mustard seed is exceptional in that it demonstrates a "quadruple tradition", meaning that in addition to Matthew and Luke, the parable is also found in Mark,[21] and in the Gospel of Thomas 20. This multiple attestation is one of the reasons that John P. Meier counts it among the so-called happy few that he accepts as authentic to the historical Jesus.[22] Following the "memory approach," I am not interested in speculative reconstructions concerning the so-called historical Jesus,[23] and focus on the synoptic tradition as varying forms of the parable of the remembered Jesus.

I do believe that there was a sayings source Q, which included this parable given the verbatim overlaps between Matthew and Luke. Following our Mainz Approach, which works with the Q-hypothesis without reconstructing the precise wording of Q,[24] I refrain from presenting a "Q version" of the text. Instead, I give a synopsis only from Mark, Matthew, and Luke. From the viewpoint of redaction criticism, Matthew's version can be seen as a connection or even conflation of the versions in Mark and Q. Carlston states: "By conflating Mk and Q he has made the text into something different from either."[25]

---

[21] There are different explanations about the tradition history of this parable. Some argue for an oral tradition behind the different versions, see Harvey K. McArthur, "The Parable of the Mustard Seed," *CBQ* 33 (1971): 209 n. 201; others for different stages of a literal development, see Franz Kogler, *Das Doppelgleichnis vom Senfkorn und Sauerteig in seiner traditionsgeschichtlichen Entwicklung. Zur Reich-Gottes-Vorstellung Jesu und ihren Aktualisierungen in der Urkirche* (Würzburg: Echter, 1988); Ivor H. Jones, *The Matthean Parables: A Literary and Historical Commentary*, NovTSup 80 (Leiden: Brill, 1995), 322–8; on the double tradition of Q and Mark, see Rudolf Laufen, *Die Doppelüberlieferungen der Logienquelle und des Markusevangeliums*, BBB 54 (Königstein-Bonn: Peter Hanstein Verlag, 1980), 174–97 (on the mustard seed).

[22] John P. Meier, *A Marginal Jew. Volume V, Probing the Authenticity of the Parables* (New Haven: Yale University Press, 2016), 230–40. According to Meier "the parable also meets the criterion of coherence" (239).

[23] See my argument addressing Meier in Ruben Zimmermann, "Memory and Jesus' Parables: J.P. Meier's Explosion and the Restoration of the 'Bedrock' of Jesus' Speech," *JSHJ* 16 (2018): 156–72.

[24] See for details Ruben Zimmermann, "Metaphorology and Narratology in Q Exegesis: Literary Methodology as an Aid to Understanding the Q Text," in *Metaphor, Narrative, and Parables in Q*, WUNT 315, ed. D. T. Roth, R. Zimmermann, and M. Labahn (Tübingen: Mohr Siebeck 2014), 3–10, and Dieter Roth, *Parables in Q* (London: T&T Clark, 2018), 39–44.

[25] Charles E. Carlston, *The Parables of the Triple Tradition* (Philadelphia: Fortress Press, 1975), 26.

Table 1

Mark 4:30–32	Matthew 13:31–32	Luke 13:18–19
Καὶ <u>ἔλεγεν</u>· πῶς <u>ὁμοιώσωμεν</u> τὴν <u>βασιλείαν</u> <u>τοῦ θεοῦ</u> ἢ ἐν τίνι αὐτὴν παραβολῇ θῶμεν;	Ἄλλην παραβολὴν παρέθηκεν αὐτοῖς <u>λέγων</u>· ὁμοία ἐστὶν ἡ βασιλεία τῶν οὐρανῶν	<u>Ἔλεγεν</u> οὖν· τίνι ὁμοία ἐστὶν ἡ βασιλεία <u>τοῦ θεοῦ</u> καὶ τίνι <u>ὁμοιώσω</u> αὐτήν; 19 ὁμοία ἐστὶν
31 ὡς **κόκκῳ σινάπεως**, ὃς ὅταν <u>σπαρῇ</u> ἐπὶ τῆς γῆς,	**κόκκῳ σινάπεως**, ὃν λαβὼν ἄνθρωπος <u>ἔσπειρεν</u> ἐν τῷ ἀγρῷ αὐτοῦ·	**κόκκῳ σινάπεως**, ὃν λαβὼν ἄνθρωπος ἔβαλεν εἰς κῆπον ἑαυτοῦ,
μικρότερον ὂν **πάντων τῶν σπερμάτων** τῶν ἐπὶ τῆς γῆς, 32 καὶ **ὅταν** σπαρῇ, ἀναβαίνει καὶ γίνεται **μεῖζον** πάντων **τῶν λαχάνων** καὶ ποιεῖ <u>κλάδους</u> μεγάλους, ὥστε δύνασθαι ὑπὸ τὴν σκιὰν αὐτοῦ	32 ὃ **μικρότερον** μέν ἐστιν **πάντων τῶν σπερμάτων**, **ὅταν** δὲ <u>αὐξηθῇ</u> **μεῖζον τῶν λαχάνων** ἐστὶν καὶ <u>γίνεται</u> δένδρον, ὥστε ἐλθεῖν	καὶ <u>ηὔξησεν</u> καὶ <u>ἐγένετο</u> εἰς δένδρον,
τὰ πετεινὰ τοῦ οὐρανοῦ κατασκηνοῦν.	**τὰ πετεινὰ τοῦ οὐρανοῦ** καὶ κατασκηνοῦν ἐν τοῖς <u>κλάδοις</u> αὐτοῦ.	καὶ **τὰ πετεινὰ τοῦ οὐρανοῦ** <u>κατεσκήνωσεν</u> ἐν τοῖς κλάδοις αὐτοῦ.

Mark–Matthew–Luke Overlap
Matthew–Luke Overlap (Q)
Mark–Matthew Overlap
<u>Mark–Luke Overlap</u>
Same semantems, but different in grammatical form

He also said, "With what can we compare the kingdom of God, or what parable will we use for it? 31 (it is) like a mustard seed, which, when it is sown upon the earth, is the smallest of all the seeds on earth;	He put before them another parable: "The kingdom of heaven is like a mustard seed that someone took and sowed in his field; 32 it is the smallest of all the seeds,	He said therefore, "What is the kingdom of God like? And to what should I compare it? It is like a mustard seed that someone took and sowed in the garden;

32 yet when it is sown it grows up and becomes the greatest of all shrubs, and puts forth large branches, so that the birds of the heaven can make nests in its shade."	but when it has grown it is the greatest of shrubs and becomes a tree, so that the birds of the air come and make nests in its branches."	it grew and became a tree, and the birds of the air made nests in its branches."

2.1. Text: Analyzing Narrative Elements and Context[26]

There are only very few elements which can be found *expressis verbis* in all three versions (marked **bold**), the Kingdom, the mustard seed and the birds of heaven. Regarding the plot of the narrative, however, there is a solid coherency: the mustard seed is sown into the ground, it grows up and becomes an adult plant (tree/shrub). Finally, the birds of heaven come and make nests.

Let me first have a closer look at the parable according to Mark, which here is the most extended version, and only mention briefly the version of Matthew and Luke. The parable in Mark consists of two parts, each of which is introduced using the same formula. The mustard seed becomes involved in the plot in that it is sown (v. 31: ὃς ὅταν σπαρῇ; v. 32: καὶ ὅταν σπαρῇ). This sowing process is clearly important, for otherwise it would not be mentioned again in the second part. Logically, it is unnecessary in the first part because the act of sowing is immaterial to the size of the mustard seed.[27] And in the next part, the mention of sowing is, in fact, stylistically misplaced because the second part is primarily about the growth of the plant and thus about processes that take place long after sowing.

The two parts have a parallel structure with which the contrast can be sharpened. The mustard seed is "the smallest of all the seeds on the earth" (μικρότερον ὂν πάντων τῶν σπερμάτων) and will become "the greatest of all shrubs" (μεῖζον πάντων τῶν λαχάνων). The addition of πᾶς turns the comparative into a superlative: that which is smaller than "all" is the smallest and that which is greater than "all" is the greatest. The central contrast, thus, is that of the extreme smallness of the mustard seed to the extreme greatness of the mustard shrub, but then both parts are described even more precisely. Though the superlatives are missing in the double tradition, the contrast between the seed and the tree is still evident.[28]

---

[26] See for more details my interpretation in Zimmermann, *Puzzling the Parables*, 240–59.
[27] Gos. Thom. 20 presents the parable in this way: "The disciples said to Jesus, 'Tell us what the Kingdom of Heaven is like.' He said to them, 'It is like a mustard seed, the smallest of all seeds. But when it falls on tilled soil, it produces a great plant and becomes a shelter for birds of the sky'" (trans. according to http://www.sacred-texts.com/chr/thomas.htm). See Uwe-Karsten Plisch, *Gospel of Thomas* (Peabody, MA: Hendrickson, 2008).
[28] See Roth, *Parables in Q*, 301.

In the first place, sowing takes place "upon the earth" and the mustard seed is smaller than all the seeds "on earth." In this ἐπὶ τῆς γῆς is mentioned twice, as if to construct a framing element. In the second part, the mustard seed becomes the subject and the tense changes to the present. It grows (ἀναβαίνει) and its own activity is underlined by the "putting forth" (ποίειν) of the large branches. The fact that μέγας appears again at the end of this phrase (κλάδους μεγάλους) emphasizes the size as the goal of this process of growth. Everything happens smoothly and naturally, and extremely fast. In the previous parable of the "self-growing seed" (Mark 4:26–29), the relationship of narrated time to narrative time had already revealed a stunning time lapse and now the dynamics increase. Whereas Mark 4:28 outlines the individual stages of growth (seed–stalk–head–full grain), the observer in Mark 4:30–32 scarcely has time to imagine the growth process from the "smallest" to the "greatest." There is not even enough time to draw breath between the sowing of the seed and the final, huge shrub.

The final part is attached to the rest of the parable like a postscript. The partial verse is closely related to the second part syntactically and in its contents, so that one could also speak of the second part having two segments. However, it also has a certain independence due to the special vocabulary and the new motif. The conjunction ὥστε indicates that the consequence of this massive growth process will now be revealed. Contrary to what one would expect in a rural society or following the parable of the sower in Mark 4:3–9 or the growing seed (Mark 4:26-29), the praise is not for the high crop yield. Instead, this mustard shrub, which itself is so full of life, becomes a source of life for other creatures. This shift in accent can be described quite precisely by means of character analysis. The passive formulation (being sown) presumes the presence of a sower who throws the seeds onto the earth. This character is, however, not explicitly identified by Mark, which is different from Matt 13:31 and Luke 13:18 where overt reference is made to an ἄνθρωπος. The man, however, does not play an important role, neither in Q, Matthew, nor Luke.[29]

The focus of the parable is clearly the mustard itself, which, at the latest in v. 32, must be regarded as an independent character for here the actions of the mustard seed are narrated: it grows up, becomes…and makes (literally from ποιεῖν) branches. Here the mustard seed is a character[30] that develops a certain degree of complexity because it is subject to a very fast process of development and change.

The growth, however, is not the end in itself. In the third section new characters are introduced: "birds" come and "live" in the large branches rather than simply perching on them. Many translators imagine nests built by the birds,[31] which certainly is a viable option from the reception of the parable. Matthew also interprets the parable in this way when he says ὥστε ἐλθεῖν τὰ πετεινὰ τοῦ

---

[29] See Craig Blomberg, *Interpreting the Parables*, 2nd ed. (Downers Grove, IL: IVP Academic, 2012), 284; Roth, *Parables in Q*, 301.

[30] See Blomberg, *Parables*, 391: "The main 'character'…is the small plant—the seed.…"

[31] The NRSV translates Mark 4:32 as follows: "…so that the birds of the air can make nests in its shade."

οὐρανοῦ καὶ κατασκηνοῦν ἐν τοῖς κλάδοις αὐτοῦ ("so that the birds of heaven come and make nests in its branches," Matt 13:32). However, if we read Mark 4:32 very carefully, we see that he does not say that the birds nest "in the branches." Instead they build the nests in (beneath) the shade (ὑπὸ τὴν σκιὰν αὐτοῦ). This catches our attention. Are these water birds or flightless birds who look to the shade of the mustard bush for protection for their nests on the ground? But why, then, are the birds explicitly identified as birds of the air or heaven? Is there perhaps a deeper meaning in the formulation "in the shade?"

And do these birds in fact build nests? The *terminus technicus* νοσσεύω ("built a nest," see Ezek 31:6),[32] which is found in Greek and biblical writings, is missing here. The term κατασκηνόω, in particular, which occurs only once in the New Testament (Acts 2:26)[33] outside the parable and its parallels (Matt 13:32; Luke 13:19), is a verb used frequently in the Septuagint in translation from the Hebrew שָׁכַן (schachan), where it occurs only once in connection with birds.[34] Otherwise κατασκηνόω stands for people "living" as well as, theologically, for the indwelling of God in people, for example in the tabernacle, the temple, or on Zion (e.g. Zech 2:14–15; 8:3; 11QT 29:8–10).[35] In view of this double semantic, we must ask whether the neutral "birds of the air" as found in the NRSV is a correct translation of τὰ πετεινὰ τοῦ οὐρανοῦ. Clearly, it is meant to create more realism. Certainly, birds are often identified in creation as the animals that populate the heavens (Gen 2:19; LXX Ps 103:12). However, the term οὐρανος stands for heaven ambiguously, as is indicated by the complementary assignment of "heaven and earth" that becomes noticeable with the two-fold mention of γῆ ("earth").

If we look at these spatial details semantically, what we have is the furthest span of the entire world that is occupied by the small mustard seed (see Mark 13:27, 31). Furthermore, in the Gospel of Mark, heaven is not only the place of angels (Mark 12:25; 13:32) and apocalyptic events (Mark 13:25). In Mark 1:10 it was introduced as the origin of the heavenly voice that can be identified with God the Father. Correspondingly, while performing miracles, Jesus looks up to heaven (Mark 6:41; 7:34: "looking up to heaven") and speaks clearly of "the Father in Heaven" (ὁ πατὴρ ὑμῶν ὁ ἐν τοῖς οὐρανοῖς, Mark 11:25). Heaven is the divine sphere. That which is particularly clear in the parable of the mustard seed in Matthew (Matt 13:31–32: βασιλεία τῶν οὐρανῶν - τὰ πετεινὰ τοῦ οὐρανοῦ), who

---

[32] Further references are Jer 31:28 (LXX); Dan 4:12 (καὶ ἐν αὐτῷ τὰ πετεινὰ τοῦ οὐρανοῦ ἐνόσσευον, Dan 4:21).

[33] The noun ἡ κατασκήνωσις is also found in Q/Luke 9:58; Matt 8:20 and is usually translated as "nest," analogous to the den of a fox. However, this is also factually incorrect because birds' nests are normally used for raising young but not for protection and escape, as the fox uses its den.

[34] See Ps 103/104:12: ἐπ᾽ αὐτὰ τὰ πετεινὰ τοῦ οὐρανοῦ κατασκηνώσει ἐκ μέσου τῶν πετρῶν δώσουσιν φωνήν ("By the streams the birds of the air have their habitation; they sing among the branches" [Ps 104:12 NRSV]).

[35] See Bernd Janowski, "Die Einwohnung Gottes in Israel: Eine religions- und theologiegeschichtliche Skizze zur biblischen Schekina-Theologie," in B. Janowski and E. E. Popkes, *Das Geheimnis der Gegenwart Gottes: Zur Schechina-Vorstellung in Judentum und Christentum*, WUNT 318 (Tübingen: Mohr Siebeck, 2013), 3–40.

is known to speak of the "kingdom of heaven" (instead of "of God"), is also true for Mark.

With the reference to the "birds of the heaven", the parable creates a link to the "kingdom of God" in the introduction. Ultimately, the level of reality has already become lucent for the religious dimension at which the parable aims metaphorically. The birds of the heaven can be regarded as a transfer signal that is added to the eternal para-textual introduction and thus underlines the metaphoric character of the text. Therefore, the kingdom of God is explained not only by the smallness and the growth but ultimately also by the fact that the bush is a habitat.

2.2. Reality: Mapping the Socio-historical Background

For the historical background, we must take an excursion into botany. What kind of a plant is found in the parable? Is the extreme contrast between the small seed and the shrub that grows from it realistic or is it an extraordinary rhetorical exaggeration? Where did such a plant grow? Was it a well-known plant or is Jesus using some special knowledge in order to give his message more emphasis?

The Greek term τὸ σίναπι (*sinapi*, "mustard") used in the text is a collective term for various plants.[36] It corresponds to the Hebrew חַרְדָּל; *hareᵉdāl* or Aramaic חַרְדְּלָא; *hareᵉdelā*. The rabbis differentiate linguistically between *ḥardal baladi* (common or native mustard) and *ḥardal mazri* (Egyptian mustard, see also Pliny, *Nat.* XIX 171), but also admit that the two kinds of mustard cannot be distinguished visually.[37]

Even if we cannot clearly identify the mustard of ancient times with the kinds that we know today, we can create plausible analogies that lead us to greater understanding.[38] Today we differentiate between "white mustard" (*sinapis alba*), "field mustard" (*sinapis arvensis*), "black mustard" (*brassica nigra*) and the so-called "mustard tree" (*salvadora persica*). Is it plausible that the version of the parable in Q (Matthew/Luke) points towards a "mustard tree" because we read "and becomes a tree" (Matt 13:32: καὶ γίνεται δένδρον/Luke 13:19: καὶ ἐγένετο εἰς δένδρον)? Even if the "mustard tree" has been used as a reference point for the parable in some scholarly literature,[39] the classification of mustard as a "vegetable crop" or "annual" (v. 32: λάχανον, see Rom 14:2) argues against

---

[36] Synonyms for the term are νᾶπυ (*napy*) or σίναπις (*sinapis*). On the following, see Georg Gäbel, "Mehr Hoffnung wagen (Vom Senfkorn): Mk 4,30par," in *Kompendium der Gleichnisse Jesu*, ed. R. Zimmermann et al., 2nd ed. (Gütersloh: Gütersloher Verlagshaus, 2015), 330–2.

[37] The Halakhic law prohibiting the mixing of different seeds during sowing (Lev 19:19; Deut 22:10), therefore, did not apply to these two types of seeds (*m. Kil.* 1:2). See Gustaf Dalman, *Arbeit und Sitte in Palästina II: Der Ackerbau* (Hildesheim: Bertelsmann, 1928), 293; Paul Billerbeck and Hermann L. Strack, *Kommentar zum Neuen Testament aus Talmud und Midrasch I: Das Evangelium nach Matthäus*, 2nd ed. (Munich: Beck, 1926), 668–9.

[38] Kogler, *Doppelgleichnis*, 48–51; Frank N. Hepper, *Pflanzenwelt der Bibel: Eine illustrierte Enzyklopädie* (Stuttgart: Deutsche Bibelgesellschaft, 1992), 133.

[39] This interpretation was considered in the nineteenth century; see particularly John Forbes Royle, "On the Identification of the Mustard Tree of Scripture," *Journal of the Royal Asiatic Society* 8.15 (1846): 113–37; Adolf Jülicher, *Die Gleichnisreden Jesu II*, 2nd ed. (Tübingen: Mohr Siebeck, 1910), 575–6; François Bovon, *Das Evangelium nach Lukas II: Lk 9,51–14,35*, Evangelisch-katholischer Kommentar zum Neuen Testament 3/2 (Zurich: Benziger, 1996), 413–14.

this interpretation. As such, Mark agrees with the ancient agrarian handbooks that classify mustard as a garden vegetable plant (see Theophrastus, *Hist. plant.* VII 1:1; Pliny, *Nat.* XX 236; Columella, *Rust.* XI 3).[40]

Thus, we are left with black mustard, white mustard, and field mustard, all of which are possibilities as they all occur frequently in Israel as wild plants or weeds.[41] If we consider the sharp contrast between the "smallest" and the "largest," we have an argument for "black mustard" (*brassica nigra*). The seeds of this plant are very small, with a diameter of only one millimeter. The white mustard seed is twice as large as that of black mustard. Furthermore, the black mustard bush grows larger than the others. Dalman reports that mustard bushes at the Sea of Galilee had a height of up to 2.5 to 3 meters[42] and a height of over 2 meters was not unusual. The field mustard plant (*sinapis arvensis*), in contrast, grows to a height of only 1 meter. The trunk of a fully grown black mustard bush can be as thick as an arm. The top of the bush has many branches which produce numerous yellow flowers, out of which develop long fruits bearing many seeds.[43] It is easy to imagine that birds would nest in such plants or that they provided good shade.

The ancient sources identify the special characteristics of the mustard plant.[44] Pliny in particular describes its fast germination and propagation. Once the plant has taken root, it is very difficult to remove (Pliny, *Nat.* XIX 170–71; XX 237–40).

Rabbinical literature also often used the size of mustard as a point of comparison. The mustard seed is identified as the smallest unit (*m. Naz.* 1:5; *m. Nid.* 5:2; *y. Ber.* 5:1, 8d; *b. Ber.* 31a); according to *y. Pe'ah* 7:4, 20b, a fully grown bush was so large that one could cover the roof of a cottage with three of its branches. According to *y. Pe'ah* 7:4, 20b, a fully grown bush once reached the size of a fig tree. Even if this is an exaggeration, it demonstrates that in Judaism, the size of the mustard bush was proverbially known.

To sum up: in ancient times and around the Sea of Galilee, mustard was a well-known plant that was often cultivated but also grew as a weed. While its general characteristics of consumption (spiciness) may have contributed to its metaphorical use, the parable in Mark 4:30–32 seems to limit itself to two aspects. One aspect is its size, as a sharp contrast is drawn between the very small seed and the meter-tall plant. This is found in particular in the case of "black mustard" (*brassica nigra*). On the other hand, the parable mentions the aspect

---

[40] For the rabbis, mustard is also a cultivated plant that was sown in the fields (*m. Kil.* 3:2; *t. Kil.* 2:8), as stated in Matt 13:31: ἔσπειρεν ἐν τῷ ἀγρῷ αὐτοῦ ("sowed in his field").
[41] Dalman has provided evidence for all three types being found in Israel. See Gustaf Dalman, *Arbeit und Sitte in Palästina I: Jahreslauf und Tageslauf Frühling und Sommer* (Hildesheim: Bertelsmann, 1928; reprint Hildesheim: Georg Olms Verlag, 1987), 369–70; Dalman, *Ackerbau*, 293–4; Hepper, *Pflanzenwelt*, 47: "in Massen als Unkraut wachsen."
[42] Dalman, *Frühling*, 369; Dalman, *Ackerbau*, 293. It is not always clear that Dalman has "black mustard" in view.
[43] See Michael Zohary, *Pflanzen der Bibel: Vollständiges Handbuch*, 3rd ed. (Stuttgart: Calwer, 1995), 93. See also *Fauna and Flora of the Bible: Prepared in Cooperation with the Committee on Translations of the United Bible Societies*, 2nd ed. (London: UBS, 1980), 145–6; Joachim Jeremias, *Die Gleichnisse Jesu*, 6th ed. (Göttingen: Vandenhoeck & Ruprecht, 1962), 147.
[44] See August Steier, "Senf," PW Supplement 6 (1935): 815–16.

of its fast growth and impressive form which remind one of a tree based on the trunk and the branches.

2.3. Tradition: Exploring Stock Metaphors and Symbols

The examination of the traditional use of metaphors shows that, despite mustard being common in the Jewish writings of the Hebrew Bible, in the Qumran texts, and in the Greek writings of Early Judaism, it has no role in religious language. Mustard was not chosen as a point of comparison in religious discourse. In other words, the parable of the mustard seed is truly a fresh or "bold" metaphor.[45]

In contrast, "sowing" and "growing" are used more frequently as metaphors in the tradition. "Sowing and reaping" are frequently contrasted with each other—in the wisdom tradition there is a close connection between acting and the consequences of those actions and in prophecy the harvest is used as an image for the temporal or eschatological judgment (of God). There is a certain logical consistency and stringency in the fact that sowing and harvesting are connected. Along these lines, Prov 22:8 states: "Whoever sows injustice will reap calamity" (ὁ σπείρων φαῦλα θερίσει κακά).[46] The regularity of the image of sowing and reaping was common in ancient times, as is demonstrated by similar references in Greek writings. Thus, we often find statements such as "you have sown shame and reaped misfortune" (Gorgias in Arist., *Rhet.* 3:3 [1406b 10]; Plato, *Phaedr.* 260d; cf. Plut., *Mor.* 2:182a; 2:394e), "one reaps the fruit one sows" (*CPG* 2:774), or that the wicked "sow injustice and reap impiety" (Philo, *Conf.* 152). References in the New Testament demonstrate that this idea was also well-known in the New Testament era and could be specified quantitatively, for example in 2 Cor 9:6: "The point is this: the one who sows sparingly will also reap sparingly, and the one who sows bountifully will also reap bountifully." Taking this background into account, the contrast described in Mark 4:30–32 is even greater as it does not call upon the expected consistency (he who sows small will also have a small plant and a small harvest). Instead, the expected regularity is breached: even though one has sown small seeds, what grows will be great. Similarly surprising is the discourse about trees and bushes that grow in hiding and from which a shoot will grow to an everlasting plantation (1QH XVI 5–6, 10–11):[47] "…its leaves [will be pasture] for all winged birds" (1QH XVI 9).

Finally, we can recognize the expression "birds of the heavens" (τὰ πετεινὰ τοῦ οὐρανοῦ) as being an established saying. The nesting of birds of the heavens in the branches or in the shade goes back to a group of motifs that appears frequently in

---

[45] See Petra von Gemünden, *Vegetationsmetaphorik im Neuen Testament und seiner Umwelt: Eine Bildfelduntersuchung*, Novum testamentum et orbis antiquus 18 (Göttingen: Universitätsverlag, 1993), 200, 419–20; similarly Gäbel, "Hoffnung," 332–3; more recently Ryan S. Schellenberg, "Kingdom as Contaminant? The Role of Repertoire in the Parables of the Mustard Seed and the Leaven," *CBQ* 71 (2009): 527–43.
[46] See also Job 4:8; Sir. 7:3.
[47] See 1QH XVI (*olim* VIII):4–12 (cf. 1QH XIV [*olim* VI]:15–17).

three Old Testament texts: Dan 4:7–9, 11, 18–19 (LXX)/Dan 4:10–12, 14, 21–22 (Theodotion); Ezek 17:22–24 and Ezek 31:6.[48] To cite simply one example:

> Under it (the great tree = King Nebuchadnezzar) the wild beasts lodged, and in its branches (κλάδοις) the birds of heaven dwelt (τὰ ὀρνέα τοῦ οὐρανοῦ κατεσκηνοῦν). (Dan 4:18)[49]

These examples (as also in Matt 13 and Luke 13) each deal with a tree; nevertheless, the image of the animals living "in the shade" (Ezek 17:23) of the tree as well as the mention of the nesting "birds" are linguistically so striking that any reader of the parable who is also familiar with the writings of Israel will necessarily be reminded of them when reading Mark 4. This is then intensified by the parable's introduction, which calls up the semantic field of the kingdom. Presumably drawing on the ancient oriental motif of the "World Tree," each of the three prophetic passages is about an image for kingdom and sovereignty: in Ezek 17:1–24 it is the king of Israel, in Ezek 31:1–18 the Pharaoh, in Dan 4:1–34 the Babylonian ruler. In each case, however, the image is linked to the prediction of humiliation and downfall, which are interpreted as the consequences of royal arrogance and abuse of power. Only after the felling of the old tree will a new beginning be possible in that a new tree will grow out of a branch in which *all* birds can live. In Ezekiel 17 it is stated thus:

> Thus says the Lord GOD: I myself will take a sprig from the lofty top of a cedar; I will set it out. I will break off a tender one from the topmost of its young twigs; I myself will plant it on a high and lofty mountain. ²³ On the mountain height of Israel I will plant it, in order that it may produce boughs and bear fruit, and become a noble cedar. Under it *every kind of bird will live; in the shade of its branches will nest winged creatures of every kind.* ²⁴ All the trees of the field shall know that I am the LORD. I bring low the high tree, I make high the low tree; I dry up the green tree and make the dry tree flourish. I the LORD have spoken; I will accomplish it. (Ezek 17:22–24 NRSV)

Targum Ezek 17:22–23, a significantly later text, even interprets the tree messianically:

> Thus says the Lord God, I Myself will bring near *a child from the kingdom of the house of David which is likened to* the lofty cedar, *and I will establish him from among his children's children; I will anoint and establish him by*

---

[48] There are later references to this motif in 2 Bar. 36, 39–40 (with reference to Ezek 17) and in *1 En.* 90:30–33 (here particularly the eschatological collection of animals and birds but without the motif of the tree); 1QH 14:14–16; 16:4–9; the Qumran texts are fully quoted in Klyne Snodgrass, *Stories with Intent: A Comprehensive Guide to the Parables of Jesus*, 2nd ed. (Grand Rapids: Eerdmans, 2018), 217.

[49] According to the Greek translation by Theodotion.

My Memra on a high and exalted mountain. On the *holy* mountain of Israel will I *establish him, and he shall gather together armies and build fortresses and become a mighty kingdom.*[50]

Against the background of this polarizing-prophetic tradition, there are two things that resonate in the metaphor of the nesting birds: judgment in the case of a false ruler and the human abuse of power as well as hope in view of God's intervention which promises salvation even beyond the borders of Israel.

2.4. Meaning: Summarizing Analysis (Interpretive Scope)

What meaning is created by connecting the aspects of linguistic form, the insights into the real history, and the linguistic tradition of the parable? In contrast to many exegetes, who narrow down the wide horizon of possible meanings,[51] I will consider various interpretations and will substantiate each on its own merits.

2.4.1. Parable of Encouragement: Everything Must Start Small But it Can Grow (Strengthening Faith). The linguistic structure of the text is particularly influenced by the contrast between "small" and "great" or following Mark between "the smallest" and "the greatest." The contrast is made as large as possible by the comparison with all seeds and shrubs. In doing this, the parable succeeds in creating a seemingly paradoxical concurrence of surprise and familiarity.

Anyone from a rural society is familiar with mustard. This applies equally to the postulated first hearers of the parable in Israel because mustard occurs quite commonly at the Sea of Galilee. Thus, even a child should know that a mustard seed is very small and that it grows into a very large bush. This experience from daily life is then used to teach a theological lesson and it is in this lesson that we find the surprise.

Usually, the religious language of the tradition makes use of the logical consistency of seed, growth, and harvest in order to indicate the consequences of human behavior or even to point out the eschatological judgment. Therefore, nature comparisons are often made in an ethical context.[52] Man will reap that which he sows (Gal 6:7; 2 Cor 9:6). He who sows small, will reap small. However, the message in Mark 4:30–33 is the complete opposite: even though the seed that is sown is small, the harvest will be great!

This is not only a surprising turn; it is also reassuring, especially for those who at the moment (can) only see the small seed. Thus, with regard to the "kingdom of God" as the object of comparison, the parable provides reassurance. If the kingdom of God is really as it is described here, its perhaps current minuteness or

---

[50] See Samson H. Levey, *The Targum of Ezekiel Translated, with a Critical Introduction, Apparatus, and Notes*, The Aramaic Bible 13 (Wilmington, DE: Michael Glazier, 1987). I am grateful to K. Snodgrass for discovering this text, see Snodgrass, *Stories with Intent*, 664–5.
[51] See, for instance, Ernest van Eck, *The Parables of Jesus the Galilean: Stories of a Social Prophet* (Eugene, OR: Wipf & Stock, 2016), 79: "The Mustard Seed is not a parable of growth or contrast that envisages an apocalyptic, eschatological kingdom."
[52] See, for instance, Matt 6:34, the parable of the Tree and the Fruits.

invisibility does not need to be discouraging for it will be like the mustard seed. Ultimately, it will be great and it will grow quickly and sturdily, as the listeners can see from their daily lives. Thus, we can count this parable as one of the parables of growth,[53] which dominate the entire fourth chapter of the Gospel of Mark—beginning with the parable of the sower (Mark 4:3–9), continuing with the allegorical interpretation of that parable (4:13–20) and the parable of the growing seed (4:26–29), and culminating with the parable of the mustard seed. All of these parables are linked by the conviction that the kingdom of God is connected to a development process comparable to the process of growth in nature. Lischer correctly speaks of the "principle of growth."[54] Beyond this, however, the parables have striking emphases, each of which sets a different accent. In contrast to Mark 4:3–9, the lack of a sower or any other person in Mark 4:30–32 is remarkable. For Blomberg, Mark "makes explicit what is already implicit in Q, that the man and the woman[55] have no significant role to play in the two short similes."[56] This idea gains plausibility above all in view of the context in Mark 4:26–29. Anyone reading the Gospel chronologically has just learned that the kingdom of God is like the "seed" that grows on its own without any contribution from man. This characteristic is sustained and intensified in Mark 4:30. Even though no one digs, fertilizes or even waters, the kingdom of God grows to an unexpected size.

To whom could this appeal be directed? Perhaps to people who suffer from overzealousness and are delusional concerning the feasibility of a plan or project? The end of the parable in particular, however, does not resemble a call for humility or passivity. Perhaps it is aimed at people who feel insignificant and discouraged.

According to Kirk, "the growth image of a tiny seed becoming a large tree… express[es] the self-understanding of the Q group."[57] Roth follows this sociological reading by stating that "at present the group is insignificant and hidden, but it will grow and be marvellously revealed."[58] In the context of Mark, the focus might shift to the growth of faith. The hearers or readers of the parable are encouraged or even comforted if they are despairing at the diminutiveness of their faith.[59] Mark 9:42 (ἕνα τῶν μικρῶν τούτων τῶν πιστευόντων, "one of these little ones who believe") demonstrates that "smallness" can also be linked

---

[53] See Nils A. Dahl, "Parables of Growth," in *Jesus in the Memory of the Early Church* (Minneapolis: Augsburg, 1976), 132–66.
[54] See Richard Lischer, *Reading the Parables: Interpretation: Resources for the Use of Scripture in the Church* (Louisville, KY: Westminster John Knox Press, 2014), 75.
[55] With regard to the parable of the leaven, which is most probably combined with the parable of the Mustard Seed in Q/Luke 13:18–19; see on the gender couplet-motif in Q-parables, Roth, *Parables in Q*, 325–6.
[56] Blomberg, *Parables*, 391. Blomberg sees a unity of the parables of the mustard seed and the leaven, as is seen in Q/Luke 13:18–21.
[57] Alan Kirk, *The Composition of the Sayings Source: Genre, Synchrony, and Wisdom Redaction in Q*, NovTSup 91 (Leiden: Brill, 1998), 303.
[58] Roth, *Parables in Q*, 324.
[59] According to Lischer, Mark 4 as a whole can be read as "mirror[ing] the believer's life in the kingdom, in which hope, joy, abundance, and loss coexist with no logic other than the logic of Jesus' own story." Lischer, *Reading the Parables*, 76.

to faith, speaking in addition of a challenge to the "little" ones who believe, the consequence of which is drastic punishment. As an early interpreter of the parable, Matthew is clearer in this respect—he utilizes the image of the mustard seed directly for faith and for the community. The only other reference of the term "mustard seed" (outside of the parables) is found in connection with a statement of faith: "He said to them, "Because of your little faith. For truly I tell you, if you have faith the size of a mustard seed, you will say to this mountain, 'Move from here to there,' and it will move; and nothing will be impossible for you'" (Matt 17:20).

The size of the mustard seed is again the subject. The smallness of the mustard seed is brought into parallel with the "little faith" but not as a reproach. Instead, it is meant as encouragement and comfort:[60] even this little faith is sufficient to cause great things to happen (move mountains). It cannot be said with certainty whether the little faith also permits a direct connection to the "little ones" in the community. However, it would permit a direct connection to Mark 9:42. Matthew characterizes certain people in the community as the "little ones" (Matt 18:6, 10) and, in the discourse on the church, explicitly wants to integrate or protect them. The fact that they have angels "in heaven" (Matt 18:10) fits into the heavenly dimension of the parable. In Mark, the little ones remind us inevitably of children, whom Jesus places centrally as the exemplary recipients of the kingdom of God (Mark 10:14–15). Therefore, it is not surprising that in religious education, children are appealed to in particular through the parable of the mustard seed.

2.4.2. *Parable of hope: There is a goal that will be great (eschatological-ecclesiastic aspect).* The above considerations lead to another possible interpretation, which, despite a certain overlap with the first, must be regarded on its own merits. Here, the emphasis shifts from the beginning of the process to its end. The core of the interpretation is no longer the smallness of the mustard seed but rather its unbelievable development into the greatest shrub or a tree. We will look at two aspects of this: the temporal and the relational dimension.

The growth of the mustard shrub occurs at a very fast pace and in the present, as is underlined by the present tense of the verbs. The mustard seed becomes not only something great, but—at least with the tree—something unexpected. As a reference for the mustard seed, the "kingdom of God" also has a temporal dimension in Mark. It is anticipated (Mark 15:43) and its coming is proclaimed, even in Jesus's very first public speech: "The time is fulfilled, and the kingdom of God has come near!" (Mark 1:15). Mark 9:1 expresses an extreme imminent expectation: "And he said to them, 'Truly I tell you, there are some standing here who will not taste death until they see that the kingdom of God has come with power.'" If the parable is meant to be an explanation for the kingdom of God,

---

[60] In contrast, the version in Q/Luke 17:5–6, which is formulated in the subjunctive and thus expresses a reproach: the apostles said to the Lord, "Increase our faith!" The Lord replied, "If you had faith the size of a mustard seed, you could say to this mulberry tree, 'Be uprooted and planted in the sea,' and it would obey you."

we cannot ignore this temporal dimension—the events in Mark 4:30–32 carry us away. The seed has scarcely fallen to earth when it is suddenly a huge shrub that is greater than all plants and is inhabited by birds.

The actual goal, however, is not realized in the growth of the plant. Instead the goal is that the mustard shrub becomes a habitat for others. At this point the relational dimension comes into play. In Mark, the kingdom of God is seen as a room that can be entered. At the same time, one can imagine it as a sovereign domain in which one can participate. Thus, the kingdom becomes a metaphor for a new community. It seems to be difficult, however, for some people, for example the rich, to enter this community (Mark 9:47; 10:23–25).

In view of this insecurity, the parable is a sign of hope. The mustard shrub, which seemingly grew on its own, offers space to "live" in and shade in which to settle down. To think only of animals is to miss the fact that the parable, as any metaphoric text, can and must be related to people and thus to the human community. The mustard shrub becomes a center of attraction for others. It invites us to spend time in its shade, thus removing the dynamics of time. The explicitly formulated "living" is not something that takes place quickly. Thus, a residential community grows up in its shade. The kingdom of God provides space for a new social community. This must not necessarily be regarded with an ecclesiastic interpretation, which in my opinion would not be suitable for Mark.[61]

This community can at the very least break through the usual borders because, in the Jewish exegesis, "birds" were used as a symbol for Gentiles[62] and the background of tradition (see below) also explicitly links eschatological dimensions (animal peace; motif of pilgrimage) to living in the shade. We can also come to an understanding of why more recent ecclesiastical interpretations are inspired by the parable, even if, in my opinion, a missionary concept is foreign to the parable.[63] It goes without question, however, that the parable has the potential for eschatological-ecclesiastic interpretation. It promises the hope of community.

---

[61] In the Q Parable, Wendy Cotter looks at the Q group that must be strengthened in view of the hostilities during the mission. See Wendy Cotter, "The Parables of the Mustard Seed and the Leaven: Their Function in the Earliest Stratum of Q," *Toronto Journal of Theology* 8 (1992): 45–8. On the contrary, that is often the interpretation of Matt 13:31–32; see, e.g., Otto Kuss, "Zum Sinngehalt des Doppelgleichnisses vom Senfkorn und Sauerteig," *Biblica* 40 (1959): 97; Paul Zingg, *Das Wachsen der Kirche: Beiträge zur Frage der lukanischen Redaktion und Theologie* (Freiburg: Universitätsverlag, 1974), 106–7.

[62] See *1 En.* 90:30, 33, 37; *Midr. Ps.* 104:10. See also Thomas W. Manson, *The Teaching of Jesus: Studies of its Form and Contents* (Cambridge: Cambridge University Press, 1959), 133; see more recently also Joel Marcus, *Mark 1–8: A New Translation with Introduction and Commentary*, Anchor Bible 27 (New York: Doubleday, 2000), 324: "These intertextual linkages suggest that the birds in our parable may symbolize Gentiles" (also 331). For K. Snodgrass these readings are allegorical interpretations: "None of this has much basis." Snodgrass, *Stories with Intent*, 223.

[63] Thus, for example, an almost missionary-ecclesiastic interpretation in Blomberg, *Parables*, 395: "the tiny seed has grown into a remarkably large mustard bush, but to this day it is no majestic cedar tree.... God is still planting seeds around the world." Referring to Peter R. Jones, *Studying the Parables of Jesus* (Macon, GA: Smyth & Helwys, 1999), 92, he warns of a "too numerous" or "powerful" church: "Respect the 'infinitude of the little.' Obsession with size is obscene."

2.4.3. Parable of protest: the alternate world—religious-political dimension (sociological aspect).

Finally, this miniature narrative carries one further dimension of interpretation. Jesus chooses a simple plant—a roadside weed—as a point of comparison for the kingdom of God. Such an image possesses explosive power.[64] It is not the size of the plant but its simplicity, its commonness, that challenges us to reflect. The mustard is implicitly contrasted with the fig tree or the grape vine, which were the classic symbols of Israel. This contrast is revealed in the context of Mark's Gospel because the overwhelming growth of the anonymous mustard shrub (Mark 4:30–32) is in opposition to the withering of the fig tree at Jesus's entrance to Jerusalem (Mark 11:13, 20–21). Furthermore, there is the parable of the vineyard in Mark 12:1–12. This bridge between the mustard and the fig tree is certainly a problematic classification that, like the linking of Mark 4 and Mark 12, has repeatedly led to anti-Jewish interpretations. Does the contrast between the plants create a conscious provocation for the Jewish listeners?

According to Ernest van Eck, the detail as recounted in Luke that the mustard seed is planted in a garden (κῆπος) could be read as a provocation towards the Jewish temple elite:

> By planting the mustard seed in the garden, the man thus violates the law of diverse kinds, and pollutes the garden. The garden is unclean, a symbol of chaos.... An ordered kingdom has been replaced by a chaotic and polluted kingdom.... As such, the kingdom of God is dangerous and deadly. In time it will take over the ordered and unpolluted garden (ordered society) of the kingdom of the Temple. Order is turned into chaos; the kingdom of God is taking over the kingdom of the Temple.[65]

This reading also has plausibility in Mark because the term used for the branches of the mustard shrub (ὁ κλάδος) is used only one other time in the Gospel of Mark—in the parable of the fig tree in the Markan eschatological discourse: "From the fig tree learn its lesson: as soon as its branch becomes tender and puts forth its leaves, you know that summer is near" (Mark 13:28). With regard to this context, perhaps we can even refer to the flavor of the mustard, which may be on the minds of the addressees. It correlates to the flavor of the salt, which occurs in Mark and which he uses eschatologically and ecclesiastically as a metaphor (Mark 9:49–50).

However, the parable's potential for meaning does not exhaust itself in the religious fields of reference. In the scope of Roman tyranny in the first century, it is not possible to speak neutrally of the "kingship of God." Instead, this

---

[64] One of the first interpretations along these lines can be found in Robert Funk, "Looking-Glass Tree is for the Birds," *Interpretation* 27 (1973): 3–9. Jesus created a burlesque and satire of all pride. Similarly Bernard Brandon Scott, *Hear then the Parable: A Commentary on the Parables of Jesus* (Minneapolis: Fortress Press, 1989), 71–3.

[65] Ernest van Eck, "When Kingdoms Are Kingdoms No More: A Social-Scientific Reading of the Mustard Seed (Lk 13:18–19)," *Acta Theologica* 33 (2013): 244.

depicts an alternative world that must stand in contrast to the "kingdom of the Romans." This political undertone is intensified, above all, by the previously noted reference of the parable to the Old Testament pre-texts (Dan 4; Ezek 17; 31, see above). The "birds of heaven"—especially in combination with mention of a tree (Q, Matthew, Luke)—carry with them, from the distant texts of tradition, the seeds of protest at the political abuse of power. Daniel 4:7–9, 11, 18–19; Ezek 17:22–24 and Ezek 31:6 (see also 1QH 16:4–9) all speak of the image of a tree and the birds living in its boughs. In each case, the interpretation is a king and his reign. In Dan 4:1–34 it is the Babylonian king, in Ezek 17:1–24 the king of Israel and in Ezek 31:1–18 the Pharaoh.

Warren Carter used these political undertones in particular for his anti-imperial interpretation of Matt 13:31–32.[66] According to Carter, the trees mentioned in the Jewish traditions "symbolize the power and rule of nations and their kings, sometimes sanctioned by God and sometimes strongly opposed by God. Either way, it is significant that in these traditions, all the trees/empires are subjected to God's sovereignty."[67] He concludes: "The central claim expressed through the image of the tree in these narratives is that God exercises control over human empires and reign."[68]

The Matthean parable metaphorically talks about the "empire of the heavens" (v. 31) and compares it with a great tree. The power and presence of God's empire are proclaimed to an addressee who is currently suffering under the power of the Roman Empire. As Carter pointed out, the entire Gospel of Matthew reflects the conflict with Rome's Empire. This context brings a specific meaning of the parable of the mustard seed to the fore: "the negotiation of Rome's Empire by Jesus' followers." God brings empires down. But "God also uses Rome to punish Jerusalem, particularly its elite leadership, allies of Rome, for rejecting Jesus."[69]

That which is apparent in Matthew through the addition of the tree symbolism can just as easily already exist in Mark.[70] As one of the first interpreters of the parable, Matthew makes us aware of one aspect that we might otherwise not notice. The kingdom of God represents an alternative world to that of the political

---

[66] See Warren Carter, "Matthew's Gospel, Rome's Empire, and the Parable of the Mustard Seed (Matt 13:31-32)," in *Hermeneutik der Gleichnisse Jesu: Methodische Neuansätze zum Verstehen urchristlicher Parabeltexte*, ed. R. Zimmermann, WUNT 231 (Tübingen: Mohr Siebeck, 2011), 181–201; R. Funk also reads the parable against the Old Testament kingdom symbolism, see Funk, "Looking-Glass Tree," 3–9. E. Van Eck, on the other hand, although arguing for a political reading denies any allusion to these Old Testament traditions (van Eck, "Kingdoms," 242; van Eck, *Parables*, 80), in order to avoid any eschatological reading of the parable.
[67] Carter, "Mustard Seed," 198.
[68] Ibid., 200.
[69] Ibid., 200.
[70] Along these lines is Adela Y. Collins, "The Discourse in Parables in Mark 4," in Zimmermann, ed., *Hermeneutik*, 521–38. Jacobus Liebenberg, "The Parable of the Mustard Seed in the Synoptic Tradition and the Gospel of Thomas," in *The Language of the Kingdom and Jesus: Parable, Aphorism, and Metaphor in the Sayings Material Common to the Synoptic Tradition and the Gospel of Thomas*, BZNW 102 (Berlin: de Gruyter, 2001), 276–335, however, denies any reference in that direction and points to other occurrences of "the birds of the air" in the New Testament (like Matt 6:26; 8:20/Luke 9:58; Luke 8:5) as ordinary reality.

rulers of the time. This is supported by the fact that the interpretation of the parable of the sower (Mark 4:13–20) could also involve this political dimension.[71]

In accordance with the criticism of the title "son of David," Jesus rides into Jerusalem on a donkey and not on a horse. Correspondingly, it is no coincidence that a garden weed such as mustard is chosen to describe the new kingdom instead of a fig tree or cedar. While the mustard grows, the fig tree withered (Mark 11:20–21). We must agree with Bovon's conclusion that "It is symptomatic for the theology of Jesus that he did not choose the proud cedar but rather the humble mustard in order to express this hope. The one evokes a lordly power, the other perhaps a welcoming, friendly community."[72] The criticism of the reigning class, however, is more radical than may be justified for a political anti-imperial reading of the parable because the political meaning cannot be built on Markan crucifixion theology, which must distance itself from exaggerated political expectations.

3. Concluding Remarks

Parables are metaphorical texts. Within the process of interaction between the different semantic domains, they open up horizons of meaning. In the semantic process of germination and growth, the multiplication of meaning takes place. This can be seen all the more clearly when we read the different versions of the parable side by side, as we have just done.

There might be many other interpretations of this parable. After my advocacy of a multiple interpretation, there is no need to curtail this process. Let me conclude by quoting Levine: "The parable of the Mustard Seed has put forth so many branches of interpretation that the birds of heaven could build multiple nests and still have room for expansion."[73]

In other words, and taking up the imagery which entitled this paper, the growth of the mustard seed is still going on and far away from a final harvest. It is, however, already possible to pick some fruit from time to time. By doing so, we realize that polyvalent interpretation will produce manifold yields.

---

[71] In the interpretation of the "failure to bear fruit" in Mark 4:13–20, Weissenrieder sees an allusion to the Roman propaganda that depicts the emperor as the country's bearer of fruit. She supports this theory with numismatic material in Judea and Syria from 29–44 C.E. See Annette Weissenrieder, "Didaktik der Bilder: Allegorie und Allegorese am Beispiel von Mk 4,3–20," in Zimmermann, ed., *Hermeneutik*, 494–520.

[72] Bovon, *Lukas*, 416: "Es bleibt dabei symptomatisch für die Theologie Jesu, daß er nicht die stolze Gestalt der Zeder, sondern die bescheidene des Senfs wählte, um diese Hoffnung auszudrücken. Das eine evoziert die herrscherliche Macht, das andere vielleicht die gastliche, freundliche Gemeinschaft." Similarly Collins, "Discourse," 537: "The author of Mark has chosen to place this simile in a climactic position in order to parody overblown messianic expectations.... [T]he most difficult aspect of the mystery of the kingdom of God in Mark is the revelation that the messiah, Jesus, must suffer and die."

[73] Levine, *Short Stories*, 152.

Bibliography

Barthes, Roland G. "La mort de l'auteur." In *Oeuvres Complètes*, edited by É. Marty. Paris: Seuil, 1994.

Billerbeck, Paul, and Hermann L. Strack, *Kommentar zum Neuen Testament aus Talmud und Midrasch I: Das Evangelium nach Matthäus.* 2nd ed. Munich: Beck, 1926.

Blomberg, Craig L. *Interpreting the Parables.* 2nd ed. Downers Grove, IL: IVP Academic, 2012.

Bovon, François. *Das Evangelium nach Lukas II: Lk 9,51–14,35.* Evangelisch-katholischer Kommentar zum Neuen Testament 3/2. Zurich: Benziger, 1996.

Buntfuß, Markus. *Tradition und Innovation: Die Funktion der Metapher in der theologischen Theoriesprache.* Theologische Bibliothek Töpelmann 84. Berlin: de Gruyter, 1997.

Carlston, Charles E. *The Parables of the Triple Tradition.* Philadelphia: Fortress Press, 1975.

Carter, Warren. "Matthew's Gospel, Rome's Empire, and the Parable of the Mustard Seed (Matt 13:31–32)." In *Hermeneutik der Gleichnisse Jesu: Methodische Neuansätze zum Verstehen urchristlicher Parabeltexte*, edited by R. Zimmermann, 181–201. 2nd ed. WUNT 231. Tübingen: Mohr Siebeck, 2011.

Collins, Adela Y. "The Discourse in Parables in Mark 4." In *Hermeneutik der Gleichnisse Jesu: Methodische Neuansätze zum Verstehen urchristlicher Parabeltexte*, edited by R. Zimmermann, 521–38. 2nd ed. WUNT 231. Tübingen: Mohr Siebeck, 2011.

Cotter (SJ), Wendy J. "The Parables of the Mustard Seed and the Leaven: Their Function in the Earliest Stratum of Q." *Toronto Journal of Theology* 8 (1992): 37–51.

Crossan, John D. *Cliffs of Fall: Paradox and Polyvalence in the Parables of Jesus.* New York: Seabury Press, 1980.

Dahl, Nils A. "Parables of Growth." In *Jesus in the Memory of the Early Church*, 141–66. Minneapolis: Augsburg, 1976.

Dalman, Gustaf. *Arbeit und Sitte in Palästina I: Jahreslauf und Tageslauf Frühling und Sommer.* Hildesheim: Bertelsmann, 1928. Reprint Hildesheim: Georg Olms Verlag, 1987.

Dalman, Gustaf. *Arbeit und Sitte in Palästina II: Der Ackerbau*, Hildesheim: Bertelsmann, 1928. Reprint Hildesheim: Georg Olms Verlag, 1987.

Dannhauer, Johann C. *Idea boni interpretis et malitiosi calumniatoris.* 4th ed. Strassburg: Argentorati, 1652.

Eco, Umberto, Richard Rorty, Jonathan Culler, and Christine Brooke-Rose. *Interpretation and Overinterpretation.* Edited by S. Collini. Cambridge: Cambridge University Press, 1992

Eco, Umberto. *The Limits of Interpretation.* Bloomington: Indiana University Press, 1990.

Fauna and Flora of the Bible: Prepared in Cooperation with the Committee on Translations of the United Bible Societies. 2nd ed. London: UBS, 1980.

Forbes Royle, John. "On the Identification of the Mustard Tree of Scripture." *Journal of the Royal Asiatic Society* 8.15 (1846): 113–37.

Fritz, Gerd. *Historische Semantik.* Sammlung Metzler 313. 2nd ed. Stuttgart/Weimar: Metzler, 2006.

Funk, Robert W. "The Looking-Glass Tree is for the Birds." *Interpretation* 27 (1973): 3–9.

Gäbel, Georg. "Mehr Hoffnung wagen (Vom Senfkorn): Mk 4,30par." In *Kompendium der Gleichnisse Jesu*, edited by Ruben Zimmermann et al., 327–36. 2nd ed. Gütersloh: Gütersloher Verlagshaus, 2015.

Gadamer, Hans-Georg. "Klassische und Philosophische Hermeneutik." In *Wahrheit und Methode: Ergänzungen und Register*, 92–117. 2nd ed. GW 2. Tübingen: Mohr Siebeck, 1993.

Geeraerts, Dirk. *Diachronic Prototype Semantics: A Contribution to Historical Lexicology*. Oxford: Clarendon Press, 1997.

Gemünden, Petra von. *Vegetationsmetaphorik im Neuen Testament und seiner Umwelt: Eine Bildfelduntersuchung*. Novum testamentum et orbis antiquus 18. Göttingen/Freiburg i. Br.: Universitätsverlag, 1993.

Hedrick, Charles W. *Many Things in Parables: Jesus and His Modern Critics*. Louisville, KY: Westminster John Knox Press, 2004.

Hepper, Frank N. *Pflanzenwelt der Bibel: Eine illustrierte Enzyklopädie*. Stuttgart: Deutsche Bibelgesellschaft, 1992.

Iser, Wolfgang. *Der Akt des Lesens: Theorie ästhetischer Wirkung*. Uni-Taschenbücher 636. 4th ed. Munich: Fink, 1994.

Janowski, Bernd. "Die Einwohnung Gottes in Israel: Eine religions- und theologiegeschichtliche Skizze zur biblischen Schekina-Theologie." In *Das Geheimnis der Gegenwart Gottes: Zur Schechina-Vorstellung in Judentum und Christentum*, edited by B. Janowski and E. E. Popkes, 3–40. WUNT 318. Tübingen: Mohr Siebeck, 2013.

Jeremias, Joachim. *Die Gleichnisse Jesu*. 6th ed. Göttingen: Vandenhoeck & Ruprecht, 1962.

Jones, Ivor H. *The Matthean Parables: A Literary and Historical Commentary*. NovTSup 80. Leiden: Brill, 1995.

Jones, Peter R. *Studying the Parables of Jesus*. Macon, GA: Smyth & Helwys, 1999.

Jülicher, Adolf. *Die Gleichnisreden Jesu I/II*. 2nd ed. Tübingen: Mohr Siebeck, 1910. Reprint Darmstadt: Wissenschaftliche Buchgesellschaft, 1963.

Kirk, Alan. *The Composition of the Sayings Source: Genre, Synchrony, and Wisdom Redaction in Q*. NovTSup 91. Leiden: Brill, 1998.

Kogler, Franz. *Das Doppelgleichnis vom Senfkorn und Sauerteig in seiner traditionsgeschichtlichen Entwicklung. Zur Reich-Gottes-Vorstellung Jesu und ihren Aktualisierungen in der Urkirche*. Würzburg: Echter, 1988.

Kuss, Otto. "Zum Sinngehalt des Doppelgleichnisses vom Senfkorn und Sauerteig." *Biblica* 40 (1959): 641–53.

Laufen, Rudolf. *Die Doppelüberlieferungen der Logienquelle und des Markusevangeliums*. BBB 54. Königstein-Bonn: Peter Hanstein Verlag, 1980.

Levey, Samson H. *The Targum of Ezekiel Translated, with a Critical Introduction, Apparatus, and Notes*. The Aramaic Bible 13. Wilmington, DE: Michael Glazier, 1987.

Levine, Amy-Jill. *Short Stories by Jesus: The Enigmatic Parables of a Controversial Rabbi*. New York: Harper One, 2014.

Liebenberg, Jacobus. "The Parable of the Mustard Seed in the Synoptic Tradition and the Gospel of Thomas." In *The Language of the Kingdom and Jesus. Parable, Aphorism, and Metaphor in the Sayings Material Common to the Synoptic Tradition and the Gospel of Thomas*, 276–335. BZNW 102. Berlin: de Gruyter, 2001.

Lischer, Richard. *Reading the Parables: Interpretation: Resources for the Use of Scripture in the Church*. Louisville, KY: Westminster John Knox Press, 2014.

Luther, Susanne, and Ruben Zimmermann, eds. *Studienbuch Hermeneutik: Bibelauslegung durch die Jahrhunderte als Lernfeld der Textinterpretation: Portraits—Modelle—Quellentexte*. Gütersloh: Gütersloher Verlagshaus, 2014.

Manson, Thomas W. *The Teaching of Jesus: Studies of its Form and Contents*. Cambridge: Cambridge University Press, 1959.

Marcus, Joel. *Mark 1–8: A New Translation with Introduction and Commentary*. Anchor Bible 27. New York: Doubleday, 2000.
McArthur, Harvey K. "The Parable of the Mustard Seed." *CBQ* 33 (1971): 198–210.
Meier, John P. *A Marginal Jew. Volume V: Probing the Authenticity of the Parables*. New Haven: Yale University Press, 2016.
Oldenhage, Tania. *Parables for Our Time: Rereading New Testament Scholarship after the Holocaust*. Oxford: Oxford University Press, 2002.
Plisch, Uwe-Karsten. *Gospel of Thomas*. Peabody, MA: Hendrickson, 2008.
Ricœur, Paul. "Philosophische und Theologische Hermeneutik." In *Metapher: Zur Hermeneutik religiöser Sprache*, edited by P. Ricœur and E. Jüngel, 24–45. Munich: Kaiser, 1974.
Roth, Dieter T. *The Parables in Q*. London: T&T Clark, 2018.
Schellenberg, Ryan S. "Kingdom as Contaminant? The Role of Repertoire in the Parables of the Mustard Seed and the Leaven." *CBQ* 71 (2009): 527–43.
Schleiermacher, Friedrich D. E. *Hermeneutik und Kritik*. Suhrkamp Taschenbuch Wissenschaft 211. Edited and introduced by M. Frank. 7th ed. Frankfurt a. M.: Suhrkamp, 1999.
Schottroff, Luise. *The Parables of Jesus*. Translated by Linda M. Maloney. Minneapolis: Fortress Press, 2006
Scott, Bernard Brandon. *Hear then the Parable: A Commentary on the Parables of Jesus*. Minneapolis: Fortress Press, 1989.
Shillington, V. George, ed. *Jesus and His Parables: Interpreting the Parables of Jesus Today*. Edinburgh: T. & T. Clark, 1997.
Snodgrass, Klyne. *Stories with Intent: A Comprehensive Guide to the Parables of Jesus*. Grand Rapids, MI: Eerdmans, 2008, 2nd ed, 2018.
Sparn, Walter. "Johann Conrad Dannhauer (1603–1666): Allgemeine und Biblische Hermeneutik." In *Studienbuch Hermeneutik: Bibelauslegung durch die Jahrhunderte als Lernfeld der Textinterpretation*, edited by R. Zimmermann and S. Luther, 187–97. Gütersloh: Gütersloher Verlagshaus, 2014.
Steier, August. "Senf." PW Supplement 6 (1935): 812–17.
Straus, Erwin. *Vom Sinn der Sinne: Ein Beitrag zur Grundlegung der Psychologie*. 2nd ed. Berlin: Springer, 1978.
Thurén, Lauri. *Parables Unplugged: Reading the Lukan Parables in Their Rhetorical Context*. Minneapolis: Fortress Press, 2014.
Tolbert, Mary A. *Perspectives on the Parables: An Approach to Multiple Interpretations*. Philadelphia: Fortress Press, 1979.
Van Eck, Ernest. "When Kingdoms are Kingdoms No More: A Social-scientific Reading of the Mustard Seed (Lk 13:18–19)." Acta Theologica 33 (2013): 226–54.
Van Eck, Ernest. *The Parables of Jesus the Galilean: Stories of a Social Prophet*. Eugene, OR: Wipf & Stock, 2016.
Weinrich, Harald. "Münze und Wort: Untersuchungen an einem Bildfeld." In *Sprache in Texten*, 276–90. Stuttgart: Klett, 1976.
Weissenrieder, Annette. "Didaktik der Bilder: Allegorie und Allegorese am Beispiel von Mk 4,3–20." In *Hermeneutik der Gleichnisse Jesu: Methodische Neuansätze zum Verstehen urchristlicher Parabeltexte*, edited by R. Zimmermann, 494–520. 2nd ed. WUNT 231. Tübingen: Mohr Siebeck, 2011.

Zimmermann, Ruben. "Bildersprache verstehen oder Die offene Sinndynamik der Sprachbilder: Einführung." In *Bildersprache verstehen: Zur Hermeneutik der Metapher und anderer bildlicher Sprachformen: Mit einem Geleitwort von H.-G. Gadamer*, edited by R. Zimmermann, 13–54. Übergänge 38. Munich: Fink, 2000.

Zimmermann, Ruben. *Geschlechtermetaphorik und Gottesverhältnis: Traditionsgeschichte und Theologie eines Bildfelds in Urchristentum und antiker Umwelt.* WUNT 2/122. Tübingen: Mohr Siebeck, 2001.

Zimmermann, Ruben. "Metaphorology and Narratology in Q Exegesis: Literary Methodology as an Aid to Understanding the Q Text." In *Metaphor, Narrative, and Parables in Q*, edited by D. T. Roth, R. Zimmermann, and M. Labahn, 3–30. WUNT 315. Tübingen: Mohr Siebeck, 2014.

Zimmermann, Ruben. *Puzzling the Parables of Jesus. Methods and Interpretation.* Minneapolis: Fortress, 2015.

Zimmermann, Ruben. "Memory and Jesus' Parables: J. P. Meier's Explosion and the Restoration of the 'Bedrock' of Jesus' Speech." *JSHJ* 16 (2018): 156–72.

Zingg, Paul. *Das Wachsen der Kirche: Beiträge zur Frage der lukanischen Redaktion und Theologie.* Freiburg: Universitätsverlag, 1974.

Zohary, Michael. *Pflanzen der Bibel: Vollständiges Handbuch.* 3rd ed. Stuttgart: Calwer, 1995.

HARVEST IMAGERY IN Q PARABLES

Dieter T. Roth

When encountering an essay, the title of which contains a reference to "Q Parables," two legitimate questions may very well arise. First, how is Q, the posited second main source alongside Mark for Matthew and Luke in the so-called two-document hypothesis, being envisioned? And second, how is a parable being defined? In the conference presentation of the material in this chapter, I followed these questions by jokingly stating, "Thankfully, these are very simple questions, as neither Q studies nor parables scholarship has any noteworthy controversies."[1] Of course, even a cursory glance at the vast literature interacting with these topics reveals that the questions are anything but simple and uncontroversial. In fact, in my recent monograph *The Parables in Q*, from which this chapter draws, I stated that given the complexity of and complications inherent to scholarly forays into these areas of scholarship, perhaps, rather than speaking of the *field* of research on the parables in Q, it may be more appropriate to speak of the *minefield* of such research![2] Though space does not permit the provision of a complete roadmap to how I have attempted to navigate this minefield, it is important to provide a summary overview of my methodological approach. Only then can the discussion move towards analyzing the striking use of harvest imagery in several Q parables and the implications one can draw from it concerning elements of the teachings and theological perspectives of Q.

1. Considering Q

When I first began my own work on Q,[3] I came across a 1985 article entitled "A Literary Folkloristic Methodology for the Study of Meaning in Personal Narrative," written by folklore studies professor Sandra K. Dolby-Stahl. In this

---

[1] The paper was presented at the 2019 SBL International Meeting in Rome (July 1–5, 2019) in a session organized by the Synoptic Gospels Section.
[2] Dieter T. Roth, *The Parables in Q*, LNTS 582 (London: T&T Clark, 2018), 4. This monograph had its genesis in my *Habilitationsschrift* submitted at the Johannes Gutenberg-Universität Mainz in 2016. References to material taken from this publication, in a summarized or slightly edited and updated form, can be found in the notes to the ensuing discussion.
[3] See the longer discussion of the issues presented here in Roth, *Parables in Q*, 23–44.

article she made reference to "the never-ending struggle to determine what a text means, what is or is not a part of the text," and "what in fact *is* a text at all."[4] It seems to me that these comments are also rather appropriate for Q studies. The question of what is or is not a part of the text (in particular on the word level) and the question of what in fact *is* a text at all are both particularly significant and relevant when considering Q. In several publications, I have argued that though I remain fully convinced that the two-document (or two-source) hypothesis remains the most persuasive suggested solution to the Synoptic problem (hence I advocate for Q), I am rather skeptical about the ability of scholarship, in many cases, to reconstruct the actual wording of Q and especially of the Q parables.[5] For this reason, and based on what could be referred to as "internal evidence" (that is, evidence of the problem from the nature of Q reconstructions themselves)[6] and "external evidence" (that is, evidence of the problem arising from

---

[4] Sandra K. Dolby-Stahl, "A Literary Folkloristic Methodology for the Study of Meaning in Personal Narrative," *Journal of Folklore Research* 22 (1985): 45–69 (here 45).

[5] See, e.g., Dieter T. Roth, "'Master' as Character in the Q Parables," in *Metaphor, Narrative, and Parable in Q*, ed. Dieter T. Roth, Ruben Zimmermann, and Michael Labahn, WUNT 315 (Tübingen: Mohr Siebeck, 2014), 371–96 and Dieter T. Roth, "Die Parabeln in der Logienquelle: 'Alte' Probleme und 'Neue' Ansätze," in *Built on Rock or Sand? Q Studies: Retrospects, Introspects and Prospects*, ed. Christoph Heil, Gertraud Harb, and Daniel Smith, BTS 34 (Leuven: Peeters, 2018), 193–212.

[6] It is rather striking that when one looks at the influential Q reconstructions found in James M. Robinson, Paul Hoffmann, and John S. Kloppenborg, *The Critical Edition of Q: Synopsis Including the Gospels of Matthew and Luke, Mark and Thomas with English, German, and French translations of Q and Thomas*, Hermeneia (Minneapolis: Fortress Press, 2000), or Harry T. Fleddermann, *Q: A Reconstruction and Commentary*, BTS 1 (Leuven: Peters, 2005), regardless of whether, for a given parable, Matthew and Luke have ca. 20% (the parallels for Q 6:47–49 [Houses Built on Rock or Sand]), 35% (Q 15:4–5a, 7 [The Lost Sheep]), 60% (the parallels for Q 7:31–35 [This Generation and the Children of Wisdom]), 80% (the parallels for Q 10:2 [Workers for the Harvest]), or 98% (the parallels for Q 16:13 [God or Mammon]) of their texts verbatim, the reconstructions found in *The Critical Edition of Q* and Fleddermann contain texts that reflect essentially 100% agreement with the words and syntax of either Matthew or Luke. This reality is not surprising when one recognizes that, unless one resorts to conjecture, a text reconstructed from Matthew and Luke cannot offer any wording beyond the wording found in either Matthew or Luke. In this way, however, regardless of the number of words actually shared by Matthew and Luke, the reader is given the strong impression that within individual pericopes the entirety of Q's wording can be found in the wording of Matthew and Luke. This impression is only furthered by the fact that since *The Critical Edition of Q* and Fleddermann are working within essentially the same methodological paradigm, their word-level reconstructions are very similar. As John Kloppenborg, "Review of Harry T. Fleddermann, *Q: A Reconstruction and Commentary*," *BTB* 37 (2007): 137–8 (here 137), noted, Fleddermann's "reconstruction of the wording of Q differs little from that of the International Q Project and where there are differences, little or nothing hangs on those differences from an exegetical point of view." The resolution of the variants between Matthew and Luke, in practice, reduces to following either one, or the other, or some combination of both. Thus, though perhaps it is not the case on the theoretical level (for there certainly is sophisticated and nuanced reflection in scholarly works concerning the issue of reconstructing the words of Q), on the practical level of actually reconstructing the text, it appears that the operative, and problematic, assumption is not only that when Matthew and Luke agree in their wording they have preserved the wording of Q, but also that when Matthew and Luke disagree in their wording either Matthew or Luke has somehow preserved the wording of Q. In fact, the notes that accompany the reconstruction in *The Critical Edition of Q*, for example, constantly ask "Luke's X or Matthew's Y?" reinforcing the impression that it is always either one or the other that contains the wording of Q, and never really neither. Michael Wolter has also drawn attention to this problem

the thought experiment of reconstructing Mark from Matthew and Luke),[7] I have become convinced that attempting to reconstruct the original words of Q and then exegeting those words just like one would when working with a critical text of Mark, Matthew, Luke, or any other early Christian gospel, is often not possible for Q.[8] For this reason, it is my view that such a model simply cannot be the most productive way to attempt to move the study of the Q parables forward. It is

---

in "Reconstructing Q?," *ExpTim* 115 (2004): 115–19, and Michael Wolter, *Das Lukasevangelium*, HNT 5 (Tübingen: Mohr Siebeck, 2008), 13.

[7] See, e.g., with different emphases and purposes, Craig Evans, "Authenticating the Words of Jesus," in *Authenticating the Words of Jesus*, ed. Bruce Chilton and Craig A. Evans, NTTS 28 (Leiden: Brill, 1999), 3–14; C. S. Rodd, "The End of the Theology of Q?," *ExpTim* 113 (2001): 5–12; C. S. Rodd, "The Theology of Q Yet Again: A Reply to the Responses of Christopher Tuckett and Paul Foster," *ExpTim* 114 (2002): 80–5; Eric Eve, "Challenging Q," *ExpTim* 113 (2002): 408–9; Eric Eve, "Reconstructing Mark: A Thought Experiment," in *Questioning Q*, ed. Mark Goodacre and Nicholas Perrin (London: SPCK, 2004), 89–114. Often overlooked in discussions of this "thought experiment" is F. Crawford Burkitt, who as early as 1906 observed "We see, clearly enough, that we could not have reconstructed the Gospel according to S. Mark out of the other two Synoptic Gospels, although between them nearly all of Mark has been incorporated by Matthew and Luke. How futile, therefore, it is to attempt to reconstruct those other literary sources which seem to have been used by Matthew and Luke, but have not been independently preserved" (*The Gospel History and Its Transmission* [Edinburgh: T. & T. Clark, 1906], 17; see also F. Crawford Burkitt, "Review of Adolf von Harnack, *Sprüche und Reden Jesu*," *JTS* 31 [1907]: 454–9). Nearly a century later, Jens Schröter similarly concludes, "The attempt to reconstruct Mk from Mt and Lk would lead inevitably to a text that would differ to a significant extent from the one that we compile from the manuscripts of Mark" (*Jesus und die Anfänge der Christologie: Methodologische und exegetische Studien zu den Ursprüngen des christlichen Glaubens*, Biblisch-Theologische Studien 47 [Neukirchen-Vluyn: Neukirchener Verlag, 2001], 94–5 [translations here and throughout are my own]). The "experiment" was carried out in detail by Joseph Allen Weaks, "Mark Without Mark: Problematizing the Reliability of a Reconstructed Text of Q" (Ph.D. diss., Brite Divinity School, 2010). When considering specifically the parables in the triple tradition, and simply using the text of NA[28] for heuristic purposes, the Parable of the Sower in Mark 4:3–9 (Matt 13:3–9//Luke 8:5–8) or the Parable of the Wicked Tenants in Mark 12:1–12 (Matt 21:33–46//Luke 20:9–18), e.g., are *impossible* to reconstruct from Matthew or Luke, since fully one-fourth or one-third of Mark's words, respectively, are not found in either Matthew or Luke.

[8] The present forum unfortunately does not allow for an extended reply to some recent criticism of my position by Olegs Andrejevs. Though I am appreciative of much in his study *Apocalypticism in the Synoptic Sayings Source*, WUNT 2/499 (Tübingen: Mohr Siebeck, 2019), the brief discussion of "The Study of Q as a Reconstructed Text" (pp. 3–11) unhelpfully groups my discussion and concerns at this point with that of Rodd and Weaks and implies that by presenting the argument concerning the inability of reconstructing the Markan wording based on Matthew and Luke, I have not understood the "deficiency of its logic" (p. 6). It is disappointing that Andrejevs did not here interact with any of the data summarized above in nn. 5 and 6 nor seem to recognize that these data include multiple layers of argumentation. Furthermore, even when Andrejevs interacts slightly more extensively with my work in an article published after his monograph ("The 'Reconstructed Mark' and the Reconstruction of Q: A Valid Analogy?," *BTB* 50 [2020]: 83–91), at several points I do not recognize the argument I am supposedly making and most of his counter-arguments betray that he has not fully grasped the nature of the arguments that I do, or at least am attempting, to make. Perhaps I had not been as clear as I had hoped in the published presentations of my argument. Finally, in a review of my monograph, Andrejevs "wonders whether the author is not attempting to stake a nonexistent middle ground between engaging Q—which would mean grappling with its text—and studying its reception by the canonical Gospels" (Review of Dieter T. Roth, 'The Parables in Q', *BTB* 50 [2020]: 62–3 [here 63]). Of course, Andrejevs is entitled to believe that there is "nonexistent middle ground" in whatever way he is conceiving of this ground, but the entire point of my extensive argument is to present a different paradigm for engaging Q precisely *by* studying it through Matthew and Luke. The main elements of my approach appear in summary form throughout this chapter.

important to note that although I am arguing that scholarship should be skeptical about reconstructions of the precise wording of Q parables, I am not advocating the position that the Q parables were not found in a written text nor would I contend that Q is largely inaccessible.[9] I also do not wish to restrict analysis of Q to those texts where very high verbal agreement theoretically might create less doubt about the wording of Q nor only engage in some type of "word study" of minimal Q.[10] I also do not wish to pursue appeals to different versions of Q (i.e., Q^{Mt} or Q^{Lk}) as an explanation for significant variants. Rather, I would argue that even as one may continue to appreciate and appropriate the insights found in the source-critical and redaction-critical model of approaching Q,[11] a possible way forward is to alter the conception of "textual reconstruction." Such a shift in thinking (and here the question at the outset, "What in fact is a text at all?," resurfaces) would result in approaching the "text" of the Q parables via Matthew and Luke, without envisioning a recovery of the precise, original *words on a page* of Q found somewhere *behind* Matthew and Luke, but to recover an "intertext" *between* Matthew and Luke. Here it is important to recognize that "intertextuality," as observed by Renate Lachmann, "is the semantic interchange, the contact between texts literary and non-literary."[12] Such semantic interchange and contact *can*, of course, occur on the word level, but it also occurs on many other levels, including narrative structures and techniques, images, stylistic devices, characters, motifs, and so forth.[13] It is particularly these other levels beyond the precise words, incorporated and expanded upon by Matthew and Luke in their Gospels, which may reveal insight into Q, and especially the Q parables, without the

---

[9] For a helpful discussion of how even passages in Matthew and Luke with low verbatim agreement do not necessarily point to an oral Q, see John S. Kloppenborg, "Variation in the Reproduction of the Double Tradition and an Oral Q?," *ETL* 83 (2007): 53–80.

[10] Thus, I would not want to follow Thomas Bergemann, *Q auf dem Prüfstand*, FRLANT 158 (Göttingen: Vandenhoeck & Ruprecht, 1993), 60, in restricting Q to "a source defined by significant agreement in wording" with the corollary that "all passages that do not meet this criterion may not be attributed to Q." Schmid had already pointed out the wide range of verbal agreement in Matthew's and Luke's use of Mark, so it is not surprising that a similar phenomenon is observable in their use of Q: Joseph Schmid, *Matthäus und Lukas. Eine Untersuchung des Verhältnisses ihrer Evangelien* (Freiburg: Herder, 1930), 188.

[11] One helpful component to Q reconstructions in their present state is, as Kloppenborg, "On Dispensing with Q? Goodacre on the Relation of Luke to Matthew," *NTS* 49 (2003): 210–36 (here 224), observes: the "text of Q obviously shares some elements with Matthew, but it also has elements that appear in Luke; what it lacks are those features that appear to be Matthean and Lukan editorializing." Even if one questions the extent to which the reconstructed text actually represents the wording of Q, the careful analysis highlighting Matthean and Lukan editorializing is extremely helpful from a negative vantage point, namely, the identification of words and phrases likely *not* in Q.

[12] Renate Lachmann, "Cultural Memory and the Role of Literature," *European Review* 12 (2004): 165–78 (here 173).

[13] This understanding of intertextuality is somewhat different from the one set forth by Franz Schnider, "Das Gleichnis vom verlorenen Schaf und seine Redaktoren: Ein intertextueller Vergleich," *Kairos* 19 (1977): 146–54 (here 146), when he states, "the intertextual comparison of texts must begin methodologically, as every comparison of texts, with a synchronic description of the text and then explain diachronically the historical development of the text." As such, Schnider approaches "intertextuality" essentially as a question of recognizing redaction. In addition, this emphasis on the redactional development also simply assumes that Luke's version is closest to Q and that the differences in the Matthean version are to be understood as Matthean redaction (p. 147).

challenge, and, at times, impossibility of reconstructing the exact and original wording of Q. Of course, such an analysis cannot function on an entirely "wordless" level; however, there is, I would submit, a fundamental difference between conceiving of the "text of Q" as a reconstruction of the original wording and approaching it as an intertextual, metaphorical and narrative realm, so to speak, accessible through Matthew and Luke.[14] Thus, when I am considering harvest imagery in Q parables, it is not merely "harvest wording" in which I am interested, though such wording is important. Instead, it is the entirety of harvest imagery as gleaned (pun intended) from Matthew and Luke in the double tradition.

2. Considering Parables

Turning briefly to the second issue surrounding the understanding and identification of parables, there has been a tremendous amount of work done on this issue over the past fifteen years or so at the Johannes Gutenberg-Universität Mainz. Ruben Zimmermann, in particular, is to be credited with providing truly significant and helpful insights for the study of parables.[15] An especially notable contribution can be found in the application of modern genre theory in order to think through and formulate a definition of a parable that does justice to the wide range of texts identified as such in antiquity and the New Testament, without becoming so broad and wide-ranging so as to no longer be helpful. Here I would simply like to highlight the definition as set forth in Zimmermann's 2015 work, *Puzzling the Parables of Jesus*:[16]

A *parable* is a short narratival (1) fictional (2) (text) that is related in the narrated world to known reality (3) but, by way of implicit or explicit transfer signals, makes it understood that the meaning of the narration must be differentiated from the literal words of the text (4). In its appeal dimension (5) it challenges the reader to carry out a metaphoric transfer of meaning that is steered by contextual information (6).[17]

On the basis of this definition, I have identified two parables of John the Baptist, one of the Centurion, and 24 parables of Jesus in Q.[18] Once again, an exhaustive discussion is not possible within the confines of this chapter, though

---

[14] Clearly such an endeavor requires a shift in the reigning paradigm of Q studies and challenges the assumption behind such statements as Robert A. Derrenbacker, "Review of Dale C. Allison Jr., *The Intertextual Jesus: Scripture in Q*," *CBQ* 64 (2002): 150–1 (here 151), observes, "Any treatment of Q's use of Scripture must presuppose a specific reconstruction of the wording of the sayings source."

[15] As noted by Klyne Snodgrass in his chapter "Recent Contributions to Parable Interpretation" in the second edition of his massive work, *Stories with Intent: A Comprehensive Guide to the Parables of Jesus*, 2nd ed. (Grand Rapids, MI: Eerdmans, 2018), 569: "Ruben Zimmermann is the most prolific contributor to parable research in the past *twenty* years' (emphasis original).

[16] See the longer discussion of a variety of issues related to defining a "parable" in Roth, *Parables in Q*, 7–21.

[17] Ruben Zimmermann, *Puzzling the Parables of Jesus: Methods and Interpretation* (Minneapolis: Fortress Press, 2015), 137.

[18] See Roth, *Parables in Q*, 18–21.

attention can be given to the harvest imagery in at least several exemplary Q parables.

3. Harvest Imagery in Q Parables of John the Baptist

Christopher Tuckett has rightly pointed out: "One of the more surprising features of Q is the amount of space devoted to John the Baptist. John's preaching is set out in detail in Q 3:7–9 and in 3:16f., and a long section a little later in Q (7:18–35) discusses the position of John in some detail."[19] In fact, a comparison of Matthew and Luke reveals that the preaching in which the two parables spoken by John the Baptist are found may have formed part of the opening sayings of Q,[20] leading Ernst Bammel to comment that "it is even more surprising that a document that is supposed to consist merely of sayings of Jesus starts with sections dealing with John."[21] The first of John's parables relates that "the ax is lying at the root of the trees; every tree therefore that does not bear good fruit is cut down and thrown into the fire" (Q 3:9) and the second concerns the "Coming One": "His winnowing fork is in his hand, to clear his threshing floor and to gather the wheat into his granary; but the chaff he will burn with unquenchable fire" (Q 3:17). Though much could be said about these parables, two points are particularly significant for the present study.

First, in the parables spoken by John the Baptist, he employs two harvest images involving fruit on trees and wheat on a threshing floor, both readily understandable in an agrarian context, in order to present images of future, yet proximate, judgment. It is striking that "fire" is introduced as a catchword that serves to connect the parables, and furthermore, in the second parable, both Matthew and Luke refer to a fire that is ἄσβεστος. Though a metaphoric transfer of the "fire" imagery can already occur through its use in the Jewish tradition to depict judgment[22] or the

---

[19] Christopher Tuckett, *Q and the History of Early Christianity* (Edinburgh: T. & T. Clark, 1996), 108. For extensive discussion of John the Baptist's parables in Q, see Roth, *Parables in Q*, 57–77.

[20] Risto Uro, "John the Baptist and the Jesus Movement: What Does Q Tell Us?" in *The Gospel Behind the Gospels*, ed. Ronald A. Piper, NovTSup 75 (Leiden: Brill, 1995), 231–57 (here 234), expresses this view more strongly: "The comparison of Matthew and Luke makes it obvious that Q opened with a collection of John's sayings." In any case, both Matthew and Luke identify the preaching as that of John the Baptist and it is generally accepted that this identification was also found, in some form, in Q. See, e.g., Harry Fleddermann, "The Beginning of Q," *SBLSP* 24 (1985): 153–9; Gerd Häfner, *Der verheißene Vorläufer: Redaktionskritische Untersuchung zur Darstellung Johannes des Täufers im Matthäusevangelium*, SBB 27 (Stuttgart: Katholisches Bibelwerk, 1994), 35; and John S. Kloppenborg, "City and Wasteland: Narrative World and the Beginning of the Sayings Gospel (Q)," *Semeia* 52 (1990): 145–60 (here 149–51). Ron Cameron, "'What Have You Come Out To See?': Characterizations of John and Jesus in the Gospels," *Semeia* 49 (1990): 35–69 (here 37), however, contends "Q 3:7–9, 16–17 do not explicitly mention John by name. Although the embedded contexts of these verses in Matthew and Luke identify the speaker as John (the Baptist), the extant text of Q does not make that identification explicit." The reference to "the extant text of Q" presumably means the Q reconstruction accepted by Cameron.

[21] Ernst Bammel, "Seminar Report: The Baptist in Early Christian Tradition," *NTS* 18 (1971): 95–128 (here 99).

[22] E.g., in the HB, Isa 10:16–17; 66:24; Nah 1:6; Zeph 1:18; and Mal 4:1, or in other Second Temple texts such as 1QpHab X, 5, 13; 1QH^a III, 29–34; 1QS II, 8; *1 En.* 10:6; 54:1–2; 90:24–25; 100:9; 102:1; *Jub.* 9:15; 36:10; *Pss. Sol.* 15:4–5, 6–7, 10–15; and *4 Ezra* 7:36–38.

burning of chaff being used as an image of the destruction of the wicked,[23] the reference to πυρὶ ἀσβέστῳ alludes to a *Bildfeld*[24] linking God's judgment, wrath, or anger with a fire that cannot be quenched (e.g., Isa 66:24; Jer 4:4; 7:20; 17:27; 21:12; Amos 5:6).[25] As John Nolland observes, "The word [ἀσβέστῳ] protrudes somewhat from the imagery as an allegorical element designed to evoke images of the fire of God's irreversible final judgment."[26]

Second, there is an important element involving the agent active in the harvest/judgment imagery that is, in my estimation, often overlooked. In the first parable, not only is it literally impossible for one ax to be laid at the root of numerous trees and the "chopping down" action of one ax to be applied simultaneously to multiple trees,[27] but the wielder of the ax is not explicitly identified. Since, however, the apparently immediately preceding verse in Q (Matt 3:9//Luke 3:8) explicitly identifies God as the one who is able to "raise up" children of Abraham from rocks, I would contend that the reader or hearer of Q is to a certain extent guided towards viewing the passive construction, as reflected in both Matthew and Luke, as a divine passive. As such, it would be appropriate to conclude that it

---

[23] E.g., Isa 5:24; Nah 1:10; Obad 18; and Mal 3:19. A further instance of קשׁ being burned can be found in Isa 47:14, though here the LXX reads φρύγανον. On Mal 3:19 being recalled in John's "portrait of what is to come," see John S. Kloppenborg Verbin, *Excavating Q: The History and Setting of the Sayings Gospel* (Minneapolis: Fortress Press, 2000), 122. Rightly cautious, however, of a tendency, at times, to connect Q 3:17 almost exclusively to Mal 3:19 (see, e.g., Jeffrey A. Trumbower, "The Role of Malachi in the Career of John the Baptist," in *The Gospels and the Scriptures of Israel*, ed. Craig A. Evans and W. Richard Stegner, JSNTSup 104 [Sheffield: Sheffield Academic Press, 1994], 28–54 [here 35–6]), is Dale C. Allison, Jr., *The Intertextual Jesus: Scripture in Q* [Harrisburg, PA: Trinity Press International, 2000], 124), who states, "John's word about judgment may not allude to any one text in particular but rather illustrate a natural concatenation of traditional eschatological motifs." See also the comments of James D. G. Dunn, "John the Baptist's Use of Scripture," in Evans and Stegner, eds., *The Gospels and the Scriptures of Israel*, 42–54 (here 49).

[24] Though there is no precise English term for a *Bildfeld*, the term "stock metaphor" comes quite close. As such, one can observe the creation of a *Bildfeldtradition* in which "a traditional coupling of metaphorical domains" takes place (Zimmermann, *Puzzling the Parables*, 204). For further observations, see Roth, *Parables in Q*, 53–4.

[25] In each instance a negation involving the verb σβέννυμι appears in the LXX. See also the imagery in Isa 34:9–10. Again cautioning against drawing a direct connection between Q 3:17 and only one verse, in this instance Isa 66:24, is Allison, *Intertextual Jesus*, 227–8.

[26] John Nolland, *The Gospel of Matthew: A Commentary on the Greek Text*, NIGTC (Grand Rapids, MI: Eerdmans, 2005), 149. See also John Nolland, *Luke*, 3 vols., WBC 35 (Dallas, TX: Word Books, 1989–93), 1:152–3. Also, see R. T. France, *The Gospel of Matthew*, NICNT (Grand Rapids, MI: Eerdmans, 2007), 115, who views the words as one of two sets of terms that point "beyond the pictorial scene to the reality it signifies" (διακαθαίρω/διακαθαρίζω being the other), and Richard Valantasis, *The New Q: A Fresh Translation with Commentary* (New York: T&T Clark, 2005), 48, who speaks of "inextinguishable fire" having "cosmic connotations." Though the "cleansing" may convey purification or refining as in Mal 3:2–3, John Kloppenborg, "The Power and Surveillance of the Divine Judge in the early Synoptic Tradition," in *Christ and the Emperor: The Gospel Evidence*, ed. Gilbert Van Belle and Joseph Verheyden (Leuven: Peeters, 2014), 147–84 (here 159 n. 37), points out that despite the verbs διακαθαίρω or διακαθαρίζω not being common, there are examples of cognate nouns appearing in papyri and referring to the pruning of plants in P.Soter. 4.24–28 and P.Strass. IX 872.7–9.

[27] It appears that the depiction of the judging ax within the context of eschatological urgency has impacted the manner in which the image is presented. As Nolland, *Luke*, 1.149, puts it, "a single ax at the root of many trees does not make for good visual imagery, but suits the eschatological temper of John's warning."

is, in fact, God who has laid the ax and who is preparing to "cut down" the trees not bearing fruit.[28] In the second parable, the agent is explicitly identified as the "Coming One," who, within the context of Q, is undoubtedly to be understood as Jesus.[29] Thus, I would argue that Q, based on the sense of a divine passive, presents God as the prosecutor of judgment in John the Baptist's first parable, but in his second parable assigns this role to the "Coming One," that is to Jesus. If this interpretation is correct, John's parables, within a "harvest" context, already create a direct connection between God's activity and Jesus's activity, a connection that is also found in the "sending" imagery in Q 10:2 and 3, for example.[30] It would appear, therefore, that the harvest imagery in John's parables is used in Q not only to highlight the theme of judgment right at or near the outset of Q, but also to equate the activity of God and that of Jesus within this context. That is to say, Q sets the stage for its proclamation with parabolic harvest imagery employed for both eschatological and theological purposes.

---

[28] In the Lukan context, Joel B. Green, *The Gospel of Luke*, NICNT (Grand Rapids, MI: Eerdmans, 1997), 177, states, "Following as it does so closely the use of God as subject in 3:8, the undeclared subject of 'to cut down' in 3:9 is presumably divine as well." In the Matthean context, W. D. Davies and Dale C. Allison, Jr., *The Gospel According to Saint Matthew*, 3 vols., ICC (Edinburgh: T. & T. Clark, 1988–97), 1:309 simply assert, "God is implicitly the agent of the passive"; similarly Blaine Charette, *The Theme of Recompense in Matthew's Gospel*, JSNTSup 79 (Sheffield: JSOT Press, 1992), 123 n. 1; Marius Reiser, *Die Gerichtspredigt Jesu: Eine Untersuchung zur eschatologischen Verkündigung Jesu und ihrem frühjüdischen Hintergrund*, NTAbh 23 (Münster: Aschendorff, 1990), 164; and Elisabeth Sevenich-Bax, *Israels Konfrontation mit den letzten Boten der Weisheit: Form, Funktion und Interdependenz der Weisheitselemente in der Logienquelle* (Altenberge: Oros, 1993), 276. I. Howard Marshall, *The Gospel of Luke: A Commentary on the Greek Text*, NIGTC (Exeter: Paternoster Press, 1978), 141, is slightly more cautious: "The passive form of the verb may signify that God is the active subject."

[29] See Paul Hoffmann, *Studien zur Theologie der Logienquelle*, 3rd ed., NTAbh 8 (Münster: Aschendorff, 1982), 33: "[Q] identifies the judge with the (coming as Son of Man) earthly Jesus." Claus-Peter März, "Zum Verständnis der Gerichtspredigt in Q," in *Weltgericht und Weltvollendung: Zukunftsbilder im Neuen Testament*, ed. Hans-Josef Klauck, QD 150 (Freiburg: Herder, 1994), 128–48 (here 137), similarly concludes: "In the context of the source, Jesus is undoubtedly the referent." See also Darrell L. Bock, *Luke*, 2 vols., BECNT 3 (Grand Rapids, MI: Baker Books, 1994–96), 1:324: "Jesus separates between people, and the winnowing fork is in his hand already," and W. F. Albright and C. S. Mann, *Matthew*, AB 26 (Garden City: Doubleday, 1971), 27: "This verse emphasizes the role of the Messiah in judgment when he comes with his baptism." Michael Tilly, *Johannes der Täufer und die Biographie der Propheten: Die synoptische Täuferüberlieferung und das jüdische Prophetenbild zur Zeit der Täufers*, BWANT 137 (Stuttgart: Kohlhammer, 1993), 78, contends that the "historical John" would have identified the "Coming One" as God and not as Jesus. This position is also cautiously advanced by Stephanie von Dobbeler, *Das Gericht und das Erbarmen Gottes*, BBB 70 (Frankfurt: Athenäum, 1988), 76–7, 144–7. T. W. Manson, *The Sayings of Jesus* (London: SCM Press, 1949), 41, however, disagrees with this sentiment, "The language of v. 16 is not the kind that John would have used of God." Be that as it may, the question of what was "originally" meant by John in his preaching, though interesting to consider, is, however, irrelevant for the identification in Q for "in Christian circles, and certainly in Q, ὁ ἐρχόμενος was identified with Jesus (as Q 7:18–23 shows)." Cf. John Kloppenborg, *The Formation of Q: Trajectories in Ancient Wisdom Collections*, SAC (Philadelphia, PA: Fortress Press, 1987), 104; see also Kloppenborg, *Excavating Q*, 391. For a survey of the various figures identified with the "Coming One" in scholarship, see Sevenich-Bax, *Israels Konfrontation*, 307–11, who herself also sees the term referring to Jesus as the Son of Man.

[30] In Q 10:2 the "Lord of the Harvest," generally understood symbolically to represent God, is petitioned to send workers into the field and in Q 10:3 Jesus sends out his followers like sheep among wolves.

4. Harvest Imagery in Q Parables of Jesus

Following these opening parables by John the Baptist, Q contains a significant number of parables spoken by Jesus. Interestingly, it seems that the first of these involving harvest imagery, namely the Parable of a Tree Being Known by Its Fruit (Q 6:43–44), picks up the fruit imagery from John's opening parable.[31] The well-known parable indicates that a good tree cannot produce bad or rotten fruit and a rotten tree cannot produce good fruit. A tree is known by its fruit. Harvest imagery then continues to be used in the observation that a "bunch of grapes" (σταφυλή) [in Matthew] or a "fig" (σῦκον) [in Luke] cannot be gathered from a thorny plant. Nor can a "bunch of grapes" (σταφυλή) be gathered from a "thorny bush" (βάτος) [in Luke] or a "fig" (σῦκον) be gathered from a "thistle" (τρίβολος) [in Matthew]. Despite these differences, and regardless of what the actual reading was in Q,[32] the fundamental point is the same: it is impossible to gather, to harvest, fruit from weeds.[33]

The parable clearly contains a general observation, presented in antithetical parallelism, involving a harvest-related image of a tree and its fruit.[34] The focus of the imagery in this general observation falls upon the nature of the fruit produced based upon the nature of the tree as no good tree produces bad fruit and vice versa.[35] When one turns to the specific instance or illustration of the general observation, it is worth noting that this illustration, regardless of whether it preceded or followed the comments about the tree and its fruit, only extrapolates upon the preceding or ensuing depiction of the "bad" tree. Thus, in this specific situation the implied narrative imagines a thorny weed or plant, the complication of such a plant not bearing fruit, resulting in the recognition of the folly of ever attempting or expecting to find fruit on such plants.[36]

---

[31] The longer discussion from which the following paragraphs are drawn can be found in Roth, *Parables in Q*, 238–46.

[32] Fleddermann, *Q: Reconstruction*, 302, rightly states that attempting to reconstruct Q here "involves many extremely difficult decisions" and observes that "some scholars like Schmid and Schulz decide not to decide; and Marshall despairs of any literary solution, appealing to oral variants." Fleddermann himself, however, is convinced that "the situation is not quite as desperate" as some have feared, though the question of just how "desperate" the reconstruction issues are at this point may be debated, I would suggest that refraining from pursuing the precise wording of Q and instead elucidating the general image, appears to be, if I am permitted yet another pun, a more fruitful approach.

[33] See Siegfried Schulz's, *Die Spruchquelle der Evangelisten* (Zurich: Theologischer Verlag, 1972), 317, view: "A decision concerning which of the respective, opposing pairs is earlier is hardly possible...and also objectively completely inconsequential."

[34] See also the comments in Ronald A. Piper, *Wisdom in the Q-Tradition: The Aphoristic Teaching of Jesu*, SNTSMS 61 (Cambridge: Cambridge University Press, 1989), 48.

[35] It is interesting to note here that "producing fruit" implies the passage of time even if this temporal element is not narrated. See also Dierk Starnitzke, "Von den Früchten des Baumes und dem Sprechen des Herzens (Vom Baum und seinen Früchten): Q 6,43–45 (Mt 7,16–20; 12,33–35 / Lk 6,43–45 / EvThom 45)," in *Kompendium der Gleichnisse Jesu*, ed. Ruben Zimmermann (Gütersloh: Gütersloher Verlagshaus, 2007), 81–91 (here 81).

[36] On this final point, see also Marshall, *Luke*, 273. Alan Kirk, *The Composition of the Sayings Source: Genre, Synchrony, and Wisdom Redaction in Q*, NovTSup 91 (Leiden: Brill, 1998), 174, comments that "the framing of the example as a rhetorical question helps coerce the assent of the auditors."

Though there are "harvesters" implied in the background of Q 6:44, no emphasis is placed upon these stock characters themselves as the parable instead highlights a particular activity and especially the imagery of an "impossible harvest." For this reason, and as is also the case in John the Baptist's parable of the Ax at the Root of the Trees, it is the trees who function as a type of "character" in this parable. Though Q 6:43–44, in and of itself, can be understood simply on the agricultural level, the intratextual connection to John the Baptist's parable as well as the content of Q 6:45 reveal that there is imagery with symbolic significance involving "trees" and "fruit" undergirding the parable. Though here the trees are not being threatened by the action(s) of the divine ax-wielder as in John the Baptist's parable, the same determination of the character of the tree via its fruit is found in both parables. This is the case even though in Q 3:9 it was the presence or absence of "good fruit" that functioned as a type of "character trait," and here the presence of "good" or "bad" fruit reveals the nature of the "character."

It is striking that even though the imagery, once again, draws on common images that would have been part and parcel of everyday life for anyone living in an agrarian culture, the parable only highlights the quality of the tree as determinative for the quality of the fruit, completely ignoring other factors, such as drought, heat, or cold, that could negatively affect the growth of fruit.[37] That no other factors are mentioned leads to the emphasis being placed upon what could be referred to as "internal" and not "external" factors, a point that becomes significant for the use of the parable in Q.

It is true that these verses are an example of the type of passage (along with Q 3:9; 17:37; and 10:2) that Tuckett points out could be simply "some kind of 'proverb' or relatively banal statement about the way the world is" when isolated from its context.[38] In other words, "Q 6:43–45 says that good trees produce good fruit, and bad trees bad fruit," a reality observable in any field, in any place, at any time.[39] Of course, as true as this statement is, Q is saying significantly more through this parable, as there is every indication that it was found in the context of a good or bad person bringing forth good or bad treasure and about speech being determined by the state of one's heart (Matt 12:34//Luke 6:45). That is to say, Q appears here to have chosen to use harvest imagery in a parable to make the point that one reveals one's own character through the actions one takes, the deeds one performs, and especially the speech that crosses one's lips.[40]

A second parable of Jesus that I would like to mention is the Parable of the Workers for the Harvest found in Q 10:2.[41] If one considers the plot development

---

[37] See also Starnitzke, "Von den Früchten," 83.
[38] Tuckett, *Q and the History of Early Christianity*, 350.
[39] Ibid.
[40] See Michael Labahn, "Das Reich Gottes und seine performativen Abbildungen: Gleichnisse, Parabeln und Bilder als Handlungsmodelle im Dokument Q," in *Hermeneutik der Gleichnisse Jesu: Methodische Neuansätze zum Verstehen urchristlicher Parabeltexte*, ed. Ruben Zimmermann in collaboration with Gabi Kern, WUNT 231 (Tübingen: Mohr Siebeck, 2008), 259–82 (here 266).
[41] The longer discussion from which the following paragraphs are drawn can be found in Roth, *Parables in Q*, 274–86.

of the account, the initial situation explicitly mentions a harvest, and one that is described as πολύς. This statement, however, is immediately followed by a complication, namely that there is a paucity of workers (οἱ δὲ ἐργάται ὀλίγοι).[42] Since the timing or the size of the harvest cannot be changed, the only variable that can be altered is the number of workers sent out to bring the harvest in. Thus, the plot's transforming action unfolds with a call to petition the lord of the harvest (κύριος τοῦ θερισμοῦ) to send workers into the harvest.[43] At this point the parable simply breaks off. The hearer or reader is not told if more workers were sent and thus does not know the fate of the harvest. The ultimate outcome is apparently not of interest, resulting in an emphatic focus upon the appeal to *petition* for an increase in the number of workers as it is the last plot element presented before the parable abruptly ends.

Also of significance is that in this parable, and differently from numerous other Q parables, the hearer is included as a "character" through the imperative addressed to her or him. When the hearer or reader of this parable is confronted with the imperative δεήθητε, she or he is drawn into the parable and admonished to direct a request to the "lord of the harvest." In the parable, at least on the surface, one group of individuals is to petition that another group be sent to bring in the harvest. Though this is often considered to be an indication that the Q context is one after the initial missionary context, perhaps it is not as obvious at it seems to some that only "settled" groups could be petitioning "the lord" to send workers into the harvest.[44] I. Howard Marshall, for instance, observed that "it

---

[42] Ruben Zimmermann, "Folgenreiche Bitte! [Arbeiter für die Ernte] Q 10,2 [Mt 9,37f/Lk 10,2/ EvThom 73]," in Zimmermann, ed., *Kompendium der Gleichnisse Jesu*, 111–18 (here 111), thus rightly observes, "In this way, it is less the joy concerning a large harvest that is brought to expression and rather a problem that is immediately pointed out."

[43] Both Matthew and Luke refer to a petition to "cast out" (ἐκβάλλω) these workers. This is different from, e.g., Matt 20:2 where the sending is described with the more expected ἀποστέλλω. Giovanni B. Bazzana, *Kingdom of Bureaucracy: The Political Theology of Village Scribes in the Sayings Gospel Q*, BETL 274 (Leuven: Peeters, 2015), 88, has pointed out that the oddity of this term is "an element that is not noted by commentators working on Q 10,2." On the basis of usage found in Egyptian papyri (BGU 16 2602 and P.Mich. 11 618), Bazzana observes that the term is used in Egypt to describe compulsory work done on dikes or canals. Though such work is obviously not in view in Q, he argues that "Q 10,2 contains two implicit elements that may well have rendered easier for its author this creative use of imagery and phrases evoking liturgies," namely the "urgency" of the work and the "hierarchical structure" implied by the term κύριος τοῦ θερισμοῦ (*Kingdom of Bureaucracy*, 95). As a result, Bazzana posits that "the occurrence of ἐκβάλλω within the image of a harvest in urgent need of a larger workforce makes most sense if we think that the groups within which the text was authored and then circulated were composed of people acquainted with the specific Greek terminology for liturgies and for the management of liturgical services" (ibid.).

[44] David R. Catchpole, *The Quest for Q* (Edinburgh: T. & T. Clark, 1993), 159, though seeing vv. 2 and 3 arising out of different contexts, also cautions against driving a wedge between "the mission of the wandering charismatics" in a Jewish setting and a "church mission" aimed at the conversion of Gentiles He prefers to speak of "a settled but charismatic church sponsoring a charismatic mission" (*Quest for Q*, 160); however, even here one could inquire just how "settled" a church must be in order to pray. In any case, Q, as available to Matthew and Luke, does not reflect a group of exclusively itinerant workers or "wandering charismatics" (for cautionary comments on making too much of the "itinerancy" model for understanding Q, see Kloppenborg, *Excavating Q*, 211). Richard A. Horsley with Jonathan Draper, *Whoever Hears You Hears Me: Prophets, Performance, and Tradition in Q* (Harrisburg, PA: Trinity Press International, 1999), 242, rather directly state

is in fact missionaries themselves who are most conscious of the need for more workers."⁴⁵ It is even possible, as Zimmermann notes, that while petitioning the lord of the harvest, those involved in such petitioning may themselves become more acutely aware of the need and end up presenting themselves as workers to be sent into the field.⁴⁶ In any case, though there are several interesting elements that could be discussed in a character analysis of the ἐργάται mentioned in the petition, the figure most relevant for present purposes is the "lord of the harvest" mentioned in both Matthew and Luke.⁴⁷

One encounters this character in the parable as both the owner of the harvest and the figure who has the authority to send workers into the field. As such, the sending is actually dependent upon him. At the same time, that the parable specifically refers to petitioning this "lord" to send the laborers so that the large harvest, or better *his* large harvest, is not lost raises the question of why such a petition should be necessary. Is the absent owner's ignorance concerning the circumstances of the harvest due to his being foolish or disinterested?⁴⁸ Or is it rather that this curiosity presses the addressee to consider that the act of petitioning reveals the fact that the resolution to the problem lies completely within the hands of the "lord" and that one is dependent upon him to act? In this way, perhaps the parable uses the petition to prompt reflection on a position of dependence in a situation involving something more than an economic concern and in a reality beyond an annual grain harvest.⁴⁹

---

their problem with approaches locating vv. 2 and 3 in different contexts, contending that "the move from a petition to "the lord of the harvest" to send out (more) laborers in Q 10:2 to the declaratory sending of (more) laborers in 10:3 would be only appropriate if not expected. Detection of a discrepancy between these two closely related steps in the standard mission discourse is an inappropriate application of modern Western logic of literary compositional consistency and is perhaps rooted in a lack of class analysis."

⁴⁵ Marshall, *Luke*, 416.

⁴⁶ Zimmermann, "Folgenreiche Bitte!," 116. It is therefore not quite clear that "Q 10:2 indicates that there must be some kind of "base community" that sends out workers, rather than workers forming groups"; cf. Alicia Batten, "More Queries for Q: Women and Christian Origins," *BTB* 24 (1994): 44–51 (here 47).

⁴⁷ Some elements of the following discussion concerning this "lord" or "master" draw on Roth, "'Master' as Character in the Q Parables," 375–7, 392.

⁴⁸ Kloppenborg, "Power and Surveillance," 164, states that "the scenario used by Q is a standard one in the agricultural realm" (assuming that an absentee landlord is in view). Even if this view is correct, the papyri that Kloppenborg cites in support of his statement, namely PSI VI 345 and P.Cair.Zen. 1 59049.3–4, only make mention of a request to send ten guards during the harvest time and of a manager requesting that the owner send someone to collect the hay since he is otherwise occupied. It seems to me that a request for guards or a representative to collect the hay is not quite the same scenario as the one presented in this parable as the landlord described in the papyri seems fully aware of the state of his fields and what the harvest requires. More generally, see Seán Freyne, *Galilee from Alexander the Great to Hadrian 323 B.C.E. to 135 C.E.* (Wilmington, DE: Michael Glazier; Notre Dame: University of Notre Dame Press, 1980), 156–70, for discussion of the difficulties of ascertaining the agricultural situation in Galilee. Joachim Habbe, *Palästina zur Zeit Jesu: Die Landwirtschaft in Galiläa als Hintergrund der synoptischen Evangelien* (Neukirchen-Vluyn: Neukirchener Verlag, 1996), 107, contends that the reference to a large estate in Luke 10:2 seems more likely to refer to the Jezreel Valley or Judea than to Galilee.

⁴⁹ Here Jens Eder's, *Die Figur im Film: Grundlagen der Figurenanalyse* (Marburg: Schüren, 2008), 213, comment seems particularly a propos, namely that when one is confronted with information

In any case, it is quite clear that the key image of this parable is the "harvest." The parable, as seen through Matthew and Luke, begins with a description of the θερισμός as πολύς, then refers to a κύριος τοῦ θερισμοῦ, and finally highlights that it is to this landlord that the harvest belongs (θερισμός αὐτοῦ). Thus, not only does the image appear repeatedly in rapid succession, it also appears at the outset, in the middle, and at the end of this brief parable, further underscoring its significance. Remarkably, the joy that would normally be associated with the blessing *of* a large harvest is immediately tempered in the parable by the paucity of workers *for* the harvest. The fact that there is an inadequate number of workers to bring the harvest in out of the field presents the very real danger of the harvest being lost or ruined.[50] It is important to note that the primary emphasis in the parable is not on a need existing because the harvest is *near*, but rather because the harvest is *large*.[51] Though on some level there may well be an implicit sense of urgency, especially in the light of the rich background in the HB and Second Temple literature of the time of the harvest as the time of God's eschatological judgment (cf. Isa 18:5; Joel 4:13; Mic 4:12; Isa 27:12; 2 Bar. 70:2; *4 Ezra* 4:28–32),[52] the danger of losing the harvest in the imagery of the parable is not first and foremost due to a lack of time, it is due to a lack of workers. There is a plentiful harvest that, *without workers*, may be lost.[53] Even though a temporal element is not entirely absent, the fact remains that the focus is not on the temporal nearness of the harvest nor is there any explicit reference to judgment of any sort in this parable. Q may very well assume that the time of the harvest, understood eschatologically, has come and that there is a certain urgency in bringing the harvest in; nevertheless, the temporal element remains in the background. Once again,

---

concerning a character that results in a certain level of cognitive dissonance, the result is that one either ignores or reinterprets the disturbing information, or modifies the model or framework within which one views the character. See also Zimmermann, "Folgenreiche Bitte!," 115.

[50] For comments on the loss of a harvest, see 1 Sam 12:17; Prov 26:1; and Theophrastus, *Caus. plant.* 4.13.6.

[51] For this reason, when Hoffmann, *Studien zur Theologie*, 291–2, states that "not the "size of the mission field" but rather the pressing time leads to the petition of the Lord of the Harvest to send laborers for his harvest," he is incorrect, or at least unbalanced, in his conclusion. See also the overriding emphasis on "apocalyptic" issues in Schulz, *Die Spruchquelle*, 410–11. Also critical of these views is Marshall, *Luke*, 416: "the saying explicitly points to the greatness of the task." See, further, David P. Moessner, *Lord of the Banquet: The Literary and Theological Significance of the Lukan Travel Narrative* (Minneapolis, MN: Fortress Press, 1989), 135. Jens Schröter, *Erinnerung an Jesu Worte: Studien zur Rezeption der Logienüberlieferung in Markus, Q und Thomas*, WMANT 76 (Neukirchen-Vluyn: Neukirchener Verlag, 1997), 170, observes, "The emphasis lies…not only on the harvest, but on the unbalanced relationship between its size and the paucity of available workers."

[52] Markus Tiwald, *Wanderradikalismus Jesu erste Jünger—ein Anfang und was davon bleibt*, ÖBS 20 (Frankfurt: Peter Lang, 2002), rightly cautions against moving too quickly into judgment imagery with the term θερισμός as only in Isa 18:5 is it used in the LXX as a metaphor for judgment. Nevertheless, the harvest imagery as image for the eschatological judgment, as Tiwald also recognizes, is clear. See also the discussion in Joachim Jeremias, *The Parables of Jesus*, 2nd ed., trans. S. H. Hooke (London: SCM Press, 1972), 119, where he comments, "Harvest and vintage symbolize in particular the Last Judgement with which the New Age begins."

[53] See the comments of Hermann-Josef Venetz, "Bittet den Herrn der Ernte: Überlegungen zu Lk 10,2//Mt 9,37," *Diakonia* 11 (1980): 148–61 (here 152–3).

the primary component is not the *time/nearness* of the harvest, but rather the *size* of the harvest.⁵⁴ The harvest is πολύς.⁵⁵

It is important to note that at the conclusion of the parable, it does not merely "point to a way out of the difficulty by tracing the Christian mission back to God who as Lord of the harvest calls and sends laborers into his mission."⁵⁶ In fact, of central import to the parable is that there is a clear demand for action on the part of the hearer. It is quite significant that when considering the nature of this action it becomes apparent that the action required is one that, when performed, expresses overt dependence upon the "lord." Action is indeed required, but it is the "dependent" action of petition; this petition must be offered, but ultimately the plentiful harvest can only be brought in if the "lord" hears the plea for more workers and sends them.⁵⁷ Harry Fleddermann rightly notes that "the ultimate initiative for the mission, and its success, lies not with the disciples, nor even with Jesus, but with God, the Lord of the harvest," that, as such, "the command to pray to the Lord of the harvest opens up the prayer theme" found in the ensuing pericopes.⁵⁸ Ultimately, however, this issue of dependence is foundational for the instructions and ethical considerations that follow in the mission discourse and for the attitude that the Q group is to embrace, not only in terms of their approach to any "mission,"⁵⁹ but also in terms of their discipleship. It must always be performed in a posture of dependence.⁶⁰

---

⁵⁴ Though much of Tiwald's discussion of the mission discourse in Q is helpful, his perspective that "there is essentially only one thread woven throughout the Missions Discourse: the *Naherwartung* of the *basileia*" may be overemphasizing that which is actually found in the *background* and not the *foreground* of this image (*Wanderradikalismus*, 159).

⁵⁵ Picking up on this point, and consonant with observations made above, Michael Wolter, *Lukasevangelium*, 378, notes, "The more precise description of θερισμός with πολύς…makes it clear that the issue here is not the size of the mission field but the size of the expected yield," contra Dieter Lührmann, *Die Redaktion der Logienquelle*, WMANT 33 (Neukirchen-Vluyn: Neukirchener Verlag, 1969), 60.

⁵⁶ Fleddermann, *Q: Reconstruction*, 429.

⁵⁷ See also the sentiment of Rudolf Laufen, *Die Doppelüberlieferungen der Logienquelle und des Markusevangeliums*, BBB 54 (Bonn: Peter Hanstein, 1980), 286, that "at the beginning of every sending is the κυρίος τοῦ θερισμοῦ, who himself elects his ἐργάται and who the community can only petition for such workers."

⁵⁸ Fleddermann, *Q: Reconstruction*, 430.

⁵⁹ See my conclusion in Dieter T. Roth, "Missionary Ethics in Q 10:2–12," in *Sensitivity to Outsiders: Exploring the Dynamic Relationship between Mission and Ethics in the New Testament and Early Christianity*, ed. Jacobus Kok et al., WUNT 2/364 (Tübingen: Mohr Siebeck, 2014), 81–100 (here 96–7).

⁶⁰ Though the issue cannot be pursued further here, there has been considerable discussion concerning the relationship between the instructions of the Q mission discourse and Cynic philosophy (see the brief overview and references in Roth, "Missionary Ethics," 93–4). In terms of at least one point, however, Tuckett has underscored the "radical difference" between the ethos in Q and among Cynics: "With cynics, the ethos is to give up one's possessions and live a life of austerity and physical deprivation in the belief that life as such will provide true and lasting happiness and fulfillment. Moreover the ideal for the cynic is a life of self-sufficiency (αὐτάρκεια) and independence from the rest of society. In Q the ethos is radically different: it is to encourage not independence, but dependence—upon God" (*Q and the History of Early Christianity*, 389).

5. Conclusion

Though there are further parables employing harvest imagery that possibly could be discussed—birds who do not sow, reap, or store food in barns are mentioned in the Parable of the Fowl and the Flowers (Q 12:24, 27–28); a mustard seed is sown in, not surprisingly, the Parable of the Mustard Seed (Q 13:18–19); and there is the idea of salt being useful for soil in the Parable of the Salt (Q 14:34–35)[61]—at the very least the parables discussed here have shown the potential that lies in a consideration of harvest imagery in the Q parables, especially in the light of an intertextual approach to Q and a broader, genre-sensitive approach to parables. And if I may be permitted a final harvest image, an image I also employed at the conclusion of my monograph, perhaps the approach advocated here can be seen as the planting of new methodological trees in the field of research on Q, new trees that may bring forth fruitful insights concerning the various themes and teachings found in Q, so that in the end both the trees and their fruit can be judged as being "good."[62]

Bibliography

Albright, W. F., and C. S. Mann. *Matthew*. AB 26. Garden City: Doubleday, 1971.
Andrejevs, O. *Apocalypticism in the Synoptic Sayings Source*. WUNT 2/499. Tübingen: Mohr Siebeck, 2019.
Andrejevs, O. "The 'Reconstructed Mark' and the Reconstruction of Q: A Valid Analogy?" *BTB* 50 (2020): 83–91.
Andrejevs, O. "Review of Dieter T. Roth, *The Parables in Q*." *BTB* 50 (2020): 62–3.
Bammel, E. "Seminar Report: The Baptist in Early Christian Tradition." *NTS* 18 (1971): 95–128.
Batten, A. "More Queries for Q: Women and Christian Origins." *BTB* 24 (1994): 41–51.
Bazzana, G. B. *Kingdom of Bureaucracy: The Political Theology of Village Scribes in the Sayings Gospel Q*. BETL 274. Leuven: Peeters, 2015.
Bergemann, T. *Q auf dem Prüfstand*. FRLANT 158. Göttingen: Vandenhoeck & Ruprecht, 1993.
Bock, D. L. *Luke*. 2 vols. BECNT 3. Grand Rapids: Baker Books, 1994–96.
Burkitt, F. C. *The Gospel History and its Transmission*. Edinburgh: T. & T. Clark, 1906.
Burkitt, F. C. "Review of Adolf von Harnack, *Sprüche und Reden Jesu*." *JTS* 31 (1907): 454–9.
Cameron, R. "'What Have You Come Out To See?' Characterizations of John and Jesus in the Gospels." *Semeia* 49 (1990): 35–69.
Catchpole, D. R. *The Quest for Q*. Edinburgh: T. & T. Clark, 1993.
Charette, B. *The Theme of Recompense in Matthew's Gospel*. JSNTSup 79. Sheffield: JSOT Press, 1992.
Davies, W. D., and Dale C. Allison, Jr. *The Gospel According to Saint Matthew*. 3 vols. ICC. Edinburgh: T. & T. Clark, 1988–97.

---

[61] Discussion of these parables can be found in Roth, *Parables in Q*, 198–211, 298–312, 320–7, 211–19.
[62] Ibid., 408.

Derrenbacker, R. A. "Review of Dale C. Allison Jr., *The Intertextual Jesus: Scripture in Q*." *CBQ* 64 (2002): 150–1.
Dobbeler, S. von. *Das Gericht und das Erbarmen Gottes*. BBB 70. Frankfurt: Athenäum, 1988.
Dolby-Stahl, S. K. "A Literary Folkloristic Methodology for the Study of Meaning in Personal Narrative." *Journal of Folklore Research* 22 (1985): 45–69.
Dunn, J. D. G. "John the Baptist's Use of Scripture." In *The Gospels and the Scriptures of Israel*, edited by Craig A. Evans and W. Richard Stegner, 42–54. JSNTSup 104. Sheffield: Sheffield Academic Press, 1994.
Eder, J. *Die Figur im Film: Grundlagen der Figurenanalyse*. Marburg: Schüren, 2008.
Evans, C. "Authenticating the Words of Jesus." In *Authenticating the Words of Jesus*, edited by Bruce Chilton and Craig A. Evans, 3–14. NTTS 28. Leiden: Brill, 1999.
Eve, E. "Challenging Q." *ExpTim* 113 (2002): 408–9.
Eve, E. "Reconstructing Mark: A Thought Experiment." In *Questioning Q*, edited by Mark Goodacre and Nicholas Perrin, 89–114. London: SPCK, 2004.
Fleddermann, H. "The Beginning of Q." *SBLSP* 24 (1985): 153–9.
Fleddermann, H. T. *Q: A Reconstruction and Commentary*. BTS 1. Leuven: Peters, 2005.
France, R. T. *The Gospel of Matthew*. NICNT. Grand Rapids: Eerdmans, 2007.
Freyne, S. *Galilee from Alexander the Great to Hadrian 323 B.C.E. to 135 C.E.* SJCA 5. Wilmington: Michael Glazier; Notre Dame: University of Notre Dame Press, 1980.
Green, J. B. *The Gospel of Luke*. NICNT. Grand Rapids: Eerdmans, 1997.
Habbe, J. *Palästina zur Zeit Jesu: Die Landwirtschaft in Galiläa als Hintergrund der synoptischen Evangelien*. Neukirchen-Vluyn: Neukirchener Verlag, 1996.
Häfner, G. *Der verheißene Vorläufer: Redaktionskritische Untersuchung zur Darstellung Johannes des Täufers im Matthäusevangelium*. SBB 27. Stuttgart: Katholisches Bibelwerk, 1994.
Hoffmann, P. *Studien zur Theologie der Logienquelle*. 3rd ed. NTAbh 8. Münster: Aschendorff, 1982.
Horsley, R. A., with J. Draper, *Whoever Hears You Hears Me: Prophets, Performance, and Tradition in Q*. Harrisburg, PA: Trinity Press International, 1999.
Jeremias, J. *The Parables of Jesus*. 2nd ed. Translated by S. H. Hooke. London: SCM Press, 1972.
Kirk, A. *The Composition of the Sayings Source: Genre, Synchrony, and Wisdom Redaction in Q*. NovTSup 91. Leiden: Brill, 1998.
Kloppenborg, J. S. "City and Wasteland: Narrative World and the Beginning of the Sayings Gospel (Q)." *Semeia* 52 (1990): 145–60.
Kloppenborg, J. S. *The Formation of Q: Trajectories in Ancient Wisdom Collections*. SAC. Philadelphia: Fortress Press, 1987.
Kloppenborg, J. S. "On Dispensing with Q? Goodacre on the Relation of Luke to Matthew." *NTS* 49 (2003): 210–36.
Kloppenborg, J. S. "The Power and Surveillance of the Divine Judge in the Early Synoptic Tradition." In *Christ and the Emperor: The Gospel Evidence*, edited by Gilbert Van Belle and Joseph Verheyden, 147–84. Leuven: Peeters, 2014.
Kloppenborg, J. S. "Review of Harry T. Fleddermann, *Q: A Reconstruction and Commentary*." *BTB* 37 (2007): 137–8.
Kloppenborg, J. S. "Variation in the Reproduction of the Double Tradition and an Oral Q?" *ETL* 83 (2007): 53–80.
Kloppenborg Verbin, J. S. *Excavating Q: The History and Setting of the Sayings Gospel*. Minneapolis: Fortress Press, 2000.

Labahn, M. "Das Reich Gottes und seine performativen Abbildungen: Gleichnisse, Parabeln und Bilder als Handlungsmodelle im Dokument Q." In *Hermeneutik der Gleichnisse Jesu: Methodische Neuansätze zum Verstehen urchristlicher Parabeltexte*, edited by Ruben Zimmermann in collaboration with Gabi Kern, 259–82. WUNT 231. Tübingen: Mohr Siebeck, 2008.

Lachmann, R. "Cultural Memory and the Role of Literature." *European Review* 12 (2004): 165–78.

Laufen, R. *Die Doppelüberlieferungen der Logienquelle und des Markusevangeliums.* BBB 54. Bonn: Peter Hanstein, 1980.

Lührmann, D. *Die Redaktion der Logienquelle.* WMANT 33. Neukirchen-Vluyn: Neukirchener Verlag, 1969.

Manson, T. W. *The Sayings of Jesus.* London: SCM Press, 1949.

Marshall, I. H. *The Gospel of Luke: A Commentary on the Greek Text.* NIGTC. Exeter: Paternoster Press, 1978.

März, C.-P. "Zum Verständnis der Gerichtspredigt in Q." In *Weltgericht und Weltvollendung: Zukunftsbilder im Neuen Testament*, edited by Hans-Josef Klauck. QD 150. Freiburg: Herder, 1994.

Moessner, D. P. *Lord of the Banquet: The Literary and Theological Significance of the Lukan Travel Narrative.* Minneapolis: Fortress Press, 1989.

Nolland, J. *The Gospel of Matthew: A Commentary on the Greek Text.* NIGTC. Grand Rapids: Eerdmans, 2005.

Nolland, J. *Luke.* 3 vols. WBC 35. Dallas, TX: Word Books, 1989–93.

Piper, R. A. *Wisdom in the Q-Tradition: The Aphoristic Teaching of Jesus.* SNTSMS 61. Cambridge: Cambridge University Press, 1989.

Reiser, M. *Die Gerichtspredigt Jesu: Eine Untersuchung zur eschatologischen Verkündigung Jesu und ihrem frühjüdischen Hintergrund.* NTAbh 23. Münster: Aschendorff, 1990.

Robinson, J. M., P. Hoffmann, and J. S. Kloppenborg. *The Critical Edition of Q: Synopsis Including the Gospels of Matthew and Luke, Mark and Thomas with English, German, and French translations of Q and Thomas.* Hermeneia. Minneapolis: Fortress Press, 2000.

Rodd, C. S. "The End of the Theology of Q?" *ExpTim* 113 (2001): 5–12.

Rodd, C. S. "The Theology of Q Yet Again: A Reply to the Responses of Christopher Tuckett and Paul Foster." *ExpTim* 114 (2002): 80–5.

Roth, D. T. "'Master' as Character in the Q Parables." In *Metaphor, Narrative, and Parable in Q*, edited by Dieter T. Roth, Ruben Zimmermann, and Michael Labahn, 371–96. WUNT 315. Tübingen: Mohr Siebeck, 2014.

Roth, D. T. "Missionary Ethics in Q 10:2–12." In *Sensitivity to Outsiders: Exploring the Dynamic Relationship between Mission and Ethics in the New Testament and Early Christianity*, edited by Jacobus Kok et al., 81–100. WUNT 2/364. Tübingen: Mohr Siebeck, 2014.

Roth, D. T. "Die Parabeln in der Logienquelle: 'Alt' Probleme und 'Neue' Ansätze." In *Built on Rock or Sand? Q Studies: Retrospects, Introspects and Prospects*, edited by Christoph Heil, Gertraud Harb, and Daniel Smith, 193–212. BTS 34. Leuven: Peeters, 2018.

Roth, D. T. *The Parables in Q.* LNTS 582. London: T&T Clark, 2018.

Schmid, J. *Matthäus und Lukas. Eine Untersuchung des Verhältnisses ihrer Evangelien.* Freiburg: Herder, 1930.

Schnider, F. "Das Gleichnis vom verlorenen Schaf und seine Redaktoren: Ein intertextueller Vergleich." *Kairos* 19 (1977): 146–54.

Schröter, J. *Erinnerung an Jesu Worte: Studien zur Rezeption der Logienüberlieferung in Markus, Q und Thomas*. WMANT 76. Neukirchen-Vluyn: Neukirchener Verlag, 1997.

Schröter, J. *Jesus und die Anfänge der Christologie: Methodologische und exegetische Studien zu den Ursprüngen des christlichen Glaubens*. Biblisch-Theologische Studien 47. Neukirchen-Vluyn: Neukirchener Verlag, 2001.

Schulz, S. *Die Spruchquelle der Evangelisten*. Zurich: Theologischer Verlag, 1972.

Sevenich-Bax, E. *Israels Konfrontation mit den letzten Boten der Weisheit: Form, Funktion und Interdependenz der Weisheitselemente in der Logienquelle*. Altenberge: Oros, 1993.

Snodgrass, K. *Stories with Intent: A Comprehensive Guide to the Parables of Jesus*. 2nd ed. Grand Rapids, MI: Eerdmans, 2018.

Starnitzke, D. "Von den Früchten des Baumes und dem Sprechen des Herzens (Vom Baum und seinen Früchten): Q 6,43–45 (Mt 7,16–20; 12,33–35 / Lk 6,43–45 / EvThom 45)." In *Kompendium der Gleichnisse Jesu*, edited by R. Zimmermann, 81–91. Gütersloh: Gütersloher Verlagshaus, 2007.

Tilly, M. *Johannes der Täufer und die Biographie der Propheten: Die synoptische Täuferüberlieferung und das jüdische Prophetenbild zur Zeit der Täufers*. BWANT 137. Stuttgart: Kohlhammer, 1993.

Tiwald, M. *Wanderradikalismus Jesu erste Jünger – ein Anfang und was davon bleibt*. ÖBS 20. Frankfurt: Peter Lang, 2002.

Trumbower, J. A. "The Role of Malachi in the Career of John the Baptist." In *The Gospels and the Scriptures of Israel*, edited by Craig A. Evans and W. Richard Stegner, 28–54. JSNTSup 104. Sheffield: Sheffield Academic Press, 1994.

Tuckett, C. *Q and the History of Early Christianity*. Edinburgh: T. & T. Clark, 1996.

Uro, R. "John the Baptist and the Jesus Movement: What Does Q Tell Us?" In *The Gospel Behind the Gospels*, edited by Ronald A. Piper, 231–57. NovTSup 75. Leiden: Brill, 1995.

Valantasis, R. *The New Q: A Fresh Translation with Commentary*. New York: T&T Clark, 2005.

Venetz, H.-J. "Bittet den Herrn der Ernte: Überlegungen zu Lk 10,2//Mt 9,37." *Diakonia* 11 (1980): 148–61.

Weaks, J. A. "Mark Without Mark: Problematizing the Reliability of a Reconstructed Text of Q." Ph.D. dissertation. Brite Divinity School, 2010.

Wolter, M. *Das Lukasevangelium*. HNT 5. Tübingen: Mohr Siebeck, 2008.

Wolter, M. "Reconstructing Q?" *ExpTim* 115 (2004): 115–19.

Zimmermann, R. "Folgenreiche Bitte! [Arbeiter für die Ernte] Q 10,2 [Mt 9,37f/Lk 10,2/ EvThom 73]." In *Kompendium der Gleichnisse Jesu*, edited by R. Zimmermann, 111–18. Gütersloh: Gütersloher Verlagshaus, 2007.

Zimmermann, R., ed. *Kompendium der Gleichnisse Jesu*. Gütersloh: Gütersloher Verlagshaus, 2007.

Zimmermann, R. *Puzzling the Parables of Jesus: Methods and Interpretation*. Minneapolis: Fortress Press.

Written and Unwritten Obligations: Dependency Relations in Early Roman Galilee*

Douglas E. Oakman

Thirty-five years ago, I presented "Jesus and Agrarian Palestine: The Factor of Debt" at a national Society of Biblical Literature meeting. Debt also played a role in my thinking for my published dissertation *Jesus and the Economic Questions of His Day*.[1] Moreover, Martin Goodman had just a few years previously argued that debt was a significant factor in the Judean-Roman War of 66–70 CE.[2]

While Goodman could point to the *prosbul* attributed to Hillel and the burning of the Jerusalem archives by the insurgents in 66 CE as evidence for this social factor in Judea, he stated in his 1982 article that "Galilee lacked such a wide division between economic classes [as Judea did] and had a safety valve for the landless poor in emigration to the cities of the Decapolis, while Galilean bandits before the outbreak of revolt tended to attack foreigners rather than the richer members of their own society."[3] In recent arguments about the social character of early Roman Galilee, archaeologists like Mordechai Aviam have also minimized Galilean social stratification and claimed that "Archaeology does not confirm the picture of a half-starved peasant as the typical Galilean."[4] David Fiensy, likewise, says "I cannot conclude that pervasive indebtedness existed in Galilee in the

---

* This chapter was originally delivered as a paper in the "Economics of the Biblical World" Section of the 2019 Society of Biblical Literature in San Diego, CA.
[1] Douglas E. Oakman, "Jesus and Agrarian Palestine: The Factor of Debt," in *Society of Biblical Literature 1985 Seminar Papers*, ed. Kent Harold Richards (Atlanta, GA: Scholars Press, 1985), 57–73; idem, *Jesus and the Economic Questions of His Day*, Studies in the Bible and Early Christianity 8 (Lewiston, NY: Edwin Mellen Press, 1986).
[2] Martin Goodman, "The First Jewish Revolt: Social Conflict and the Problem of Debt," *JJS* 33 (1982): 417–27.
[3] Ibid., 418.
[4] Mordechai Aviam, "People, Land, Economy, and Belief in First-Century Galilee and Its Origins: A Comprehensive Archaeological Synthesis," in *The Galilean Economy in the Time of Jesus*, ed. David A. Fiensy and Ralph K. Hawkins (Atlanta, GA: Society of Biblical Literature, 2013), 29; see also now various perspectives in David A. Fiensy and James Riley Strange, eds., *Galilee in the Late Second Temple and Mishnaic Periods*, 2 vols. (Minneapolis, MN: Fortress Press, 2014–15).

earlier part of the first century CE, and that it served as historical and economic backdrop to the ministry of Jesus."[5]

In my 1985 paper I assumed too much about debt in Roman Galilee, based largely upon the Judean evidence. Thus, the specific focus of my inquiry in this chapter will be Galilee at the turn of the eras and the historical figure of Jesus. What I hope to offer are a number of observations and considerations to urge that agrarian debt was indeed an important social reality in Jesus's Galilean context, and a significant factor in Jesus's historical praxis. Further, the argument of this essay is that both written debt records and unwritten personal obligations embodied in patronage politics have to be taken into account, and that both were important tools of early imperial domination.[6] In other words, obligation and indebtedness were all part and parcel of vertical dependency and power relations leveraging production for the benefit of the various elite groups. It is important to realize that culture, family, and economy were all embedded in politics as the governing social variable for most people.[7]

The main lines of evidence for early Roman Galilee today are both literary and archaeological. Here are included pre-70 traditions in the Synoptic Gospels (especially Q, the Galilean traditions in Mark, and Jesus's parables), together with Josephus and the rabbis.[8] Both Josephus and the synoptic evangelists write in the post-temple period, but contain recollections stemming back to the Herodian period. Likewise, some of the rabbinic traditions retain valuable information. Archaeology, however, has yielded competing arguments and social pictures. But what is clear from the material record is that both Judean and Herodian interests, under a Roman aegis, were at play. A fuller review of archaeological evidence for social stratification is provided in my 2012 book, *The Political Aims of Jesus*.[9] All of these sources have been sifted, and will continue to require critical interpretation. It is clear, nonetheless, that we must still embrace the hazard of interpretive inference, usefully informed by comparative social science data and models.

---

[5] David A. Fiensy, "Jesus and Debts: Did He Pray About Them?" in *Christian Origins and the Ancient Economy* (Eugene, OR: Cascade Books, 2014), 66.

[6] For a discussion of patronage in first-century Palestine, see Bruce J. Malina, "Patron and Client: The Analogy Behind Synoptic Theology," in *The Social World of Jesus and the Gospels* (London: Routledge, 1996), 143–75; John H. Elliott, "Patronage and Clientage," in *The Social Sciences and New Testament Interpretation*, ed. Richard L. Rohrbaugh (Peabody, MA: Hendrickson Publishers, 1996), 144–56; more generally, Richard P. Saller, *Personal Patronage Under the Roman Empire* (Cambridge: Cambridge University Press, 1982).

[7] On the importance of politics (coercive social power) as a primary social variable in early Roman Galilee, see Douglas E. Oakman, "The Galilean World of Jesus," in *The Early Christian World*, ed. Philip F. Esler, 2nd ed. (London: Routledge, 2017), 97–120 (here 99–101).

[8] For references to Q (the Sayings Source), these two works have been consulted: James M. Robinson, Paul Hoffmann, and John S. Kloppenborg, eds., *The Critical Edition of Q* (Minneapolis, MN: Fortress Press; Leuven: Peeters, 2000), and James M. Robinson, Paul Hoffmann, and John S. Kloppenborg, *The Sayings Gospel Q in Greek and English with Parallels from the Gospels of Mark and Thomas* (Minneapolis, MN: Fortress Press, 2002). Q references reflect very early material in the Jesus traditions and his likely social context and experience.

[9] Douglas E. Oakman, *The Political Aims of Jesus* (Minneapolis, MN: Fortress Press, 2012), 49–59.

Because of the limited nature of the evidence for our knowledge of Galilean debt in this period, and the conflicting interpretations that have produced competing pictures, a model of dependency relations in early Roman Galilee is a first desideratum for analysis.

1. Dependency Model, and Various Replications

Dependency implies a superior with vertical power over an inferior with little power, and with notable differences in the types of material goods held and exchanged. According to Moses Finley, elites put their wealth into land, storehouse, or loans. They aim to control land for material self-sufficiency, evidenced in the storehouse, have capital from various sources, and lend in the interest of further control of labor.[10]

Table 2

Patronage politics—involving both unwritten and written institutional forms	
Patron expects loyalty, specifies various unwritten obligations for the client ("other duties as assigned"), single-stranded means absentee lord and one-sided exploitation	Mark 12:1–9/Gos. Thom. 65—Parable of the Tenants; Josephus, *B.J.* 2.168—cities of the Herods honoring the Emperor (Caesarea Maritima, Tiberias, Caesarea Philippi, Julias, etc.)
Multi-stranded (very tight personal bonds) vs. single-strand (absentee landlords in cities)	Josephus, *Life* 204, 259—Josephus hailed twice as benefactor and savior by the Galileans; cf. Q 12:42—the "faithful and wise" *oikonomos*
Control of land, lake, and other productive resources	
Imperial direct taxation/Royal House	Mark 12:17; Tacitus, *Ann.* 2.42; Josephus, *B.J.* 2.95; *A.J.* 14.203—*Tributum soli, tributum capitus*, client taxation
Temple tax and tithes in Galilee	Matt 17:27; Josephus, *Life* 63, 80; *m. Šeqal.* 1:3
Direct tax collection by slaves and city elites	Matt 18:23–24; Josephus, *B.J.* 2.405? *Life* 69, 296
Indirect taxes taken for imperial/royal houses	Josephus, *B.J.* 2.287, 292—John of Caesarea (tolls on trade)
Farmed by *telonai* under fixed contracts	Mark 2:14—Levi (transit tolls or fisher contracts)

---

[10] Moses I. Finley, *The Ancient Economy*, updated ed. (Berkeley, CA: University of California Press, 1999).

Peasant hatred for the cities, landlords control land production and rents, imperial and royal control of harvest and storehouses	Acts 12:20; Josephus, *Life* 71, 99, 119, 143, 375
Tenant or village owes fixed or shared rent in kind, payment at harvest taken into landlord's storehouse	Mark 12:1–9/Gos. Thom. 65; Luke 12:16–20; Matt 13:24–30; *m. Baba Meṣ.* 9; *b. Meṣ.* 9.14—liens against the harvest
Control of capital	
Control of Mediterranean and land commerce	Caesarea Maritima, Caesarea Philippi, *Via maris*, Jericho (Zacchaeus)
Archives	Josephus, *Life* 17; *B.J.* 2.427; 7.54–62
Banks/Tables (controlled by elites)—source of loans, money exchanged for a commission	Q 19:13, 23—*pragmateia* through Galilean tables *epi trapezan*; Mark 11:15; Josephus, *Life* 28
Control of labor	
Taxation, rents, liens, tenancy agreements	Josephus, *B.J.* 2.428; 7.61 *archeia*—"sinews of the city'; Luke 16:5–7—fixed rents in kind
Harvest—need for labor on estates (landless). Was there also corvée labor on estates?	Matt 20:1–3; Josephus, *A.J.* 18.274—"harvest of banditry'

Agrarian economy requires land and labor as essential factors of production. Ruling elites of the early Roman Empire in the east controlled nearly all land either directly or indirectly, and also capital from commerce. Moses Finley observed that ancient elites preferred to place their capital in land, in the strong box, or out on loan.[11] Obligations incurred under provincial patronage politics and land tenure arrangements could also be enhanced by money debts incurred through the tables (that is, banks) controlled by the local elites. This aspect is seen, for example, in the Q parable of the Entrusted Money where business loans garner control over cities or estates, but are of little benefit to the peasant. Josephus could even refer to the Jerusalem archives where debt contracts were stored as the "sinews of the city" (*B.J.* 2.428). So, the dependency model attempts a categorization of interrelated vertical dependencies as discussed selectively in what follows.

2. Galilee and Debt

Turning now to obligation and debt in early Roman Galilee, recent help in thinking about Greco-Roman indebtedness in general has come from the

---

[11] Ibid., 116.

economist Michael Hudson.[12] Hudson, along with many previous students of agrarian societies, knows that peasant debts and arrears are often interminable once they have been initiated by natural disasters or money loans or any other kinds of loans. Essentially, all the village peasant has to offer is labor, with few valuables of any long-term worth. Further, the peasant aims at consumption of a (mostly) annual product; taxes, rents, liens, payments must be taken from the harvest. The peasant producer lives literally from ground to mouth and from seed to harvest, year after year. In his *Antiquities* (18.274), Josephus recounts that because of the agricultural strike against Caligula's statue, unsown land threatened both the annual tribute and yielded a "harvest of banditry." Because of this natural pressure, James Scott saw the moral economy of the peasant as aiming at stability and predictability, shored up by intra-familial generosity.[13] Likewise, Hudson sees most agrarian indebtedness as "arrears on paper," and argues that ancient Near Eastern debt amnesties aimed to restore productivity by removal of such arrears.[14] Silver debts of commerce, a commerce sponsored by and benefiting the ruling elites alone, were never forgiven. To this may be added that arrears of farmed taxes or default on fixed tax contracts would likely lead to imprisonment or slavery. However, slavery made more sense in preserving for the master the labor potential of the debtor.

Hudson also argues persuasively that the Greco-Roman political arrangements handed most power over to the creditor oligarchies, a fact lamented by Livy and Plutarch, among others.[15] For Republican Rome, this was especially evident with the rise of the Equestrians and *publicani*. But it is also evident in the policies of the early Empire in the east that replaced the publicans and placed peasant villagers under local elites in client kingdoms or cities, and charged those local elites with collection of Roman tribute. Other local taxes and rents—in money and kind—were left to reward provincial elites for their loyalty. We see in the picture of the Herods for over a century an intent of political self-preservation and self-enrichment, and monumental building to honor their patron emperors.

These priorities did not earn them any love from the village. Of Herod the Great, Josephus reports: "He had not ceased to adorn neighboring cities that were inhabited by foreigners although this led to the ruin and disappearance of cities located in his own kingdom" (Josephus, *A.J.* 17.306 LCL). Both Agrippa I and

---

[12] Michael Hudson, "Entrepreneurs: From the Near Eastern Takeoff to the Roman Collapse," in *The Invention of Enterprise: Entrepreneurship from Ancient Mesopotamia to Modern Times*, ed. David S. Landes, Joel Mokyr, and William J. Baumol (Princeton, NJ: Princeton University Press, 2010), 8–39; idem, *...and Forgive Them Their Debts: Lending, Foreclosure and Redemption from Bronze Age Finance to the Jubilee Year* (Dresden: ISLET-Verlag, 2018).

[13] James C. Scott, *The Moral Economy of the Peasant: Rebellion and Subsistence in Southeast Asia* (New Haven, CT: Yale University Press, 1976), vii, 3, 18, et passim.

[14] Hudson, *Forgive Them Their Debts*, x, xxv; for ancient predatory lenders "subsistence land became alienable.... Credit became a lever to deprive its customary holders of their tenure rights," 67. Royal amnesties in the ancient Near Eastern (e.g., by Hammurabi, 143–48; or such as depicted in Lev 25, pp. 213–20; or in the Ptolemaic rescript of the Rosetta Stone, p. 178) were intended to restore rural productivity.

[15] Hudson, *Forgive Them Their Debts*, xxvi, offers portraits of Lycurgus and Solon in the U.S. House of Representatives, based on Plutarch, *Lycurgus*; *Solon* 7–8 and Livy, 52–53, p. 223.

II likewise patronized Beirut, and the latter's subjects were reported to hate him (*A.J.* 19.335–36; 20.211–12); indeed, Acts 12 narrates that Agrippa I regularly supplied Phoenician cities with grain. It is reasonable to think such policy was carried on by Antipas as well. Further, Josephus makes clear that the Galilean peasantry hated both Sepphoris and Tiberias (*Life* 99, 143, 375). Mendel Nun notes that Susita/Hippos "supplied Tiberias with agricultural produce," and that "the frequently used local expression 'as from Tiberias to Susita'…points to the close connection between the two cities," a fact verified when Josephus escapes by boat from Tiberias to Susita (Josephus, *Life* 153).[16] These notices strongly suggest that oligarchic landlord control of produce overrode local peasant concerns for subsistence.

The temple tax was paid in Tyrian silver, the money of commerce; the Roman poll tax was assessed in silver *denarii*. Collection of direct taxes for Rome was the responsibility of provincials—royal slaves or city elites (especially the *deka protoi* or ten chief men whose wealth secured the tax amount owed (Josephus, *Life* 69, 296; cf. *B.J.* 2.405, 407); indirect taxes of various sorts were also farmed by contract to *telonai* (Mark 2:14–15; Luke 18:13; 19:2).[17] Local mints produced only token coppers.[18] The control of mints by Caesar, and the permission for client rulers in the provinces to mint only copper money, produced what I call "batteries of power" (by Gresham's Law).[19] This means that token money kept silver in the cities and houses of the imperial elites, and that money worked under conditions of agrarian production to leverage goods in kind for the benefits of the royal house, cities, and landlords. Bad money drove out the goods from the village larders.

Taxes and rents had, to a certain degree, to be paid in kind to ensure the material security of the local estate owners. Fiensy notes that Eleazar ben Harsom received rents in kind from Asochis, and that Jerusalem taxes in kind were collected from Asochis, Zebulon, and Magdala. Not without reason, then, Peter Brown has called storehouses "the economic villains of antiquity."[20] For

---

[16] Mendel Nun, *Ancient Anchorages and Harbours Around the Sea of Galilee* (Kibbutz Ein Gev, Israel: Kinnereth Sailing Co., 1988), 12.

[17] *Deka protoi*: see Emil Schürer, *The History of the Jewish People in the Age of Jesus Christ (175 B.C.–A.D. 135)*, A New English Version, ed. Geza Vermes, Fergus Millar, Matthew Black, and Martin Goodman, 3 vols. (Edinburgh: T. & T. Clark, 1973–87), 2:180 n. 518. Also reflective of a tax function of such eminent men are the twelve *dynatoi* with John the *telonēs* in Caesarea (Josephus, *B.J.* 2.292). For *telonai* as farmers of indirect taxes, see John Donahue, "Tax Collectors and Sinners: An Attempt at an Identification," *CBQ* 33 (1971): 39–61.

[18] Danny Syon, *Small Change in Hellenistic-Roman Galilee*, Numismatic Studies and Researches 11 (Jerusalem: The Israel Numismatic Society, 2015).

[19] Gresham's Law is usually summarized as "Bad money drives out the good." The law is named after Thomas Gresham (1519–1579), who first articulated this theory about circulation of mixed-valued monetary systems. Douglas E. Oakman, "Batteries of Power: Coinage in the Judean Temple System," in *In Other Words: Essays on Social Science Methods and the New Testament in Honor of Jerome H. Neyrey*, ed. Anselm C. Hagedorn, Zeba A. Crook, and Eric Stewart, SWBA, Second Series 1 (Sheffield: Sheffield Phoenix Press, 2007), 171–85. Further discussions can be found in these resources: Robert Mundell, "Use and Abuses of Gresham's Law in the History of Money," *Zagreb Journal of Economics* 2 (1998): 3–38; Amelia Carolina Sparavigna, "Some Notes on the Gresham's Law of Money Circulation," *International Journal of Sciences* 3, no. 2 (2014): 80–91, https://www.ijsciences.com/pub/pdf/V320140220.pdf, accessed 03/02/2021.

[20] David A. Fiensy, "Did Large Estates Exist in Lower Galilee?," in David Fiensy, *Christian Origins and the Ancient Economy* (Eugene, OR: Cascade Books, 2014), 107. Cf. Peter Brown, *Through the*

even if the landlord was generous during years of famine or blight, relief only meant that the tentacles of obligation grew stronger for the better years. Absentee landlords, managing estates through stewards, increased the opportunities for predatory extractions from villagers. And the more that estates require fixed rents, the more the pressure is upon the steward and village cultivator. Conversely, multi-stranded relations between landlord and cultivator will perhaps issue in share-contracts that distribute the risk within "the vertical family."

The exact shape and distribution of tenancy relations in early Roman Galilee can only be inferred by educated guesses. John Kloppenborg, in several very careful studies, argues that tenancies had increased in number during the Hellenistic period in Palestine.[21] The Zenon Papyri attest to vineyards and royal tenants in Upper Galilee in the early Hellenistic period. Such arrangements would naturally have been known to the Hasmoneans and Herods. Of course, the parable of the Tenants appears in the Synoptic Gospels (Mark 12:1–11) and in the Gospel of Thomas (65). The Mishnah knows of fixed and share contract arrangements (e.g., *m. B. Meṣ.* 9). The story of the Dishonest Steward in Luke 16 attests to fixed debt contracts in kind, probably within the context of large estate management. Gildas Hamel discusses the scenario of a share rental in *t. Baba Meṣ.* 9:14—everyone owed (except the landlord) gets a cut at the harvest before what remains is shared between landlord and tenant.[22]

Even the lack of evidence for a mass of starving peasants cannot obviate the fact of agrarian social stratification in Roman Galilee. This stratification at the top included the royal interests of the Herods and their people, the interests of the Jerusalem temple and priestly families in Galilee, along with those of others in Sepphoris and Tiberias.

The *Life* of Josephus (78) indicates that he was in Galilee to keep peace (with intent to prevent rebellion against Rome), and underlying the narrative are indications of his patronage politics. Upon his arrival in Galilee, for instance, tithes (in arrears?) were brought to him and his compatriot priests Joazar and Judas, but Josephus himself refused to take them. He later refers to 70 leading men, the *protoi* of Galilee, held hostage "under the guise of friendliness" to ensure the loyalty of Galilee—that is, they became clients under his political patronage. The Gospel of Mark likewise identifies the *megistanes*, the chiliarchs, and the *protoi*. Their attendance at Antipas's invitation made them royal clients indebted to the patron king. The *protoi* seem to be the heads of villages and towns. Within the

---

Eye of a Needle: Wealth, the Fall of Rome, and the Making of Christianity in the West, 350–550 AD (Princeton, NJ: Princeton University Press, 2012), 14.

[21] John S. Kloppenborg, "The Growth and Impact of Agricultural Tenancy in Jewish Palestine (III BCE–I CE)," *Journal of the Economic and Social History of the Orient* 51 (2008): 31–66; idem, "The Dishonoured Master (Luke 16,1–8a)," *Biblica* 70 (1989): 474–95; also, *The Tenants in the Vineyard: Ideology, Economics, and Agrarian Conflict in Jewish Palestine*, WUNT 195 (Tübingen: Mohr Siebeck, 2006). It should be noted that no peasant or peasant village is ever free of "taxation." See the models of tenant dynamics in Douglas E. Oakman, *Jesus and the Peasants*, Matrix: The Bible in Mediterranean Context (Eugene, OR: Cascade Books, 2008), 22, 28.

[22] Gildas Hamel, *Poverty and Charity in Roman Palestine, First Three Centuries C.E.*, Near Eastern Studies 23 (Berkeley, CA: University of California Press, 1990), 154–63. Hamel especially stresses the connection between tenancy and debt as an elite control mechanism.

royal establishment was Herod Antipas's mercenary army led by the commanders (chiliarchs and centurions). The *megistanes* are then the great nobles supported by large estates. The presence of so many stewards and bailiffs in Jesus's parables indicates that absentee landlords were commonplace in the cities.[23]

Josephus designates the large mass of the population as "the Galileans," a grouping headed by the 70 chief men.[24] He reports that they hated both Sepphoris and Tiberias. Josephus, in fact, says that Justus of Tiberias was not only burning the villages of the Decapolis, but also was hated by the Galileans for what they had suffered from him. Bandits like the *archilestes* Jesus were clearly an outgrowth of landless elements and indices of agrarian discontent. Both the city of Sepphoris and Josephus struck deals with the bandits to keep them at bay, and commoners feared them (*Life* 77, 105, 206). Jesus of Nazareth, too, associated with many landless people including the fishers of the Lake of Galilee. Their relations of dependency with landlords come into focus, for instance, in the Parable of the Vineyard Laborers.

Josephus twice mentions in his *Life* that he was called benefactor and savior by the Galileans (204, 259). Friendship is patron–client language, and Josephus was evidently in their good graces until he went over to Vespasian. I argue that Josephus's maneuverings before the arrival of Vespasian were intended to avert war and especially to protect the Galilean village labor along with Judean landed interests. Interestingly, Josephus, the client of Nero's consort Poppeia (*Life* 16), later becomes the client of Nero's general![25]

The fact that the royal archives and tables—after their transfer by Nero from Tiberias to Sepphoris—were not burned as they were in Jerusalem suggests that debt records carried through and beyond the war as a political control mechanism over village labor. Recall again, that Josephus calls such record archives the "sinews of the city" (and that similar archives existed in Syrian Antioch, cf. *B.J.* 7.61).

---

[23] For a similar loyalty test of analogous ruling groups, see Josephus, *A.J.* 20.26–28, where Queen Helena summons landed nobles, royal satraps, and military commanders (τοὺς μεγιστᾶνας καὶ τῆς βασιλείας σατράπας καὶ τοὺς τὰς δυνάμεις πεπιστευμένους) to attest their obeisance to Izates upon his royal succession.

[24] On the identity of *hoi Galilaioi*, see Solomon Zeitlin, "Who Were the Galileans? New Light on Josephus' Activities in Galilee," *JQR* 64 (1973/1974): 189–203. Joseph Armenti and Louis Feldman have given convincing arguments *against* Zeilin's identification of the term with a political faction and *for* the term's meaning as the peasants of Galilee: Joseph Armenti, "On the Use of the Term 'Galileans' in the Writings of Josephus Flavius: A Brief Note," *JQR* 72 (1981): 49; Louis Feldman, "The Term 'Galileans' in Josephus," *JQR* 72 (1981): 51.

[25] On Josephus's motives during the war, Shaye J. D. Cohen, *Josephus in Galilee and Rome: His Vita and Development as a Historian* (Leiden: E. J. Brill, 1979), provides a lengthy discussion. Was he the partisan general as he portrays himself in *War*? Or was he in Galilee to preserve the peace as he says in the *Life* (17–23)? In the end, Cohen, contra Laqueur, seems to opt for some version of the former scenario—namely, that Josephus was there trying to organize a resistance among an amalgam of social elements (230–31). The present essay stresses that Judean and especially priestly interests in Galilee were ill served by rebellion against Rome. With regard to his relations with Sepphoris, a Judean city, Josephus only seems(?) to have opposed its Romanophile interests (*Life* 346–48), but this is in service of his polemic against Justus. Josephus makes clear that Sepphoris built fortification walls and allowed a Roman garrison access to protect its own interests. Prior to 70 CE, Sepphoris was clearly a Judean center, given the evidence of archaeology. Cf. Mark Chancey and Eric M. Meyers, "How Jewish Was Sepphoris in Jesus' Time?," *BAR* 26, no. 4 (July/August 2000): 23, 27, and Schürer, *The History of the Jewish People*, 172–6.

3. Jesus and Debt

Turning now to evidence of the early Jesus traditions and contemplating the historical praxis of Jesus, what comes into focus is a strong critique of a "Mammon Ethic." Hudson helps to explicate how this Mammon Ethic—that is, elite security established through estate storehouse and tightly bonded producers—overtook Galilee after the coming of Pompey.[26] With provincial *publicani* banished in the late Republic, as mentioned, imperial policy turned over tax and debt control to provincial elites—in Galilee the Herods, the Temple elites, and the cities. Jesus's association with *telonai* like Levi (or Luke's fictional Zacchaeus) become signposts for understanding both Jesus's critique and his interest in the behavior of the system's enforcers.[27]

The very presence of copper coinage in an agrarian setting would foster money debts. Interestingly, coin densities (as determined by surveys) increase around administrative towns and the cities, where they might have more of the economic exchange function. For instance, many coins were found at Jotapata/Yodefat, including Neronian *denarii*, but few coins and no silvers from this period turned up at nearby Khirbet Qana. This flow of coppers to the towns and cities—implied by the densities of coin finds—associates provincial money far more with elites and their agents.[28]

Table 3

Coin Densities for Select Towns and Cities in Galilee					
Place	300–200 BCE	200–125 BCE	125–63 BCE	63–70 CE	Totals
Capernaum	0	3	2	7	12
Bethsaida	53	105	35	12	205
Jotapata	2	184	397	84	667
Qana	0	12	9	2	23
Magdala	3	2	233	188	426
Tiberias	3	7	7	47	64
Hippos	7	30	26	59	122
Sepphoris	4	45	194	278	521
Nazareth	0	0	11	4	15
Scythopolis	61	83	93	141	378

[26] Hudson, "Entrepreneurs," 8–39.
[27] Jesus's association with Levi by the lake is likely historical. Whether Zacchaeus the *architelonēs* was literally in Jericho is doubtful, although he certainly represents a known type. See also the reference to John the *telonēs* of Caesarea in Josephus, *B.J.* 2.287, 292.
[28] The data for coin densities are drawn from Syon, *Small Change in Hellenistic-Roman Galilee*, 34–7. His discussion of silver and gold money helpfully indicates the association of "precious metals" with elite-determined values and elite social strata.

Note in the table that Capernaum, Qana, and Nazareth are an order of magnitude different from the political centers Bethsaida, Jotapata, Magdala, and Sepphoris. Tiberias is an outlier because it was only founded in the early first century. It is possible that find-counts are proportional to ancient populations or contingent on modern areas excavated. Still, the data can also support the view that the political leverage of money (taxes, rents, loans) for the Galilean peasants was more predominant than any limited economic exchange value. From this political angle, the injurious agrarian import of the parable of the Entrusted Money becomes clear, that is, by linking loans with control of estates or cities. Further, to trade up from produce in kind to coin, then from copper to silver, clearly advantaged the controlling groups. The Q 11:11 saying about giving a son a stone instead of bread may be an indirect reference to money. Markets in Galilee were for the most part local and utilitarian.[29] The Q-saying about sparrows being sold in the market (12:6) is more lament than evidence of dynamic economic exchange.

The saying of Jesus in Q 12:59 must refer to personal execution with the *antidikos* or creditor on the way to the judge with the debtor; "making friends" therefore would imply the establishment of a patronage-bond akin to slavery, else the debtor will be thrown into debtor's prison. Corroboration for the existence of such executions and imprisonments is also given by the parable of the Unforgiving Servant in Matthew 18. Both of these instances can be regarded as evidence for the Galilean context of Jesus—including royal tax contracts, personal executions, and private loans enforced by courts.[30]

That Jesus eats with "tax collectors and debtors" speaks to his subversive praxis of asking the tax farmers and collectors to write down the debts for their indebted. The reference to "eating with tax collectors and debtors" belongs to the earliest strata of the Jesus traditions. In Mark 2:15–16, Jesus's commensality with tax collectors draws the ire of the Pharisees, who represent the financial interests of Jerusalem in Galilee (recall Josephus the Pharisee here as well; and recall enmity in the parable of the Pharisee and the Publican).[31] Q 7:34 also makes reference to Jesus as a friend of "tax collectors and debtors" in the context

---

[29] Hayim Lapin documents city and rural markets based upon Talmudic evidence in *Economy, Geography, and Provincial History in Later Roman Palestine*, TSAJ 85 (Tübingen: Mohr Siebeck, 2001), 130–7.

[30] It is an open question whether Hillel's Judean *prosbul* obtained in Galilee. However, see Lyndon Drake, "Did Jesus Oppose the *prosbul* in the Forgiveness Petition of the Lord's Prayer?" *NovT* 56 (2014): 233–44, who argues that the *prosbul* antedated Hillel and that Jesus did in fact oppose its legal fiction (debt contracts held by a court could circumvent the seventh-year release mandated in Deut 15). If true, then the Q scribes were likely familiar with such court enforcement of debt contracts in the scenario of Q 12:59.

[31] This point is based in part upon Anthony J. Saldarini's arguments that pre-70 Pharisees/scribes were "retainers" or functionaries for the elites, in *Pharisees, Scribes and Sadducees: A Sociological Approach* (Wilmington, DE: Michael Glazier, 1988), 46–7, 284, 296. Q 11:42–43 and Mark 12:38 associate Pharisees/scribes with temple taxation and markets. See also the discussion of John S. Kloppenborg, "Literary Convention, Self-Evidence and the Social History of the Q People," *Semeia* 55 (1991): 98.

of eating and drinking. While Matthew and Luke can understand the phrase as a hendiadys with moral or honor–shame import, late New Testament and early Christian traditions drop the reference. The term *hamartolos* has usually been discussed in the literature in negative moral terms, and this may be so, but the Aramaic words *chovah/chovayin* that *hamartia/hamartaloi* translate, as often noted, can denote the materially indebted. For instance, in the story of Simon the Pharisee in Luke 7, why does Jesus tell a parable about two debtors in response to a moral evaluation? We might surmise that the woman has been liberated from a sex slavery imposed by her indebted father and now expresses her gratitude to her benefactor Jesus. Or perhaps, the money debt for the nard—loaned by the woman's master—has been annulled. Notice that the 500 *denarii* would have been close to the price of the alabaster jar of *myrrhos*.[32]

Importantly, in the table prayer of Jesus, bread—debt forgiveness—and deliverance from creditor courts are linked. The second part of the prayer refers centrally to material concerns and along with the address to "*Abba*" is the core of Jesus's historical prayer.[33] If we interpret the fifth petition from the vantage point of the contract system, then a significant agenda of the meal with tax collectors and debtors comes into focus. The sympathetic scribes of the *telonai* ask for release from their fixed debt just as they are easing the burdens of their debtors. Likewise, with Luke 16:1–7 and v. 13, this hidden transcript of subversive debt relief surfaces into public view. The cooking of the written books delivers unwritten benefits to grateful debtors who embrace "as friends" another kind of patronage.[34]

Implicit in these notices, then, is what I will call Jesus's critique of the Mammon Ethic. With this ethic embodied in the ruling groups of early Roman Galilee, we see various absentee landlords trusting in land, storehouse, loans, and whose agents are normally a vexation to the village producer. The service of Mammon and the inverse of unrelieved debt leads to unreliable vertical patronage. Conversely, Jesus articulates a reverse patronage in persuading the enforcers to provide help and relief to their indebted. In the parable of the Rich Fool (Luke 12:13–21), not only is the storehouse as self-sufficient security in view, but the landlord is depicted as a thief of what could benefit others. Further, "you cannot serve God and Mammon" effectively signifies the misplaced trust of the landlord class. The root of the Semitic word Mammon, *'aman*, suggests trust in such

---

[32] A similar reference to an *alabastron myrhou* occurs in Mark 14:3, worth 300 *denarii*. On the sale of a daughter, see Catherine Hezser, *Jewish Slavery in Antiquity* (Oxford: Oxford University Press, 2005), 86–7 and 233–46 on *m. Soṭ.* 33, and Josephus, *A.J.* 3.282.
[33] For arguments that the Father-address and Second Table are the original Prayer of Jesus, in the context of court- and creditor-enforced debt-bondage, see Douglas E. Oakman, *Jesus, Debt, and the Lord's Prayer* (Eugene, OR: Cascade Books, 2014), Chapter 3. Michael Hudson, *Forgive Them Their Debts*, 9–15, also argues that Jesus promoted debt forgiveness. Interestingly, Hudson links Isa 61, Jesus's sermon in Luke 4, and Jubilee debt remission in 11Q Melch. How Luke would have known Dead Sea texts is a pertinent question, but certainly Isa 61 was influential in Luke's presentation about Jesus.
[34] Kloppenborg, "The Dishonoured Master," 491.

security arrangements.[35] For the landlord class, these involve patronage, estates, storehouses, and loans delivered through agents or the tables of the bankers.

4. Conclusion

In this return to the matter of debt in first-century Galilee, I have come to see Jesus as a subversive and practical mitigator, an efficacious broker, not an advocate of eschatological utopia.[36] His activity of impugning the interests of the ruling classes could quite naturally lead to a cross, as he himself notes in Q 14:27. However, in light of my belief that he read his context through the analogy of the Exodus, status quo play-it-safe was insufficient.[37] Reliance even on a softened reverse patronage was inadequate. Hence, I also see him in the end as pointing toward a more horizontal, family-like reciprocity of fictive kin, just as we see in the early Jesus groups. What Jesus was doing had to get him in trouble with the ruling classes. He was doing things that weakened the iron-clad bonds of the rulers, written or unwritten, so that they might fear loss of their own material security and so to speak self-sufficiency.

In closing, it is good to recall again that the debt archives in Galilee were not destroyed as in Jerusalem. Landlord and creditor interests prevailed. What James Scott talks about as the security-first orientation of peasants also allows them to be easily co-opted by elite interests. Where Josephus largely succeeded in defusing a rebellion rooted in Galilean peasant discontent, forty-some years earlier, the Galilean peasant, Jesus of Nazareth, spoke and acted against those same elite interests. In the end, his challenges to written and unwritten obligation offended the majesty of Rome, and he suffered the capital consequences of one who dared to advocate what the Romans called "New Tables."[38]

---

[35] Oakman, *Political Aims of Jesus*, 99–102; idem, "The Radical Jesus: You Cannot Serve God and Mammon," *BTB* 34 (2004): 122–9. See also the discussion in Ronald A. Piper, "Wealth, Poverty, and Subsistence in Q," in *From Quest to Q: Festschrift James M. Robinson*, ed. Ronald A. Piper, BETL 146 (Leuven: Leuven University Press, 2000), 235, and references there to Honeyman and Fitzmyer discussing the etymology of the Semitic word *mamon*.

[36] Albert Schweitzer's view of Jesus as apocalyptic or eschatological prophet has been emphasized in contemporary Jesus studies by scholars like Dale Allison, Bart Ehrman, and N. T. Wright. My own dissent is rooted in the belief that the earliest layer of Q and most of the parables of Jesus do not attest such preoccupation. Moreover, Jesus himself was not a literate scribe like those at Qumran, and more likely as a Galilean peasant he was centrally concerned with concrete and immediate material matters as described in this chapter. For similar reservations about Jesus and apocalypticism, see John S. Kloppenborg and Leif E. Vaage, "Early Christianity, Q and Jesus: The Sayings Gospel and Method in the Study of Christian Origins," *Semeia* 55 (1991): 7–8. For my further views about the scribes of the early Jesus traditions, see Douglas E. Oakman, *The Radical Jesus, the Bible, and the Great Transformation*, Matrix: The Bible in Mediterranean Context (Eugene, OR: Cascade Books, 2021), 89–115.

[37] Oakman, *Political Aims of Jesus*, 94–7.

[38] The serious gravity of advocating New Tables (Lat. *tabulae novae*) in the eyes of Roman elites was enunciated in the late Roman Republic by the Catiline Orations of Cicero and Sallust's *Bellum Catilinae* 21. See also, the *OCD* s.v. "Sergius Catilina, Lucius." Josephus records that Judean insurgents proclaimed release from debts in order to strengthen their rebellion against Rome (*B.J.* 2.427); and cf. his reference to Simon son of Giora (*B.J.* 4.508).

Bibliography

Armenti, J. "On the Use of the Term 'Galileans' in the Writings of Josephus Flavius: A Brief Note." *JQR* 72 (1981): 45–9.
Aviam, M. "People, Land, Economy, and Belief in First-Century Galilee and Its Origins: A Comprehensive Archaeological Synthesis." In *The Galilean Economy in the Time of Jesus*, edited by David A. Fiensy and Ralph K. Hawkins, 5–48. Atlanta, GA: Society of Biblical Literature, 2013.
Brown, P. *Through the Eye of a Needle: Wealth, the Fall of Rome, and the Making of Christianity in the West, 350–550 AD*. Princeton, NJ: Princeton University Press, 2012.
Chancey, M., and E. M. Meyers. "How Jewish Was Sepphoris in Jesus' Time?" *BAR* 26, no. 4 (2000): 18–33, 61.
Cohen, S. J. D. *Josephus in Galilee and Rome: His Vita and Development as a Historian*. Leiden: E. J. Brill, 1979.
Donahue, J. "Tax Collectors and Sinners: An Attempt at an Identification." *CBQ* 33 (1971): 39–61.
Drake, L. "Did Jesus Oppose the *prosbul* in the Forgiveness Petition of the Lord's Prayer?" *NovT* 56 (2014): 233–44.
Elliott, J. H. "Patronage and Clientage." In *The Social Sciences and New Testament Interpretation*, edited by Richard L. Rohrbaugh, 144–56. Peabody, MA: Hendrickson, 1996.
Feldman, L. "The Term 'Galileans' in Josephus." *JQR* 72 (1981): 50–2.
Fiensy, D. A. "Did Large Estates Exist in Lower Galilee?" In *Christian Origins and the Ancient Economy*, 98–117. Eugene, OR: Cascade Books, 2014.
Fiensy, D. A. "Jesus and Debts: Did He Pray About Them?" In *Christian Origins and the Ancient Economy*, 59–66. Eugene, OR: Cascade Books, 2014.
Fiensy, D. A., and J. R. Strange, eds. *Galilee in the Late Second Temple and Mishnaic Periods*. 2 vols. Minneapolis, MN: Fortress Press, 2014–15.
Finley, M. I. *The Ancient Economy*. Updated edition, with a new foreword by Ian Morris. Sather Classical Lectures 43. Berkeley, CA: University of California Press, 1999.
Goodman, M. "The First Jewish Revolt: Social Conflict and the Problem of Debt." *JJS* 33 (1982): 417–27.
Hamel, G. *Poverty and Charity in Roman Palestine, First Three Centuries C.E.* Near Eastern Studies 23. Berkeley, CA: University of California Press, 1990.
Hezser, C. *Jewish Slavery in Antiquity*. Oxford: Oxford University Press, 2005.
Hudson, M. *...and Forgive Them Their Debts: Lending, Foreclosure and Redemption from Bronze Age Finance to the Jubilee Year*. Dresden: ISLET-Verlag, 2018.
Hudson, M. "Entrepreneurs: From the Near Eastern Takeoff to the Roman Collapse." In *The Invention of Enterprise: Entrepreneurship from Ancient Mesopotamia to Modern Times*, edited by D. S. Landes, J. Mokyr, and W. J. Baumol, 8–39. Princeton, NJ: Princeton University Press, 2010.
Josephus. Translated by H. St. J. Thackeray et al. 10 vols. LCL. Cambridge, MA: Harvard University Press, 1926–65.
Kloppenborg, J. S. "The Dishonoured Master (Luke 16, 1–8a)." *Biblica* 70 (1989): 474–95.
Kloppenborg, J. S. "The Growth and Impact of Agricultural Tenancy in Jewish Palestine (III BCE–I CE)." *Journal of the Economic and Social History of the Orient* 51 (2008): 31–66.
Kloppenborg, J. S. "Literary Convention, Self-Evidence and the Social History of the Q People." *Semeia* 55 (1991): 77–102.

Kloppenborg, J. S. *The Tenants in the Vineyard: Ideology, Economics, and Agrarian Conflict in Jewish Palestine*. WUNT 195. Tübingen: Mohr Siebeck, 2006.

Kloppenborg, J. S., and L. E. Vaage. "Early Christianity, Q and Jesus: The Sayings Gospel and Method in the Study of Christian Origins." *Semeia* 55 (1991): 1–14.

Lapin, H. *Economy, Geography, and Provincial History in Later Roman Palestine*. TSAJ 85. Tübingen: Mohr Siebeck, 2001.

Malina, B. J. "Patron and Client: The Analogy Behind Synoptic Theology." In *The Social World of Jesus and the Gospels*, 143–75. London: Routledge, 1996.

Mundell, R. "Use and Abuses of Gresham's Law in the History of Money." *Zagreb Journal of Economics* 2 (1998): 3–38.

Nun, M. *Ancient Anchorages and Harbours Around the Sea of Galilee*. Kibbutz Ein Gev, Israel: Kinnereth Sailing Co., 1988.

Oakman, D. E. "Batteries of Power: Coinage in the Judean Temple System." In *In Other Words: Essays on Social Science Methods and the New Testament in Honor of Jerome H. Neyrey*, edited by A. C. Hagedorn, Z. A. Crook, and E. Stewart, 171–85. SWBA Second Series 1. Sheffield: Sheffield Phoenix Press, 2007.

Oakman, D. E. "The Galilean World of Jesus." In *The Early Christian World*, edited by Philip F. Esler, 97–120. 2nd ed. London: Routledge, 2017.

Oakman, D. E. "Jesus and Agrarian Palestine: The Factor of Debt." In *Society of Biblical Literature 1985 Seminar Papers*, edited by K. H. Richards, 57–83. Atlanta, GA: Scholars Press, 1985.

Oakman, D. E. *Jesus and the Economic Questions of His Day*. Studies in the Bible and Early Christianity 8. Lewiston, NY: Edwin Mellen Press, 1986.

Oakman, D. E. *Jesus and the Peasants*. Matrix: The Bible in Mediterranean Context. Eugene, OR: Cascade Books, 2008.

Oakman, D. E. *Jesus, Debt, and the Lord's Prayer*. Eugene, OR: Cascade Books, 2014.

Oakman, D. E. *The Political Aims of Jesus*. Minneapolis, MN: Fortress Press, 2012.

Oakman, D. E. "The Radical Jesus: You Cannot Serve God and Mammon." *BTB* 34 (2004): 122–29.

Oakman, D. E. *The Radical Jesus, the Bible, and the Great Transformation*. Matrix: The Bible in Mediterranean Context. Eugene, OR: Cascade Books, 2021.

Piper, R. A. "Wealth, Poverty, and Subsistence in Q." In *From Quest to Q: Festschrift James M. Robinson*, edited by R. A. Piper, 219–64. BETL 146. Leuven: Leuven University Press, 2000.

Robinson, J. M., P. Hoffmann, and J. S. Kloppenborg, eds. *The Critical Edition of Q*. Minneapolis: Fortress Press; Leuven: Peeters, 2000.

Robinson, J. M., P. Hoffmann, and J. S. Kloppenborg, eds. *The Sayings Gospel Q in Greek and English with Parallels from the Gospels of Mark and Thomas*. Minneapolis, MN: Fortress Press, 2002.

Saldarini, A. J. *Pharisees, Scribes and Sadducees: A Sociological Approach*. Wilmington, DE: Michael Glazier, 1988.

Saller, R. P. *Personal Patronage Under the Roman Empire*. Cambridge: Cambridge University Press, 1982.

Schürer, E. *The History of the Jewish People in the Age of Jesus Christ (175 B.C.–A.D. 135)*. A New English Version. Edited by G. Vermes, F. Millar, M. Black, and M. Goodman. 3 vols. Edinburgh: T. & T. Clark, 1973–87.

Scott, J. C. *The Moral Economy of the Peasant: Rebellion and Subsistence in Southeast Asia*. New Haven, CT: Yale University Press, 1976.

Sparavigna, A. C. "Some Notes on the Gresham's Law of Money Circulation." *International Journal of Sciences* 3, no. 2 (2014): 80–91, https://www.ijsciences.com/pub/pdf/V320140220.pdf, accessed 03/02/2021.

Syon, D. *Small Change in Hellenistic-Roman Galilee*. Numismatic Studies and Researches 11. Jerusalem: The Israel Numismatic Society, 2015.

Zeitlin, S. "Who Were the Galileans? New Light on Josephus' Activities in Galilee." *JQR* 64 (1973/1974): 189–203.

A Realistic Reading of the Parable of the Lost Coin in Q: Gaining or Losing Even More?

Ernest van Eck

1. Introduction

C. H. Dodd, in his reading of the parables, treated the parables as didactic stories, explored their eschatological dimensions, and focused on the original intention of the parables in their historical settings. Dodd insisted that the parables should be heard by the modern interpreter as they were heard by Jesus's original first-century Jewish Palestinian audience. This approach culminated in his now well-known definition of a parable as a "metaphor or simile *drawn from nature or common life*, arresting the listener by its *vividness or strangeness*."[1]

Dodd's definition of a parable informs a realistic reading of the parables in two ways. First, a realistic reading of the parables takes as point of departure that the parables are stories *drawn from nature or common life*, that is, stories to be read against the backdrop of the social realia (cultural scripts of socio-cultural features) invoked by a given parable. From this perspective, the parables of Jesus are stories about shepherds attending to flocks of sheep and not stories about Jesus looking for lost sinners (Luke 15:4–6), day laborers being hired to work in a vineyard and not God who invites Gentiles to become part of the kingdom (Matt 20:1–15), and servants whose debt are released and not God who forgives abundantly (Matt 18:23–33). As put by Kloppenborg, we have to consider that

---

[1] C. H. Dodd, *The Parables of the Kingdom* (New York: Charles Scribner's Sons, 1961), 5 (emphasis added). See also Ruben Zimmermann's definition in "Die Gleichnisse Jesu: Eine Leseanleitung zum Kompendium," in *Kompendium der Gleichnisse Jesu*, ed. Ruben Zimmermann (Munich: Gütersloher Verlagshaus, 2007), 3–45 (here 25): "Eine Parabel is ein kurzer narrativer…fiktionaler Text, der in der erzählten Welt auf bekannte Realität…bezogen ist." Arland J. Hultgren, *The Parables of Jesus: A Commentary* (Grand Rapids, MI: Eerdmans, 2000), 9, is of the same opinion: "The subject of the parables is typically the familiar everyday life: men and women working, losing, and finding; fathers and sons in strained and joyous relationships; kings, rich men, and slaves in stereotypical roles; domestic animals, seeds, plants, vineyards, leaven, and the like."

possibility that in the parables "a vineyard or a shepherd...is just a vineyard or a shepherd."[2]

Applied to the parable of the Lost Coin, the woman searching for her lost coin is not a metaphor for God, as has been argued, for example, by Hultgren, Boucher, or Blomberg.[3] The woman also does not reveal "vital information about the character of God"[4] or show metaphorically what "Jesus is doing," that is, "finding/saving the lost ones."[5] From the point of view of a realistic reading, the woman is just a (peasant) woman, not looking for a sinner or the lost, but a coin with the value of 1 drachma.

Since a realistic reading of the parables focuses on the social realia invoked by each parable, the focus of the reading is the socio-cultural features drawn from nature or common life that form the backdrop of a specific parable. A realistic reading of the Lost Coin, therefore, asks questions such as the following: Was the woman, owning 10 drachmas, poor or rich? Does she have a husband or not? What does her house look like? Did she own the house? Why was it necessary to light a lamp to look for the coin? Who were her neighbors? What was the value of a drachma? More important even, what was the buying power of 1 drachma? Was it normal to light up a lamp to look for something like a coin? What was the woman's status? Hultgren, for example, poses some of these questions, but argues that "all these questions are actually beside the point of a good story."[6] Blomberg shares this sentiment: "Other details in these two parables (the Lost Sheep and Lost Coin)—the wilderness and the shepherd's home, or the lamp with what the women searches her house—*add nothing to the meaning of the narratives* but simply act as the logical 'stage props' for the action of the main characters."[7] For a realistic reading of the parables, to the contrary, any detail in a parable that in some way or other relates to its socio-cultural background, is deemed as important.

The second way in which Dodd's definition of a parable informs a realistic reading of the parables is the *vividness or strangeness* of details (social realia) in a parable that created meaning for the original hearers listening to the parable. The first audiences of Jesus's parables, as Kloppenborg has argued, most probably had native knowledge of the social realia referred to in the parables.[8] For them,

---

[2] John S. Kloppenborg, *Synoptic Problems: Collected Essays*, WUNT 329 (Tübingen: Mohr Siebeck, 2014), 490.

[3] Hultgren, *Parables of Jesus*, 64. Cf. Craig Blomberg, *Interpreting the Parables* (Downers Grove, IL: InterVarsity Press, 2012), 214; Madeleine Boucher, *The Mysterious Parable* (Wilmington, DE: Michael Glazier, 1981), 98.

[4] Klyne Snodgrass, *Stories with Intent: A Comprehensive Guide to the Parables of Jesus* (Grand Rapids, MI: Eerdmans, 2008), 111.

[5] John Dominic Crossan, *The Power of Parable: How Fiction by Jesus became Fiction about Jesus* (New York: HarperOne, 2012), 38, 40.

[6] See Hultgren, *The Parables of Jesus*, 66: "Does [the woman] live alone and own [the house] as a private dwelling (which would indicate wealth)? Is it provided for her? Does she live with others in the house, or does she have an apartment within a house? Does she have other assets? Is she a widow?"

[7] Blomberg, *Interpreting the Parables*, 216 (emphasis added).

[8] Kloppenborg, *Synoptic Problems*, 2.

the mention of a peasant home most probably would have invoked a very vivid picture, as well as celebrations with neighbors. The lighting of lamp to look for a lost coin, however, with the mere value of 1 drachma, would that have been seen as normal or strange? And if it was considered strange, or abnormal, was that the "surprise" in the parable that, for them, carried its meaning? Moreover, as Levine has argued, that what seems odd (strange or abnormal) to the modern reader might have been perfectly normal to the first hearers of a parable, and what may seem normal to the modern reader might have been perceived as odd or surprising to the first hearers of a parable.[9]

To distinguish between "normal" and "abnormal" social practices and realities in any given parable, knowledge of the cultural scripts and social *realia* embedded in the parable is indispensable to understand what message the parable wanted to convey. And for this, as will be argued and indicated below, information provided by Roman-Egypt documented papyri is indispensable.

To get to the social context of the Lost Coin, which is vividly expressed by its content (Dodd), socio-cultural information available in documented papyri can be used to identify the possible social realities and practices (cultural scripts) invoked by the parable. Knowledge of these social realia will then help the modern reader to identify what is *vivid* ("normal") in the parable, and what most probably is strange ("abnormal"). And what is strange, most probably, will in some way or other lead the modern reader to the intended meaning of the parable.

2. The Socio-cultural Background of the Lost Coin

When details in the parable of the Lost Coin (e.g., the lamp or the house in which the coin got lost) are considered as beside the point of a good story,[10] or mere logical stage props to facilitate the actions of the characters in the parable,[11] the social realia invoked by the parable is obviously not deemed as an important contributor to a possible meaning of the parable in its originating setting. Moreover, since most available interpretations of the parable read it in its literary context, taking Luke's allegorical application of a Jesus parable as cue, it is not surprising that only scant references to the socio-cultural background of the parable can be found in available interpretations.

When these interpretations do refer to the social realia invoked by the parable, the focus is on the status of the woman, the house, why the woman possesses ten drachmae, and the value of a drachma. The woman is either described as poor,[12]

---

[9] Amy-Jill Levine, *Short Stories by Jesus: The Enigmatic Parables of a Controversial Rabbi* (San Francisco: HarperOne, 2014), 1.
[10] Hultgren, *The Parables of Jesus*, 66.
[11] Blomberg, *Interpreting the Parables*, 216.
[12] Boucher, *The Mysterious Parable*, 98; Hultgren, *The Parables of Jesus*, 66; Annette Merz, "Last und Freude des Kehrens (Von der verlorenen Drachme)—Lk 15,8–10," in Zimmermann, ed., *Kompendium der Gleichnisse Jesu*, 610–17 (here 612).

or well-off,[13] and married or unmarried.[14] The house in which the coin got lost is described as small,[15] with no windows for natural lighting,[16] or with small windows with a low door or opening letting in limited natural light.[17] The woman thus had to light a lamp to look for the coin, most probably lodged in one of the many cracks of the floor, even if the search took place during daylight.[18]

Why was the woman in possession of ten drachmae? Some argue that the lost coin was part of the woman's headdress bedecked with coins as part of her dowry,[19] while others see this possibility, based on evidence from *m. Kelim* 12:7, as ill-founded.[20] Schottroff, in her turn, believes that the woman worked for the money. Regarding the value of a drachma, there is more or less unanimity among interpreters of the parable: a drachma was the equivalent of the denarius,[21] more or less equaling a peasant's subsistence wage for a day's work,[22] and, according to Schottroff, enough money to buy food for two days.[23]

3. The Socio-Cultural Background of the Lost Coin and the Use of Papyri

In the recent past some parable scholars, who are interested in reading the parables in their original setting, started using papyri from early Roman Egypt as a source that gives evidence to the social realia and social practices that are presupposed by the parables.[24] These papyri—with due allowance made for

---

[13] Klyne Snodgrass, *Stories with Intent: A Comprehensive Guide to the Parables of Jesus* (Grand Rapids, MI: Eerdmans, 2008), 113; Levine, *Short Stories*, 42. Snodgrass further describes the woman as "probably just a typical woman one would find in any Galilean village" (p. 113). What this means, and on what evidence this is based, is not clear.

[14] Luise Schottroff, *The Parables of Jesus*, trans. L. M. Maloney (Minneapolis, MN: Augsburg, 2006), 154.

[15] Merz, "Freude," 612; Schottroff, *Parables*, 153; Snodgrass, *Stories with Intent*, 113.

[16] Hultgren, *The Parables of Jesus*, 67; Joachim Jeremias, *The Parables of Jesus*, trans. S. H. Hooke (London: SCM Press, 1972), 135; Simon J. Kistemaker, *The Parables: Understanding the Stories Jesus Told* (Grand Rapids, MI: Baker Books, 1980), 175; Schottroff, *Parables*, 154.

[17] Jeremias, *The Parables of Jesus*, 135; Kistemaker, *The Parables*, 175; Snodgrass, *Stories with Intent*, 114.

[18] Merz, "Freude," 612; Snodgrass, *Stories with Intent*, 114.

[19] E. F. F. Bishop, *Jesus of Palestine: The Local Background to the Gospel Documents* (London: Lutterworth Press, 1955), 191; Jeremias, *The Parables of Jesus*, 134; Kistemaker, *The Parables*, 174; Bernard B. Scott, *Hear Then the Parable: A Commentary on the Parables of Jesus* (Minneapolis, MN: Fortress Press, 1989), 311–12.

[20] Snodgrass, *Stories with Intent*, 114.

[21] Schottroff, *Parables*, 154. This rough equivalency is confirmed by Josephus in his *Jewish Antiquities* 3.193 and 18.312. See, further, Hultgren, *Parables of Jesus*, 66.

[22] Hultgren, *The Parables of Jesus*, 67; Scott, *Hear Then*, 311; Snodgrass, *Stories with Intent*, 113.

[23] Schottroff, *Parables*, 154.

[24] Giovanni Bazzana, "Basileia and Debt Relief: The Forgiveness of Debts in the Lord's Prayer in the Light of Documentary Papyri," *CBQ* 73 (2011): 511–25; idem, "Violence and Human Prayer to God in Q 11," *HTS* 70, no. 1 (2014): 1–8; John S. Kloppenborg, "The Parable of the Burglar in Q: Insights from Papyrology," in *Metaphor, Narrative, and Parables in Q*, ed. D. T. Roth, R. Zimmermann, and M. Labahn, WUNT 315 (Tübingen: Mohr Siebeck, 2014), 287–306; Kloppenborg, *Synoptic Problems*; idem, *The Tenants in the Vineyard: Ideology, Economics, and Agrarian Conflict in Jewish Palestine*, WUNT 195 (Tübingen: Mohr Siebeck, 2006); Ernest van Eck, *The Parables of Jesus the Galilean: Stories of a Social Prophet* (Eugene, OR: Cascade Books, 2016);

differences between Roman Egyptian and Roman Palestinian socio-cultural practices—provide ancient *comparanda* on the practices and social realities which the parables of Jesus presuppose.[25] These papyri also usually are our most plentiful, and sometimes only, resource to identify the social realia and social practices embedded in any given parable.[26] Using these papyri also can help the interpreter of a parable "to get clear on the most basic meanings of the images in question (invoked by the parable) before moving to abstract, symbolic or allegorical meanings."[27] Using these papyri, therefore, can help to answer the question whether the woman in the parable indeed functions as a symbol or metaphor for God or simply should be seen as a peasant woman looking for a lost coin.[28] In short, using papyri from early Roman Egypt as a source that gives evidence to the social realia and social practices that are presupposed by the parables, facilitates a realistic reading of the parables.

Erin Vearncombe, in her 2014 article, has done an extensive realistic reading of the parable of the Lost Coin (Q 15:8–10), using early Roman Egypt papyri.[29] Starting with the question why the woman in the parable was in possession of ten coins, she indicates that a wealth of papyri attest to the fact that women owned, controlled and disposed property such as "houses, parts of houses, workshops, sums of money, and objects such as furniture, slaves, animals, equipment and tools, clothing, jewelry, produce and provisions."[30] Although the parable is not explicit about whether the woman lives alone or not, some papyri do indicate that some women lived alone, and that women could experience stress in the absence of a male family member (P.Bad. 4.48; P.Flor. 3.332). Papyrological evidence thus confirms that it could be customary for women to possess sums of money, own dwellings, and live alone.[31]

Regarding the relative value of ten coins (ten drachmae), she agrees with most scholars that the value of 1 drachma is more or less equivalent to the Roman

---

idem, "Realism and Method: The Parables of Jesus," *Neotestamentica* 51 (2017): 163–84; Ernest van Eck and John S. Kloppenborg, "The Unexpected Patron: A Social-scientific and Realistic Reading of the Parable of the Vineyard Laborers (Mt 20:1–15)," *HTS* 71, no. 1 (2015): 1–11; Ernest van Eck and R. J. Van Niekerk, "The Samaritan 'brought him to an inn': Revisiting πανδοχεῖον in Luke 10:34," *HTS* 74, no. 4 (2018): 1–11.

[25] Kloppenborg, "The Parable of the Burglar in Q," 289; Erin K. Vearncombe, "Searching for a Lost Coin: Papyrological Backgrounds for Q 15,8–10," in Roth, Zimmermann, and Labahn, eds., *Metaphor, Narrative, and Parables in Q*, 307–37 (here 314).
[26] Kloppenborg, *Synoptic Problems*, 2.
[27] Ibid., 490.
[28] The answer to this question obviously relates to a reading of the parable in the originating setting it was first told by Jesus (27–30 CE), or a reading of the parable in its literary setting in Luke (or Q). With regards to the latter, the following remark of Kloppenborg, *Synoptic Problems*, 515, cannot not be relevant enough: "It is clear from the editing of the parables by the Synoptic evangelists themselves that they did not treat the parables as fresh and lively narratives, combining the everydayness of Palestinian village society with playful inversions and resonant metaphors; instead, the parables offered mere surfaces upon which to inscribe instructions on salvation history, Christology, ecclesiology and morals."
[29] Vearncombe, "Searching for a Lost Coin," 307–37.
[30] Vearncombe, "Papyrological Backgrounds," 314; see, e.g., P.Bad. 2.35; P.Mert. 2.83; P.Brem. 63; P.Tebt. 2.389; P.Oxy. 1.114, 6.932; P.Berl.Dem. 3142.
[31] Vearncombe, "Papyrological Backgrounds," 314–17.

denarius. From available papyri it seems that wages for agricultural tasks was in the range of 4 obols per day (1 drachma = 6 obols), and even if it was 1 drachma, it was not a "generous amount, meeting bare subsistence needs only."[32] Working with this equation, Vearncombe estimates that the 10 drachmae of the woman was the equivalent of perhaps two weeks of work. As such, the "characterization of the woman in the parable as poor would be very appropriate."[33]

Turning to household maintenance, evidence from papyri indicates that it was a regular part of the upkeep of a dwelling (e.g., P.Mil.Vogl. 2.77). References to lamps are scant in available papyri, but one papyrus (P.Corn 1 = SB 3.6796) gives a very detailed record of lamp oil assigned to the entourage of a certain Apollonius, down to an eight of a kotyle, with 1 kotyle (= one twelfth of a chous) equalling approximately 0.27 liters. Importantly, this record indicates "that lamp oil was monitored precisely, with amounts being carefully measured."[34] Vearncombe continues: "Her lighting of the lamp in order to search for the coin is significant, however; lamp oil seems to have been carefully managed, and in a situation where a single drachma was worth a search, in a subsistence-level circumstance, the lighting of a lamp was not a negligible or insignificant action."[35]

Vearncombe next discusses the coins as property of the woman, indicating that evidence from the papyri describing the content of dowries refutes the possibility that the lost coin was part of a headdress that formed a part of the woman's dowry, as was argued before (see, e.g., P.Mich. 2.121).[36] It also seems that the action of searching and finding was a quite common practice, attested to in several papyri (see, e.g., P.Mich. 1.26, 1.74, 8.503; P.Tebt. 3.1; P.Corn. 48; P.Oxy. 14.1680). Evidence from available papyri, finally, indicates that relationships between neighbors were not always amicable and without problems. Neighbors at times may have been the subject to some surveillance, and at times suspected of theft (see SB 12.11125, 16.12326; P.Oxy. 10.1272). As such, the celebration after the coin has been found, which was a normal event, also could have served to eliminate the possibility of theft.[37]

3.1. Price of Oil and Daily Usage

Vearncombe's excellent study makes two further observations that are important for a realistic reading of the Lost Coin. First, she indicates that it seems that the use of lamp oil was monitored precisely, with amounts being carefully measured.

---

[32] See ibid., 318–19, and P.Mich. 5.355; P.Col. 4.66; P.Cair.Zen. I.59028, IV.59748; P.Lond. I.131.
[33] Ibid., 320. In Douglas Oakman's estimate, *Jesus and the Peasants* (Eugene, OR: Cascade Books, 2008), 44, two denarii represented around three weeks' worth of food for one person and, in terms of a family of four, 2 denarii would stretch from a week to a week-and-a-half for a family. A year's supply of food for a family of four thus required between 60 and 122 denarii. When other necessities such as clothes, taxes and religious dues are also taken into consideration, 250 denarii per annum (22 denarii per month) was a poverty-level income. Vearncombe (p. 319) more or less concurs with Oakman in her estimate: 300 denarii would have been an annual subsistence wage for a family of six.
[34] Ibid., 321.
[35] Ibid.
[36] Ibid., 321–2.
[37] Ibid., 323.

Second, she remarks that, considering that the woman lived at a subsistence-level, her lighting of the lamp in order to search for a coin with a value of 1 drachma is significant. Why was a meticulous measuring of lamp oil used, and why was the woman's lighting of a lamp significant? To answer these questions, it is important to determine, as far as possible, what the price of lamp oil was and what quantities were used by an individual or a household on a daily basis. With this information available, one can then calculate how much it cost to light a lamp in a house, or to look for a lost coin.

As will be indicated below, available papyri contain a vast amount of information that can help with these kind of calculations. First, however, it is necessary to establish the units by which liquid volume was measured. This is needed, not only to calculate the cost of lamp oil per volume used, but also as a guide for liquid volumes used in available papyri. While the primary volume unit used to quantify amounts of dry goods used was the artaba (ἀρτάβη), the volume of liquids, such as wine and oil, was quantified by the metrētēs (μετρητής). A metrētēs was usually equivalent in volume to a jar known as a keramion (κεράμιον). A metrētēs was further divided into the chous (χοῦς), and equalled 12 chous. The chous was then subdivided into 12 kotylai (κοτύλαι; sing. κοτύλη).[38] According to Aristophanes, a κοτύλη equaled half a ξέστης (ἡμίξεστον), with a ξέστης equalling the Roman sextarius (measured as half a chous).[39] If a chous had a volume of 2.9 liters,[40] the volume of the different liquid measures can be indicated as follows:[41]

Table 4

Measurement	Relative volume	Volume in liters
μετρητής/metrētēs	12 chous	34.8 liter
χοῦς/chous	12 κοτύλαι	2.9 liter
ξέστης/xeston	6 κοτύλαι	1.446 liter
κοτύλη/kotyle	1/12 chous	0.241 liter

---

[38] See also LSJ, s.v. χοῦς, where the volume of a χοῦς is equated to 12 κοτύλαι. Cf. D. B. Sandy, *The Production and Use of Vegetable Oils in Ptolemaic Egypt* (Atlanta, GA: Scholars Press, 1989), 9–10. See also P. W. Pestman, *The New Papyrological Primer* (Leiden: Brill, 1994), 49; K. Maresch, *Bronze und Silber: Papyrologische Beiträge zur Geschichte des Währung im ptolemäischen und römischen Ägypten bis zum 2. Jahrhundert n. Chr.* (Cologne: Westdeutscher Verlag, 1996), 187; B. Hayden, "Price Formation and Fluctuation in Ptolemaic Egypt" (Ph.D. diss., University of Chicago; Chicago, 2018), 279–80.

[39] κοτύλη δέ ἐστιν εἶδος μέτρου, ὃ λέγομεν ἡμεῖς ἡμίξεστον. A kotyle is a kind of measure, which we say is a half xeston (Aristophanes, *Plut.* 436b). For other Roman units of measurement, see: W. C. A. Smith, *A New Classical Dictionary of Greek and Roman Biography, Mythology, and Geography partly based upon the Dictionary of Greek and Roman Biography and Mythology* (New York: Harper & Brothers, 1951), 1024.

[40] Hayden, "Price Formation", 279; Pestman, *New Papyrological Primer*, 48.

[41] Smith, *New Classical Dictionary*, 1024, is of the opinion that 1 chous equalled a volume of 3.27 litres. Vearncombe's measurement of 1 kotyle as equalling 0.27 litres is most probably based on Smith's estimated volume of 1 chous. In the following the measurement used in Pestman's *The New Papyrological Primer* is used: 1 chous equals 2.9 litres.

What was the price of oil used for lighting? In determining the price of oil used for lighting, one must take into consideration that only oil produced from sesame and castor seeds were used for cooking, lighting, and potentially, medicine.[42] In available papyri, oil produced from these seeds is distinguished by the terms σησάμινος (sesame oil) and κίκιον (castor oil).[43] Also, where ἔλαιον is found in the papyri of this period, meaning one kind of oil, the presumption is that sesame oil is meant.[44] A search in available documented papyri for σησάμινος, κίκιον, and ἔλαιον (and their derivatives), where price per volume is also mentioned, yields the following information that can be used to get an indication of the price for lamp oil.

In available documented papyri, we have two occurrences of σησάμινος.[45] In P.Rev. 40.12[46] (Arsinoite nome, 259 BCE), the price for sesame oil (σησάμινον) is indicated as 48 drachmae per metrētēs (i.e., 8.275 obols per liter),[47] and in P.Rev. 40.15 it is indicated as 2 obols per kotyle (8.298 obols per liter). References to castor oil (κίκιον) occurs more often in documented papyri, and in most cases the price per liter is indicated as more or less 48 drachmae per liter. This, for example, is the case in P.Rev. 40.15–16 (Arsinoite nome, 259 BCE) and in P.Col.Zen. I.21.4[48] (= P.Col. 3.21; Memphis, 257 BCE), a letter from Nikon, agent of Apollonios, to Panakestor, in which he complains about the loss of castor oil given to some donkey drivers. In P.Rev. 53.15, the price of castor oil (κίκιον) is indicated as 2 obols per kotyle, the same as the price for sesame oil (σησάμινον) in P.Rev. 40.15. In some cases, a lower price is indicated. In P.Rev. 40.13 the price for 1 metrētēs of castor oil is 30 drachmae (i.e., 5.172 obols per liter), and in P.Rev. 53.20 it is indicated as 19 drachmae and 2 obols per metrētēs (3.333 obols per liter). In PSI IV 531.8 the price of 1 χαλμαιαν τοῦ ἐλαίου is priced at 1 drachma and 4.5 obols, but since it is not clear what a χαλμαιαν measures, a

---

[42] Hayden, "Price Formation," 423.
[43] B. P. Grenfell and J. P. Mahaffy, *The Revenue Laws of Ptolemy Philadelphus* (Oxford: Clarendon Press, 1896), 132; Hayden, "Price Formation," 425; D. B. Sandy, *The Production and Use of Vegetable Oils in Ptolemaic Egypt* (Atlanta, GA: Scholars Press, 1989), 18–19.
[44] Sandy, *Vegetable Oils*, 19.
[45] Hayden, "Price Formation," 430.
[46] P.Rev. 40.9–20 reads as follows:
πωλήσουσι δὲ τὸ ἔλαι[ο]ν ἐν τῆι χώραι ⟦τοῦ μὲν⟧
10 \τό τε/ σησάμινον καὶ τὸ κν[ή]κινον \καὶ τοῦ κίκιος καὶ τοῦ κολυκυντίνου καὶ ἐπελλυχνίου/ πρὸς χαλκὸν
τὸμ μετρητὴν τὸν [δωδε]κάχουν (δραχμῶν) μη,
⟦τοῦ δὲ κίκιος καὶ κολοκ[υνθίνο]υ καὶ \ἐ/πελλυχνίου⟧
⟦τὸμ μετρητὴν (δραχμῶν) λ⟧ τὴν δὲ κοτύλην (διωβόλου), ἐ[ν Ἀ]λεξανδρείαι δὲ κ[αὶ] τῆι Λιβύηι πάσηι
15 τοῦ σησ[α]μίν[ου] \καὶ τοῦ κίκι[ος]/ τὸμ με[τρη]τὴν (δραχμῶν) μη, \τὴν δὲ κοτύλην (διωβόλου)/,
⟦καὶ τοῦ⟧
⟦κ[ί]κιος τὸμ μ[ετ]ρητὴν [(δραχμῶν)] μη⟧ \{τὴν}/ καὶ πα[ρέ]ξουσιν ἱ[κανὸ]ν τοῖς [βου]λομένοις
ὠνεῖσθαι π[ω]λο[ῦ]ντες
δι[ὰ χώ]ρας ἐν [π]άσαις ταῖς πόλεσιν [καὶ κώ]μαις [....]σ.μ[..μ]ἐτ[ρ]οις τοῖς ἐξετα[σθεῖσιν] ὑπό
20 [τοῦ οἰκονόμου καὶ τοῦ ἀν]τιγραφέω[ς].
[47] The price per liter is calculated by using the volumes in Table 4, with 1 drachma equaling 6 obols. In this case, for example, 48 drachmas equal 288 obols, divided by 1 metrētēs (34.8 liters), equaling 8.275 obols per liter.
[48] P.Col.Zen I.21.4 reads as follows: "ἢ [τὸ] κίκ[ι] ἢ τὴν τιμὴν (δραχμὰς) δ. καὶ ἀποδότω Κρότωι."

price per liter cannot be calculated. References to castor oil are also found in SB XXIV 16067 and UPZ II 158, but since no unit of measurement is given, it also cannot be used to calculate a price per liter.

Turning to the occurrences of ἔλαιον, we have four references in the Oxyrhynchus papyri. In P.Oxy. 4.736.15 (Oxyrhynchus, 1 CE),[49] the price of oil is indicated as 1 chous for 4 drachmae and 4 obols, thus a price of 8.965 obols per liter. In P.Oxy 4.739.11 and 16 (1 CE), the price for a chous is respectively set at 4 drachmae and 2 obols (ἐλαίου χοῦς (δραχμαὶ) δ (διώβολον); i.e., 9.655 obols per liter) and 4 drachmae and 3 obols (ἐλα[ίου] (δραχμαὶ) δ (τριώβολον); i.e., 10 obols per liter). P.Oxy. 4.819.15 (1 CE) sets the price of 1 chous at 5 drachmae, thus a price of 10.344 obols per liter. In P.Fay. 101 v.1.9 (Euhemeria from the Arsinoite nome; 18 BCE), the price for 1 choenix of oil is given as 5 drachmae.[50] The choenix is a dry measure, but equals more or less 0.9463 liters of liquid volume. If this volume is taken as equivalent to the choenix, the price will be 6.211 obols per liter. P.Petr. 3.137 (third century BCE; Arsinoite nome), finally, has six references to the price of oil as 4 obols (ἔλαιον τέταρτον ὀβολοῦ; see P.Petr. 3 137.1.4, 9, 16, 21; 2.10, 16). Here we are set with a challenge, since the papyrus does not give the unit of measure; although the price is referenced several times, these references do not help in determining the price of oil per liter.

From the figures above it seems that from 279 BCE up to 1 CE, the price of oil was somewhere between 3.3 and 10.33 obols per liter, with 8.2 obols per liter (1 drachma and 2 obols) more or less the mean figure.[51] Taking into consideration that prices, over time, normally increase, a price of more or less 10 obols per liter in the first century would be a good estimation (see P.Oxy 4.739.11, 16; 4.819.15).

Some texts do differ quite drastically from this number. In P.Tebt. 3.885 and 3.891, for example, prices of 2880, 4032, 7200, and even 8640 drachmae per metrētēs, are mentioned. These prices, according to Hayden, may be due to dramatic price increases that at times did occur, and also may be related to the status of the buyer or the relationship between buyer and seller.[52] Josephus (*Life* 75–76), for example, relates the incident during which John of Gischala heard that 80 sextarii (40 choes) of oil was sold in Caesarea for 4 drachmae. He then bought all the oil, and resold it at price of 1 drachma for a chous, thus making a huge profit. He also, according to Josephus (*B.J.* 2.590–93), pretended that Jews staying in Syria were only allowed to use oil produced in their homeland, and therefore got permission to send oil to some Jews living in Syria. By buying oil in bulk, at times as much as 4 amphorae, at a low price and selling it at a much higher price, he again made a noteworthy profit. Trading in oil seems to have been a normal economic activity, as can be detected from several papyri that have

---

[49] P.Oxy. 4.736.15 reads as follows: "χβ. ἐλαίου χο(ὸς) α (δραχμαὶ) δ (τετρώβολον)."
[50] P.Fay 101 v.1.9 reads as follows: "(γίνονται) (δραχμαὶ) κθ. καὶ τιμ(ῆς) ἐλαίου χοί(νικος) α (δραχμαὶ) ε."
[51] In calculations to follow pertaining the daily use of oil, the figure of 8.2 obols per liter (1 drachma and 2 obols) will be used.
[52] Hayden, "Price Formation," 433.

toll receipts for oil as content,[53] as well as several ostraca that contain custom passes for the export of wine and oil.[54] It also seems that, because the trade in oil made such huge profits, at times the price was set by ordinance.[55] This, however, did not stop sellers from overcharging buyers.[56]

Available ostraca and papyri also indicate that oil for cooking and lighting was a necessary commodity. Several papyri, for example, contain delivery orders for oil,[57] and in contracts with (professional) nurses to look after the sick or in contracts to rear children, almost all of these contracts include the provision of oil for cooking and lighting.[58] Being a necessity, sometimes oil-makers were not allowed to move from nome to nome, since such movement could have led to a scarcity of oil in certain nomes.[59]

Turning to oil-use patterns, documented papyri contain some information that can help in determining the amount of oil most probably used per individual per day. First, it seems that it was not uncommon practice for wills, in the form of a contract, to include a stipulation on the provision of oil. In P.Mich. 5.321 (Tebtynis, in the Arsinoite nome, 42 CE), Orseus, son of Nestnephis, divides his property amongst his four children. Although the legal division is to be made after his death, the heirs actually take over their inheritance at once, as is clear from the fact that his eldest son, Nestnephis, agrees to pay to his father 12 drachmae a year for oil. In P.Mich. 5.322a (Tebtynis, in the Arsinoite nome, 46 CE), also a will in

---

[53] See BGU 13.2306 (51 CE), BGU 13.2307 (first century), and BGU 13.2309 (99–100 CE), all from Soknopaiu Nesos in the Arsinoite nome.

[54] See, for example, O.Berenike 1.4 (26–75 CE), O.Berenike 1.26 (25–75 CE), O.Berenike 1.28 (33–70 CE), and O.Berenike 1.87 (26–75 CE).

[55] In P.Tebt. III, pt. I 703.174–182 (Tebtynis, in the Arsinoite nome; 210 BCE), Zenodoros, the dioiketes, gives instructions to the oikonomos that oil should not be sold for more than the fixed price:

πρὸς διαρίπτειν. μελέτω δέ σοι καὶ [ἵ]να τὰ [ὤ-]
175 για μὴ πλείονος πωλῆται τῶν διαγεγραμ- [μ]ένων τιμῶν· ὅσα δ᾽ ἂν ἦι τιμὰς οὐχ ἑστη- [κ]υίας ἔχοντα, ἐπὶ δὲ τοῖς ἐργαζομένοις
[ἐσ]τὶν τ[άσ]σειν \ὰς/ ἂν βο[ύ]λωνται, ἐξεταζέσ- [θ]ω καὶ τοῦτο μὴ παρέργως, καὶ τὸ σύμ
180 μετρον ἐπιγένημα [[τα]] τάξας τῶν πω- [λ]ουμένων φορτίων συνανάγκα[[ι]]ζε τοὺς
.[.]..κου[..].ς τὰς διαθέσεις ποιεῖσθα[ι].

Take care that commodities not be sold for more than the prices fixed by ordinance. Examine closely all those which do not have fixed prices, and those for which it is up to the traders to set (the price) as they wish, and after you prescribe a moderate profit for the goods that are being sold, you must make the ... dispose of them (tr. from Hayden, "Price Formation," 211).

[56] See Chr.Wilck. 300.1–4 (Alexandria; 217 BCE):

1 Ὧρος Ἁρμάει χαίρειν. προσπέπτωκέ μοι παρὰ πλειόνων τῶν ἐκ τοῦ νομ[οῦ] καταπεπλευκότων τὸ ἔλαιον π[ωλ]εῖσθαι πλείονος τιμῆς τῆς ἐν τῶι προστάγμα[τι] διασεσαφημένης, παρὰ δὲ σοῦ οὐθ[ὲ]ν ἡμῖν προσπεφώνηται οὐδ᾽ Ἰμούθηι τ[ῶι] υἱῶι ἐπὶ τῶν τόπων μεταδεδώκα[τ]ε

Horos to Harmais, greeting. I have heard from many of those who have sailed down from the nome that oil is being sold at a higher price than what was made clear in the ordinance, but nothing from you has been reported to me, nor have you communicated to Imouthes my son, who is on location (trans. from Hayden, "Price Formation," 212).

[57] See, for example, O.Mich. 1.55 (Arsinoite nome; 6 CE) and O.Mich. 2.772, 774, and 775 (Karanis, in the Arsinoite nome; 2 BCE).

[58] See, for example, C.Pap.Gr. 1.9 (Alexandria, 5 BCE) and C.Pap.Gr. 1.24 (Oxyrhynchus, 87 CE), for contracts with nurses, and C.Pap.Gr. 1.13 (Alexandria, 30 BCE–14 CE) and P.Ryl. 2.178 (Hermopolis, 127 CE) for contracts relating to the rearing of children.

[59] See P.Rev. 44–46 in Hayden, "Price Formation," 97.

the form of a contract, the sons, daughters, and grandsons of Psyphis and Tetosiris are required to provide their parents with wheat, money for clothing and other expenses, as well as 6 kotylai of oil per month, that is, an amount of 2 drachmae per month.[60] P.Mich. 5.355dupl (Tebtynis, in the Arsinoite nome, 1 CE) contains the same kind of provision for oil. The text, consisting of a contract between Heron, son of Haryotes, and the weaver Harmiysis, son of Petesouchos, stipulates that Harmiysis will work for Heron for a period of two years, and that Heron will pay Harmiysis, as part of the payment for his labor, an annual amount of 28 drachmae for oil (i.e., approximately 14 obols or 2 drachmae and 2 obols per month). Although these texts give an indication of the monthly amount expected for oil, it cannot be used to indicate monthly consumption, simply because one cannot assume that the expected amounts covered the total expenditure for the monthly use of oil. What the texts do affirm, however, is that oil was such a necessary commodity that it was most probably common that wills and payment agreements made explicit provision to cover the cost of the use of oil.

There are, however, documented papyri that can help to indicate the approximate daily use of oil per individual. Above, reference was already made to SB 3.6796, in which the entourage of a certain Apollonius received a daily allowance of six-and-a-quarter kotylai of lamp oil, that is, 1.5 liters a day, equalling 12.3 obols. Several other papyri that have expense accounts as content contain the same kind of information. In P.Cair.Zen. 4.59704.30 (Philadelphia, in the Arsinoite nome, 263–229 BCE), it is indicated that Apollonios' employees were given an allowance of 4 obols per day for castor oil (0.5 liters per day, equalling 4 obols per day). P.Mich. 2.123 (Tebtynis, from the Arsinoite nome; 46 CE), an account of the expenditure of Kronion, son of Apion, and his colleague Eutychas for the period 14–24 December 46 CE, indicates that their total expenditure on oil for the 10-day period was 349 obols, that is, 0.423 liters per person per day, amounting to a cost of 3.5 obols per day. P.Mich. 2.127 (Tebtynis, from the Arsinoite nome, 46 CE), finally, gives a figure of 180 obols for the expenditure on oil by Kronion and Eutychas for the period between 1 September 45 to 17 January 46 CE (i.e., 1.5 obols per day).

The above papyri indicate that the expenditure on oil was between 1.5 and 4 obols per day. These figures, however, only give evidence of the use of oil for cooking, since the daily expenditure in these texts is almost always given with the cost of food (e.g., vegetables) or the preparation of food. Interestingly, P.Mich. 2.123 mentions that on three specific evenings the respective amounts of 4, 2 and 2 obols were spent on oil for the night scribes, and P.Mich. 2.128.24 indicates the cost of 4 obols of oil for night scribes on 19 September 46 CE. Clearly, lighting was expensive, increasing the amount an individual had to spend on oil. The remark of Vearncombe, namely that the woman's lighting of the lamp in order to search for a coin with the value of 1 drachma, is therefore significant,

---

[60] If we take the cost of oil as 8.2 obols per liter, it comes down to a payment of 2 drachmae (1 drachma and 5.1 obols) per month.

especially in a subsistence-level circumstance. As will be indicated below, it indeed was "not a negligible or insignificant action."[61]

4. The Lost Coin and Q

Several scholars have noted that that one of the typical stylistic features of Q is the tendency to pair men with women by means of gender paired illustrations.[62] Although scholars do not always agree on the number of gendered doublets in Q, the following doublets are normally indicated: Q 11:31–32 (Queen of the South and men of Nineveh); Q 12:24–28 (those who farm and those who spin); Q 12:51–53 (father against son, mother against daughter); Q 13:18–21 (the parables of the Mustard Seed and Leaven; a man sowing and a woman making bread); Q 15:4–10 (the parables of Lost Sheep and Lost Coin; a man losing a sheep and a woman losing a coin); Q 17:27 (marrying and being married); and Q 17:34–35 (two men on one couch and two women grinding).[63]

Although Q 15:4–10 (the parables of Lost Sheep and Lost Coin) is included as one of the gendered doublets in Q, Q 15:8–10 (the parable of the Lost Coin) is a debatable parable when it comes to Q. Some scholars argue that the Lost Coin is either Lukan *Sondergut*,[64] or a Lukan creation as a sequel to the parable of the Lost Sheep (Lk 15:4–7).[65] Kloppenborg, however, has argued convincingly that the Lost Coin should be considered as being part of Q.[66] First, like the other gendered doublets in Q, the parable is associated with the Lost Sheep in Q.[67]

Second, the basic structure of the Lost Coin is parallel to the Lost Sheep in Luke, a consistent feature of the gendered doublets in Q. Third, the possibility of

---

[61] Vearncombe, "Papyrological Backgrounds," 321.
[62] William E. Arnal, "Gendered Couplets in Q and Legal Formulations: From Rhetoric to Social History," *JBL* 116 (1997): 75–94; Alicia Batten, "More Queries for Q: Women and Christian Origins," *BTB* 24, no. 2 (1994): 44–51 (here 47–9); John S. Kloppenborg, *Excavating Q: The History and Setting of the Sayings Gospel* (Minneapolis, MN: Fortress Press, 2000), 97; Vearncombe, "Papyrological Backgrounds," 312.
[63] Batten, "More Queries," 47–9, lists the six instances mentioned; Arnal, "Gendered Couplets," 82, adds Q 7:29–30, 34 (Jesus's association with tax collectors and prostitutes) and Q 14:26–27 (in which one is exhorted to hate father and mother, son and daughter) to Batten's list, while Kloppenborg, *Excavating Q*, 97, and Vearncombe, "Papyrological Backgrounds," 312, exclude Q 12:51–53 from the list of Batten.
[64] See, for example, Joseph A. Fitzmyer, *The Gospel According to Luke X–XXIV*, AB 28 (New York: Doubleday, 1985), 1073; Hultgren, *The Parables of Jesus*, 64; T. W. Manson, *The Sayings of Jesus* (Cambridge: Cambridge University Press, 1951), 283.
[65] See, for example, Rudolf Bultmann, *History of the Synoptic Tradition*, trans. J. Marshall (Oxford: Blackwell, 1963), 171; Harry T. Fleddermann, *Q: A Reconstruction and Commentary* (Leuven: Peeters, 2005) 772; Michael Goulder, *Luke: A New Paradigm* (Sheffield: Sheffield Academic Press, 1989), 604.
[66] Kloppenborg, *Excavating Q*, 96–8.
[67] According to Dieter T. Roth, *The Parables in Q* (New York: T&T Clark, 2018), 320, and Jens Schröter, *Erinnerung an Jesu Worte: Studien zur Rezeption der Logienüberlieferung in Markus, Q und Thomas* (Neukirchen-Vluyn: Neukirchener Verlag, 1997), 321 n. 76, it is difficult, if not impossible to ascertain the precise location of the parable of the Lost Coin in Q. Alan K. Kirk, *The Composition of the Sayings Source: Genre, Synchrony, and Wisdom redaction in Q* (Leiden: Brill, 1998), 304, however, argues the opposite. See also Crossan, *The Power of Parable*, 38, who calls the parables of the Lost Sheep and Lost Coin in Q a "deliberate pair."

the Lost Coin stemming from L (Lukan *Sondergut*), is "extremely unlikely," since it would be incredible that "Q and some completely independent source would contain two parables that were almost in identical form."[68] Also important for inclusion in Q, is that both parables cohere with the poor village or small-town environment reflecting the socio-economic situation of Q.[69] Finally, the parable was most probably omitted by Matthew because it would have been difficult to use the parable, like the parable of the Lost Sheep, in the context of pastoral exhortation in which he uses the Lost Sheep.[70] Based on these arguments, in what follows it is assumed that the Lost Coin is part of Q.

5. The Lost Coin: A Realistic Reading

Positioning the Lost Coin in Q, as part of a gendered doublet, has a definite bearing on its possible meaning, as is the case with the other gendered doublets in Q. In Q 11:31–32, the Queen of the South will rise up with the men of this generation at the judgment and condemn them; so will the men of Nineveh. In Q 12:24–28, those who farm should be like the ravens who do not farm. They are not anxious because God feeds them. This should also be the attitude of those who spin. Because Jesus brings division, father will turn against son, and so mother against daughter (Q 12:51–53). In the days of the Son of Man, men will be given in marriage as will women (Q 17:27), and one man will be taken from two lying in bed. So it will be with two women grinding (Q 17:34–35). What happens or will happen in the first part of the doublet, happens or will happen in the second part. Put differently, the meaning of the second part of the doublet is determined by the first part. As put by Kloppenborg, "The pairing of the parables (and other sayings of Jesus), which perhaps first took place in the Sayings Gospel, represents an important interpretive manoeuvre."[71]

This is especially clear from Q 13:18–21, the parables of the Mustard Seed and Leaven, and very importantly, two parables as is the case in Q 15:4–10 (the parables of Lost Sheep and Lost Coin). A clue to interpret these two parables, apart from their placement as a double illustration, is the way in which they are structured. The structure of the Mustard Seed is paralleled in the Leaven, and the creation of this parallel stresses that the kingdom of God is the focus of both

---

[68] Kloppenborg, *Excavating Q*, 97.
[69] See also Vearncombe, "Papyrological Backgrounds," 314–24, who indicates that typical social realia offered by papyrological evidence grounds the parable in the social location of Q.
[70] So David R. Catchpole, *The Quest for Q* (Edinburgh: T. & T. Clark, 1993), 190–4; Helmut Koester, *Ancient Christian Gospels: Their History and Development* (Harrisburg, PA: TPI, 1990), 148; Jan Lambrecht, *Once More Astonished: The Parables of Jesus* (New York: Crossroad, 1981), 38–41; Alfred F. Loisy, *Les évangiles synoptiques* (Chez l'auteur, Ceffonds, Près Montier-en-Der, 1908), 138; C. G. Montefiore, *The Synoptic Gospels* (London: MacMillan, 1909), 984; Athanasius Polag, *Fragmenta Q: Textheft zur Logienquelle* (Neukirchen-Vluyn: Neukirchener Verlag, 1979), 26, 72; Hans Weder, *Die Gleichnisse Jesu als Metaphern: Traditions- und Redaktionsgeschichtliche Analysen und Interpretatonien* (Göttingen: Vandenhoeck & Ruprecht, 1984), 170, who argue for the inclusion of the Lost Coin in Q.
[71] Kloppenborg, *Synoptic Problems*, 542.

parables, specifically its rapid and dramatic growth.[72] This is also the point of view of Arnal and Roth: what links the couplet is the fact of growth,[73] or "what is insignificant and hidden...will grow and be marvelously revealed."[74] Elsewhere, I have presented a realistic reading of the Mustard Seed, and argued that the Q-version of the parable (Q 13:18–19), since it does not contain the smallest–largest comparison, is not a parable of growth. Rather, the kingdom is compared to a mustard seed planted in a garden, meaning that the garden becomes polluted because of the "law of diverse kinds." Moreover, once planted, a mustard seed turns into a shrub that tends to take over, since it very soon grows out of control. As such, as a comparison to the kingdom, the kingdom is polluted, includes the impure, and takes over.[75] When this interpretation of the Mustard Seed is applied to the parable of the Leaven (Q 13:20–21), it confirms Q's "important interpretive manoeuvre": leaven—a symbol of moral evil, corruption, and uncleanness—hid in three pecks of meal turns that what is unleavened (pure) to what is leavened (i.e., impure, corrupt and unclean); a process that cannot be stopped.[76] Thus, again the kingdom is compared with that what is polluted and impure, that what is out of control, and that what cannot be stopped until everything is corrupt and unclean (ἕως οὗ ἐζυμώθη ὅλον, Luke 3:21). As such, the meaning of the Leaven parallels that of the Mustard Seed. A garden becomes impure, wheat becomes impure. And those things that make the garden and wheat impure, are out of control and cannot be stopped.

Is this also the case with the parables of the Lost Sheep and Lost Coin? Does the meaning of the parable of the Lost Sheep also preempt the meaning of the Lost Sheep? Using social realia invoked by these two parables, attested in available papyri, it seems to be the case. The social and economic registers presupposed by the Lost Sheep, attested by social comparanda provided by available documented papyri, are that a flock of hundred sheep was a medium-sized flock that most probably belonged to one or more than one owner, and that shepherds were contracted to care for the flock. The sheep thus did not belong to the shepherd who practiced a despised trade. Shepherds were rendered unclean and seen as robbers, criminals, and thieves, were unsupervised, transient, and armed, and were often associated with bandits and agitators. Wages paid to shepherds were poor; and the intrinsic value of a sheep, relative to a shepherd's wage, was high. Shepherds earned more or less 16 drachmae per month, and the intrinsic value of a male sheep was more or less 10 drachmae and that of a female sheep 18–20 drachmae. Thus, since shepherds were held accountable for livestock losses, the

---

[72] Both are introduced by a question, the formula introducing the comparison is similar, both involved an agent that takes mustard or leaven, both of the principal verbs are aorist, both represent unusual choices, both focus on the element of growth, and in both cases the result is extraordinary (see ibid., 54, 543).

[73] Arnal, "Gendered Couplets," 82.

[74] Roth, *The Parables in Q*, 324.

[75] E. van Eck, *The Parables of Jesus*, 79–83; cf. John Dominic Crossan, *The Historical Jesus: The Life of a Mediterranean Jewish Peasant* (San Francisco: Harper Collins Publishers, 1991), 278–9.

[76] Bernard B. Scott, "The Reappearance of Parables," in *Listening to the Parables of Jesus*, ed. E. F. Beutner (Santa Rosa, CA: Polebridge Press, 2007), 95–119.

shepherd had no other option than to go and look for the lost sheep. By doing this, he took a huge risk by leaving 99 sheep behind. Finding one lost sheep could also mean losing the 99 he left behind. The chance he took, however, paid off. A lost sheep was found, wages were secured, and when the shepherd went home after his contract expired, there was reason to celebrate. As such, the kingdom became visible in the risky and unexpected action of an unexpected person. A despised shepherd, by taking a chance, made sure that everybody has enough. Seeking, that could have resulted in losing, resulted in gaining. In the parable of the Lost Coin, the same theme of gaining or losing is present.

In the Lost Sheep parable, the focus is the actions of a shepherd, and in the Lost Coin the focus is on the actions of a woman. In both parables this is unexpected—a despised shepherd and a female, not a male. The social background of the shepherd and the woman, based on papyrological evidence, is the same. A shepherd's wage of 16 drachmae per month was well below a poverty-level income,[77] and given the relative value of 10 drachmae and the woman's behavior regarding the 1 drachma in the parable, she is also poor and "living at or near subsistence."[78] In both cases, when the sheep and drachma get lost, a risk is taken to find that what was lost. The shepherd risks 99 sheep for the sake of one, and the woman risks 9 drachmae for the sake of one. Why?

As demonstrated by available papyrological evidence, the price of oil used for lighting was more or less 10 obols per liter in the first century, with the cost of cooking and food between 1.5 and 4 obols per day. Lighting a lamp for a night or part of a night seems to amount to 2 to 4 obols. Thus, looking for a coin with the worth of 1 drachma easily could have cost more than 1 drachma, if not found soon after a lamp was lit. Looking for one sheep risked the loss of 99 sheep, and lighting a lamp risked the loss of 9 drachmae.

This is why the woman's search is described with the adverb ἐπιμελῶς (Q 15:8). Contra Vearncombe and Hultgren,[79] the woman is described as searching diligently because she has to find the lost coin as soon as possible. If not done attentively or carefully, the search could cost more than that what was lost. This, then, is also the reason why she rejoices and celebrates with her female friends and neighbors (τὰς φίλας καὶ γείτονας, Luke 15:9) when she finds the lost coin. The risk she took paid off; less was spent on what was found. And therefore, as is the case with the Lost Sheep, she invites her friends and neighbors to come and rejoice with her (συγχάρητέ μοι, Q 15:9; see Q 15:6 for the Lost Sheep). Her risk

---

[77] Van Eck, *The Parables of Jesus*, 137.
[78] Vearncombe, "Papyrological Backgrounds," 318, 336. It is not stated in the parable that the woman was married, or lived on her own. If she lived on her own, and therefore was responsible for the income of the family (like the shepherd), her situation would have even been more desperate. Cf. K. E. Bailey, *Poet and Peasant: A Literary-Cultural Approach to the Parables in Luke* (Grand Rapids, MI: Eerdmans, 1976), 103–4.
[79] According to Vearncombe, "Papyrological Backgrounds," 322–3, the adverb ἐπιμελῶς was added by Luke to facilitate a metaphorical interpretation of the parable. It becomes "the interpretative key for the metaphoric understanding of the parable," that is, the woman as a symbol for God. Hultgren, *The Parables of Jesus*, 67, describes the woman as acting ἐπιμελῶς because she has to light a lamp in a house that has no windows or natural lighting.

was warranted, and now everybody has enough. The kingdom is visible in the risky and unexpected action of an unexpected person. A poor woman, by taking a chance to end up with even less than she has, made sure that everybody has enough.

Bibliography

Aristophanes. *Lysistrata, Thesmophoriazusae, Ecclesiazusae, Plutus.* Translated by B. B. Rogers. LCL. Cambridge, MA: Harvard University Press, 1925.
Arnal, W. E. "Gendered Couplets in Q and Legal Formulations: From Rhetoric to Social History." *JBL* 116 (1997): 75–94.
Bailey, K. E. *Poet and Peasant: A Literary-Cultural Approach to the Parables in Luke.* Grand Rapids, MI: Eerdmans, 1976.
Batten, A. "More Queries for Q: Women and Christian Origins." *BTB* 24, no. 2 (1994): 44–51.
Bazzana, G. B. "Basileia and Debt Relief: The Forgiveness of Debts in the Lord's Prayer in the Light of Documentary Papyri." *CBQ* 73 (2011): 511–25.
Bazzana, G. B. "Violence and Human Prayer to God in Q 11." *HTS* 70 (2014): 1–8.
Bishop, E. F. F. *Jesus of Palestine: The Local Background to the Gospel Documents.* London: Lutterworth Press, 1955.
Blomberg, C. L. *Interpreting the Parables.* Downers Grove, IL: InterVarsity Press, 2012.
Boucher, M. I. *The Mysterious Parable.* Wilmington, DE: Michael Glazier, 1981.
Bultmann, R. *History of the Synoptic Tradition.* Translated by J. Marshall. Oxford: Blackwell, 1963.
Catchpole, D. R. *The Quest for Q.* Edinburgh: T. & T. Clark, 1993.
Crossan, J. D. *The Historical Jesus: The Life of a Mediterranean Jewish Peasant.* San Francisco: Harper Collins, 1991.
Crossan, J. D. *The Power of Parable: How Fiction by Jesus became Fiction about Jesus.* New York: HarperOne, 2012.
Dodd, C. H. *The Parables of the Kingdom.* New York: Charles Scribner's Sons, 1961.
Fitzmyer, J. A. *The Gospel According to Luke X–XXIV.* AB 28. New York: Doubleday, 1985.
Fleddermann, H. T. *Q: A Reconstruction and Commentary.* Leuven: Peeters, 2005.
Goulder, M. D. *Luke: A New Paradigm.* Sheffield: Sheffield Academic Press, 1989.
Grenfell, B. P., and J. P. Mahaffy. *The Revenue Laws of Ptolemy Philadelphus.* Oxford: Clarendon Press, 1896.
Hayden, B. "Price Formation and Fluctuation in Ptolemaic Egypt." Ph.D. dissertation. University of Chicago, 2018.
Hultgren, A. J. *The Parables of Jesus: A Commentary.* Grand Rapids, MI: Eerdmans, 2000.
Jeremias, J. *The Parables of Jesus.* Translated by S. H. Hooke. London: SCM Press, 1972.
Kirk, A. K. *The Composition of the Sayings Source: Genre, Synchrony, and Wisdom Redaction in Q.* Leiden: Brill, 1998.
Kistemaker, S. J. *The Parables: Understanding the Stories Jesus Told.* Grand Rapids, MI: Baker Books, 1980.
Kloppenborg, J. S. *Excavating Q: The History and Setting of the Sayings Gospel.* Minneapolis, MN: Fortress Press, 2000.

Kloppenborg, J. S. "The Parable of the Burglar in Q: Insights from Papyrology." In *Metaphor, Narrative, and Parables in Q*, edited by D. T. Roth, R. Zimmermann, and M. Labahn, 287–306. WUNT 315. Tübingen: Mohr Siebeck, 2014.

Kloppenborg, J. S. *Synoptic Problems: Collected Essays*. WUNT 329. Tübingen: Mohr Siebeck, 2014.

Kloppenborg, J. S. *The Tenants in the Vineyard: Ideology, Economics, and Agrarian Conflict in Jewish Palestine*. WUNT 195. Tübingen: Mohr Siebeck, 2006.

Koester, H. *Ancient Christian Gospels: Their History and Development*. Harrisburg, PA: TPI, 1990.

Lambrecht, J. *Once More Astonished: The Parables of Jesus*. New York: Crossroad, 1981.

Levine, A.-J. *Short Stories by Jesus: The Enigmatic Parables of a Controversial Rabbi*. San Francisco: HarperOne, 2014.

Loisy, A. F. *Les évangiles synoptiques*. Chez l'auteur, Ceffonds, Près Montier-en-Der, 1908.

Manson, T. W. *The Sayings of Jesus*. Cambridge: Cambridge University Press, 1951.

Maresch, K. *Bronze und Silber: Papyrologische Beiträge zur Geschichte des Währung im ptolemäischen und römischen Ägypten bis zum 2. Jahrhundert n. Chr.* Cologne: Westdeutscher Verlag, 1996.

Merz, A. "Last und Freude des Kehrens (Von der verlorenen Drachme)—Lk 15, 8–10." In *Kompendium der Gleichnisse Jesu*, edited by Ruben Zimmermann et al., 610–17. Gütersloh: Gütersloher Verlagshaus, 2007.

Montefiore, C. G. *The Synoptic Gospels*. London: MacMillan, 1909.

Oakman, D. E. *Jesus and the Peasants*. Eugene, OR. Cascade Books, 2008.

Pestman, P. W. *The New Papyrological Primer*. Leiden: Brill, 1994.

Polag, A. *Fragmenta Q: Textheft zur Logienquelle*. Neukirchen-Vluyn: Neukirchener Verlag, 1979.

Roth, D. T. *The Parables in Q*. New York: T&T Clark, 2018.

Sandy, D. B. *The Production and Use of Vegetable Oils in Ptolemaic Egypt*. Atlanta, GA: Scholars Press, 1989.

Schottroff, L. *The Parables of Jesus*. Translated by L. M. Maloney. Minneapolis, MN: Augsburg, 2006.

Schröter, J. *Erinnerung an Jesu Worte: Studien zur Rezeption der Logienüberlieferung in Markus, Q und Thomas*. Neukirchen-Vluyn: Neukirchener Verlag, 1997.

Scott, B. B. *Hear Then the Parable: A Commentary on the Parables of Jesus*. Minneapolis, MN: Fortress Press, 1989.

Scott, B. B. "The Reappearance of Parables." In *Listening to the Parables of Jesus*, edited by E. F. Beutner, 95–119. Santa Rosa, CA: Polebridge Press, 2007.

Smith, W. C. A. *A New Classical Dictionary of Greek and Roman Biography, Mythology, and Geography Partly Based upon the Dictionary of Greek and Roman Biography and Mythology*. New York: Harper & Brothers, 1951.

Snodgrass, K. R. *Stories with Intent: A Comprehensive Guide to the Parables of Jesus*. Grand Rapids, MI: Eerdmans, 2008.

Van Eck, E. *The Parables of Jesus the Galilean: Stories of a Social Prophet*. Eugene, OR: Cascade Books, 2016.

Van Eck, E. "Realism and Method: The Parables of Jesus." *Neotestamentica* 51, no. 2 (2017): 163–84.

Van Eck, E., and J. S. Kloppenborg. "The Unexpected Patron: A Social-scientific and Realistic Reading of the Parable of the Vineyard Laborers (Mt 20:1–15)." *HTS* 71 (2015): 1–11.

Van Eck, E., and R. J. Van Niekerk. "Life in its Unfullness: Revisiting ἀναίδειαν (Lk 11:8) in the Light of Papyrological Evidence." *Verbum et Ecclesia* 37 (2017): 1–10.

Van Eck, E., and R. J. Van Niekerk. "The Samaritan 'brought him to an inn': Revisiting πανδοχεῖον in Luke 10:34." *HTS* 74, no. 4 (2018): 1–11.

Vearncombe, E. K. "Searching for a Lost Coin: Papyrological Backgrounds for Q 15,8–10." In *Metaphor, Narrative, and Parables in Q*, edited by D. Roth, R. Zimmermann, and M. Labahn, 307–37. WUNT 315. Mohr Siebeck, Tübingen, 2014.

Weder, H. *Die Gleichnisse Jesu als Metaphern: Traditions- und Redaktionsgeschichtliche Analysen und Interpretatonien*. Göttingen: Vandenhoeck & Ruprecht, 1984.

Zimmermann, R. "Die Gleichnisse Jesu: Eine Leseanleitung zum Kompendium." In *Kompendium der Gleichnisse Jesu*, edited by R. Zimmermann, 3–45. Munich: Gütersloher Verlagshaus.

In Ferment:
Is Jesus's Parable of the Leaven Hyperbolic or True to Life?*

J. R. C. Cousland

Ἄλλην παραβολὴν ἐλάλησεν αὐτοῖς · Ὁμοία ἐστὶν ἡ βασιλεία τῶν οὐρανῶν ζύμῃ, ἣν λαβοῦσα γυνὴ ἐνέκρυψεν εἰς ἀλεύρου σάτα τρία ἕως οὗ ἐζυμώθη ὅλον.

³³ He told them another parable: "The kingdom of heaven is like yeast that a woman took and mixed in with three measures of flour until all of it was leavened."

The introduction of this volume stresses the need to examine the *realia* reflected in the parables. In the case of the parable of the Leaven this concern applies not only to its individual features, but to the parable as a whole. One of the perennial questions raised by the parable is whether it is offering a description of an everyday event, a characteristic instance of Jesus's use of hyperbole, or a circumstance that is unusual but within the bounds of possibility. Because of the parable's brevity and the very limited details it provides, certitude will inevitably remain elusive. Nevertheless, this chapter will argue that the parable is neither commonplace nor hyperbolic. Rather, the parable describes a scenario that could conceivably take place, but one that is out of the ordinary in the events it describes. As such, it describes the outworking of the Kingdom: one that is seemingly quotidian in its process, but extraordinary in its manifestations. To do this, the parable deliberately streamlines the breadmaking process, minimizes human involvement, and focuses exclusively on the leavening of the flour, with the leavening likened to God's own active involvement in the world.

---

* This study considers only the versions of the parable in Matthew and Luke. I follow Simon Gathercole, *The Gospel of Thomas: Introduction and Commentary*, TENTS 11 (Leiden: Brill, 2014), 180, and Mark Goodacre, *Thomas and the Gospels* (Grand Rapids, MI: Eerdmans, 2012), 187–91, in regarding Thomas' version as reliant on the canonical versions in Matthew and Luke.

1. Hyperbole and Everyday Events

The view that the parable is not to be taken literally finds its classic expression in the analysis of Joachim Jeremias: "no housewife would bake so vast a quantity of meal." Instead, he contends that those features of the parable that transcend the bounds of actuality "are meant to tell us that we have to do with divine realities."[1] Jeremias' view seems to be echoed by Arland Hultgren, who remarks that in the parable of the Leaven it is "evident" that "hyperbole is being used." The problem with Hultgren's assertion is that what he means by hyperbole is not really "evident" at all.[2] While it is frequently remarked that "hyperbole" is a characteristic feature of Jesus's parables, as well as of his apophthegms, scholars do not appear to use the term consistently.[3] At points, "hyperbole" seems to be construed simply as a synonym for "exaggeration." Yet the word "exaggeration" is far from precise: it can embellish a factual occurrence—as when one claims, "I caught a five-pound salmon with my flyrod" (when the salmon was really only three pounds) or it can describe an impossible claim—"I caught a great blue whale with my flyrod."

Strictly speaking, hyperbole can only pertain to the second alternative. In *On Style*, Demetrius flatly remarks that every "instance of hyperbole is impossible" (πᾶσα δὲ ὑπερβολὴ ἀδύνατος, *Eloc.* 161). Demetrius' assertion is echoed by *The New Princeton Encyclopedia of Poetry and Poetics*, which defines hyperbole as "an extravagant statement used to express strong emotion, not intended to be understood literally."[4] Hence, if one describes part or all of a parable as hyperbolical, the implication is that it is not intended to be interpreted literally. On this reading, Hultgren, like Jeremias, would be arguing that the parable goes beyond the bounds of actuality. Yet, it is not at all clear that this is what Hultgren or other commentators actually mean when they say that the parable of the Leaven is hyperbolical, and this lack of certitude impedes a clear understanding of the parable and its interpretation.

Is, then, the account in the parable of the Leaven possible or impossible? Realistic or hyperbolical? Everyday or extraordinary? By way of answer, one can consider the leavening in the parable from at least five different perspectives:

---

[1] Joachim Jeremias, *The Parables of Jesus*, trans. S. H. Hooke, rev. ed. (London: SCM Press, 1972), 147. The German reads: "Diese den Rahmen der Wirklichkeit überschreitenden Züge (…σάτα τρία: so riesige Mengen verbäckte keine Hausfrau Mehl) wollen sagen: es handelt sich um Realitäten Gottes!" Cf. Joachim Jeremias, *Die Gleichnisse Jesu*, 11th ed. (Göttingen: Vandenhoeck & Ruprecht, 1998), 146. The description of the woman (γυνή) in the parable as a *Hausfrau* goes back at least as far as Adolf Jülicher, *Die Gleichnisreden Jesu*, 2 vols. (Freiburg: Mohr, 1899), 577.

[2] Arland J. Hultgren, *The Parables of Jesus: A Commentary* (Grand Rapids, MI: Eerdmans, 2000), 407.

[3] On the place of hyperbole in Jesus's sayings, see Paul Ricoeur, "Biblical Hermeneutics," *Semeia* 4 (1975): 29–148 (here 99). Cf. further, Klyne Snodgrass, *Stories with Intent: A Comprehensive Guide to the Parables of Jesus*, 2nd ed. (Grand Rapids, MI: Eerdmans; Cambridge, MA: Paternoster Press, 2018), 18; John P. Meier, *A Marginal Jew, Volume 5: Probing the Authenticity of the Parables* (New Haven, CT: Yale University Press), 42–3. Norman A. Huffman, "Atypical Features in the Parables of Jesus," *JBL* 97 (1978): 207–20 (here 207–8, 220).

[4] *The New Princeton Encyclopedia of Poetry and Poetics*, ed. Alex Preminger and T. V. F. Brogan (Princeton, NJ: Princeton University Press, 1993), 546, s.v. "Hyperbole."

(1) an "everyday" occurrence; (2) an event that is out of the ordinary run of affairs; (3) an extremely improbable happening; (4) a miraculous circumstance, normally impossible; (5) a figurative assertion not intended to be taken literally, such as the statement, "I've told you a million times not to exaggerate."[5] The following discussion, therefore, will investigate the underlying realia of the parable to determine which of the above perspectives is best suggested by its provisional contexts. The word "contexts" is used here deliberately: because the parable of the Leaven is so abbreviated and provides its audience with so few tertiary details, it necessitates positing a number of hypothetical contexts to attempt to frame its underlying meaning. A further difficulty arises from the diverse and diffuse nature of the evidence. Breadmaking was a fundamental constituent of existence in the ancient Mediterranean world and its periphery, so it is not surprising that the evidentiary record treating it is widely disseminated over time and space. While some of the features of breadmaking are relatively uniform, other traits differ significantly from region to region and period to period. As a result, any reconstruction will be a limited approximation, built on inference. Nevertheless, such inferments may help to prevent some uncritical retrojections of modern-day understandings of breadmaking onto the ancient Mediterranean world.[6] For this reason, the following examination will begin with ancient, roughly contemporaneous accounts of breadmaking to provide a framework for contextualizing the parable of the Leaven.

2. Breadmaking in Antiquity

The pseudo-Virgilian poem, the *Moretum*, includes an account of breadmaking that is roughly contemporaneous with Jesus's parable. The account has obvious poetic (epic!) flourishes, but these do not likely impinge on the poem's subject matter. It helpfully offers a fuller description of the breadmaking process, and serves as an instructive counterpart to the parable of the Leaven.[7]

2.1. Moretum

> On the ground was poured a poor heap of corn: from this he [Simulus the farmer] helps himself to as much as the measure, which runs to twice eight pounds in weight, would hold. And now he goes and takes his place at the mill; and on a tiny shelf, firmly fastened on the wall for such needs, he places his trusty lamp [...]. Next he summons his hands to the work, which he allots to this side or to that: the left is devoted to supplying the

---

[5] This category overlaps with the literary device known as "adynaton," which works by "magnifying an event by comparison with something impossible," *New Princeton Encyclopedia*, 9.
[6] Although an uncommon word, "inferment," meaning the "action of inferring," appears in the *OED*, s.v.
[7] Cf. A. J. Kenney, *The Ploughman's Lunch = Moretum: A Poem Ascribed to Virgil* (Bristol: Bristol Classical Press, 1984). On various approaches to the *Moretum*, see William Fitzgerald, "Labor and Laborer in Latin Poetry: The Case of the *Moretum*," *Arethusa* 29 (1996): 389–418.

grain, the right to plying the mill. The right hand, in constant circles, turns and drives the wheel (the grain, bruised by the stones' swift blows, runs down); the left, at intervals, relieves her wearied sister and changes places. Now he sings rustic songs, and with rude strains solaces his toil; at times he shouts to [his slave] Scybale.... Her he calls, and bids her place fuel on the fire to burn, and over the flame heat cold water. When the task of grinding has come to its due end, he pours out the meal, transfers it by hand into a sieve and shakes: the black husks remain on the upper side; the flour, clean and pure, sinks down, filtering through the crevices. Then straightway on a smooth table he lays it out, pours warm water on it and packs together the now mingled moisture and meal into lumps which he turns over and over till they are hardened and cohere through the action of hand and liquid, from time to time sprinkling salt thereon. And now he lifts the kneaded mixture and with open palms spreads it out into its rounded shape which he marks into quadrants, stamped out at equal intervals. Then he puts it in the hearth. (*Moretum* 16–49)[8]

Two other brief accounts of breadmaking can be found in the writings of Cato the Elder and Seneca. Cato provides a succinct recipe: "Wash your hands and a bowl thoroughly. Pour meal into the bowl, add water gradually, and knead thoroughly. When it is well kneaded, roll out and bake under a crock" (*On Agriculture* LXXIV).[9] Seneca, referencing Posidonius, provides a description of the origins of breadmaking as follows:

someone placed two rough stones, the one above the other, in imitation of the teeth, one set of which is stationary and awaits the motion of the other set. Then, by the rubbing of the one stone against the other, the grain is crushed and brought back again and again, until by frequent rubbing it is reduced to powder. Then this man sprinkled the meal with water, and by continued manipulation subdued the mass and moulded the loaf. This loaf was, at first, baked by hot ashes or by an earthen vessel glowing hot; later on ovens were gradually discovered and the other devices whose heat will render obedience to the sage's will. (*Epistle* 90.23)[10]

There are obvious and significant differences between these accounts and the parable; they all provide more background to the breadmaking process, and the *Moretum*, especially, recounts it in considerable detail. Moreover, all three describe the making of *unleavened* bread. Nevertheless, these accounts provide a valuable encapsulation of the various stages involved in breadmaking. Based

---

[8] Virgil, *Aeneid: Books 7–12. Appendix Vergiliana*, trans. H. Rushton Fairclough and G. P. Goold, rev. ed., LCL (Cambridge, MA: Harvard University Press, 2000), ll.16–49.
[9] *Cato. De Re Rustica. Varro: De Re Rustica*, trans. H. B. Ash and W. D. Hooper, LCL (Cambridge, MA: Harvard University Press, 1967).
[10] Seneca, *Epistles 66–92*, trans. Richard M. Gummere, LCL (Cambridge, MA: Harvard University Press, 1920).

on these accounts, the following examination will provide a succinct overview of these stages to provide a framework in which to situate the parable of the Leaven.

2.2. Grain

The breadmaking process begins with the selection of grain. Pliny the Elder, Galen, and Athenaeus attest to the extraordinary diversity of breads and of grains used for breadmaking that had currency in the ancient Mediterranean sphere.[11] For its part, the Mishnah lists five types of grain that were commonly made into bread: wheat, barley, emmer, millet, and oats.[12] Of them, wheat was by far the most popular, followed by barley, and the parable of the Leaven reflects this choice: the word ἄλευρα signifies wheat flour.[13]

There are several reasons for wheat's widespread popularity. Even though barley and wheat bread have a similar nutritional value, wheat bread has a pleasant taste, it is easily digested and, compared to barley, it has a 25 to 30 percent higher extraction rate.[14] The latter is the percentage of grain that actually becomes flour after the milling process. Most importantly as far as leavened bread is concerned, wheat flour has a gluten content, which enables the bread to rise. Gluten is derived from two of the proteins that occur in wheat, gliadin and glutenin. When mixed with water, these proteins form gluten, which constitutes the rubbery mass of wheat-dough when it is mixed and kneaded, and which gives the bread its characteristic lightness.

For these reasons, wheat was worth about twice as much as barley (cf. 2 Kgs 7:1, 16; Josephus, *B.J.* 5.427; *m. Ketub.* 5:8) and was typically the bread of the wealthy. It was also favored in cultic practice, and *solet*, the finest wheat flour, figured prominently in the offerings made in the Temple.[15]

2.3. The Breadmaker

The above accounts of breadmaking are unusual insofar as they describe a male as the breadmaker, even if he has assistance from a female slave, as is the case with Scybale. Male bakers, including male slaves, were not uncommon, especially in larger cities, but it was atypical for a laborer to do his own baking. Generally speaking, within the Mediterranean domestic context—including Jewish communities—women were almost universally regarded as the breadmakers of a

---

[11] Athenaeus, *Deip.* 3.108–116; Galen, *On the Powers of Foods* 1.78–79; Pliny, *Nat.* 18.27–29. Athenaeus lists some 70 varieties of wheat bread alone. Table IV in Marie-Claire Amouretti, *Le pain et l'huile dans la Grèce antique* (Paris: Les Belles Lettres, 1986), 284, provides a list of the standard Greek terms for some of these products.

[12] See *m. Hallah* for restrictions on eating such grains in fermented form on Passover.

[13] H. Blümner, *Technologie und Terminologie der Gewerbe und Künste bei Griechen und Römern*, 4 vols., rev. ed. (Leipzig: Teubner, 1912; repr. Hildesheim: Olms, 1969), 1:52, 68. Cf. Amouretti, *Le pain et l'huile*, 126. The term chiefly used for barley was ἄλφιτα.

[14] Magen Broshi, *Bread, Wine, Walls and Scrolls*, JSPSup 36 (Sheffield: Sheffield Academic Press, 2001), 124–5.

[15] According to Naum Jasny, "The Daily Bread of the Ancient Greeks and Romans," *Osiris* 9 (1950): 227–53 (here 242), *solet* was the "best ground [wheat] product in antiquity."

household.[16] The Mishnah, for instance, is revealing about breadmaking. In its descriptions of the process, the text will suddenly switch the pronoun to "she," stipulating that "she" is to do this and that. And, in fact *Mishnah Ketuboth* explicitly asserts that grinding flour and baking bread are, along with other tasks, the "works which the wife must perform for her husband."[17] If, however, a woman has the good fortune to bring a female servant with her when she weds, then these breadmaking duties will devolve onto her female servant (*m. Ket.* 5:5).

2.4. Milling

As the *Moretum* indicates, grinding grain was one of the most onerous tasks associated with breadmaking: the breadmaker changes hands frequently as he grinds, and whiles away the tedious process by singing songs. For much of the ancient Mediterranean, handmills (querns) were the most common method of grinding grains, having come into general use in the Hellenistic period.[18] As the *Moretum* and Seneca's account suggest, the handmill consisted of two flat, circular stones (ca. 18 inches to 2 feet in diameter), with the smaller of the two set on top, and a central peg joining the two and serving as the axis. A central hopper allowed for the introduction of grain and, as the upper stone was rotated, the grain was slowly ground into flour.[19] According to one reconstruction, the milling process took half to three quarters of an hour just to grind one pound of wheat.[20]

As just noted, women were the ones usually tasked with grinding the grain.[21] Matthew and Luke quote Jesus as saying, "Two women will be grinding at the mill; one is taken and one is left" (Matt 24:41).[22] It is likely that Jesus is describing a domestic scene here, where women take turns rotating the handmill and introducing grain into the hopper. Matthew was also clearly aware of the existence of other, much larger mills that were often powered by donkeys.[23] The type of millstone (μύλος ὀνικὸς) that he mentions at 18:6 would have been the upper half of a large quern. These large mills were a far more efficient technique

---

[16] J. Bottéro, *The Oldest Cuisine in the World: Cooking in Mesopotamia* (Chicago: University of Chicago Press, 2004), 77; S. Krauss, *Talmudische Archäologie* (3 vols.; Leipzig, 1910; repr., Hildesheim: Georg Olms, 1966), 1:95; August Mau, "Bäckerei," *PW* 2 (1909), cols. 2734–2743.

[17] Although it is not mentioned here, sifting the grain and flour through a sieve was also one of the primary tasks of breadmaking, as the *Moretum* illustrates. Cf. *m. Kel.* 15:3 and, metaphorically, Luke 22:31.

[18] On domestic grinders in the ancient Near East, see the text cited in Bottéro, *Oldest Cuisine*, 78. Cynthia Shafer-Elliott, "Baking Bread in Ancient Judah," *BAR* 45, no. 4 (2019): 59–64, includes pictures of a built-in grinder in an iron-age house from Tell Halif. See, in addition, L. A. Moritz, *Grain Mills and Flour in Classical Antiquity* (Oxford: Clarendon Press, 1958), Plate 11, for illustrations of handmills.

[19] Gustav Dalman, "Grinding in Ancient and Modern Palestine," *The Biblical World* 19 (1902): 9–18 (here 9–12).

[20] Jasny, "Daily Bread," 242.

[21] Blümner, *Technologie*, 1:21.

[22] Luke's version is similar, stating that "There will be two women grinding together" (Luke 17:35), but it makes no reference to their being at "the mill" (ἐν τῷ μύλῳ, Matt 24:41).

[23] Moritz, *Grain Mill*, 12. See Plate 13 for examples of millstones. Cf. *Gos. Phil.* 45 and Apuleius, *Metam.* 9.11–12, where Lucius in his guise as a donkey gives an "autobiographical" account of the process and of the wretchedness of the slaves forced to engage in it.

for grinding grain. Estimates of their rate of production range between 22 and 55 pounds of grain per hour.[24] Clearly, if the woman of the parable could be envisioned as having access to a mill of this kind, she would have saved herself many tedious hours of work with a handmill. Sharon Lea Mattila reports that one of these large querns has been excavated at Capernaum, though it postdates the time of Jesus.[25] These large mills were typically linked to bakeries, with smaller mills situated in the common courtyard of multiple households (*m. B. Bat.* 3:5), or alternatively within individual houses (*m. B. Bat.* 2:1).

2.5. Kneading/Additions of Water and Salt

As the *Moretum* demonstrates, water and salt were regular constituents in the preparation of the dough. The addition of warm water had a dual purpose. First, the water transformed the flour into a malleable mass of dough that could be readily worked with the hands. Second, in the case of leavened bread dough, the warmth of the water facilitated the fermentation process, allowing the microorganisms to break down the carbohydrates in the flour. Without the addition of water, breadmaking was not possible. Likewise, kneading the flour together with the water was absolutely essential to the breadmaking process, since it transformed the wheat proteins into gluten—i.e., the flour into dough.

The addition of salt to dough was also a regular occurrence because, in addition to adding savor to the bread itself, it expedited the leavening process.[26] Technically speaking, salt improved the enzymatic action involved in the kneading process, which then provided more starch for the micro-organisms to convert into sugar.[27] Of course, the ancients would not have known why adding warm water and salt were so effective—they simply knew that they worked.

Once the dough was adequately kneaded, it could be rolled out flat with tools such as rolling pins, then inserted into bread molds or fashioned into loaves by hand (*Gos. Thom.* 96), and laid out on bakers' boards to rise (*m. Kelim* 15:2). Dalman postulates that, "As the baking is done in the forenoon, the dough is kneaded in the first hours of the morning, perhaps between 2 and 3 o'clock in the night. Then women will begin with grinding about midnight."[28]

---

[24] Jan Theo Bakker and Bernhard Meijlink, "Introduction," in *The Mills-Bakeries of Ostia: Description and Interpretation*, ed. Jan Theo Bakker (Amsterdam: Gieben, 1999), 1–15 (here 14). For ancient reliefs depicting donkey mills and querns, see Nicolas Monteix, *Les lieux des métier. Boutiques et ateliers d'Herculanum* (Rome: École Française de Rome, 2010), 135–4 and figs. 60–69.

[25] Sharon Lea Mattila, "Capernaum, Village of Nahum, from Hellenistic to Byzantine Times," in *Galilee in the Late Second Temple and Mishnaic Periods*, ed. David A. Fiensy and James Riley Strange, 2 vols. (Minneapolis, MN: Fortress Press, 2015), 1:217–57 (here 234).

[26] Gustaf Dalman, *Arbeit und Sitte in Palästina* (Gütersloh, 1935; repr. Hildesheim: Georg Olms, 1964), 4:56: "Das Salz ist auch hier für jedes normale Brot selbstverständliche Voraussetzung." See further, Blümner, *Technologie*, 1:60; Krauss, *Talmudische Archäologie*, 1:76.

[27] F. Heinrich, "Cereals and Bread," in *The Routledge Handbook of Diet and Nutrition in the Roman World*, ed. P. Erdkamp and C. Holleran (London: Routledge, 2018), 101–15 (here 106).

[28] Dalman, "Grinding," 13.

2.6. Baking the Bread

Once the dough—leavened or unleavened—was readied for baking, it could be prepared in a number of ways. As Seneca indicates, it could be baked in the ashes of a fire or on (or under) a piece of crockery. From the Iron Age onward ovens for baking bread were a commonplace in Palestine and its several varieties remained largely unchanged in their essentials through Second Temple and Talmudic periods even up until modern times. The *tanur* (תנור) was a conical structure in which a fire was built and bread baked on its sides.[29] By contrast, the *tabun* "was a dome-shaped installation made of clay, with a round opening through which unbaked bread was inserted and set on a bed of red-hot stones."[30]

The *tabun* was often shared among several houses within a common courtyard, typically on the periphery to keep its smoke away from the habitations. Both ovens were distinguished from the household stoves, which were usually situated inside the house beneath the chimney, and provided access for cooking pots and other vessels for food preparation.[31] In wealthier houses, the number of outdoor ovens could be multiple: the courtyard of the "Herodian House" in Jerusalem, for instance, features four ovens.[32]

2.7. Bakeries

Given the very substantial amount of flour that the parable specifies, the question arises whether Jesus could be referencing a bakery or at least some of the facilities provided by a bakery, such as large mills, mixing troughs, work areas, and ovens. Although Jasny affirms that "every Jewish family in Palestinian cities baked its own bread," it is more likely that households in cities and towns also availed themselves of bakeries and especially the ovens (*furni*) where they could bring their own dough to bake.[33] The Hebrew Bible (1 Sam 8:13; Jer 37:21; Hos 7:4) and the Mishnah (*m. Demai* 2:4; 5:1, 3–4; *m. Makš.* 2:8) also provide substantial evidence for the presence of bakeries in Jewish communities. Despite the limited archaeological evidence for ancient bakeries in Palestine, abundant evidence, especially from Pompeii, Ostia, and Rome, provides valuable insights into their nature and variety.[34] Many dozens of bakeries existed, and ranged from single-owner shops to assembly-line operations employing a dozen or more workers or slaves. The extensive and detailed iconographical record depicts each stage of the baking process.[35]

---

[29] S. Avitsur, "The Way to Bread," *Tools and Tillage* 2 (1975): 228–41 (here 237).
[30] Yizhar Hirschfeld, *The Palestinian Dwelling in the Roman-Byzantine Period* (Jerusalem: Franciscan Printing Press/Israel Exploration Society, 1995), 141.
[31] Ibid., 274.
[32] Ibid., 58.
[33] Jasny, "Daily Bread," 252; cf. S. Avitsur, "Way to Bread," 234.
[34] On bakers or bakeries in the ancient Mediterranean, see Bakker, *Ostia, passim*; Bottéro, *Oldest Cuisine*, 82; Monteix, *Les lieux des métier*, 143–54 and figs. 68–72.
[35] Andrew Wilson and Katia Schörle, "A Baker's Funerary Relief from Rome," *Papers of the British School at Rome* 77 (2009): 101–23, featuring multiple images.

Taken together, the above sketch of breadmaking provides a representative, if necessarily abbreviated, outline of the process in Palestine and the ancient Mediterranean world. As such, it suggests a number of contexts in which to situate the parable of the Leaven. Yet, startlingly, apart from this background, the chief insight that these contexts provide is negative in the sense that they provide an overview of everything that is *not* included in the parable. Remarkably, *none* of the above processes is actually mentioned by the parable—not grinding, not sifting, not kneading, not forming loaves, and not baking.[36] And whereas the *Moretum*, Seneca, and Cato all focus on the production of unleavened bread, the parable is fixated solely on the leavening process. Why this is the case will be considered next.

3. The Parable of the Leaven

3.1. Leaven

Although it is not mentioned in the *Moretum*, Seneca, or Cato, leaven was a fundamental component of ancient breadmaking. The distinction between leavened and unleavened bread was already well established the ancient Near Eastern period, where the dough was sometimes fermented using the barm (froth) from beer or soured soup (cf. Pliny, *Nat.* 18.68). The *Epic of Erra* 1:57 already distinguishes the two types of bread by claiming that the "best city bread [which was prepared with care, leavened and raised] cannot compare with the pancake baked under ashes."[37] By the turn of the Common Era, leavened bread came to be prized more highly.

But precisely what does the parable mean by the term leaven (ζύμη)? The common identification of yeast with leaven is misleading because, as BDAG rightly notes, it "popularly suggests a product foreign to ancient baking practice."[38] Instead of the baking yeast that is commonly used today (*Saccharomyces cerevisiae*), ancient leaven was more akin to a modern sourdough "starter," consisting of dough that had been fermented by wild, airborne yeast (*Saccharomyces exiguus*) and various lactobacilli. The final product—*seor* (שׂור)—was so sour that it could not be eaten on its own. Instead, it would be added to a mass of unleavened dough and water, producing *hametz* (חמץ) or leavened dough—the same *hametz* that had to be eliminated from Jewish households annually in preparation for Passover (cf. Exod 12:15; 23:15; Deut 16:3–4).[39]

In antiquity various techniques were employed to initiate this fermentation process: grain could be steeped in water, wine, or wine lees for several days.

---

[36] The *Gospel of Thomas'* mention of loaves is likely secondary.
[37] *Epic of Erra* 1:57; translation and gloss by Bottéro, *Oldest Cuisine*, 47–8. The passage from the *Epic* further implies that "city bread" would have been prepared by bakers, while the "pancakes" would have been prepared by soldiers or rustics.
[38] BDAG, s.v. ζύμη.
[39] D. Kellermann, "חמץ," *TDOT* 4:487–511 (here 489–90); M. Jastrow, *A Dictionary of the Targumim, the Talmud Babli and Yerushalmi, and the Midrashic Literature* (1903; repr., Peabody, MA: Hendrickson, 2006), 1505; S. Krauss, *Talmudische Archäologie*, 1:99–100.

Alternatively, certain additions (e.g., apples, mouldy bread, flour made from bitter vetch or chickling) could be mixed with the flour to advance the process.[40] Pliny the Elder states that in his time leaven was made from flour, salt was kneaded in, and the resulting mixture boiled and reduced to a sort of porridge which was left until it went sour (Pliny, *Nat.* 18.104). He adds that the most common means of fermentation saw that a piece of dough from the previous batch was retained and used to sour the dough (Pliny, *Nat.* 18.102–4). As Dalman indicates, this was also the customary practice for leavening bread amongst Jews.[41] The retained piece of dough would become more potent with the passage of time, and would be stored in wooden or earthen containers.[42] If, after Passover or for some other reason a family needed to obtain a fresh supply of *seor*, it could be obtained from gentile households or bakeries (*m. Hal.* 1:7). The Tosefta, in fact, provides evidence of leaven being sold in bulk by Gentiles (*t. Pesah.* 2:14).

What precisely happens during the leavening process? F. Heinrich offers an instructive overview:

> During fermentation, dough "rises" as the microorganisms consume part of the carbohydrates. The enzyme amylase, which converts starches into sugars that the microorganisms can consume, plays an important facilitating role in this process. It occurs naturally in cereals, but today it is added for better performance; traditional practices such as adding salt, however, also improve enzymatic action. As the microorganisms consume the sugars, they excrete alcohol (which is lost during baking) and carbon dioxide (CO^2). Because of their unique rheological properties (water absorption capacity, cohesivity, viscosity and elasticity) gluten are able to catch this CO^2 in bubbles by stretching out, creating the desired airy, more voluminous bread.[43]

The presence of carbon dioxide bubbles accounts for the characteristic increase in size that is associated with panary fermentation. In addition to the dough's increased size, other changes occur: the mishnaic tractate *Pesahim* minutely describes the gradual transformations occasioned by the fermentation process. It identifies *si'ur* [*seor*] as partially fermented dough, while *sidduk* is wholly fermented dough:

> What *is si'ur*? [Dough on which streaks appear] like the horns of a locust. And *sidduk*? [Dough] on which the cracks are all tangled together. So R. Judah. But the Sages say: …what is *si'ur*? [Dough] whose surface turns palid [*sic*] like a man's face when his hair stands on end.[44]

---

[40] Pliny, *Nat.* 18.102–4; *m. Ter.* 10:2; *b. Pesah.* 45b11.
[41] Dalman, *Arbeit*, 4:53–4. His plate #13 illustrates a small basket that Bedouins used to store the *seor*.
[42] Krauss, *Talmudische Archäologie*, 1:93, affirms that it lasts about three weeks (that is, if it is not "refreshed" with more flour and water). The *Geoponica* 2.33 gives a recipe for making dried leaven cakes that will last for a year.
[43] Heinrich, "Cereals and Bread," 106.
[44] *The Mishnah*, trans. Danby, *m. Pes.* 3:5.

While these descriptions are a trifle poetic—not to say fanciful—they indicate that in the face of the annual need to expel *hametz* from their households prior to Passover, Jesus's audience would very likely have been familiar with fermentation in its various stages and guises.[45]

The time involved for the leavening is not often specified in our sources. One passage from the Jerusalem Talmud suggests that it could take longer than a whole day's journey: "The women of Lydda knead their dough, go out and pray [in Jerusalem] and were back before their dough was leavened" (*j. Ma'aś.* 5:2 56a17).[46] Several passages from the Mishnah point to a shorter time-frame. In the mishnaic tractate *Pesahim*, for instance, R. Gamaliel remarks that on festival-days, "three women may knead [unleavened] dough at the same time and bake it in the same oven one after another," without fear of it becoming fermented during the process (*m. Pesah.* 3:4). Similarly, dough offerings that were thought to be tainted with *hametz* were to be left until evening to see whether they became leavened (*m. Pesah.* 3:3).

In Matthew and Luke, the parable focuses emphatically on this leavening process. This emphasis on process contrasts noticeably with others of Jesus's parables where human agency receives far more prominence and attention. Like the parable of the Seed Growing Secretly (Mark 4:26–29), human involvement is at a minimum. While farming and breadmaking are both labor-intensive activities, one would not guess this fact from either parable. Human activity is downplayed in favor of the dough's extraordinary growth. In the leaven parable, the dominant focus is on the growth process that transpires from the time the woman "hides" the leaven until the whole is leavened, that is, *until* (ἕως οὗ) the dough's leavened character is no longer hidden. The ending of the parable—ἕως οὗ ἐζυμώθη ὅλον—marks the end of the process and similarly marks the point at which the leaven was no longer "hidden," and *could* no longer be hidden. After her initial appearance in the parable, the woman is not mentioned again, and her absence means that the emphasis is almost wholly on the resultant activity of the leaven.

This emphasis is very different from the version of the parable found in the *Gospel of Thomas*. Where Matthew and Luke have Jesus compare the kingdom with leaven, in Thomas' parable it is a woman who is compared with the kingdom of the Father. Thomas' express focus on the woman highlights her agency and power, since she initiates three actions within the parable, compared to just two actions in the canonical version.[47] Her activity not only sets the leavening in motion, but her involvement also continues over the course of the breadmaking process, culminating in her production of "large loaves." Her role here, therefore, is strongly associated with the successful production of actual loaves of bread—not just with leavening the dough. The woman's activity, therefore, is explicitly

---

[45] S. Safrai and M. Stern, *The Jewish People in the First Century*, 2 vols., CRINT 1 (Assen: Van Gorcum, 1976), 2:808–9.

[46] The trip to Lydda (Lod) was regarded as a one-day journey; cf. *m. M.Sh.* 5:2.

[47] For the woman as "catalyst," see B. E. Reid, "Beyond Petty Pursuits and Wearisome Widows: Three Lukan Parables," *Int* 56 (2002): 284–94 (here 287).

integrated into the larger enterprise of bread-making, while this is not the case in the canonical version.

Hence, Thomas' emphasis on the woman in the parable suggests a conscious concern to correlate human with divine agency. The woman in Thomas' parable (perhaps under the influence of the woman with the jar of flour in *Gos. Thom.* 97) has been deliberately accorded something of a divine role and she is directly engaged in advancing the kingdom through her actions. In doing so, she takes on aspects of the persona of God and his intervention in the world. Thomas' perspective here is thus almost antithetical to the canonical versions, where the divine agency occurs in the operation of the kingdom in the ζύμη. To be sure, the leaven is hidden in the dough by the woman, and the actual transformation in the parable occurs with the fermentation of the whole: from ζύμη to ἐζυμώθη ὅλον. This global transformation is entirely due to the inscrutable operation of the leaven / kingdom: the mass of dough simply grows *automatē*—one "does not know how" (Mark 4:27). This entire process, moreover, is mysterious. While, it is certainly true that leavening (like the growth of a seed) was an every-day event and could be taken for granted, at the same time, the forces that enabled this growth were obscure and simply not understood. So, too, with the operation of the kingdom. Its growth was also accomplished by the working of God and was largely independent of human operations. Humans may set the process in motion, but the outcome is ordained by God.

Thomas' version of the parable also highlights the issue of contrast, which is explicitly emphasized in the *Gospel of Thomas'* mention of "little leaven" and "great loaves" (*Gos. Thom.* 96).[48] While the contrast in the canonical version of the parable is more muted, it allows for two sorts of contrast—between the leaven and the amount of dough, and also between the mass of unleavened dough, and that same dough in its final leavened state. The leavening in the parable, therefore, portrays the activity of the kingdom both in terms of process and of contrast.

This depiction of the leavening process returns us to the question of the realia of the parable and to just how exaggerated the details of the parable actually are. Here, a number of the parable's features come to the fore: (1) its literary form; (2) the exceptional amount of the flour involved in the breadmaking process; (3) the parable's unusual use of ἐγκρύπτω and its failure to mention the addition of water in the leavening process. All three of these features have a bearing on the "reality" of the parable and will be addressed seriatim.

3.2. Literary Form

Is the leavening described in the parable an everyday, commonplace event? The form of the parable would suggest otherwise; it speaks to the singularity of the leavening of the large amount of flour. The parable's use of the aorist tense distinguishes it as a narrative (*Parabel*) rather than as a similitude (*Gleichnis*).

---

[48] Gathercole, *Thomas*, 546–7; Uwe-Karsten Plisch, *The Gospel of Thomas. Original Text with Commentary* (Stuttgart: Deutsche Bibelgesellschaft, 2008), 212–13.

As is typical for a *Parabel*, Jesus presents a narrative consisting of one specific instance where a woman introduces leaven into the flour. While it is possible that the event described may have happened multiple times, the parable only provides warrant for supposing that it happened once. Hence, the actual form of the parable necessarily stresses the distinctiveness of this event, and does not treat it as a commonplace or everyday occurrence. On this reading, the leavening of the three satas can be viewed as something entirely *sui generis* or as an event out of the ordinary course of affairs. Unlike, for instance, Mark's parable of the Mustard Seed or the Seed Growing Secretly, it is not portrayed as a regular occurrence, but as a singular event—a singularity that may well highlight its exceptional character.

3.3. The Exceptional Amount of Flour in the Parable

The chief difficulty with the parable's plausibility is the seemingly large amount of flour that Jesus describes. If a lone *Hausfrau* in a poor household were suddenly called upon to leaven three satas of flour, she would be faced with various difficulties. Would she have access to such an extensive amount of wheat? Would she have to grind all of it herself with a handmill? If so, she would be faced with days and days of labor. If she had to leaven the dough indoors, would she have had sufficient space or vessels of a sufficiently large size to knead that amount of dough readily? If she only had access to a small bake oven, would she have been able to bake all the loaves? In short, given the multiple difficulties the woman might have faced, is Jesus indicating that she is presented with an impossible or hyperbolical situation?

This may well be the case. Nevertheless, it is necessary to emphasize once again that the parable is *exclusively* concerned with the leavening of the dough. It does not mention any of the other circumstances related to breadmaking: it says nothing about the woman having to grind the flour or, for that matter, even having to knead it. Nor does it say anything about the woman being a *Hausfrau*—this is entirely a presupposition of Jeremias, Jülicher, and other interpreters. Nor does the parable provide any indication whatever that it is mirroring everyday domestic events—such a supposition would uncritically accept C. H. Dodd's longstanding supposition that parables describe "everyday" events.[49]

All the γυνή is said to do is hide the leaven within three measures of flour. If she is conceived of as a baker, leavening such an amount would hardly seem problematic. Yet, even if she is interpreted as a *Hausfrau*, there were likely avenues by which a housewife could accomplish such a task. This issue hinges on a variety of factors: (1) the actual amount of three satas, (2) possession of the necessary implements, (3) the possibility of coworkers, and (4) the influence of Gen 18:6 on the parable. These factors will now be considered in order.

---

[49] C. H. Dodd. *The Parables of the Kingdom* (London: Nisbet & Co., 1935), 16. For a succinct criticism of Dodd's assumption, see Karl-Heinrich Ostmeyer, "Gott knetet nicht (Vom Sauerteig) Q 13.20f. (Mt 13,33 / Lk 13.20f. / EvThom 96)," in *Kompendium der Gleichnisse Jesu*, ed. Ruben Zimmermann (Gütersloh: Gütersloher Verlagshaus, 2007), 185–92 (here 189–90).

3.3.1. *The Amount of Three Satas.* The first question concerns the amount of flour. Given the instability of metrics over various geographical regions and the course of centuries, what would a saton have signified in first-century Palestine? The answer is far from straightforward because, as Magen Broshi has argued, the actual amounts in a saton were inconsistent.[50] Where the proportions of the measurements to each other were generally established, the saton was the counterpart of the seah, and 3 satas / seahs constituted one ephah. What is problematic is that the amount represented by a saton / seah varies. *Mishna Menahoth*, for instance, relates that five seahs according to the Jerusalem measure are equivalent to six seahs of the Wilderness [or "desert"] measure (7.1).[51] Drawing on Epiphanius' *Treatise on Weights and Measures*, Angelo Segrè concludes that "the Jews used three *sata*: a *saton* of 20 *sextarii italici*, a *modius italicus* of 16 *sextarii*, and a *saton* of *sextarii italici*."[52] He calculates the amounts as 13.10, 10.91, and 8.73 liters respectively.[53] On this reckoning, the three satas of the parable could amount to 39.3, 32.73, or 26.19 liters.

The same problem in variation concerns the relation of the saton / seah to the modius. Josephus relates that the saton is equivalent to one and a half Italian modii (ἰσχύει δὲ τὸ σάτον μόδιον καὶ ἥμισυ Ἰταλικόν. *A.J.* 9.86), which would equate to 12.9 liters.[54] By contrast, Epiphanius in his *Treatise on Weights and Measures* asserts that a saton "is an overfull *modius*, so that the *modius* is full and because of the overfullness a quarter of a *modius* (more)"—that is, one and a quarter modii.[55] And to complicate matters further, Daniel Sperber, drawing on the Mishnah and Talmud, estimates that one Mishnaic seah was equivalent to two Italian modii.[56] These calculations would make a saton equivalent to 10.7, 12.9, or 17.2 liters, making three satas equal to 32.1, 38.7, or 51.6 liters. Taken cumulatively, these figures suggest that certitude about the quantity of flour in the parable is difficult to establish, seeing as the amount could range anywhere from 26.19 to 51.6 liters. Scholars often argue for a figure in the high thirties, which is a plausible compromise.[57] On the basis of his figures, Sperber estimates that

---

[50] Broshi, *Bread*, 121. *M. Men.* 7:1 relates that one ephah constitutes three seahs.
[51] See the discussion in Daniel Sperber, "Costs of Living in Roman Palestine," *Journal of the Economic and Social History of the Orient* 8 (1965): 248–71 (here 266–8).
[52] Angelo Segrè, "A Documentary Analysis of Ancient Palestinian Units of Measure," *JBL* 64 (1945): 357–75.
[53] Ibid., 360.
[54] Cf. R. P. Duncan-Jones, "The Choenix, the Artaba and the Modius," *ZPE* 21 (1976): 43–52 (here 52), who argues that an Italian modius was equivalent to 8.6185 liters. Yet, as he also points out, the various types of modius also differed in size considerably.
[55] James Elmer Dean, ed., *Epiphanius' Treatise on Weights and Measures: The Syriac Version*, Studies in Ancient Oriental Civilization 1 (Chicago: University of Chicago Press, 1935), §21 (Greek text), p. 137, cf. 41. Sperber, "Costs of Living," 268 n. 2 cites other instances where a saton is 1 and 3/8 of a modius.
[56] Sperber, "Costs of Living," 268.
[57] Dalman, *Arbeit*, 4:56, estimates the amount as 36.44 liters, while Klaus Berger, *Manna, Mehl und Sauerteig. Korn und Brot im Alltag der frühen Christen* (Stuttgart: Quell Verlag, 1993), 50, proposes 39 liters. Franz Kogler, *Das Doppelgleichnis vom Senfkorn und vom Sauerteig in seiner traditionsgeschichtlichen Entwicklung. Zur Reich-Gottes-Vorstellung Jesu und ihren Aktualisierungen in der Urkirche*, FB 59 (Würzburg: Echter Verlag, 1988), 61, concurs and lists

there were roughly 22 loaves per seah, based on Livy's calculation of 22 loaves per modius.[58]

The actual amount of leaven in the parable is not specified, except in the *Gospel of Thomas* version (96), which refers to "a little bit (*kouei*) of yeast," where the Coptic *kouei* corresponds to the Greek *mikron*.[59] The elder Pliny is more precise about the needed ratio: "The Greeks have decided that two-thirds of an ounce of leaven is enough for every two half-pecks (*binos semodios*) of flour" (*Nat.* 18.102), which, according to Blümner, works out to "about 2/3 of a pound per modius"[60] While not precisely a "little bit," proportionately speaking, two pounds of leaven still constitutes a small fraction of three satas.

Despite these calculations, Sperber needs to be taken seriously when he cautions that it is "manifestly evident that there were a number of different standards current at the same time (and at different times), and that metrological writings are only approximate and (consequently) diverse when dealing with these matters."[61]

With this caveat, how realistic, then, is it for a woman to leaven this amount of flour? Dalman estimates the three seahs "as possibly the largest amount that a woman baking could work with."[62] If he is correct, the leavening seems to fall somewhere between the two degrees of plausibility noted above at the outset of this chapter, namely—(2) an out-of-the-ordinary event, or (3) an extremely improbable happening.

3.3.2. *Possession of the Necessary Implements.* The question also arises about whether there would have been spaces and vessels sufficiently large to accommodate the working of three seahs of flour. Typical Palestinian houses were not noted for their excessive size or their extensive array of cooking vessels. Would a woman possessed of such a prodigious amount of flour have been able to deal with it in one single operation? The Mishnah provides indications that accommodation could be made for substantial amounts of dough. Kneading could take place in various parts of a house, including an upper room (*m. 'Ohal.* 5:4), but shared courtyards also frequently had kneading troughs in common. *Mishnah Kelim* seems to refer to three different sizes of kneading trough: "There are three kinds of kneading-troughs: [the] kneading-trough [holding] from two *logs* {i.e. one twelfth of a *seah*} to nine *kabs* {one and a half *seahs*} which when cracked is *susceptive to treading-contact-uncleanness*, [that which when] whole

---

a number of other scholars who also estimate the amount as ca. 39 liters. By contrast, Jülicher, *Gleichnisreden Jesu*, 577, calculates the amount as 20 liters.

[58] Sperber, "Costs of Living," 269.
[59] Plisch, *Thomas*, 212.
[60] Pliny, *Natural History* V, trans. H. Rackham, LCL (Cambridge, MA: Harvard University Press, 1950), 18.102: "Graeci in binos semodios farinae satis esse bessem fermenti constituere." Cf. Blümner, *Technologie*, 1:58.
[61] Sperber, "Costs of Living," 268.
[62] Dalman, *Arbeit*, 56: "als das grösste Mass, mit dem eine backende Frau etwa arbeiten könnte." Here Dalman echoes Jülicher, *Gleichnisreden Jesu*, 577, except that Dalman estimates the amount of flour as nearly double that of Jülicher—36 versus 20 liters.

is *susceptive to corpse-uncleanness* and that which holds the prescribed measure [of forty *seahs* liquid or sixty *seahs* grain] is *unsusceptive to any uncleanness whatever*" (*m. Kel.* 24:3).[63] The last of these seems more suited to storage than kneading (cf. the list of containers mentioned at *m. Kel.* 15:1), but presumably the second type of trough would have been of a size intermediate between the other two and, therefore, capable of holding more than just one and a half seahs. Other mishnaic tractates refer to large wooden kneading troughs (*m. Kel.* 25:7), as well as to kneading troughs that were joined together to provide a more capacious vessel (*m. Parah* 5:9), in addition to "baker's boards"—long trestles designed for kneading and forming the dough that were found in bakers' establishments, but also figured among private householders (*m. Kel.* 15:2). The general impression that the Mishnah provides, therefore, is that the wherewithal existed to prepare an extensive amount of dough.

3.3.3. *Women Co-workers.* While the parable stipulates that it is "a woman" who initiates the leavening process, it is also possible that the preparation of the dough was not confined to one person. As noted above, the *Moretum* indicates that there was involvement of a slave girl in the process, even though the story remarks that it was "a man" who baked the bread. So, it is not out of the question that the parable also envisages assistance from others. While this assistance would not likely have been in the form of slaves, there are various indications from the Iron Age onwards that women typically engaged in the baking processes together.[64] Carol Meyers notes that ethnographic data of Iron Age Israel specify that the tedious grain processing tasks were "often performed in gendered workgroups, in which women of one household and even of neighbouring households gather together to grind, knead, and bake."[65] And as noted above, Matthew and Luke both allude to two women grinding grain together, and the Mishnah and Tosefta also provide a number of references where women work together at winnowing, sifting, and grinding grain (*m. Sheb.* 5:9; *m. Toh.* 7:4; *t. Nid.*). In *m. Pesaḥ.* 3:4, three women are described as working collectively in the baking process: "three

---

[63] *Mishnayot*, trans. Philip Blackman, 2nd ed., 7 vols. (Gateshead: Judaica Press, 1990), 6:152.
[64] Aubrey Baadsgaard, "A Taste of Women's Sociality: Cooking as Cooperative Labor in Iron Age Syro-Palestine," in *The World of Women in the Ancient and Classical Near East*, ed. B. A. Nakhai (Newcastle upon Tyne: Cambridge Scholars Press, 2008), 13–44; Carol Meyers, "From Field Crops to Food: Attributing Gender and Meaning to Bread Production in Iron Age Israel," in *The Archaeology of Difference: Gender, Ethnicity, Class and the "Other" in Antiquity: Studies in Honor of Eric M. Meyers*, ed. D. Edwards and T. McColloch, AASOR 60/61 (Boston: ASOR, 2007), 67–84; Carol Meyers, "Having Their Space and Eating There Too: Bread Production and Female Power in Ancient Israelite Households," *Nashim* 5 (2002): 14–44; Carol Meyers, "Material Remains and Social Relations: Women's Culture in Agrarian Households of the Iron Age," in *Symbiosis, Symbolism, and the Power of the Past*, ed. W. G. Dever and S. Gitin (Winona Lake, IN: Eisenbrauns, 2000), 425–44. While these articles are largely concerned with Iron Age, breadmaking practices (with the exception of the innovation of the rotary mill in the Hellenistic period) would have continued virtually unchanged from the Iron Age to the Common Era. See, further, Kurtis Peters, *Hebrew Lexical Semantics and Daily Life in Ancient Israel: What's Cooking in Biblical Hebrew?*, BibInt 146 (Leiden: Brill, 2016).
[65] Cf. Jer 7:18; Meyers, "Material Remains," 431. Krauss, *Talmudische Archäologie*, 1:451 n. 273, suggests that women ground in pairs because of the exhausting nature of the task.

women may knead dough at the same time and bake it in the same oven one after another." The dominant impression is that it was a commonplace for women to assist each other with their breadmaking. So, even though the parable mentions a single woman, Jesus's audience may well have assumed that the γυνή would have had assistance from other women as a matter of course. If this was the case, then the plausibility of the parable is further increased.

3.4. The Role of Genesis 18:6

Having taken these various factors into consideration, it is also worth comparing the story of the angels' visitation to Sarah and Abraham in Genesis 18, which describes Sarah preparing the same amount of dough (τρία μέτρα = סאים שלש) as the woman in the parable.[66] The passage is important because it provides a scriptural example of a single woman preparing the same amount of flour as in the parable. Scholars are divided about whether Jesus's parable is alluding to this account. Snodgrass considers the likelihood of an allusion to Gen 18:6 to be "minimal at best," whereas Robert Funk is far more open to the prospect of intertextuality.[67] The same amount is specified in each account, although different words are used—the LXX uses μέτρα instead of σάτα.

Here, upon the visitants' arrival, "Abraham hastened into the tent to Sarah, and said, 'Make ready quickly three measures of choice flour, knead it, and make cakes'" (Gen 18:6 NRSV).[68] Nothing more is said about the baking process, merely that the food prepared for the divine visitors was set before them and that they ate it (Gen 18:7).

This account resembles the parable insofar as it provides only the barest account of breadmaking, and leaves most of the details to inference. It is likely, for example, that Sarah prepared unleavened bread for her guests so that they would not have to wait many hours for the dough to rise (cf. Gen 19:3 where Lot prepares "unleavened bread" as part of the "feast" for his angelic visitors). Further, it seems that the amount of flour here is not represented as impossibly large. The counterpart to the flour—the calf sacrificed by Abraham (Gen 18:7)—would furnish a lavish and festive meal (cf. Luke 15:23)—but not one that was unduly excessive. Abraham seemingly recognizes his guests as exceptional, possibly divine, visitants, and he treats them as such, but the meal he presents them with—made from "choice flour," and a "tender and good" calf (singular)—was evidently focused at least as much on quality as on quantity. Shafer-Eliot observes that "It is difficult to know if the use of top-quality foodstuffs reflects

---

[66] The LXX reads: φύρασον τρία μέτρα σεμιδάλεως καὶ ποίησον ἐγκρυφίας. For a detailed discussion of this account in the Hebrew Bible, see especially C. Shafer-Elliott, *Food in Ancient Judah: Domestic Cooking in the Time of the Hebrew Bible* (Abingdon, TN: Routledge, 2014), 139–48.
[67] Snodgrass, *Stories with Intent*, 234; Robert W. Funk, "Beyond Criticism in Quest of Literacy: The Parable of the Leaven," *Int* 25 (1971): 149–70.
[68] Comparable amounts of dough are found elsewhere in the Hebrew scriptures, but expressed in terms of one epha rather than three seahs; איפה is translated as οιφι at Judg 6:19 (LXX οιφι ἀλεύρου ἄζυμα) and 1 Sam 1:24 (LXX οιφι σεμιδάλεως).

an ancient Near Eastern notion of the need to present the finest meal/offering to honored guests or the divine."⁶⁹

Abraham asks Sarah herself to make cakes for the angels, but asks "the servant" to prepare the calf. His directive gives the distinct impression that Sarah was to prepare the cakes herself rather than have a servant do so. On the other hand, Gen 18:8 goes on to refer to "the calf that he [Abraham] had prepared," which attributes the servant's actions to Abraham himself, so it is possible that the same was being done for Sarah, and that the bread preparation was performed by one or more of her servants (with or without her assistance). Nevertheless, the overriding impression from the text is that this woman's task (baking over butchery) was given to Sarah to perform, that she accepted it as a matter of course, and successfully prepared the bread, notwithstanding the amount of flour involved. The narrative treats the episode matter-of-factly, and there is no indication that she was faced with an impossible task.⁷⁰ If, then, this episode from Genesis was in Jesus's mind (or that of a very early tradent), it might well have suggested the amount of flour that figures in the parable—even if the parable refers to Aramaic *satas* and not the *seahs* of Gen 18:6. Similarly, if Jesus's audience was familiar with the story, it may have led them to accept the amount of flour in the parable as something familiar, albeit somewhat out of the ordinary.

Based, therefore, on the above data about the feasibility of a woman being able to leaven three satas of flour, it is likely that she would have been able to manage. This assessment is far from absolute, of course, as it is possible to envisage various circumstances where a woman would have been unable to perform the task. But, based on ancient *realia*, it is easier to envisage a variety of circumstances where a woman could leaven the dough: that she carried out the bread preparation in concert with other women, and that the kneading could readily be performed in common kneading troughs. And if Sarah could do it, why not the woman of the parable?

3.5. Kneading and the Addition of Water

The absence in the parable of any express mention of kneading, or of the addition of any water is unusual in an account that ostensibly describes the leavening of dough. These details are all mentioned in the breadmaking accounts of the *Moretum*, Cato, and Seneca, not to mention in Livy's remarks, so their absence here offers an instance where the parable departs notably from the *realia* of regular bread-making practice. Does this detail undermine the plausibility of the narrative?

It has long been recognized that the parable of the Leaven's description of a woman "hiding" (ἐνέκρυψεν) leaven in the dough is both unusual and unexpected: this verb is never used elsewhere to describe the process of mixing leaven into

---

⁶⁹ Shafer-Elliott, *Food in Ancient Judah*, 147.
⁷⁰ Shafer-Elliott overstates the case somewhat when she remarks, "*Obviously*, Sarah and the servant boy prepared the food", ibid., 140 (my emphasis).

flour or dough.[71] It is on the basis of the parable alone that the meaning of the verb is sometimes given as "mix."[72]

BDAG is—justifiably—more cautious in its definition. It defines ἐγκρύπτω as "to put into, and so out of sight," which points to the hidden dimension associated with the addition of the leaven.[73] But if this definition is taken seriously, the term's primary signification is more concerned with the leaven being hidden within the flour than with the leaven's being mixed into the flour. Even with all the mixing in the world, the leaven could not have raised the flour for the simple reason that *the leavening process would not have happened until water was added to the mixture*.[74]

Why does the parable omit this fundamental detail? Is its omission meant to highlight the miraculous effectiveness of the leaven—suggesting that, even without the addition of water, its irresistible growth could not be stayed? While such a hypothesis is possible, it is not certain that most listeners—particularly people unfamiliar with baking—would have even noticed this omission. Even those auditors who were regular bakers may have simply assumed that it was presupposed by the narrative. After all, a great many of the parable's subsequent interpreters have done the same thing.[75]

It is certainly possible that the parable's failure to mention water (and salt) is partly for the sake of brevity; to include them would have unnecessarily cluttered the stark simplicity of the parable's message. Nevertheless, the absence of these details is also intended to play down the human dimensions of the parable and focus on the divine efficacy of the leaven. As with the parable of the Seed Growing Secretly, human agents are needed primarily to jumpstart the growth process. Yet, once it has begun, humans are largely extraneous to the process until it is completed. But in the case of breadmaking (or a growing plant) this representation is not true to life—leaven not only needs to be introduced into the flour, it needs to be energetically worked to produce a glutinous dough that will rise effectively, just as plants likewise need to be watered, weeded, and tended to grow successfully. By deliberately and explicitly eliding these details, the parable is able to emphasize the hiddenness of the leaven, as well as its exceptional capacity to grow. That is to say, the canonical parable of the Leaven argues that although the kingdom of God depends on humans for its initial outworking, the growth of the kingdom is almost exclusively God's work—mysterious both in its inscrutability and in its powerful effects. The parable's pronounced avoidance of reference to the various features of breadmaking practice chronicled above, therefore, is *theological*. Where the *Moretum* and other accounts are chiefly concerned with describing the breadmaking process, Jesus's parable of the Leaven is chiefly concerned with describing the progress of the kingdom of God.

---

[71] Kogler, *Doppelgleichnis*, 183.
[72] *EDNT* 1, s.v. ἐγκρύπτω. Contrast 1 Kgs 28:24 where a woman ἔλαβεν ἄλευρα καὶ ἐφύρασεν καὶ ἔπεψεν ἄζυμα.
[73] BDAG, s.v. ἐγκρύπτω. Compare *The Cambridge Greek Lexicon*, s.v.: "put yeast into flour."
[74] See Ostmeyer, "Gott knetet nicht," 189–90, who also makes this observation.
[75] E.g., Jülicher, *Gleichnisreden Jesu*, 578.

The parable's studied omission of necessary features of breadmaking, along with the addition of exaggerated details like the three satas, indicate that it is intentionally subverting the notion that the leavening is an "everyday" event. The parable's omissions and additions are intended to set the narrative apart as exceptional.[76] In it, the quotidian clashes with the quizzical; the mundane with the marvelous; the human with the holy. While the events described are not impossible, they are sufficiently unusual to elicit questions on the part of hearers and readers. They are, in other words, pointers to God's otherwise hidden activity in their day-to-day lives. The catchword, then, that best describes the parable is not *hyperbole*, but *ambiguity*—the interplay of divine and human realities in the realm of everyday human experience.

4. Conclusions

To return, then, to the issue raised at the outset of this chapter, what do the *realia* associated with this parable suggest about its facticity? Given the five perspectives mentioned above, ranging between (1) an everyday occurrence and (5) hyperbole, which category best applies to the parable? The cumulative impression that emerges from this study is that while it certainly would not be a commonplace event, and while not every woman would have had the capability of leavening this amount of flour, this occurrence would, nevertheless, not have exceeded the "bounds of actuality." Scripture, in fact, provides a warrant for it—if Sarah could do it, as Genesis attests, the implication is that another woman should be able to do the same. Moreover, because the parable is so succinct, and focuses exclusively on the leavening of the dough, it allows for a broad spectrum of situations in which this leavening might occur. Festive occasions, such as weddings, could well require such extensive amounts of flour. And if co-operation among women in breadmaking was as widespread as it appears to have been, the large amount of flour would, perhaps, have seemed less exceptional. For these reasons it is best to propose that it falls somewhere between (2), an event that is out of the ordinary run of affairs, and (3), an extremely improbable happening.[77]

Nevertheless, the parable deliberately courts ambiguity. Three satas (whatever its precise parameters) is a very substantial amount, and it would signal to the audience that the parable is describing something considerably out of the ordinary. Likewise, the notable omission of standard breadmaking features, such as kneading the dough and the addition of water (and salt), would also point to the unusual features of this style of breadmaking. Most of all, the parable's marked de-emphasis of the breadmaker's role, and its correspondingly strong emphasis on the leaven's remarkable ability to raise such an extensive amount

---

[76] It is, of course, possible that the mention of "three satas" is indebted to later tradition and not to Jesus, but such a supposition still does not explain the parable's omissions.

[77] One might even argue that it impinges on (4), a miraculous circumstance, normally impossible, because it is not possible to leaven dough simply by hiding leaven in the flour. Since, however, the parable does not dwell on the miraculous, it is likely the hiddenness of the woman's action that is most important.

of dough, points to the profound but hidden activity of the Kingdom of God: the mysterious but irrepressible power of the kingdom at work amongst believers. Human actions may facilitate this growth in a limited fashion, but the author of this growth is God. As Paul asserts elsewhere, it is "God who gives the growth" (1 Cor 3:6).

Bibliography

Amouretti, M.-C. *Le pain et l'huile dans la Grèce antique*. Paris: Les Belles Lettres, 1986.
Avitsur, S. "The Way to Bread." *Tools and Tillage* 2 (1975): 228–41.
Baadsgaard, A. "A Taste of Women's Sociality: Cooking as Cooperative Labor in Iron Age Syro-Palestine." In *The World of Women in the Ancient and Classical Near East*, edited by B. A. Nakhai, 13–44. Newcastle upon Tyne: Cambridge Scholars, 2008.
Bakker, J. T., and B. Meijlink. "Introduction." In *The Mills-Bakeries of Ostia: Description and Interpretation*, edited by Jan Theo Bakker, 1–15. Amsterdam: Gieben, 1999.
Berger, K. *Manna, Mehl und Sauerteig. Korn und Brot im Alltag der frühen Christen*. Stuttgart: Quell Verlag, 1993.
Blümner, H. *Technologie und Terminologie der Gewerbe und Künste bei Griechen und Römern*. 4 vols. Rev. ed. Leipzig: Teubner, 1912. Repr. Hildesheim: Olms, 1969.
Bottéro, J. *The Oldest Cuisine in the World. Cooking in Mesopotamia*. Chicago: University of Chicago Press, 2004.
Broshi, M. *Bread, Wine, Walls and Scrolls*. JSPSup 36. Sheffield: Sheffield Academic Press, 2001.
Cato. De Re Rustica. Varro: De Re Rustica. Translated by H. B. Ash and W. D. Hooper. LCL. Cambridge, MA: Harvard University Press, 1967.
Dalman, G. *Arbeit und Sitte in Palästina*. Vol 4. Gütersloh, 1935. Repr. Hildesheim: Georg Olms, 1964.
Dalman, G. "Grinding in Ancient and Modern Palestine." *The Biblical World* 19 (1902): 9–18.
Dean, J. E., ed. *Epiphanius' Treatise on Weights and Measures: The Syriac Version*. Studies in Ancient Oriental Civilization 11. Chicago: University of Chicago, 1935.
Dodd, C. H. *The Parables of the Kingdom*. London: Nisbet & Co., 1935.
Duncan-Jones, R. P. "The Choenix, the Artaba and the Modius." *ZPE* 21 (1976): 43–52.
Fitzgerald, W. "Labor and Laborer in Latin Poetry: The Case of the *Moretum*." *Arethusa* 29 (1996): 389–418.
Funk, R. W. "Beyond Criticism in Quest of Literacy: The Parable of the Leaven." *Int* 25 (1971): 149–70.
Gathercole, S. *The Gospel of Thomas: Introduction and Commentary*. TENTS 11. Leiden: Brill, 2014.
Goodacre, M. *Thomas and the Gospels*. Grand Rapids, MI: Eerdmans, 2012.
Heinrich, F. "Cereals and Bread." In *The Routledge Handbook of Diet and Nutrition in the Roman World*, edited by P. Erdkamp and C. Holleran, 101–15. London: Routledge, 2018.
Hirschfeld, Y. *The Palestinian Dwelling in the Roman-Byzantine Period*. Jerusalem: Franciscan Printing Press and Israel Exploration Society, 1995.
Huffman, N. A. "Atypical Features in the Parables of Jesus." *JBL* 97 (1978): 207–20.
Hultgren, A. J. *The Parables of Jesus: A Commentary*. Grand Rapids, MI: Eerdmans, 2000.

Jasny, N. "The Daily Bread of the Ancient Greeks and Romans." *Osiris* 9 (1950): 227–53.
Jastrow, M. *A Dictionary of the Targumim, the Talmud Babli and Yerushalmi, and the Midrashic Literature.* 1903. Repr. Peabody, MA: Hendrickson, 2006.
Jeremias, J. *Die Gleichnisse Jesu.* 11th ed. Göttingen: Vandenhoeck & Ruprecht, 1998.
Jeremias, J. *The Parables of Jesus.* Translated by S. H. Hooke. Rev. ed. London: SCM Press, 1972.
Jülicher, A. *Die Gleichnisreden Jesu.* 2 vols. Freiburg: Mohr, 1899.
Kellermann, D. "חמץ." *TDOT,* 4:487–511.
Kenney, A. J. *The Ploughman's Lunch = Moretum: A Poem Ascribed to Virgil.* Bristol: Bristol Classical Press, 1984.
Kogler, F. *Das Doppelgleichnis vom Senfkorn und vom Sauerteig in seiner traditionsgeschichtlichen Entwicklung. Zur Reich-Gottes-Vorstellung Jesu und ihren Aktualisierungen in der Urkirche.* FB 59. Würzburg: Echter Verlag, 1988.
Krauss, S. *Talmudische Archäologie.* 3 vols. Leipzig, 1910. Repr. Hildesheim: Georg Olms, 1966.
Mattila, S. L. "Capernaum, Village of Nahum, from Hellenistic to Byzantine Times." In *Galilee in the Late Second Temple and Mishnaic Periods,* edited by David A. Fiensy and James Riley Strange, 2:217–57. 2 vols. Minneapolis, MN: Fortress Press, 2015.
Mau, A. "Bäckerei." *PW* 2 (1909): cols. 2734–2743.
Meier, J. P. *A Marginal Jew, Volume 5: Probing the Authenticity of the Parables.* New Haven: Yale University Press, 2016.
Meyers, C. "From Field Crops to Food: Attributing Gender and Meaning to Bread Production in Iron Age Israel." In *The Archaeology of Difference: Gender, Ethnicity, Class and the "Other" in Antiquity. Studies in Honor of Eric M. Meyers,* edited by D. Edwards and T. McColloch, 67–84. AASOR 60/61. Boston: ASOR, 2007.
Meyers, C. "Having Their Space and Eating There Too: Bread Production and Female Power in Ancient Israelite Households." *Nashim* 5 (2002): 14–44.
Meyers, C. "Material Remains and Social Relations: Women's Culture in Agrarian Households of the Iron Age." In *Symbiosis, Symbolism, and the Power of the Past,* edited by G. Dever and S. Gitin, 425–44. Winona Lake, IN: Eisenbrauns, 2000.
The Mishnah. Translated by Herbert Danby. Oxford, 1931. Repr. Peabody, MA: Hendrickson, 2011.
Mishnayot. Translated by Philip Blackman. 2nd ed. 7 vols. Gateshead: Judaica Press, 1990.
Monteix, N. *Les lieux des métier. Boutiques et ateliers d'Herculanum.* Rome: École Française de Rome, 2010.
Moritz, L. A. *Grain Mills and Flour in Classical Antiquity.* Oxford: Clarendon Press, 1958.
The New Princeton Encyclopedia of Poetry and Poetics. Edited by Alex Preminger and T. V. F. Brogan. Princeton, NJ: Princeton University Press, 1993.
Ostmeyer, K.-H. "Gott knetet nicht (Vom Sauerteig) Q 13.20f. (Mt 13,33 / Lk 13.20f. / EvThom 96)." In *Kompendiumn der Gleichnisse Jesu,* edited by Ruben Zimmermann, 185–92. Gütersloh: Gütersloher Verlagshaus, 2007.
Peters, K. *Hebrew Lexical Semantics and Daily Life in Ancient Israel: What's Cooking in Biblical Hebrew?* BibInt 146. Leiden: Brill, 2016.
Pliny, *Natural History* V. Translated by H. Rackham. LCL. Cambridge, MA: Harvard University Press, 1950.
Plisch, U.-K. *The Gospel of Thomas: Original Text with Commentary.* Stuttgart: Deutsche Bibelgesellschaft, 2008.

Reid, B. E. "Beyond Petty Pursuits and Wearisome Widows: Three Lukan Parables." *Int* 56 (2002): 284–94.

Ricoeur, P. "Biblical Hermeneutics," *Semeia* 4 (1975): 29–148.

Safrai, S., and M. Stern. *The Jewish People in the First Century*. 2 vols. CRINT 1. Assen: Van Gorcum, 1976.

Segrè, A. "A Documentary Analysis of Ancient Palestinian Units of Measure." *JBL* 64 (1945): 357–75.

Seneca, *Epistles 66–92*. Translated by Richard M. Gummere. LCL. Cambridge, MA: Harvard University Press, 1920.

Shafer-Elliott, C. "Baking Bread in Ancient Judah." *BAR* 45, no. 4 (2019): 59–64.

Shafer-Elliott, C. *Food in Ancient Judah, Domestic Cooking in the Time of the Hebrew Bible*. Abingdon, TN: Routledge, 2014.

Snodgrass, K. *Stories with Intent: A Comprehensive Guide to the Parables of Jesus*. 2nd ed. Grand Rapids, MI: Eerdmans; Cambridge, MA: Paternoster Press, 2018.

Sperber, D. "Costs of Living in Roman Palestine." *Journal of the Economic and Social History of the Orient* 8 (1965): 248–71.

Virgil. *Aeneid: Books 7–12. Appendix Vergiliana*. Translated by H. Rushton Fairclough and G. P. Goold. Rev. ed. LCL. Cambridge, MA: Harvard University Press, 2000.

Wilson, A., and K. Schörle. "A Baker's Funerary Relief from Rome." *Papers of the British School at Rome* 77 (2009): 101–23.

Telling Stories in a Violent World

Thomas E. Goud

Jesus of Nazareth urged love of enemies and turning the other cheek, but he also declared that those who live by the sword will die by the sword and that he did not come to bring peace, but a sword. That paradox is one of the more intractable problems of scholarship on Jesus, whether as historical or remembered or theologically constructed. Similarly, the parables pose questions not only about Jesus and violence, but also about whether God is to be seen as a vengeful king burning cities, slaughtering enemies, and handing slaves over to the torturers. I admit up front that I do not propose to offer a solution to those questions. This chapter is rather aimed at sketching in some of the landscape of violence as found in the parables, first by a consideration of some aspects of the social-historical context, then through an examination of the language of violence, and finally an attempt to understand the actors and victims of violence in the parables.

1. Persistence, Ubiquity, and Diversity of Violence

First-century Galilee, indeed, first-century Palestine as a whole, was a very violent place. That violence was persistent, ubiquitous, and diverse. It occurred both in the public and in the private spheres. One common image of violence, especially popular in film and television, is that of soldiers—usually, though often wrongly, portrayed as Roman legionaries—marauding through towns and villages. While there are clear instances of official action involving soldiers, a focus on political and military violence misses how widespread and diverse the experience of violence was for most of the population. In the twenty-first century we have become keenly aware of issues of systemic violence. And it is to the credit of a number of recent social-historical scholars that they have identified such patterns in the world of Jesus.[1] I begin with an overview of persistence, ubiquity, and diversity of violence.

---

[1] Various studies of "bandits" have been especially helpful. For example: Richard A. Horsley, "'By the Finger of God': Jesus and Imperial Violence," in *Violence in the New Testament*, ed. Shelly Matthews and E. Leigh Gibson (New York/London: T&T Clark, 2005), 51–80; Richard A. Horsley,

1.1. Persistence and Ubiquity

Models of historical periodization can be open to dispute, but, as Josephus realized, the period from the Maccabean revolt in the mid-second century BCE to the destruction of Jerusalem and the Temple in 70 CE forms an important historical period that saw the reassertion of independence, a decline from that position, a disastrous period of internal dissension, and a revolt to throw off foreign control. That longer period can itself be divided into at least three main sections by the arrival of the Romans in the person of Pompey in 63 BCE and the destruction of the Temple in 70 CE after four years of bloody rebellion and war. It is also helpful to mark two other dates: the rise and reign of Herod the Great (40–4 BCE) and the establishment of the Roman province of Judaea (6 CE). Every one of those dates and periods was marked by uprisings, rebellions, war, and various types of public violence.

1.1.1. From the Maccabean Revolt to the Death of Herod (167–4 BCE). The Maccabean revolt against the domination of the Seleucid empire under Antiochus IV Epiphanes spawned a substantial literature, with stories not only of the liberation of the Jewish people from domination, but also of bravery in the face of horrific mistreatment. The culmination of that perspective is especially clear in 4 Maccabees which revels in the language of torture and torment. Although the Hasmonean dynasty that ruled the newly independent nation was effective in its administration, the period from 165 BCE to the arrival of Pompey in 63 BCE was not free from wars, both internal and external—including wars of conquest and expansion—as well as betrayal and murder within the ruling family. I note only two examples.

The early part of the reign of Alexander Jannaeus (103–76 BCE) was both a time of war and a time when the people were in a state of persistent rebellion, with factions even looking to outsiders as allies against the king. After Alexander reduced Gaza, Raphia, and Anthedon to slavery, the Jewish people revolted.[2] Later, after putting down another uprising of his own people against him, Alexander is said to have crucified 800 Jews and to have slaughtered their wives and children before them while they were still alive. All the while he looked on, feasting lavishly and surrounded by his concubines (*B.J.* 1.97).

Jesus and the Spiral of Violence: Popular Jewish Resistance in Roman Palestine (Minneapolis, MN: Fortress Press, 1993); J. S. Kloppenborg, "Unsocial Bandits," in *A Wandering Galilean: Essays in Honour of Seán Freyne*, ed. Margaret Daly-Denton, Anne Fitzpatrick Mckinley, and Zuleika Rodgers (Leiden/Boston: Brill, 2009): 451–84; Seán Freyne, *Galilee From Alexander the Great to Hadrian* (Edinburgh: T. & T. Clark, 1980). While I am not persuaded by models that overstate the direct involvement and interference of Rome in ancient Palestine, and especially in the client kingdoms, I have found much to stimulate thought in the work of scholars such as Horsley and Warren Carter. In addition to the works by Horsley noted above, see Warren Carter, "Constructions of Violence and Identities in Matthew's Gospel," in Matthews and Gibson, eds., *Violence in the New Testament*, 81–108; "Resisting and Imitating the Empire: Imperial Paradigms in Two Matthean Parables," *Interpretation* 56 (2002): 260–72; "Sanctioned Violence in the New Testament," *Interpretation: A Journal of Bible and Theology* 71 (2017): 284–97.

[2] Josephus notes: "It was thought that Alexander would not have been able to crush this uprising without the use of his mercenaries" (*B.J.* 1.88).

If the behavior of Alexander Jannaeus was conspicuous for its brutality, the reign of his widow saw a number of executions and his sons Hyrcanus and Aristobulus ended up in civil war for control of the kingship. At that point Hyrcanus appealed to Pompey in Syria to aid him against his brother. When Aristobulus reneged on an agreement to pay an indemnity and surrender himself and Jerusalem, Pompey laid siege to the city, took it, and, to the horror of the Jews, entered the most holy part of the Temple. Hyrcanus was restored to the high priesthood and Aristobulus and his family taken captive. The following years saw attempts by Aristobulus and members of his family to regain control; the Roman governors of Syria put down such efforts and Hyrcanus, together with his right-hand man Antipater, remained in power (*B.J.* 1.131–54).[3] Throughout the period from Alexander Jannaeus to the arrival of Pompey (103–63 BCE) the clashes and acts of violence were found throughout the whole of the region and even frequently involved neighboring peoples.

Antipater's son, Herod, rose to power through boldness and violence. As governor of Galilee in 47 BCE, he defeated the ἀρχιληστής Ezekias and his large group of bandits (*B.J.* 1.204). Having won the support of Marcus Antonius in 42 BCE, Herod shrewdly went to Rome in 40 BCE and obtained the title of "King of the Jews" from both Antonius and the young Caesar. He then returned home to a country that was being disturbed by a number of factions, including a number of "bandits" (*B.J.* 1.304–13). Over the course of three years, Herod consolidated control of his new kingdom. The latter part of his reign was notorious for palace intrigues and royal murders and near the end of his life there was another rebellion in Jerusalem stirred up at the instigation of two experts in the traditional law. They inveighed against the golden eagle that Herod had erected over the Great Gate. When some who had been stirred up attempted to chop the eagle down, Herod, though ill, appeared and demanded that they be punished. He had the two preachers and the ones who had attempted to chop down the eagle burnt alive and others were arrested and sent off for execution (*B.J.* 1.648–55).

The last act of violence of Herod's reign was one that was intended, but not completed. He had gathered leading men from the villages throughout Judea and locked them in the hippodrome at Jericho with instructions to his wife that they were to be executed at his death. Salome, however, freed the men at Herod's death, rather than have them killed (*B.J.* 1.659–66).

1.1.2. From the Death of Herod to the Organization of Judaea as a Province (4 BCE–6 CE). At the death of Herod (4 BCE) his kingdom was divided between three of his sons with Archelaus receiving Judaea. He was immediately faced with a protest that turned violent. Popular protests erupted in Jerusalem[4] egged on especially by those who wanted to put pressure on Archelaus as well as by those who were determined to honor those who had cut down Herod's eagle and had

---

[3] I skip over the years of the Roman civil wars after the assassination of Julius Caesar.
[4] Many of the accounts of violent activity focus on Jerusalem and often occur at the great festivals of Passover (Pesach), Pentecost (Shavuot), and Booths (Sukkot).

subsequently been executed. The disturbances escalated and Archelaus's eventual response was to send his troops against the crowds as they were making sacrifice for Passover and cut them down. The result was that the festival was interrupted and the people dispersed. Archelaus then departed for Rome to receive Augustus's endorsement of his position.[5]

Sabinus, an imperial procurator in Syria, attempted with force to obtain control of royal monies in the hill-forts and stirred up a great resistance. By the time Pentecost arrived people had flooded into Jerusalem from Galilee, Idumaea, Jericho, and Peraea. Destruction and bloodshed in the city as well as the burning of part of the Temple and the plundering of the treasury by Sabinus and his troops followed.

At the same time a man named Athrongaeus stirred up a revolt in the surrounding Judaean hill country. He and his supporters carried out guerilla attacks on Romans and Jews alike and even managed to kill the centurion Arius and forty of his men near Emmaus (Ammaus).[6] When Varus arrived from Syria he burned Emmaus to the ground and advanced on Jerusalem. He rounded up insurrectionists and had some imprisoned and others crucified.[7] Simon in Peraea was a royal slave who gathered up a gang of bandits and burned a palace at Jericho. Eventually confronted by Gratus, he and his men were defeated.[8] And in Idumaea a discontented group of royal veterans roused up rebellion and engaged in war against Achiab, a cousin of the now dead king.[9]

There were also protests and uprisings in Galilee. Josephus provides a very brief account of the activities at Sepphoris of a certain Judas, the son of the former "chief bandit" Ezekias. Herod had subdued Ezekias when he was appointed to govern Galilee in 47 BCE.[10] When Varus entered the region from Syria to put down the many uprisings at the death of Herod, he burned Sepphoris and enslaved the population.[11]

1.1.3. *From the organization of Judaea as a province to Cumanus (6–52 CE).*

Although Archelaus was able through violence to put down the uprisings in Jerusalem at the time of his succession, the same was not true after some ten years of disturbances and maladministration. In 6 CE he was deposed and Augustus had Quirinius, the governor of Syria, make arrangements for Judaea to become a province with direct Roman administration under a prefect. The protests against the census spread throughout the region and saw the rise of another Judas, Judas the Galilean who is credited by Josephus with establishing what he called

---

[5] *A.J.* 17.206–18; *B.J.* 2.4–13.
[6] *A.J.* 17.278–85; *B.J.* 2.60–65. For the name and location of Emmaus/Ammaus, see Steve Mason, *Flavius Josephus: Translation and Commentary. Volume 1B: Judean War 2* (Leiden: Brill, 2008): 44 n. 388.
[7] *A.J.* 17.295; *B.J.* 2.75. Josephus puts the number of those crucified at 2,000, but his numbers are often difficult to credit.
[8] *A.J.* 17.273–77; *B.J.* 2.57–59; Tacitus, *Hist.* 5.9.2.
[9] *A.J.* 17.270–73, 297; *B.J.* 2.55, 76.
[10] *A.J.* 17.271–73; *B.J.* 2.56.
[11] *A.J.* 17.289; *B.J.* 2.68.

the Fourth Philosophy.[12] From that time on there are persistent stories of the "bandits" (λῇσται) that rose up everywhere in the region.

As the provincial seat of the governor of Judaea, Caesarea Maritima was also the site of official complaints made to him. In some instances, the crowds that assembled were large and potentially menacing. One of Pontius Pilate's first clashes with the population of his province came when he attempted to place military standards in Jerusalem. A large crowd from the surrounding area formed in Jerusalem and then went to Caesarea where they surrounded Pilate's house and lay face down on the ground for five days and nights. When he surrounded them with troops and threatened to kill them, they, to his astonishment, bared their throats and made no resistance. On that occasion, Pilate capitulated.[13]

A second protest against Pilate occurred in Jerusalem.[14] To disperse the crowd, Pilate sent soldiers among the protesters with clubs and, at a signal, had the soldiers beat them. It is, of course, during the governorship of Pilate that Jesus of Nazareth was arrested and executed as "King of the Jews" and that the insurrectionist Jesus bar Abbas and other λῇσται were captured.[15] Luke 13:1 makes a cryptic reference to Pilate mingling the blood of Galileans with their sacrifice, which may well have occurred in Jerusalem at Passover.

A clash between Pilate and the Samaritans resulted in Pilate's recall from Judaea. A charismatic individual persuaded many Samaritans that he would lead them up Mount Gerizim where he would reveal to them sacred vessels left by Moses. When a large group assembled at the base of the mountain, Pilate met them with troops. Many were killed in battle, many fled, and still others were taken prisoner and executed. The Samaritans complained to Varus, the imperial legate in Syria and he ordered Pilate to return to Rome (*A.J.* 18.85–87).

At the death of Agrippa I (44 CE), and after a brief period again under a client king, Judaea was once more put under direct administration as a province. At the first Passover of Cumanus's governorship he was in Jerusalem with a cohort of soldiers. Josephus notes that it had come to be common practice to provide a heavy guard in the city during festivals. One of the guards who was positioned on the roof of the Temple hiked up his tunic, exposing his buttocks, and farted (*B.J.* 2.224).[16] The crowd was incensed and demanded that Cumanus punish the soldier. Others began to throw stones and, to put the riot down, Cumanus ordered in heavy troops with the result that many of the people were crushed in the melee.

Finally, an incident that occurred on the border between Galilee and Samaria reveals both the geographical range of acts of violence as well as the variety of actors and types.[17] In 52 CE a group of Jews was on its way from Galilee to Jerusalem for a festival. At the border village Gema one of the Galileans

---

[12] *A.J.* 18.3–6; 20.102; *B.J.* 2.118, 433; 7.253; Acts 5:37.
[13] *A.J.* 18.55–59; *B.J.* 2.169–74. On the beginning date of Pilate's governorship, see Mason, *Judean War 2*, 139.
[14] *A.J.* 18.60–62; *B.J.* 2.175–77.
[15] Matt 18:15–16; Mark 15:6–7, 27; Luke 23:18–19, 32–33; John 18:39–40; 19:18.
[16] The parallel account in *A.J.* 20.108 claims that the soldier exhibited his genitals.
[17] *A.J.* 20.118–36; *B.J.* 2.232–46.

was killed. As a result a number of Galileans planned to attack the Samaritans, but others went to Cumanus to have him intervene and bring the murderers to justice. Cumanus did not attend to the matter and when word reached Jerusalem, a mob assembled and headed for Samaria. Included in this group were a number of people whom Josephus identifies as λῇσται under the leadership of Eleazer and Alexander. These gangs engaged in massacres and burned villages on their way. Cumanus sent troops against Eleazer's gangs and leaders from Jerusalem came and persuaded the crowds not to provoke a Roman response by attacking the Samaritans. There were some, however, who were not persuaded and there followed a period of insurgencies and what, for want of a better term, could be labeled terrorism.

Delegations from the Samaritans and from Jerusalem presented themselves to Ummidius Quadratus, the governor of Syria seeking an official intervention in the situation. Quadratus first went to Caesarea where he crucified the prisoners that Cumanus had taken. After hearing another delegation of Samaritans, he had eighteen Jews beheaded and then sent the high priests and other Jerusalem leaders as well as a group of Samaritan leaders to Claudius in Rome. He also dispatched Cumanus and the military tribune Celer to Rome. Claudius was persuaded that the Samaritans were to blame and had three prominent leaders executed. The final humiliation and brutality of this event was that Celer was sent back to Jerusalem in chains with orders that he be handed over to the Jews to be tortured, dragged around the city, and executed.

Judaea may have become a Roman *provincia*, but there was hardly any *pax Romana* in the region. The seven decades from the death of Herod to the outbreak of the revolt and war that led to the destruction of Jerusalem and the Temple provide a rich crop of incidents of rebellion, murder, military action, executions, and unrest. That unrest spread beyond the province to the neighboring regions of Samaria and Galilee, as well as across the Jordan, and south toward the Arabian peninsula. On the political front, many of those incidents were either caused by or at least exacerbated by the behavior of the governors. Finally, in 66, a widespread revolt began. This narrative only sketches bits of the history from the Maccabean revolt to the beginning of the war with Rome, but it should more than suffice to emphasize the persistence and ubiquity of violence in the region. I turn now to the diversity of that violence.

1.2. Diversity

In addition to understanding the persistence and ubiquity of violence, it is also important to note the diversity. From the incidents already noted we see examples of murder, armed revolt, beating, crucifixion, beheading, banditry, and mass protest (often turning to violence). The examples so far adduced are largely those of a public and often official nature or of the kinds of things that occur in situations akin to civil war. That does not cover the full range of experiences of violence.

1.2.1. *Beatings*. Beatings themselves were diverse in kind, ranging from public scourging as a form of corporal punishment to the abuse of female slaves who had managed to annoy their mistresses in some way.[18] Josephus and the Acts of the Apostles provide repeated examples of people being beaten for offences. In 2 Corinthians 11, Paul claims that he had received the Jewish punishment of scourging on five occasions and on three other occasions had been beaten with rods, presumably by Roman authorities. He also mentions once having been stoned.[19] These types of punishments were frequently public, precisely to intimidate others and humiliate those being punished. And those same motives of intimidation and humiliation often informed the treatment of slaves.

Slavery in the Roman world was a multifaceted phenomenon.[20] The material and psychological conditions varied widely, as did the contexts in which one might become a slave and in which one might live (or die) as a slave. But what is clear in Roman law and appears to be paralleled to a large extent among the ancient Jews is that slave bodies were to be used at the discretion of their masters with very limited restrictions on what could be done to them. There is not room here, nor is there need, to rehearse all of the aspects of slave experience of violence. It will suffice to note that slaves were routinely subjected to beatings within the household and, at times, in public spectacle.[21] Sexual exploitation of female slaves was so prevalent that they were often simply assumed to be unchaste.[22] Hezser demonstrates that the justification of corporal punishment as well as assumptions with respect to sexual exploitation of female slaves was sought in texts such as Prov 29:19 as well as Exod 21:20–21 on beating[23] and Exod 21:7–11 on purchasing a Hebrew girl to be a slave. In the latter case, there does appear to be some protection for the woman against being prostituted or abandoned.[24]

---

[18] See Catherine Hezser, *Jewish Slavery in Antiquity* (Oxford: Oxford University Press, 2006): 169ff., and Juvenal, *Sat.* 6.475–495.

[19] An incident that occurred at Lystra, Acts 14:19.

[20] In addition to Hezser, *Jewish Slavery*, Jennifer A. Glancy, *Slavery in Early Christianity* (Oxford: Oxford University Press, 2002), is always useful for any discussion of slavery in first-century Palestine.

[21] Jennifer A. Glancy, "Slaves and Slavery in the Matthean Parables," *The Jewish Quarterly Review* 82 (2000): 83, on public punishment of slaves. See also Mary Ann Beavis, "Ancient Slavery as an Interpretive Context for the New Testament Servant Parables with Special Reference to the Unjust Steward (Luke 16:1–8)," *JBL* 115 (1996): 471–88, for parallel material from New Comedy and Aesop and Phaedrus.

[22] Jennifer A. Glancy, "The Sexual Use of Slaves: A Response to Kyle Harper on Jewish and Christian *Porneia*," *JBL* 134 (2015): 215–29, argues that Hellenistic Jewish writers did not extend the use of the term *porneia* to relations with slaves and that attitudes to such extra-marital conduct was tolerated.

[23] Prov 29:19: "By mere words servants are not disciplined, for though they understand, they will not give heed." Exod 21:20–21: "When a slaveowner strikes a male or female slave with a rod and the slave dies immediately, the owner shall be punished. But if the slave survives a day or two, there is no punishment; for the slave is the owner's property."

[24] Exod 21:7–11: "When a man sells his daughter as a slave, she shall not go out as the male slaves do. If she does not please her master, who designated her for himself, then he shall let her be redeemed; he shall have no right to sell her to a foreign people, since he has dealt unfairly with her. If he designates her for his son, he shall deal with her as with a daughter. If he takes another wife to himself, he shall not diminish the food, clothing, or marital rights of the first wife. And if he does

Slaves were not only on the receiving end of violence. Since a number of slaves had positions of responsibility within households or in business and agricultural enterprises, they themselves inflicted beatings and abuse on others. Hezser cites *t. Men.* 13:21 for evidence of the slaves of the high priest Ishmael ben Fabus beating others with staves.[25] And Josephus, probably referring to the same context, provides an example of conflict that arose between the high priest and the other priests and leading men of the city. Gangs of reckless revolutionaries formed that clashed with one another and hurled stones as well as abuse. Slaves of the high priest were sent to the threshing floor to collect the tithes that should have been distributed to the priests with the result that some poor priests starved. Josephus sums the situation up: "Thus the violence of the opposing factions prevailed over all justice."[26] Hezser also draws attention to some rabbinic king parables in which nurses and pedagogues were regarded with suspicion and as potentially the greatest threat to a child.[27] Given the close interaction of nurses and pedagogues with children, there is a certain logic to that, but it is worthwhile to reflect on the impact that such anxiety might have on familial relations.

It appears that wives and children fared somewhat better in domestic contexts. There is certainly evidence that children might be beaten for disciplinary reasons, but, as Saller has argued, that was thought to be more appropriate for small children.[28] As the children grew older, the preference was for suasion rather than physical punishment.[29] At heart was the aim not to humiliate and crush the spirit of the child. Clear evidence of husbands beating wives is not readily available, but it would be naïve to think that absence of evidence is evidence of absence.

1.2.2. *Torture and Executions.* Torture was not as public as beatings and many of the instances noted in our sources are of torturing individuals to obtain evidence of criminal or subversive activity. Under Roman law, testimony from slaves had to be taken under torture,[30] but that does not account for the majority of the stories.

---

not do these three things for her, she shall go out without debt, without payment of money." Unlike the male Hebrew slave, she does not go free after six years. That no doubt reflects the assumption that she would no longer be marriageable and would therefore be especially vulnerable were she no longer part of the master's household. The obligation on the master to provide for her, even if he takes another wife is also aimed at providing some kind of protection.

[25] Hezser, *Jewish Slavery*, 126 n. 21.
[26] *A.J.* 20.181: οὕτως ἐκράτει τοῦ δικαίου παντὸς ἡ τῶν στασιαζόντων βία.
[27] Hezser, *Jewish Slavery*, 147–8.
[28] Richard P. Saller, *Patriarchy, Property and Death in the Roman Family*, Cambridge Studies in Population, Economy, and Society in Past Time (Cambridge: Cambridge University Press, 1994), 142–3; cf. Hezser, *Jewish Slavery*, 204–5.
[29] Things were not so favorable in schools. Teachers seem to have been quite quick with beatings as part of their educational "best practice." Saller, *Patriarchy*, 148–9, cites examples from authors from Martial to Augustine.
[30] On the use of torture in investigation see *Digest* 48.18; P. A. Brunt, "Evidence Given Under Torture at Rome," *Zeitschrift der Savigny-Stiftung für Rechtsgeschichte. Romanistische Abteilung* 97 (1980): 256–65, and K. R. Bradley, *Slavery and Society at Rome* (Cambridge: Cambridge University Press, 1994), 165–70.

Josephus records a number of instances where Herod the Great put people to torture who were suspected of conspiracy against him.[31] One incident is noteworthy for its savagery on the part of private individuals as well as the king. Herod's introduction of a theater, an amphitheater, and games in honor of Caesar so outraged many of his people that a conspiracy was formed to assassinate him. One of his spies learned of the plot and informed on the conspirators. They were summoned before Herod and boldly confessed, whereupon they were led off to torture and execution.[32] Shortly thereafter the spy was seized by some who were sympathetic to the conspirators and was torn apart and left for the dogs.[33]

The language of torture is richly on display in Josephus's description of all that the Essenes were willing to endure during the war with the Romans (*B.J.* 2.152-53):

> The war with the Romans put their character to every sort of test. *Racked, twisted, burnt, broken* (στρεβλούμενοί τε καὶ λυγιζόμενοι καιόμενοί τε καὶ κλώμενοι), sent through the *whole gamut of torture instruments* (διὰ πάντων ὀδεύοντες τῶν βασανιστηρίων ὀργάνων) to make them blaspheme their Lawgiver or eat some forbidden food, they refused to do either, refused too to make any cringing appeal to their abusers or shed any tears. Smiling through the pain, and teasing the *agents of their torture* (τῶν τὰς βασάνους προσφερόντων), they happily gave up their souls in the confidence that they would recover them in the future.[34]

While there are a number of examples of executions by Roman governors, the evidence for the Sanhedrin's authority with regard to capital punishment is not entirely clear for the period in question. Certain events and practices do emerge from the Rabbinic material, Josephus, and the New Testament. On occasions, whether irregularly or not, the Jewish authorities did impose at least stoning[35] and burning. In addition, the Mishnah and the Jerusalem and Babylonian Talmuds go to great length to lay out proper procedure for four types of execution: stoning, burning, strangulation, beheading.[36] In the discussion on burning, it is recorded that R. Eleazer b. Zadok claimed to have witnessed an occasion when a woman was burned by being surrounded by flammable materials. The anecdote is included because it is at odds with the procedure that required that a person to be executed by burning should be burned from the inside by forcing a burning item down the throat.[37]

---

[31] *B.J.* 1.485, 527–29, 584–86, 590–99.
[32] *A.J.* 15.289: τοιαῦτα μὲν ἐκεῖνοι τῇ προαιρέσει τῆς ἐπιβουλῆς ἐμπαρρησιασάμενοι περιστάντων αὐτοῖς τῶν βασιλικῶν ἤγοντο καὶ πᾶσαν αἰκίαν ὑπομείναντες διεφθάρησαν.
[33] *A.J.* 15.289: μετ' οὐ πολὺ δὲ καὶ τὸν ταῦτα μηνύσαντα κατὰ μῖσος ἁρπασάμενοί τινες οὐκ ἀπέκτειναν μόνον, ἀλλὰ καὶ μελιστὶ διελόντες προύθεσαν κυσίν.
[34] *B.J.* 2.152–53 (trans. Mason).
[35] Acts 7:54–60 recounts the stoning of Stephen and Josephus tells of the stoning of James (*A.J.* 20.9).
[36] *m. Sanh.* 7.2.
[37] *m. Sanh.* 7.2, b.

2. The Parables in the Contexts of Violence

In light of the persistence, ubiquity, and diversity of violence in the world of Jesus, it comes as no surprise that images of various kinds of violence turn up in the parables. In some, such as the reference to "extortioners" in the parable of the Pharisee and the tax-collector, the violence is only implicit. In others it is very overt and graphic, as in the burning of the city of those who rejected the king's invitation to his banquet or the cutting in two of the unfaithful slave. Violent images and language occur in all of the following:[38]

Mark, Matthew, Luke

Strong Man (Matt 12:29 // Mark 3:27 // Luke 11:21–22)
Tenants in the Vineyard (Matt 21:33–46 // Mark 12:1–12 // Luke 20:9–19)
Salt ([Mark 9:49–50][39] // Matt 5:13 // Luke 14:34–35)
Kingdom Divided (Mark 3:22–26 // Matt 12:22–28 // Luke 11:14–20)

Matthew, Luke

Opponent at Law (Matt 5:25–26 // Luke 12:58–59)
Two Houses (Matt 7:24–27 // Luke 6:47–49)
Corpse and Vultures (Matt 24:28 // Luke 17:37)
Beware of the Thief (Matt 24:43–44 // Luke 12:39–40)
Faithful and Unfaithful Slaves (Matt 24:45–51 // Luke 12:42–46)
Talents/Minas (Matt 25:14–30 // Luke 19:12–27)
Good and Bad Trees (Matt 7:16–20 // [Luke 6:43–45])
Wedding Feast/Banquet (Matt 22:1–14 // [Luke 14:12–24])

Matthew

Pearls to Swine (Matt 7:6)
Wheat and Tares (Matt 13:24–30, 36–43)
Dragnet (Matt 13:47–50)
Rooted Up (Matt 15:13)
Unforgiving Slave (Matt 18:23–35)

Luke

Good Samaritan (Luke 10:30–35)
Two Slaves (Luke 12:47–48)
Barren Fig Tree (Luke 13:6–9)
Widow and Judge (Luke 18:1–8)
Pharisee and Tax Collector (Luke 18:9–14)

---

[38] A word about the range of parables that I include in this study. I have followed the pattern of Ruben Zimmermann et al., eds., *Kompendium der Gleichnisse Jesu* (Gütersloh: Gütersloher Verlagshaus, 2007), in casting a broad net. In fact, I include on its own one parable that is not treated separately even in the *Kompendium*: the "Faithful and Unfaithful Slaves."

[39] Parallel passages that contain no violent language are put in square brackets.

2.1. The Language of Violence

As already noted, some of the violence in the parables listed here is implicit. So, for example, in the parable of Salt, apart from Mark's cryptic "Everything will be salted with fire," the only violence implied is that the salt that is no longer "salty" is of no use and should be thrown out. While not particularly strong language, being "thrown out" takes on more ominous nuance when placed alongside the language of being cast into "outer darkness" (Matt 22:14; 25:29) or into prison (Luke 12:59) or being thrown away like the bad stuff caught in the net (Matt 13:50). Similarly, the comment "Where the corpse is, there the vultures will gather" (Matt 24:28 // Luke 17:37) would imply something grim, even if it were not embedded in apocalyptic contexts.

Other examples include: the threat of pigs "tearing in pieces" (ῥήξωσιν, Matt 7:6); "collapse/ruin" of a house (ἡ πτῶσις, Matt 7:27; τὸ ῥῆγμα, Luke 6:49); "extortioners" (ἅρπαγες Luke 18:11); the danger of being imprisoned (εἰς φυλακήν, Matt 5:25–26 // Luke 12:58–59); and references to the master as a "severe" or "hard" man in the parable of the Talents/Minas (σκληρός, Matt 25:24; αὐστηρός, Luke 19:21).

In the next group, I place those with clearly violent language, but the violence is not directed at human beings. Of course, in a metaphorical transfer, human beings may come into consideration, but at the level of the narrative itself, the reference is to non-human things. Four parables deal with plants that have either been planted improperly or have proved to produce either bad fruit or no fruit. In the parable of the Wheat and Tares, the tares have actually been sown by the enemy and are to be gathered into bundles and burned (Συλλέξατε πρῶτον τὰ ζιζάνια καὶ δήσατε αὐτὰ εἰς δέσμας πρὸς τὸ κατακαῦσαι αὐτά, Matt 13:30). In a similar vein, Matt 15:13 states simply: "Every plant that my heavenly Father has not planted will be uprooted" (ἐκριζωθήσεται). The parable of the Good and Bad Trees occurs in both Matthew and Luke. The wording varies, but in the first part the two versions make the similar point that a tree can be determined by its fruit. At that point they diverge significantly and in Matthew's version the tree that does not bear good fruit is destined to be "cut down and thrown into the fire" (ἐκκόπτεται καὶ εἰς πῦρ βάλλεται, Matt 7:20). Luke has a longer parable about an unproductive fig tree. In that parable, the master, after three years of looking for fruit and finding none, tells the vinedresser to cut it down (ἔκκοψον). The vinedresser asks that he be allowed to tend the tree for one more year to see whether it will bear fruit at that time. If it does not, he says, "you will cut it down" (ἐκκόψεις αὐτήν, Luke 13:9). While the fate of the fig tree is not yet settled, it is clear that, if it fails to produce fruit, it will join the bad tree and the falsely planted crops in being destroyed.

The parable of the Kingdom Divided is impersonal but it serves as a transition to the parables that are explicitly about people. The language of destruction is most moderate in Mark: "If a kingdom is divided against itself, that kingdom cannot stand (οὐ δύναται σταθῆναι). And if a house is divided against itself, that house will not be able to stand (οὐ δυνήσεται...σταθῆναι). And if Satan has risen up against himself and is divided, he cannot stand, but is coming to an end (οὐ δύναται στῆναι ἀλλὰ τέλος ἔχει)" (Mark 3:24–26). In Matthew and Luke the divided kingdom is not only one that cannot stand, it in fact is "laid waste" (ἐρημοῦται, Matt 12:25 // Luke 11:17). This is the language of a city or kingdom falling in war and is a favorite of historical and geographical writers.[40] Furthermore Luke replaces the language of a house divided with the note that in such a kingdom "house falls on house" (οἶκος ἐπὶ οἶκον πίπτει).

In the parables that involve human beings we encounter the language of robbery, beating, strangling, torture, burning, enslavement, brigandage, murder, imprisonment, execution, and wholesale destruction of a city and its inhabitants.[41] The language of violence is most dense in four parables: Tenants in the Vineyard, the Wedding Feast,[42] the Unforgiving Slave, and the Good Samaritan. These four parables need to be dealt with individually and so I set them aside for the moment.

In Strong Man (Matt 12:29; Mark 3:27; Luke 11:21–22) and Beware of the Thief (Matt 24:43–44; Luke 12:39–40), the principal concern is robbery. But these two parables address the issue from opposite perspectives. In the Strong Man, the story is told from the point of view of the person who undertakes to rob the strong man and the language is that of entering, binding, and plundering (Mark and Matthew) or of attacking, conquering, stripping the armour, and dividing the spoils. Conversely, in Beware of the Thief, the story is told from the point of view of the householder (οἰκοδεσπότης) who, had he known when the thief was coming, would not have allowed his house to be broken into (διορυχθῆναι).

There is a wide variety of language available to describe beating in various forms. One of the more striking words (pardon the pun) is in the parable of the Widow and the Judge. The judge is anxious that the widow will harm him, but translators often avoid the blunt force of ὑπωπιάζῃ. The verb is used only one other time in the New Testament: "I punish my body and enslave it" (NRSV; ὑπωπιάζω μου τὸ σῶμα καὶ δουλαγωγῶ, 1 Cor 9:27). The cognate noun ὑπώπιον is more common in classical texts than the verb and one example from Cassius Dio will serve to illustrate the meaning and to reinforce the larger context of this chapter, although it involves events in Rome rather than Roman Palestine. Nero had a practice of going about the streets of Rome at night in disguise and beating and stripping those whom he encountered, outraging women and boys and even going so far as to break into homes. On one occasion, Julius Montanus, incensed at the mistreatment of his wife, attacked Nero and beat him so badly that Nero "had to remain in concealment several days by reason of the black eyes (τῶν ὑπωπίων) he had received" (61.9.3). The judge is not concerned that the widow will "wear him out," he is concerned that she will beat him.[43]

---

[40] Examples can be found in Herodotus, Thucydides, Diodorus Siculus, Dionysius of Halicarnassus, Josephus, Cassius Dio, and in Strabo and Pausanias.
[41] Absent from the list is any reference to crucifixion.
[42] Luke's parable of the Banquet lacks any violence and for this reason, among many, is sufficiently different from Matthew's royal wedding feast that it should be regarded as a separate parable altogether.
[43] See Ellen Aasland Reinertsen's discussion of this parable in this volume.

Two other parables that involve beating feature slaves. As noted earlier, slaves were regularly subject to beating and various mistreatment. The parable of Two Slaves (Luke 12:47–48) is often regarded as simply a redactional conclusion to the parable of the Faithful and Unfaithful Slaves (Luke 12:42–46),[44] but even if it is a Lukan redaction, it is sufficiently different from the earlier parable to warrant being treated separately. Furthermore, the language of violence is importantly different in the two parables. In the parable of Two Slaves both will be beaten (δαρήσεται) but the degree of beating varies, depending on whether or not the slave knowingly failed his master. Even the slave who acted in ignorance is described as having done "things deserving of blows" (ἄξια πληγῶν), but because he did not know the will of his master he is beaten with few (blows). The slave who knew the will of his master but did not ready himself and act in accordance with that will be beaten with many (blows).

Things are very different in the parable of the Faithful and Unfaithful Slaves. First, one of the slaves behaves entirely properly and is rewarded abundantly by his master. Indeed, he is introduced in the parable as "faithful and wise." The second slave in this parable not only abuses the master's trust, he goes so far as to abuse his fellow slaves; he begins to beat them (ἄρξηται τύπτειν τοὺς συνδούλους αὐτοῦ, Matt 24:49 / ἄρξηται τύπτειν τοὺς παῖδας καὶ τὰς παιδίσκας, Luke 12:45). When the master returns unexpectedly and finds what this slave is up to he does not simply beat him, but rather he "cuts him in two" (διχοτομήσει). This verb is reasonably rare outside of astronomical texts. It occurs once in Josephus, *A.J.* 8.31 in the story of Solomon proposing to cut both the living and dead babies in two in order to give half of each to the two women who both claimed to be the mother of the living baby. It also occurs in Plutarch, *Pyrrhus* 24 in a graphic description of Pyrrhus cutting an enemy in two from the top of his head down through his body and thereby instilling fear in all. And in 3 Baruch 16 we find a reference to divine punishment in an apocalyptic setting. The brutality of the language is inescapable and the parable does not aim to soften it by referring simply to some kind of metaphorical severing of individuals from the larger people of God.[45]

In Luke's parable of the Minas the violent conclusion is much more severe than the parallel parable of the Talents in Matthew. Matthew's account ends with the master ordering that the slave who had done nothing with the talent entrusted to him be thrown into outer darkness where there would be weeping and gnashing of teeth (τὸν ἀχρεῖον δοῦλον ἐκβάλετε εἰς τὸ σκότος τὸ ἐξώτερον· ἐκεῖ ἔσται ὁ

---

[44] It is even handled that way in the *Kompendium* which, in other instances, does not hesitate to treat even small pericopes independently.

[45] For example, Joel B. Green, *The Gospel of Luke* (Grand Rapids, MI: Eerdmans, 1997), 505: "Verses 46–47 paint a horrifying picture. 'Cutting in two' is known as a severe punishment. Though in the present co-text its meaning is not likely to be taken in such a literal, physical way, this does not detract from its repulsiveness." On the other hand, Klyne Snodgrass, *Stories with Intent: A Comprehensive Guide to the Parables of Jesus*, 2nd ed. (Grand Rapids, MI: Eerdmans, 2018), 502, inclines to a more literal rendering while acknowledging the paradox of "literal" reading in a metaphoric text. He calls διχοτομήσει "a gripping hyperbole to underscore the punishment of the unfaithful servant, the polar opposite of the blessing to the faithful servant."

κλαυθμὸς καὶ ὁ βρυγμὸς τῶν ὀδόντων, Matt 25:30).[46] Luke's parable begins with a nobleman heading off to receive a kingdom. He is hated by at least a portion of his subjects. The parable ends with the unproductive and frightened slave apparently suffering nothing more than the loss of that which had been entrusted to him. Instead of focusing on the slave, the king turns rather to the people who did not want him as king and his orders are: "But as for these enemies of mine, who did not want me to reign over them, bring them here and slaughter (κατασφάξατε) them before me" (Luke 19:27). Again, there is no escaping the brutality of the order and the overtones of slaughter.[47]

In the parables discussed so far, there are usually one or two types of violence involved and some limitation on the language used. That does not mean that the violence is muted, as seen with the language of bisecting and slaughter, but it is focused. I turn now to four parables in which there is a remarkable density of violent language.

2.1.1. *The Good Samaritan.* In the parable of the Good Samaritan there are five terms of violence, four of which occur in the very first sentence (Luke 10:30):

A man was going down from Jerusalem to Jericho, and fell into the hands of *robbers*, who *stripped* him, *beat* him, and went away, leaving him *half dead*.

Ἄνθρωπός τις κατέβαινεν ἀπὸ Ἰερουσαλὴμ εἰς Ἰεριχὼ καὶ λῃσταῖς περιέπεσεν, οἳ καὶ ἐκδύσαντες αὐτὸν καὶ πληγὰς ἐπιθέντες ἀπῆλθον ἀφέντες ἡμιθανῆ.

This is the only parable in which "robbers/bandits/brigands" (λῇσται) appear. This word occurs most frequently in ancient novels where the world of banditry provides plentiful material for adventure and daring.[48] It is also frequently found in geographical and historical texts and especially in the works of Josephus where it occurs more than 200 times, more than half in the *Jewish War*. By contrast, the term is very restricted in its use in the New Testament. Apart from the two uses in this parable it turns up in only three contexts in the life of Jesus, including a discourse in John 10, and once in Paul's description in 2 Corinthians 11 of his many sufferings and hardships.

In the discourse on the good shepherd in John 10, Jesus declares that the one who does not enter by the gate is a "thief and bandit" (κλέπτης ἐστὶν καὶ λῃστής,

---

[46] The phrase "weeping and gnashing of teeth" itself could also be included in a register of violent language. It occurs six times in Matthew (8:12; 13:42, 50; 22:13; 24:51; 25:30) and once in Luke (13:28). Five of the occurrences in Matthew are attached to parables: Wheat and Tares, Dragnet, Wedding Feast, Faithful and Unfaithful Slaves, and the Talents. It is possible to argue that all of these are redactional and do not belong to the parables proper, but they do point to at least one way of construing the parables and should not simply be dismissed in the interest of interpreting the parables more benignly.

[47] Zech 11:4–6. Frequent use in 2 Maccabees (5:12, 24; 6:9; 8:24; 10:17, 31, 37; 12:26) The similarities between this parable and the behavior of Archelaus upon Herod the Great's death are evocative.

[48] See Brent Shaw, "Bandits in the Roman Empire," *Past & Present* 105 (1984): 43.

10:1). He goes on to claim that "All who came before me are thieves and bandits (κλέπται...καὶ λῃσταί);[49] but the sheep did not listen to them" (10:8). The passage from 2 Corinthians has already been noted in the discussion of types of beating. In listing the many types of dangers that he had endured Paul includes being in danger from "bandits" (κινδύνοις λῃστῶν, 11:26).

The other two contexts in the life of Jesus are his cleansing of the Temple and his arrest, trial, and crucifixion. In the former he cites Jer 7:11 and accuses those in the Temple of having made it a "den of robbers" (σπήλαιον λῃστῶν).[50] In the accounts of Jesus's arrest, trial, and crucifixion the term λῇσται occurs in three distinct ways. First, when the officials come to arrest him in Gethsemane, he asks: "Have you come out with swords and clubs as against a bandit?" (ὡς ἐπὶ λῃστὴν ἐξήλθατε μετὰ μαχαιρῶν καὶ ξύλων, Luke 22:52).[51] During Jesus's trial, Pilate provides the crowd with a choice between releasing Jesus of Nazareth or Jesus Barabbas. Whereas the Synoptic Gospels describe Barabbas as a "notorious prisoner" (Matthew) who was in prison with the rebels (τῶν στασιαστῶν) who had committed murder during the insurrection" (Mark and Luke), it is John who explicitly labels Barabbas a λῃστής (John 18:40). And finally, in Mark and Matthew the two who were crucified with Jesus are identified as λῇσται.[52] Luke simply refers to them as "evildoers" (κακοῦργοι, 23:32, 33, 39). From the larger context, and taking into account the material from John as well as the Synoptic Gospels, it seems that Jesus, Barabbas, and the other two who were crucified were all swept up in the context of the ongoing disturbances that were rife throughout Palestine. Indeed, Jesus's question in the garden highlights the normalcy of using swords and clubs when rounding up such characters.

The "robbers" then stripped and beat the traveller. And they beat him so badly that he is described as being left "half dead." The uncommon word for "stripping" occurs nowhere else in Luke and the only other instances of the word in the New Testament are in Matthew and Mark in the context of Jesus being stripped of his clothing, dressed in a purple robe, and then subsequently stripped of that robe.[53] As for the beating, πληγή is used by Luke in this passage, in the one noted above about the Two Slaves, and twice in Acts 16 in the context of the official beating of Paul and Silas in Philippi. Other than that, the only New Testament writer to use this word is the author of the Revelation where it frequently means "plague."

The only other term of violence in this parable is τραῦμα (10:34). This is the only use of this word in the New Testament, although it is quite frequent in other sources, most notably in the Hippocratic corpus.[54] Is it too much of a stretch to suggest that this language would be well known to Luke the physician?

---

[49] This use of both κλέπτης and λῃστής suggests that the two words are not synonymous. Translating λῃστής as "robber" or "thief" is not adequate, especially given the clear indication in other sources that λῃσταί were involved in much more than simple robbery.
[50] Matt 21:13 // Mark 11:17 // Luke 19:46. This is the term used in the LXX of Jer 7:11.
[51] Matt 26:55 and Mark 14:48 add "to arrest me" (Ὡς ἐπὶ λῃστὴν ἐξήλθατε μετὰ μαχαιρῶν καὶ ξύλων συλλαβεῖν με;).
[52] Mark 15:27 // Matt 27:38, 44.
[53] Matt 27:28, 31 // Mark 15:20.
[54] See, for example, the ubiquitous use of τραῦμα in the treatise "On Wounds in the Head."

2.1.2. *The Wedding Feast.* Matthew's parable of the Wedding Feast also presents a dense collection of violent language, but most of the terms are quite common. Richard Bauckham has demonstrated the importance of seeing that this is not simply a story about a banquet, but it is a story about a king sending invitations to the wedding feast prepared for his son.[55] Such an invitation is, by its very nature, a political event and refusal to come from the towns under the king's rule is tantamount to insurrection. That point is made explicit in v. 6 when the people of the town abuse and even kill the messengers who are sent to them. The behavior of the invitees is described with three verbs increasing in violence: "the rest *seized* his slaves, *mistreated* them, and *killed* them." (οἱ δὲ λοιποὶ κρατήσαντες τοὺς δούλους αὐτοῦ ὕβρισαν καὶ ἀπέκτειναν.) None of these words is particularly unusual, but the piling up with the increase in severity gives the passage an especially hard tone. This sets the scene for the following verse in which the angered king determines to exact punishment on those "murderers" (φονεῖς). And his mode of punishment escalates the violence to a new level. In the banquet parables in Luke 14 and Gospel of Thomas 64, the people who refuse the invitations are not "murderers" nor do they suffer any consequence beyond the displeasure of the host and an indication that they will not be given any further opportunities to enjoy his hospitality. But in Matthew's parable, the king sends his troops against the city, destroys "those murderers" and burns their city. The response might appear to be out of proportion to the offence, but seizing, outraging, and murdering messengers who have come with invitations must also appear disproportionate.

The verb "burn" is used only here in the New Testament, but it is very common in the LXX. I draw attention only to the examples in Joshua: in 6:24, the burning of Jericho; in 8:19, the burning of Ai; in 11:9–13, burning of Mizpeh and Hazor and sparing of the other towns; and in a supplement in the LXX to 16:10, the burning of Gezer by the Pharaoh of Egypt.

In the coda to the parable, a guest turns up who does not have proper wedding attire. Again, the king's response is violent. He gives almost the same order that the master in the parable of the Talents gives: "Bind him hand and foot and cast him into the outer darkness. In that place there will be weeping and gnashing of teeth" (δήσαντες αὐτοῦ πόδας καὶ χεῖρας ἐκβάλετε αὐτὸν εἰς τὸ σκότος τὸ ἐξώτερον· ἐκεῖ ἔσται ὁ κλαυθμὸς καὶ ὁ βρυγμὸς τῶν ὀδόντων, Matt 22:13).

2.1.3. *The Tenants in the Vineyard.* This parable appears in all three Synoptic Gospels[56] and with substantial agreement in the language of violence. Kill (ἀποκτείνω), beat (δέρω), and destroy (ἀπόλλυμι) are in all three and are the heart

---

[55] Richard Bauckham, "The Parable of the Royal Wedding Feast (Matthew 22:1–14) and the Parable of the Lame Man and the Blind Man (Apocryphon of Ezekiel)," *JBL* 115 (1996): 484: "It is only because interpreters so regularly fail to register the political significance of the wedding feast of the king's son that they equally regularly find v. 7 explicable only as an allegorical reference to the destruction of Jerusalem, which has been inserted incongruously into the story"

[56] Matt 21:33–46 // Mark 12:1–12 // Luke 20:9–19. This parable has been the subject of a great deal of scholarly study not only in discussion of the parables in their own right, but also in works on violence. See, for example, David J. Neville, *The Vehement Jesus: Grappling with Troubling*

of the violent language. At least two also use terms for dishonoring/treating shamefully (ἀτιμάω), seizing (λαμβάνω) and for casting out (ἐκβάλλω). There are, of course, differences in the number of slaves sent and the number of visits made before the master decides to send his son.

For all the similarity of language and expression, each author has one unique verb for describing how the tenants treated the messengers that were sent to them. Mark has the verb κεφαλιόω which appears to be *hapax legomenon*. While injury to the head might point to a fatal injury or even to beheading, it seems preferable to give it a less severe meaning. There appears to be an escalation of violence: the first is beaten and sent away, the second is beaten about the head (but not killed) and treated shamefully, and the third is killed. Mark goes on to say that many others were subsequently sent, some of whom the tenants beat and some of whom they killed. Matthew's unique verb of violence in this parable is "to stone" (λιθοβολέω). His sequence is "beat," "kill," "stone." If the stoning did not result in death, then it seems to be at the wrong point in the sequence; if it did result in death, then it is just a variation on the simple verb of killing. It does not indicate an escalation of violence, unless stoning is regarded as a harsher form of death. As in Mark's account, Matthew then generalizes by saying that many others were subsequently sent and that the tenants treated them in the same way. The unique verb in Luke's version of the parable is τραυματίζω. It only occurs in Luke and Acts and corresponds to Luke's use of the noun τραῦμα in the parable of the Good Samaritan and may point to his medical interests.

In Matthew and Luke's versions there is a coda about the stone that the builders rejected which has become the capstone (Ps 118:22). There then follows: "The one who falls on this stone will be crushed (συνθλασθήσεται); and it will thresh (λικμήσει) anyone on whom it falls."[57] Συνθλάω clearly means to crush. It occurs a number of times in the LXX, especially in the Psalms, as a metaphor of God's power. It also occurs in two graphic instances of killing: Jael's pounding of a tent peg through Sisera's head (Judg 5:26), and a woman who threw a millstone on the head of Abimelech, thereby crushing his head and killing him (Judg 9:53).[58] The primary meaning of λικμάω is to winnow. By extension, it is frequently used in the sense of God's judgment in separating wheat from chaff.[59]

Gospel Texts (Eugene, OR: Cascade Books, 2017), and Thomas R. Yoder Neufeld, *Killing Enmity: Violence and the New Testament* (Grand Rapids, MI: Baker Academic, 2011). Any discussion of this parable is confronted by and aided by the monumental work by John Kloppenborg, *The Tenants in the Vineyard: Ideology, Economics, and Agrarian Conflict in Jewish Palestine*, WUNT 195 (Tübingen: Mohr Siebeck, 2006). For a helpful guide through much of the scholarship leading up to Kloppenborg's work and in the decade following, see Gregory R. Lanier, "Mapping the Vineyard: Main Lines of Investigation Regarding the Parable of the Tenants in the Synoptics and Thomas," *Currents in Biblical Research* 15, no. 1 (2016): 74–122.

[57] The verse appears in Luke 20:18, but the MS tradition for Matt 21:44 is divided on whether or not to include it.

[58] It is tempting to see in this the "crushing" of the person's chest as described in the Rabbinic sources for the proper procedures for stoning (*m. Sanh.* 6). This procedure involved casting the condemned person from a height to crush him in the fall. If that did not prove fatal, stones were to be cast on his chest to complete the crushing.

[59] Although the word is different, the same concept is found in John the Baptist's remark about Jesus having his winnowing fan in his hand (Matt 3:12).

2.1.4. *The Unforgiving Slave.* In the parable of the Unforgiving Slave (Matt 18:23–35) nobody dies, but there is a dense cluster of words connoting violence. Again there is the language of "seizing" (κρατήσας, v. 28), and "throwing into prison" (ἔβαλεν αὐτὸν εἰς φυλακὴν, v. 30), but there are also three new terms: "selling" (πραθῆναι, v. 25) of the person; "strangling" (ἔπνιγεν, v. 28); and handing over to "torturers" (τοῖς βασανισταῖς, v. 34). Selling of persons is not particularly remarkable language, although it is a bit difficult to see how the king expects to be repaid if the man is sold and it is also a bit difficult to see why he would hand him over to torturers. The torturers are well known figures from this period. Herod had torturers at the ready and the concept is satirized in Petronius's *Satyricon* with the boorish nouveau riche Trimalchio having torturers on his staff ready to torture any slave who might displease him.[60]

2.2. Violent Actors

In sketching the landscape of violence in the parables, it is also important to consider who actually commits the acts of violence. In the majority of cases, there is one actor and frequently that actor is impersonal or merely implied. Only in the case of the potentially violent pigs do we find non-human actors who actually initiate the violence.

In the parables of Kingdom Divided, Two Houses, and the Pharisee and Tax Collector, the destruction or abuse is inherent in the situation and is not specifically caused by an identifiable actor. The divided kingdom simply cannot stand, the house on sand will suffer ruin, and the world of the Pharisee and tax collector is one that has to endure (or be?) extortioners. Closely related are the parables where a personal actor may be assumed, but the identity is not important to the narrative. So in the case of the Strong Man, the person who will break in and bind him, that is, play the role of the robber, is "you." In the parables of Salt and Rooted Up the verbs are passive or impersonal. Presumably the fishermen are the unidentified "they" in the parable of the Dragnet. The tree that bears bad fruit will be cut down and thrown into the fire. In these parables there is no focus on the actor, simply on the act/experience and its consequences. Any understanding of these parables must focus on the violence suffered,[61] not on any violence committed. In some ways the parable of the Corpse and the Vultures is an ideal distillation of this type.

It may be appropriate to put the parable of the Two Slaves in the same group since the verbs are passive and, again, the attention is on the beating suffered, not on the one who administers the beating. Each of the slaves in this parable has a master whose will is to be obeyed, but that master plays no other explicit role.

There is a subtle shift in actor in the parable of the Barren Fig Tree. When the owner finds that, for the third year running, the tree is still unproductive, he orders the vineyard keeper to cut it down. But the keeper cleverly avoids doing

---

[60] *Satyricon* 49.6. See Barry Baldwin, "Trimalchio's Domestic Staff," *Acta Classica* 21 (1978): 87–97 and Saller, *Patriarchy*, 148.
[61] See "2.3. Suffering Violence" below.

any such harm. Instead, he offers to care for the tree and nurture it in hopes that it will produce. Of course, that outcome is not guaranteed and he is in no position to resist the owner. So he makes a deal with the owner: "If it bears fruit next year, well and good; but if not, you will cut it down (ἐκκόψεις αὐτήν)." What the owner commanded the worker to do, the worker now claims that the owner himself will do, if necessary.

Each of the parables Opponent at Law, Beware of the Thief, and the Widow and the Judge has two characters, one of whom is potentially violent. In the case of the Opponent at Law the warning is to "you" to take care and avoid being hauled off to the judge and thrown into prison. The potentially violent action of the opponent can be circumvented. The past contrafactual condition in Beware of the Thief suggests that the householder could also have circumvented the potentially violent action of his house being broken into, but he did not take the necessary action. This instance seems to show a certain carelessness on the householder's part, at least partially accounted for by ignorance. In the parable of the Widow and the Judge it is not completely clear that the widow may blacken the judge's eye. That thought is only expressed in the voice of the judge and he may be incorrect. What does remain, however, is that within the dynamics of the parable, it is at least imaginable that such could occur. Again, the threat of violence can be thwarted, if the judge responds to the widow's demand.

In the parable of the Good Samaritan the λῆσται are the only perpetrators of violence and they serve no extended function in the narrative. Although they clearly reflect a realistic context, their function in the story does not reach beyond the abuse of the traveler. That said, it is clear that the situation requires that the traveler be both a victim and, in many ways, a completely ordinary and fungible character. The identity of the bandits, the Samaritan, the priest, and the Levite are all carefully revealed, but we have no idea who the traveler was. He is simply "some person" (ἄνθρωπός τις). We can know nothing about him other than that he was travelling from Jerusalem to Jericho and that he was attacked and left to die.

The parables of the Talents and of the Minas present a number of actors, but it is primarily the master of the slaves (a nobleman about to become a king in Luke's parable) who orders his attendants to carry out the violence. He himself does not seem to get in on the act, but he is certainly responsible. As noted above, the action taken by the new king against the citizens who did not want him to rule over them is conspicuous for its severity. In Matthew's parable the agents of the master's instructions are completely unidentified and voiceless. In Luke's parable they do question the king's order that the mina be taken from the one slave and given to the slave who had ten. The unnamed attendants question the action but are told that the principle at work is that more will be given to the one that has. They do not question the king's order to round up his enemies who opposed his being king and to slaughter them in his presence.

The Wheat and the Tares works very much in the same way as the Talents and the Minas. There is both a master and his workers who are responsible for the final destruction of the tares. There is another actor, namely the master's enemy, who came and sowed the tares in amongst the wheat. While his action was meant to cause harm, it should be seen more as destructive and malicious than as violent.[62] After his initial act, the enemy disappears from the story and suffers no consequences. When the harvest comes, the master orders his workers to bind up the tares and burn them in the fire. As with the parables of the Talents and the Minas, the actors are the subordinates, but they act on the orders of the master. They are again nameless, but there is some sense of them as characters in that they do engage the master in conversation and offer to gather in the tares. The master tells them to wait so as not to uproot (ἐκριζώσητε) the wheat. That is an interesting counterpart to the Rooted Up parable in which "Every plant that my Heavenly Father has not planted will be rooted up" (Matt 15:13). Here care is taken not to uproot the plants that the master has planted, even if it means that uprooting the others may have to wait for a period of time.

The parables of the Wedding Feast, the Tenants in the Vineyard, the Faithful and Unfaithful Slaves, and the Unforgiving Slave are more complex. In each there is a master who metes out brutal punishment against others who have themselves perpetrated violence. The king in the parable of the Wedding Feast does not initiate the violence; that is done by the invitees. Their abuse and murder of his messengers, their implicit rejection of his royal position provoke him to anger and in that anger he sends troops, burns their city, and destroys them. At some level, his action, while driven by anger, can be seen as an act of justice, not simply a tyrannical response. His subsequent action in tossing out the man not properly attired is somewhat less easy to understand. All we are told is that the man without the proper garment remains silent when questioned.

As in the parable of the Wedding Feast, the master in the Tenants in the Vineyard does not initiate the violence. It is certainly possible to move outside the narrative of the parable and create a narrative that attempts to excuse the beating, abuse, and murder, but that is not in the narrative. What is more, the punishment of the tenants is not actually narrated in the parable. Instead, the question is asked, "What will the owner of the vineyard do?" In Mark and Luke, Jesus provides the answer to his own question, but in Matthew's account it is the hearers who respond: "He will put those wretches to a miserable death (κακοὺς κακῶς ἀπολέσει αὐτούς), and lease the vineyard to other tenants who will give him the produce at the harvest time." (Matt 21:41).

In the parable of the Faithful and Unfaithful Slaves we are able to see the master's behavior clearly in the face of noble action as well as in the face of violence and outrage. The slave has been entrusted not only with his master's possessions, but also with the care of others to ensure that their needs are met. The slave who rises to the challenge and shows that he will see to the needs not only of his master but of his fellow slaves as well will be richly rewarded by that master. But the other slave not only fails in his responsibility to see to the master's possessions and care for those in his charge, he actually becomes

---

[62] Of course, he may have been intending not only to spoil the crop, but also to poison the owner. See J. R. C. Cousland, "Toxic Tares: The Poisonous Weeds (Ζιζάνια) in Matthew's Parable of the Tares (Matthew 13.24–30, 36–43)," *NTS* 61, no. 3 (2015): 395–410, for discussion of the type of plant under consideration.

violent toward them. His behavior and character are revealed in his beating of fellow slaves and eating and drinking with drunkards. The master responds with remarkably violent punishment; he cuts the slave in two.

Finally, in the parable of the Unforgiving Slave there are three violent actors. Not only does the unforgiving slave behave violently and bring upon himself the actions of the king (through anonymous attendants), but we also have the introduction of the torturers.

2.3. Suffering Violence

From the language of violence and violent actors, I turn finally to those who suffer violence in the parables. The pattern of sufferings suggests three broad divisions.

2.3.1. *Nature.* In one group, especially involving impersonal characters, we find that the suffering is plainly consequent on the nature of the "victim." And so a divided kingdom or a house built on sand will suffer ruin simply because of what they are. The same is true for salt that is no longer salty, for tares, for the trash that turns up in the dragnet, and for plants that the Father did not plant. In all of these cases the very nature of the thing is cause for it being rooted up, burned, thrown out. That is the reality of the realia of these parables. Any interpretation must not attempt to evade the clear dynamics of these stories. These things fail or are destroyed because they are by nature fit for nothing else. "Where the corpse is the vultures will gather."

2.3.2. *Behavior.* In yet another group we find that rather than the nature of the actor it is the behavior that matters. These suffer, not because of what they are, but because of what they do. This group must itself be further subdivided.

In the parables of Opponent at Law, the Unjust Judge, and the Barren Fig Tree there is an opportunity to avoid any violent outcome. But that is contingent on the behavior of the one who will otherwise suffer punishment, abuse, or destruction. Closely related to this group of parables are those in which the suffering has occurred, but there is a modicum of sympathy for the victim as it seems that the behavior was not so much wicked as negligent or careless or a matter of ignorance. For example: the slave who is beaten with few blows, having failed to do his master's will because he did not know it; or the person who suffered a break in at his house because he did not know when the thief would come and did not take suitable precautions; or perhaps even the recipient of one talent/mina who in fear hid what had been entrusted to him intending to return it undiminished. In each of these cases, however, the individual is held accountable for his behavior. In the case of the ignorant slave, the text explicitly says that he, in his ignorance, did things deserving of beating (ἄξια πληγῶν).

The next group of parables includes those whose behavior is itself violent and the violence which they suffer in turn is seen as consequent on their behavior. Those invited to the royal banquet who chose instead to beat and kill the messengers, the slave who, rather than caring for the possessions and people entrusted to him, indulged himself and beat his fellow slaves, the tenants who beat and murdered those sent to them, including the owner's son, and the slave who, though relieved of an overwhelming debt, strangled and imprisoned his fellow slave, all provoked the response of the king or master or owner to whom they were accountable.

2.3.3. *Victims.* The last group is in many ways the most troubling and, arguably, appears in the parables because it is intractably rooted in the social realities of Jesus's world. These are the people who are simply and plainly the victims of violence, not because of their inherent nature nor because of their behavior. At the top of that list is the traveller in the parable of the Good Samaritan. As noted above, the identity of the bandits, the Samaritan, the priest, and the Levite are all carefully revealed, but we have no idea who the traveler was. He is simply "some person" (ἄνθρωπός τις). We can know nothing about him other than that he was travelling from Jerusalem to Jericho and that he was attacked and left to die. Any attempt to find him culpable in any way is to reach far beyond what the narrative itself will allow.

In the parables of the Faithful and Unfaithful Slaves and the Unforgiving Slave, it is the fellow slaves who suffer at the hands of one of their own. When the unfaithful slave notes that his master has been away for a long time he concludes that he can do whatever he wants and so he begins to beat his fellow slaves. As noted above, it is that behavior that makes him liable to the anger of the master and he is sundered. But what of those fellow slaves? We know only two things about them: they are slaves and they were supposed to be cared for by the one who had been left in charge. Instead they have become his victims.

A similar situation obtains with the unforgiving slave. Despite being relieved of enormous debt, he strangles and imprisons a fellow slave who owes him a small amount. In this parable we hear from the other fellow slaves. They are grieved (ἐλυπήθησαν) at the violent behavior of their fellow slave and report to the king what had happened. It is worth noting the emotional responses that the behavior of this slave provokes. When that slave pleaded for patience the king was moved to pity (σπλαγχνισθείς), but when he responded with violence, the king was moved to anger (ὀργισθείς).[63]

Finally, in the parable of the Tenants in the Vineyard the violent acts of beating, stoning, killing, and disgracing the messengers perpetrated by the tenants renders the messengers as victims. As in other parables, we know very little about these individuals. They are not given voice and we know only that they are sent to collect the fruit from the vineyard.

This group of victims of violence is in some ways the most troubling. With the parables in which violence is suffered because of nature or behavior one can see a rough justice at work. But that is not the case with these victims. Here it

---

[63] Clearly I disagree with Ernest van Eck, *The Parables of Jesus the Galilean: Stories of a Social Prophet* (Eugene, OR: Cascade Books, 2016), 161–83, who ends the parable with the rhetorical question in v. 33.

seems that the only explanation is the lamentable reality of human experience. And perhaps here as much as anywhere we see in the parables a cold reflection of the realities of life in the time of Jesus.

3. Jesus as Teller of Violent Stories

As I said at the outset, the problems of Jesus and violence are beyond the scope of this study. A few observations do emerge, however, that should form part of interpretation of these parables. The first is simply that the violence that does occur in Jesus's parables is entirely at home in the context of first-century Palestine. Even the seemingly extreme instances of burning cities and slaughtering enemies, or handing someone over to torturers are easily paralleled in the world of Jesus. The second observation is that Jesus does not avoid these settings, characters, and language. Perhaps most pointedly, he does not avoid settings in which people are treated with violence for no clear reason other than that other people have abused them; there are true victims in these stories. The third point is that however one may choose to interpret the violent parables those interpretations must face that violence square on. It will not do to diminish the violence out of squeamishness or a desire to render Jesus meek and mild. The "lamb that was slain" lived in and knew violence and we will not hear or see his teaching if we pretend that he was merely having a lovely chat in a genteel country club, a university classroom, or at a church potluck.

Bibliography

Bauckham, Richard. "The Parable of the Royal Wedding Feast (Matthew 22:1–14) and the Parable of the Lame Man and the Blind Man (Apocryphon of Ezekiel)." *JBL* 115 (1996): 471–88.

Baldwin, Barry. "Trimalchio's Domestic Staff." *Acta Classica* 21 (1978): 87–97.

Beavis, Mary Ann. "Ancient Slavery as an Interpretive Context for the New Testament Servant Parables with Special Reference to the Unjust Steward (Luke 16:1–8)." *JBL* 111 (1992): 37–54.

Bradley, K. R. *Slavery and Society at Rome.* Cambridge: Cambridge University Press, 1994.

Brunt, P. A. "Evidence Given Under Torture at Rome." *Zeitschrift der Savigny-Stiftung für Rechtsgeschichte. Romanistische Abteilung* 97 (1980): 256–65.

Carter, Warren. "Constructions of Violence and Identities in Matthew's Gospel." In *Violence in the New Testament*, edited by Shelly Matthews and E. Leigh Gibson, 80–108. New York: T&T Clark, 2005.

Carter, Warren. "Resisting and Imitating the Empire: Imperial Paradigms in Two Matthean Parables." *Interpretation* 56, no. 3 (2002): 260–72.

Carter, Warren. "Sanctioned Violence in the New Testament." *Interpretation: A Journal of Bible and Theology* 71, no. 3 (2017): 284–97.

Cousland, J. R. C. "Toxic Tares: The Poisonous Weeds (Ζιζάνια) in Matthew's Parable of the Tares (Matthew 13.24–30, 36–43)." *NTS* 61, no. 3 (2015): 395–410.

Freyne, Seán. *Galilee From Alexander the Great to Hadrian*. Edinburgh: T. & T. Clark, 1980.
Glancy, Jennifer A. "Slaves and Slavery in the Matthean Parables." *JBL* 119, no. 1 (2000): 67–90.
Glancy, Jennifer A. *Slavery in Early Christianity*. Oxford: Oxford University Press, 2002.
Glancy, Jennifer A. "The Sexual Use of Slaves: A Response to Kyle Harper on Jewish and Christian Porneia." *JBL* 134, no. 1 (2015): 215–29.
Green, Joel B. *The Gospel of Luke*. Grand Rapids, MI: Eerdmans, 1997.
Hezser, Catherine. *Jewish Slavery in Antiquity*. Oxford: Oxford University Press, 2006.
Hezser, Catherine. "Slavery and the Jews." In *The Cambridge World History of Slavery, Vol. 1*, edited by Keith Bradley and Paul Catledge, 438–55. Cambridge: Cambridge University Press, 2011.
Horsley, Richard A. "'By the Finger of God': Jesus and Imperial Violence." In *Violence in the New Testament*, edited by Shelly Matthews and E. Leigh Gibson, 51–80. New York: T&T Clark, 2005.
Horsley, Richard A. *Jesus and the Spiral of Violence: Popular Jewish Resistance in Roman Palestine*. Minneapolis, MN: Fortress Press, 1993.
Kloppenborg, J. S. "Unsocial Bandits." In *A Wandering Galilean: Essays in Honour of Seán Freyne*, edited by Margaret Daly-Denton, Anne Fitzpatrick Mckinley, and Zuleika Rodgers, 451–84. Leiden: Brill, 2009.
Kloppenborg, John S. *The Tenants in the Vineyard: Ideology, Economics, and Agrarian Conflict in Jewish Palestine*. WUNT 195. Tübingen: Mohr Siebeck, 2006.
Lanier, Gregory R. "Mapping the Vineyard: Main Lines of Investigation Regarding the Parable of the Tenants in the Synoptics and Thomas." *Currents in Biblical Research* 15, no. 1 (2016): 74–122.
Mason, Steve. *Flavius Josephus: Translation and Commentary, Volume 1B: Judean War 2*. Flavius Josephus. Leiden: Brill, 2008.
Neville, David J. *The Vehement Jesus: Grappling with Troubling Gospel Texts*. Eugene, OR: Cascade Books, 2017
Saller, Richard P. *Patriarchy, Property and Death in the Roman Family*. Cambridge Studies in Population, Economy, and Society in Past Time. Cambridge: Cambridge University Press, 1994.
Shaw, Brent D. "Bandits in the Roman Empire." *Past & Present* 105 (1984): 3–52.
Snodgrass, Klyne. *Stories With Intent: A Comprehensive Guide to the Parables of Jesus*. 2nd ed. Grand Rapids, MI: Eerdmans, 2018.
Van Eck, Ernest. *The Parables of Jesus the Galilean: Stories of a Social Prophet*. Eugene, OR: Cascade Books, 2016.
Yoder Neufeld, Thomas R. *Killing Enmity: Violence and the New Testament*. Grand Rapids, MI: Baker Academic, 2011.
Zimmermann, Ruben, Detlev Dormeyer, Gabi Kern, Annette Merz, Christian Münch, and Enno Edzard Popkes, eds., *Kompendium der Gleichnisse Jesu*. Gütersloh: Gütersloher Verlagshaus, 2007.
Zimmermann, Ruben. *Puzzling the Parables of Jesus: Methods and Interpretation*. Minneapolis, MN: Fortress Press, 2015.

οἰκοδεσπότης, κύριος, AND βασιλεύς: IDENTIFYING THOSE WITH SLAVES IN MATTHEAN PARABLES IN LIGHT OF THE LITERARY EVIDENCE AND *REALIA* OF ROMAN PALESTINE IN THE FIRST CENTURY

John Harrison

There are six parables in Matthew's Gospel that include characters who have "slaves" (δοῦλοι):[1] the Wheat and Weeds (13:24–30); the Unmerciful Slave (18:23–34); the Wicked Tenants (21:33–39), the Wedding Banquet (22:1–14); the Faithful/Wicked Slave (24:45–51), and the Talents (24:14–30).[2] Numerous studies on these specific parables and parables at large have helped to illuminate how they may have functioned either in the life of the historical Jesus and/or for the synoptic authors who composed them for their distinctive narrative purposes.[3] Many commentators have also noted aspects of slavery throughout

---

[1] Hendrick Goede lists fourteen different words found in LSJ that were used by Greeks to describe those in slavery, "Constructing Ancient Slavery as Socio-historic Context of the New Testament," *HTS* 69, no. 1 (2013): 1–7 (3). The only one of these that occurs in the Matthean parables is δοῦλος, though some figures are named (e.g. διάκονος) who likely served as slaves.

[2] For other lists of parables that contain identified "slaves" or those who are probably meant to be thought of as slaves (e.g. parable of the barren fig tree in Luke 13:6–9), see J. D. Crossan's *In Parables: The Challenge of the Historical Jesus* (New York: Harper & Row, 1973), 96–120; idem, "The Servant Parables of Jesus," *Semeia* 1 (1974): 17–32; and A. Weiser, *Die Knechtsgleichnisse der synoptischen Evangelien*, SANT 29 (Munich: Kösel, 1971).

[3] For example, see Mary Ann Beavis, "Ancient Slavery as an Interpretive Context for the New Testament Servant Parables with Special Reference to the Unjust Steward (Luke 16:1–8)," *JBL* 111, no. 1 (1992): 37–54, who draws from evidence of slaves as figures in the comedies of Plautus and the *Life of Aesop* to suggest that the tendency of some parables is to dignify the role of the slave and may even be suggesting that slaveowners identify with them (p. 54). Cf. Ernest van Eck and John S. Kloppenborg, "An Unexpected Patron: A Social-scientific and Realistic Reading of the Parable of the Vineyard Labourers (Matthew 20:1–15)," *HTS* 71, no. 1 (2015): 1–11; Ernest van Eck and Meshack Mandla Mashinini, "The Parables of Jesus as Critique on Food Shortage Systems for Vulnerable Households in Urban Townships," *HTS* 72, no. 3 (2016): 1–9; John Harrison "Weeds: Jesus' Parable and Economic and Political Threats to the Poor in Roman Galilee," *Stone-Campbell Journal* 18 (2015): 73–88; and Edmund Neufeld, "Vulnerable Bodies and Volunteer Slaves: Slave Parable Violence in the Rest of Matthew," *BBR* 30, no. 1 (2020): 41–63.

the greater Roman Empire to better appreciate the parables' background. But what is frequently missing in interpretations of these parables is any reference noting both the *realia* of slavery in Roman Palestine during the first centuries BCE and CE along with the literary evidence from the period to more narrowly characterize in social-ethnic terms who the Matthean audience (or even Jesus') might have assumed these slaves are likely serving.[4] Since some of these parables would have been heard with the assumption they reflect agricultural practices that used slaves in Palestine, this background information should be considered when determining how the parables may have been first heard by Matthew's audiences, who would have assumed a Galilean or Judean setting for them.[5]

In the present study, I briefly highlight some of the more significant literary and archaeological *realia* that indicate the type of people who owned slaves in Roman Palestine. I then suggest what this evidence might indicate about how Matthew's audience (if not the audience of the historical Jesus) would have heard these parables and envisioned the slaveowners socially, ethnically and politically. I begin with a brief introduction to some of the problems associated with defining "slaves," "slavery" and "slaveholders" in Roman society generally. I then review the details of those who are cast as figures who possess slaves in the Matthean parables before moving on to examine more closely the literary evidence and *realia* that identify those who owned slaves in Palestine. Finally, I will suggest what bearing and limitations this evidence has for describing who Matthew's audience might have conceived the social, ethnic, and political identities of these characters. I conclude that slaveholders in Matthew's parables, as the Roman Palestinian evidence also often indicates, are associated with the non-Jewish ruling class of the Roman Empire and wealthy land owners (more frequently—though not necessarily exclusively—non-Jews), which had large, commercial estates in certain areas of Palestine. The Matthean slave parables assume the status quo of slave ownership, condemn no slaveowners for any exercise of authority over their slaves and primarily utilizes them as characters Matthew's audience would have likely assumed represented the wealthy and powerful in the Roman Empire broadly and in Palestine specifically.

---

[4] Peter Garnsey, *Ideas of Slavery from Aristotle to Augustine* (Cambridge: Cambridge University Press, 1996), 103, notes that New Testament scholars before the 1990s had not been observing how to integrate the ancient ideology of slavery with studies of Jesus parables. One such ideology that he notes which could be valuable when exegeting parables is that ancient stories often used slavery as a metaphor for people who serve their passions and emotions (p. 16). Goede's more recent essay ("Constructing Ancient Slavery") provides important data for reconstructing the socio-historical context of slavery for the period of the first century CE, but does not specifically draw attention to how this information is useful for exegeting parables.

[5] None of these parables specifically designates the geographical setting of the characters, but if Matthew's audience assumed they were originally delivered by Jesus, it is reasonable they would assume he was alluding to agricultural practices his Galilean or Judean audiences were somewhat familiar with.

1. Identifying Slavery in Roman Society and in Palestine

Defining exactly what a "slave" or "slavery" was in the first-century Roman Empire is complex, leaving the concepts frustratingly ambiguous. Various approaches have been theorized to help crystalize what those in the first century would have thought about such persons. For this paper, by "slave" (δοῦλος) I am referring to those who came under the authority of one designated as a "master" or "lord" or "head of family," and came to be under their authority customarily because they were taken as a captive of war, or sold themselves into compulsory service, or had to serve as part of restitution of debt, or were born to parents who were enslaved, or were kidnapped, or were exposed infants who were collected. These were the most common ways people became enslaved throughout the Empire.

Caution should be taken, though, not to assume that the majority of those who utilized slaves ascribed to what was advocated as the "legal status" of slaves or to how certain philosophers described a slave's nature. While Aristotle and Roman policy saw slaves as a type of property similar in status to farm animals or equipment, it is never clear that this view is how most slaveowners saw them.[6] What is reasonable to assume is that the majority of slaves would have served within the traditional systems that would have characterized the institution of the household (οἶκος), however it might have been configured.[7]

Estimates of the slave population in the Roman Empire are also difficult to determine with any exact specificity. Estimates vary with regards to what percentage of people would have roles as "slaves." H. O. Maier claims that estimating at least 10% of the Empire's population was made up of slaves would be a conservative number, with a third of them living in Italy.[8] Keith Bradley has calculated that the Roman Empire had a population of roughly 50 million, out of which 5 million were slaves.[9] If these estimates are an accurate approximation, and a third of the five million (ca. 1.5 million) slaves lived in Italy, there would have been roughly three and a half million slaves in the rest of the Empire. But how would this number break down into specific locations and especially in Roman Palestine?

Based on a claim made by Galen, W. L. Westermann concluded that in Pergamum in the late-second century there was a one to three ratio of adult slaves to those in the citizen class.[10] But would such a ratio be characteristic within a region on the periphery of the Empire like Palestine? Hardly so. Considering

---

[6] J. A. Harrill, *The Manumission of Slaves in early Christianity*, 2nd ed. (Tübingen: Mohr Siebeck, 1998), 14. See, further, Aristotle's *Politics* Book 1 ch. 4 and, for an example of Roman law, see Codex Theodosianus 5.10.1.

[7] Some slaves in a household would have been known as the οἰκονόμος (one who manages the household including other slaves), see LSJ, 1204.

[8] Harry O. Maier, *New Testament Christianity in the Roman World* (Oxford: Oxford University Press, 2019), 161.

[9] Keith Bradley, "On the Roman Slave Supply and Slavebreeding," in *Classical Slavery*, ed. Moses I. Finley (London: F. Cass, 1987), 53–81.

[10] W. L. Westermann, *The Slave Systems of Greek and Roman Antiquity* (Philadelphia: American Philosophical Society, 1955), 87 n. 51. For the reference in Galen, see Galen 5:49 in *Claudii Galeni Opera Omnia*, vol. 5, ed. Gottlob Kühn (Cambridge: Cambridge University Press, 2011).

the area's ability to produce an adequate food supply, Magen Broshi calculated that Palestine in the early Roman period would not have, despite what previous calculations suggested, exceeded a million people.[11] But Pergamum's one to three ratio of slaves to adults was unlikely to apply to Palestine. Slave ownership in Roman Palestine is doubtful to have been as pervasive in the occupied territory of Jews. The vast majority of Jews in Palestine lived predominantly at a subsistence existence. Nor did Palestine have any cities comparable to the population size and wealth of Rome or to other large Roman colonies. Jerusalem, however, did have wealthy elites (Jews and non-Jews) who supported the Romans and there were also cities built by the Herodians to attract wealthy non-Jews to live in them while they invested in the region (e.g. Sepphoris and Tiberius) by buying land and creating large estates to produce food that would be shipped out across the Empire.[12] Can the ratio of slave to resident in Palestine be determined more concretely on the basis of specific evidence for the practice of slavery in Palestine based on knowing the type of people who had slaves?

There is only limited archaeological data for the existence of slavery in pre-Roman Hellenistic Palestine, even though Torah permitted Jews to have slaves, both Jewish and non-Jewish (Exod 21:1–6; Lev 25:39–55; Deut 15:12–18). The number of slaveowners and slaves was likely a lot less in Roman Palestine in the first century than in other parts of the Empire since there were very few who would have been Roman citizens (as some in Pergamum could have been) and very few wealthy collaborators with the Empire (as most Jewish high priests were).[13] Additionally, the topography and climate of Palestine were not like the agricultural conditions of Italy where large estate farms could be constructed that would utilize a sizable number of slaves. Palestine is more arid and only valleys and terraced hills could accommodate the extensive agricultural practices that would require a number of agricultural slaves.[14] Nevertheless, while it did not demonstrate the sizable ratio that one might find in other parts of the Empire, slavery in Galilee and Judea still existed—as the Gospels[15] and

---

[11] Magen Broshi, "The Population of Western Palestine in the Roman-Byzantine Period," *BASOR* 236 (1979): 1–10 (here 7).

[12] Evidence for the redistribution of land and communities in Lower Galilee under Herodian rule can be found in Morten Hørning Jensen's "Rural Galilee and Rapid Changes: An Investigation of the Socio-Economic Dynamics and Developments in Roman Galilee," *Biblica* 93, no. 1 (2012): 43–67. It should be noted, though, that the lack of archaeological evidence for large commercial farms in lower Galilee seems to suggest that these farms were not as pervasive as some scholars have contended. See David Fiensy, "Did Large Estates Exist in Lower Galilee in the First Half of the First Century CE?," *JSHJ* 10 (2012): 133–53.

[13] See Josephus, *A.J.* 20.251. The Romans tended to allow the most wealthy and local elites to exercise regional control. "High" priests (i.e. priests who were very wealthy and those most influential in governing) would have belonged to this elite group. See Richard Horsley, "High Priests and the Politics of the Roman Empire: A Contextual Analysis of the Evidence in Josephus," *JSJ* 17, no. 1 (1986): 23–55.

[14] Yohanan Aharoni and Miriam Aharoni, *The Archaeology of the Land of Israel: From the Prehistoric Beginnings to the End of the First Temple Period* (Philadelphia: Westminster Press, 1982), 4–5.

[15] For example, see the story of the centurion's slave in Matt 8 and Luke 7; possibly Chuza the overseer of Herod Antipas (Luke 8:3), Malchus the slave of the high priest (Matt 26:51; Mark 14:47;

the evidence examined below shows. There were large commercial farming estates, military personnel, and the households of the elites and the ruling class. But narrowing that number with any precise ratio goes beyond the available data.

I will now turn to the Matthean slave parables to examine what they indicate about the socio-ethnic-political identities of people as slaveowners.

2. The Matthean Parables with Slaveowners

Recent scholarship on the Matthean parables and other slave parables in the Synoptic Gospels[16] have examined and debated whether or not they reflect actual conditions of first-century Roman slavery in Palestine and whether or not they go back to the historical Jesus.[17] It is not the purpose of this essay to argue for or against the authenticity of these parables, but rather to show what Matthew's audience[18] would have likely assumed that those who had slaves in their service were and what possible implications their assumptions about these slaveowners would have had on how they heard the parables.[19]

Some research on the Matthean slave parables has focused on whether or not some slaveowners are meant to prefigure God[20] or are rather "ideal" figures with no allegorical implications.[21] There has also been debate whether or not the

---

Luke 22:51; John 18:10–11) as well as the female slave and household slaves of the high priest (Matt 26:69–71; Mark 14:66–69; Luke 22:55; John 18:16–26.

[16] Mark's Gospel has the parable of the Wicked Tenants (Mark 12:1–8) and Luke's Gospel has six parables, the Waiting Slaves (12:35–38); the Faithful/Wicked Slave (12:42–48); the Great Banquet (14:16–24); the Prodigal Son (15:11–32), the Minas (19:12–27), and the Wicked Tenants (20:9–15). The "manager" in the parable of the shrewd manager (Luke 16:1–8a) is not specified as a "slave," but does refer to the rich man as his "master" (v. 3). However, since the manager considers that he will have to either find employment as a digger or beg (v. 3) and was not beaten for poor management of the rich man's finances, he is probably not meant to be thought of as a slave.

[17] Charles Hedrick, *Many Things in Parables: Jesus and His Modern Critics* (Louisville, KY: John Knox Press, 2004); Ernest van Eck, "Realism and Method: The Parables of Jesus," *Neotestamentica* 51, no. 2 (2017): 163–84; R. Zimmermann, "Die Gleichnisse Jesu: Eine Leseanleitung zum Kompendium," in *Kompendium der Gleichnisse Jesu*, ed. R. Zimmermann (Gütersloh: Gütersloher Verlagshaus, 2007), 3–46.

[18] I assume a composition date for Matthew's Gospel after 70 CE and that the Gospel, while potentially written for a wider audience, was composed with a predominately Jewish-Christian audience living in Syrian Antioch. For a defense of this position, see John Harrison, "Matthew's Vision for Jesus' Community of Disciples," in *The New Testament Church: The Challenge of Developing Ecclesiologies*, ed. John Harrison and James Dvorak, MacMaster Biblical Studies (Eugene, OR: Pickwick Publications, 2012), 1–21 n. 1.

[19] For a closer examination of the authenticity of Matthew's parables of the Wicked Tenants, Wedding Banquet and Talents, see John P. Meier, *A Marginal Jew: Rethinking the Historical Jesus, vol. 5* (New Haven, CT: Yale University Press, 2016), 240–310. Meier does not include among his list of "authentic parables" the parable of the Faithful/ Wicked Slave since it only appears in Q and has no signs of the "independent witness" of M and L (as he suggests could be the case with the parables of the Talents/Pounds and the Great Supper/Wedding Banquet: p. 210).

[20] See Craig Blomberg, *Interpreting the Parables* (Downers Grove, IL: InterVarsity Press, 1990); Klyne Snodgrass, *Stories with Intent: A Comprehensive Guide to the Parables of Jesus*, 2nd ed. (Grand Rapids, MI: Eerdmans, 2018).

[21] W. G. Rollins, "Slavery in the NT," in *The Interpreter's Dictionary of the Bible (Supplement)*, (Nashville, TN: Abingdon Press, 1976), 832.

portrayal of slaves is meant to attack the ideology and practice of slavery.[22] But what is frequently missing in the interpretations of these parables is any reference to the evidence from Roman Palestine in the first century for reconstructing what types of people had slaves.[23]

Jennifer Glancy provides a close reading of the ideology of slavery in the Matthean parables.[24] She has shown that Matthew's parables present slaves with the type of managerial responsibilities (messengers, handling financial affairs, household management, etc.) and the experience of corporal punishment that many slaves would have encountered within Roman society. She observes that the slave parables in Matthew depict slaves who advance themselves when they act in accordance with their owners' interests.[25] Additionally, Glancy notes that Matthew's slave parables never present slaves who are working in mines (which is where many slaves in the Empire worked) or engaged in "onerous tasks common among first-century slaves."[26] Although agricultural slaves might be presumed in at least one of the Matthean parables (i.e. the Wheat and the Weeds), what one primarily finds in these parables are "elite slaves," that is, slaves who show themselves faithful and are able to accrue financial advantages for themselves.[27] Yet attention is warranted for a closer examination of the six slave parables in Matthew's Gospel to isolate any details the text might indicate about the ethnic and/or social-political situation of each slave owner.

In the parable of the Wheat and Weeds (13:24–30), the slaves belong to a man who sows in his field (v. 24). Even though the slaves question the field owner about the seed that he has sown, κύριε, οὐχὶ καλὸν σπέρμα ἔσπειρας ἐν τῷ σῷ ἀγρῷ (v. 27), it is unlikely that Matthew intends to imply that the field owner is the actual one who does the sowing of seeds.[28] Rather, since he owns the field and has slaves, he more likely had agricultural slaves who carried out the actual sowing. The slaves who are questioning the existence of the weeds in the field are other slaves than those who carried out the sowing. Whether they are managerial slaves or house slaves or both is unclear.

These other slaves address the owner of the field with the common Greek expression κύριε, which was used for a formal address (i.e. "Sir") or more specially one in the role of a "master." The term, Bietenhard suggests, indicates

---

[22] Beavis, "Ancient Slavery as an Interpretive Context"; Crossan, *In Parables*; idem, "The Servant Parables of Jesus"; Bernard Brandon Scott, *Hear Then the Parable: A Commentary on the Parables of Jesus* (Minneapolis, MN: Fortress Press, 1989), 205–80.

[23] Donald Hagner, *Matthew 1–13*, WBC (Dallas, TX: Word Books, 1993); idem, *Matthew 14–28*, WBC (Dallas, TX: Word Books, 1995); Daniel Harrington, *The Gospel of Matthew*, SP (Collegeville, MN: Liturgical Press, 2007); John Nolland, *The Gospel of Matthew*, NIGTC (Grand Rapids, MI: Eerdmans, 2005); David Turner, *Matthew*, BECNT (Grand Rapids, MI: Eerdmans, 2008).

[24] Jennifer A. Glancy, "Slaves and Slavery in the Matthean Parables," *JBL* 119, no. 1 (2000): 67–90.

[25] Ibid., 73.

[26] Ibid., 74.

[27] "Elite slavery" is an expression employed by Dale B. Martin to describe the upward mobility of slaves in his *Slavery as Salvation: The Metaphor of Slavery in Pauline Christianity* (New Haven, CT: Yale University Press, 1990). Cf., as well, Orlando Patterson, *Slavery and Social Death: A Comparative Study*, 2nd ed. (Cambridge, MA: Harvard University Press, 2018).

[28] Nolland, *Matthew*, 545.

a person who exercises legal or acknowledged authority over others.²⁹ This legal authority could exist because the person has employed someone, as in the case of the rich man and the manager in Luke's parable of the Shrewd Manager (Luke 16:1–8a), or because the person owns slaves, as in this case. Absent from the parable is any indication why the field owner takes no action against the enemy who sowed weeds into his field.³⁰

After the field owner's slaves enquire if he wants them to pull up weeds (why were the slaves who presumably sowed the wheat seed not charged with this task?), he instructs them not to, because if they do, they will inevitably uproot wheat (v. 30).³¹ The task of uprooting weeds is left to the "harvesters" (τοῖς θερισταῖς), who themselves could be either slaves or seasonal workers.³² Interestingly, the slaves are the only major figures in the parable that do not receive an allegorical identification in vv. 36–43. The text does not indicate the ethnicity of the slaveowner. He could have been assumed to be either a Jew or non-Jew. However, that the field's owner has slaves and a "barn" (ἀποθήκην)³³ and will later utilize harvesters (v. 30), who may or may not themselves be Jewish or non-Jewish slaves, suggests that the parable is envisioning a large estate that was common for commercial production of food, many of which would have been acquired by non-Jews who were enticed by Herodians to become rich by managing crop production on large sections of land in parts of Galilee.³⁴

In the parable of the Unmerciful Slave (18:23–34), the owner of slaves is a "king" (ἀνθρώπῳ βασιλεῖ) who wished to "settle accounts" (συνᾶραι λόγον). As many commentators have suggested, this story appears to be depicting an emperor who wants to know about the collection of taxes or tributes and that at least the first "slave" is responsible for the collection of an extremely large

---

²⁹ H. Bietenhard, "Lord, Master," in *NIDNTT*, ed. Colin Brown, 2 vols. (Exeter: Paternoster Press, 1976), 2:520.

³⁰ For the practice of similar "bio-terrorism" during the period, see A. J. Kerr's "Matthew 13:25: Sowing *Zizania* Among Other's Wheat: Realistic or Artificial?," *JTS* 48, no. 1 (1997): 108–9. It could be that the field owner knows he has many enemies and would not know which of them to take any action against. Snodgrass references those who have noted that the Romans even legislated against the practice of sabotaging another's field with weed seed (*Stories with Intent*, 201 n. 100).

³¹ It is often suggested that the "weeds" (ζιζάνια) refer to the popular darnel or *lolium temulentum* plant that looks similar to wheat in its early stages, see Robert McIver, "The Parables of the Weeds Among the Wheat (Matt 13:24–30, 36–43) and the Relationship between the Kingdom and the Church in the Gospel of Matthew," *JBL* 114, no. 4 (1995): 643–59 (here 647 n. 10). But the text does not indicate that the problem that the slaves have is recognizing the difference between the wheat and weeds. In fact, they do see the difference. The problem is that the weeds cannot be uprooted without disturbing the soil and possibly the roots of the wheat. There is no suggestion in the parable that the "weeds" (i.e. the children of the evil one in the allegorical interpretation) in their early stages of growth look like the "wheat" (children of the kingdom). Such an idea seems to run counter to Jesus's earlier teaching that his disciples ought to be able to tell the difference between a "good" tree and "bad" tree by looking at their "fruits" (Matt 7:17–18).

³² For details on the use of day or seasonal laborers in agricultural contexts in first-century Palestine, see John Kloppenborg, "The Growth and Impact of Agricultural Tenancy in Jewish Palestine (III BCE–I CE)," *Journal of the Economic and Social History of the Orient* 51 (2008): 31–66.

³³ BGAD, s.v. ἀποθήκη.

³⁴ See K. C. Hanson and Douglas Oakman, *Palestine in the Time of Jesus* (Minneapolis, MN: Fortress Press, 1998), 96. But for a rebuttal to these claims, see Fiensy's "Did Large Estates Exist in Lower Galilee," 136, where he defines "large" estates as anything from 50 to 1000 acres.

amount of taxes or tribute.[35] The fact that one of the slaves owes the king 10,000 talents makes it appear that the story is unlikely to be depicting an actual scenario that would occur in Palestine for a localized ruler and his financial slave. It more reasonably reflects a situation that could be imagined for the Empire at large. Later in the story, the king is described as the slave's "master" (κύριος). Curiously, the first slave never addresses the king with any title, possibly contributing to an impression of the slave's shamelessness. However, since the second slave also does not address the first slave in any formal way and that slave's character is not portrayed negatively, the absence of the address may not be significant.

It is the first slave's "fellow slaves" of the king who became outraged by his harsh treatment of the second slave who owed him much less than the first slave owed the king. They report to the king what his slave had done to one of the king's other slaves. The character of the king (emperor?) is at first harsh because he intends to have his slave and his family sold to repay part of the debt. This punishment might indicate that the king would have been thought of as a non-Jew (or at least a non-Torah observant Jew) since the Torah forbids selling a debtor's family into slavery in order to repay a debt.[36] He then, quite unexpectedly, appears to be benevolent and merciful after the slave begs for more time to repay the debt.[37] At the conclusion of the parable, his harshness reappears as he sends the slave off to the "jailers to be tortured" (v. 34).[38] The parable then provides the example of a slaveowner who represents the highest level in the social-political stratification.

In the parable of the Wicked Tenants (21:33–39), an οἰκοδεσπότης ("family-master") has a vineyard. Similar to the parable of the Wheat and Weeds, he is said to have planted the vineyard, built a wall around it, dug a winepress, and built a

---

[35] If Herod the Great, who was wealthy, was required to pay the Romans only 900 talents a year in taxes (Josephus, *A.J.* 17.11.4), the sum of 10,000 talents is significantly large, though not unheard of, as some have argued based on the reference in Josephus of a tax-farmer bidding to collect 16,000 talents for Coele-Syria, Phoenicia, Judea, and Samaria (Josephus, *A.J.* 12.175–77). I am not aware, though, of any evidence that can corroborate the view that huge taxes or tributes that were levied were managed by enslaved individuals rather than by Roman administrative support who assisted in the collection of such funds.

[36] Lev 25:39 indicates that a debtor can "sell themselves" to their creditor, but the creditor must not treat the debtor or the family that they bring with them as slaves. Rather, they are to be treated as hired laborers. Amos 2:6 refers to "Israel" selling the righteous for silver, which God condemns. Some interpreters see this reference as an allusion to enslavement for nonpayment of debts; see Douglas Stewart, *Hosea–Jonah*, WBC (Waco, TX: Word Books, 1987), 316–17. But see Avi Shveka's caution about this interpretation in his "'For a pair of shoes': A New Light on an Obscure Verse in Amos' Prophecy," *VT* 62 (2012): 95–114 (here 96–7). The Torah does, however, permit the selling of a thief who cannot make restitution into slavery (Exod 22:2). In 2 Kgs 4:1, it may be an Israelite who takes the children of a deceased prophet as repayment for an outstanding debt. Several texts in the Hebrew Bible indicate that the practice of taking a debtor's family was commonplace (e.g. Isa 50:1). But in some texts, such as Neh 5:3–5, the identity of those taking a debtor's family into slavery to compensate for a debt in not obvious.

[37] Some interpreters have seen this "forgiveness of a debt" as a heavier debt than the monetary one since it could not be repaid and therefore kept the slave indebted indefinitely to the king.

[38] For details on the violent treatment of slaves by their masters, see Glancy, "Slaves and Slavery," 67–8. This part of the parable has also caused difficulties for those interpreters who see the king as an allegorical figure for God and how he will treat followers of Jesus who do not forgive those who have sinned against them.

watchtower (21:33). The Matthean Jesus depicts a large estate that would have been similar to the common commercial farming plots that sprang up in Galilee under Herodian rule. Therefore, once again, Matthew is most likely not claiming that the οἰκοδεσπότης did the physical work himself but was responsible for having it completed by his agricultural slaves, who are not mentioned. Matthew's audiences would have likely known that while many large landowners may have carried out some of the labor necessary to establish their farm themselves, most would have used slaves in the construction.

After establishing his vineyard and renting it out to tenant farmers, the οἰκοδεσπότης then sends out one group of slaves (managerial?) to "collect the fruit" (v. 34). After the mistreatment of these slaves, the οἰκοδεσπότης sends out a second and larger group of slaves who experience that same mistreatment (v. 36). This scenario likely recalls the Herodian practice of confiscating lands once farmed by private land owners that were then sold off (or leased or given) to elite individuals, non-Jews or wealthy Jews who would collaborate with Herodian authority.[39] The new landowners could be trusted to generate a larger crop production for the Roman Empire's food consumption. While this social identity of the slaveowner is possible, there is no indication of his ethnicity.

In the parable of the Wedding Banquet (22:1–14), which resembles the parable of the Unforgiving Slave, the owner of slaves is a "king" (ἀνθρώπῳ βασιλεῖ). This king (emperor perhaps?) is described as someone who "prepared a wedding banquet" (v. 2). The specific tasks that would have been required in order to have the room and food ready for guests would have been carried out by slaves, who once again are not specified in the text. Once the room and food are ready, the king then sends out his "messenger slaves" to those who had been previously invited to come to the wedding (v. 3). But the reader is then informed that the king has not sent out all of his slaves because, recalling a similar pattern to that of the parable of the Wicked Tenants, after the slaves are rebuffed by those invited, a second group of slaves is sent out. It is not clear if by πάλιν ἀπέστειλεν ἄλλους δούλους (v. 4) the reader is to imagine that the second group of slaves outnumber the first group[40] or are merely a new batch of a similar number. Again, the second group of slaves are mistreated and killed (v. 6). After his invitation has been twice rejected and he has been dishonored when his messenger slaves were killed, the king sends an army to kill the murderers and burn their city (v. 7). In the next scene, the king tells a third group of his slaves to invite anyone they find.[41] It is also probable that another group of slaves are identified in the parable by the term διακόνοις (v. 13) since serving as attendants at meals for a king would have been one of the duties carried out by slaves. As in the case with the parable of the Unforgiving Slave, this slaveowner represents the highest level of Roman social-political stratification.

---

[39] For example, according to Josephus, *A.J.* 15.5–6, Herod confiscated the lands of the pro-Hasmonean Jewish aristocracy who had resisted his rise to power.

[40] The NIV's "more servants" probably only intends to imply "additional" slaves but is unclear.

[41] It is ambiguous whether this third group of servants are the same as the first group or an additional group.

In the parable of the Faithful/Wicked slave (24:45–51), there is a "master" (κύριος) who puts one of his slaves in charge of the others in his household and to provide them food. In the first scenario, it is imagined that the slave does what his master expects and increases his responsibility as a reward for faithful service. In the second scenario, the slave "says to himself" that the slaveowner was staying away for a long time and might not come back soon (if ever? cf. v. 48).[42] This time the slaveowner will find the slave mistreating other slaves and associating with drunkards, probably insinuating that the slave was allowing others to eat and drink without restraint from his master's supply (possibly what was set aside to be consumed by the other slaves?). The slaveowner then acts violently against the slave, either himself or more likely he has another to administer the execution. There is no indication of the ethnicity of the slaveowner or whether this slaveowner is one of those who had large commercial farming estates. Also, there is no condemnation or aspersion in the parable against the slaveowner for carrying out his action against his slave's mistreatment of others. It would have probably been assumed by Matthew's audience that the slaveowner was acting within his legal rights.

In the parable of the Talents (24:14–30), a man who was preparing to go on a journey calls his slaves to entrust his wealth to them. The man is identified as their "master" (κύριος) and the amount that he entrusted to these three slaves is eight talents (v. 15), a sizeable sum indicating the slaveowner's wealth for risk-taking investment.[43] These slaves resemble the managerial slave that one finds in the parable of the Unforgiving Slave. Nothing is stated about who is managing his household (other slaves perhaps) or where these slaves are living while this man is away. The scenario, however, readily reflects the frequent practice of non-Jews who acquired commercial undertakings in Palestine but would leave the management of land and resources to slaves while they returned to their homes elsewhere (whether in a "city" in Palestine such as Sepphoris or Caesarea Philippi or farther afield).

After a lengthy time, the man returns and wishes to "settle accounts" with them (v. 19). The first slave addresses the slaveowner as "master" (κύριε), shows that he has made for his master a profitable return of his investment, and is rewarded with additional responsibilities and a "share" in the master's happiness (v. 21). The same scenario occurs with the second slave. The third slave also addresses the slaveowner as κύριε (so there is no insinuation that the slave is disrespecting his master as in the case of the Unforgiving Slave), but he reports that he did not

---

[42] These "interior monologues" in Lucan parables always occur with characters who do not provide examples of virtuous behavior.

[43] A ταλάντον developed from being used to describe a "scale" or a "balance" to a specific weight of thirty kilograms and then to setting the value of gold, silver and copper coins. If the parable assumes silver talents, which each one would equate in value somewhere between 6,000 drachmai (Blomberg, *Interpreting the Parables*, 242) to 10,000 denarii (Kenneth Harl, *Coinage in the Roman Economy: 300 BC to 700 AD* [Baltimore, MD: The Johns Hopkins University Press, 1996], 482), then eight talents would be equivalent to 48,000 drachmai or 80,000 denarii. If a drachma was a "day's wage," as frequently depicted, the slaveowner is allocating to his three slaves enough money to employ more than 200 day-laborers for a year.

increase the master's investment. Instead, he hid it because he knew his master was a "hard man" (σκληρὸς ἄνθρωπος) and harvested where he had not sown (v. 24). The master scolds the slave and then instructs someone (another unidentified slave?) to take the talent that was entrusted to the third slave and give it to the first one. This unidentified person is then instructed to throw the unprofitable slave outside (v. 30). It is not clear what additionally is to be done to this slave. He is not given to someone to be tortured (as in the case of the Unforgiving Slave) or executed (as in the case of the Wicked Slave). Nothing explicit is stated about the slaveowner's ethnicity, though his departure again is suggestive that he would have been thought of by Matthew's audience as one of those non-Jews who acquired land or wealth in Palestine only to leave its management to slaves, who themselves could have been either non-Jews or Jews. Though he is characterized as a "hard man" who harvests where he had not sown, it does not appear that his treatment of his slave is condemned or reproached by the Matthean Jesus.

Therefore, in two of the six Matthean slave parables (the Unforgiving Slave and Wedding Feast), the slaveowners are "kings" exercising their authority powerfully; one towards his slave, who was likely an unmerciful imperial administrator, and the other towards his subjects who murder some of his messenger slaves. In both of these cases, the kings are more likely to have been understood by Matthew's audience as non-Jews (if not reminiscent of Roman emperors themselves). Neither of the parables ends with any condemnation of the actions of the one who owned the slaves. In three parables (the Wheat and Weeds, Wicked Tenants, and Talents) the slave owners are reminiscent of those who owned and worked sizeable estates that were established in Palestine, especially under Herodian rule, and who could leave their estates or wealth to be managed by the managerial slaves. The commercial farms that arose during the Herodian period were often acquired by non-Jews (and possibly even elite Jews) when they seized the opportunity to purchase (or lease or be given) land that had to be sold to cover debt, taxes or other losses. It is unclear in the parable of the Faithful/Wicked Slave whether the household is a large estate or a small house with a few slaves or whether the slaveowner or slave was Jewish or non-Jewish. So how are these slaveowners similar or dissimilar to the literary and archaeological evidence of slaveowners that come from first-century Roman Palestine?

3. Literary Evidence and Archaeological Realia for Slavery and Slaveowners in First-century Roman Palestine

Interpreting the evidence that is useful for constructing a general portrait of slavery in Roman Palestine is fraught with challenges. For example, when reading specific texts that mention the existence of slaveowners and slaves in a precise area, the author is presenting a particular narrative which can skew the information and affect its reliability or value (e.g. Josephus' depiction of Palestine).[44] It is

---

[44] Ben-Zion Rosenfeld, "Flavius Josephus and His Portrayal of the Coast (*Paralia*) of Contemporary Roman Palestine: Geography and Ideology," *JQR* 91, no. 1/2 (2000): 143–83 (here 145).

obvious at first that when investigating the archaeological remains of Palestine, what remains to be examined is often small, fragmentary and in poor condition.[45] Most notably, none of the literary or archaeological *realia* will provide all the details necessary for a coherent, specific taxonomy of the practice of slavery in Roman Palestine in the first century CE. All that is available are snippets of data or artifacts which must be combined with other research approaches and disciplines to make the most plausible portrayal with the material that exists to date.[46] Invariably, as new discoveries arise about the practice of slavery both in Palestine specifically and in the Roman Empire more generally, modifications and nuancing for any interpretive suggestions will be necessary.

The literary and archaeological evidence for slaves and who owned them in Roman Palestine is not extensive. However, what does exist is instructive for the type of social-ethnic background of many, if not the majority, of slaveowners in the region. Here I note several pieces of evidence (outside of specific individuals mentioned in the Gospels)[47] that help to more narrowly define those who had slaves. I first cite evidence for slaveowners who belonged to, not surprisingly, the Roman imperial family and their client-kings/rulers in Judea and Galilee. Then I cite the evidence for others who owned slaves, specifically wealthy priestly families living in Jerusalem and an unnamed Essene who intends to bequeath his slave to his community.

As John Gibbs and Louis Feldman have shown, Josephus provides extensive and useful insights into how slavery was practiced in first-century Palestine.[48] While Josephus' descriptions of the common practice of Roman military leaders taking Jews into enslavement after a military conquest could be examined,[49] I will focus here only on the examples Josephus supplies that are most pertinent for documenting slaveowners who belonged to the imperial family or their Roman client-kings in Palestine.

My first example is Josephus' description of Herod the Great's treatment of his slaves after his younger brother Pheroras was killed approximately 5 BCE (see *A.J.* 16.197 and *B.J.* 1.484). Pheroras was offered poison in the form of a "love potion." To discover the truth of who was behind the murder, Herod had his female slaves and freewomen tortured until a confession of a conspiracy was

---

[45] Aharoni and Aharoni, *Archaeology of the Land of* Israel, 1.

[46] Patterson suggest that researchers utilize a comparative method by paralleling what took place in other societies with a preponderance of slaves, O. Patterson, *Slavery and Social Death: A Comparative Study*, 2nd ed. (Cambridge, MA: Harvard University Press, 2018), 32. Martin, *Slavery as Salvation*, illustrates how slavery within Roman society can be understood broadly by interpreting the evidence of epigraphs and realia but does not provide evidence available from within Palestine.

[47] The centurion's slave (Matt 8:9//Luke 7:2–10); the "royal official's" slaves (John 4:51); the high priest's slave (Matt 26:51//Mark 14:47//Luke 22:50//John 18:10); another high priest's slave (John 18:26) and other slaves (John 18:18). For Caiaphas's "female-slave" (παιδίσκη), see Matt 26:69// Mark 14:66–69//Luke 22:56). For the high priest's "female door-keeper" (θυρωρός) who may have likely been a slave, see John 18:16. There is also a curious text in Luke where Jesus supposes one of his disciples having a slave (Luke 17:7–10).

[48] John G. Gibbs and Louis H. Feldman, "Josephus' Vocabulary for Slavery," *JQR* 76, no. 4 (1986): 281–310.

[49] See, for example. *B.J.* 1.68, which mentions Jews of Sepphoris who were taken as slaves by general Caius after they resisted Varus, the governor of Syria.

obtained.⁵⁰ This reference provides evidence of an Idumean (though ruler of the Jewish people) Roman-client king as a slaveowner. Herod would stand at the top of the social stratification in Roman Palestine. Though Josephus often emphasizes Herod's reputation for being violent and suspicious to highlight Herod's poor character as a ruler, he nevertheless assumes that Herod, like most other slaveowners under Roman law,⁵¹ acted within his authority over his slaves when he tortured them.

In *A.J.* 18.194, Josephus comments on how Agrippa I obtained the freedom of Caius' slave Thaumastus. This slave had given Agrippa water to drink when Tiberius had him bound and had him led about as punishment for speaking ill of Tiberius. Josephus writes that Agrippa pledged to the slave to get him his freedom out of gratitude if Agrippa's fortunes were ever restored. After Tiberius' death, Caius (Agrippa's friend) permitted Thausmastus to be set free and Agrippa made him ἐπίτροπος ("manager")⁵² of his estate. But Thaumastus was not a freed man who could choose to serve or not serve Agrippa but rather became Agrippa's slave. For when Agrippa died, he willed Thaumastus (a common action that a slaveowner could take towards their slave) to his son and daughter to serve in the same capacity.

An epigraphical example from Palestine of an imperial family's ownership of a slave comes from a first-century CE ossuary that was found in Jericho. However, it does not describe a slaveowner (or even a slave) who lived in Palestine, but rather a Jew with family roots at least in Jericho who was enslaved to the imperial family. The inscription on the ossuary reads Θεοδότου ἀπελευθέρου βασιλίσσης Ἀγριπείνης ('the ossuary of Theodotos, the freed person of Queen Agrippina').⁵³ What the inscription makes clear is that Theodotos once served Queen Agrippina, whom Rachel Hachlili has identified with Agrippina the Younger, the mother of Nero, who lived from 15–59 CE.⁵⁴ Hachlili theorizes that Theodotos probably served for some time with Agrippina in Rome before he was buried in an ossuary in a family tomb in Jericho.⁵⁵ How he came into her service is not known. But this evidence does show that some Jews, who at least originated from Palestine,

---

⁵⁰ The confession is questionable though, since Pheroras had dishonored Herod by refusing to wed his daughter, Cypros whom he had agreed to marry, and instead sought the affections of a slave-concubine.
⁵¹ Bradley, *Slaves and Masters*, 133.
⁵² See also the use of ἐπίτροπος in Matt 20:8 (parable of the workers in the vineyard) and Luke 8:3 for Chuza who was ἐπίτροπος for Herod Antipas.
⁵³ This inscription is marked as JERI0007 in the Inscriptions of Israel/Palestine Catalogue (Brown University). Also see, L. Y. Rahmani, Rashut Ha-'atikot Israel, and Muze'on Yiśra'el, *A Catalogue of Jewish Ossuaries in the Collections of the State of Israel* (Jerusalem: Israel Antiquities Authority, 1994), 97.
⁵⁴ Rachel Hachlili, "The Goliath Family in Jericho: Funerary Inscriptions from a First-Century A.D. Jewish Monumental Tomb," *BASOR* 235 (1979): 31–65 (here 33). This assessment is also shared by Catherine Hezser, *Jewish Slavery in Antiquity* (Oxford: Oxford University Press, 2005), 50.
⁵⁵ Hachlili, "Goliath Family," 31–65. It is not clear who paid for the ossuary. If Agrippina or another member of the imperial family paid for the ossuary, that certainly would shed some interesting light onto how some slaveowners took care to give their slaves a burial in accordance with the customs of their tradition.

did serve as slaves to members of the imperial family and seemingly were cared enough for that their bones were allowed to be buried in a family tomb.

I turn now to literature and *realia* about slaveowners in Roman Palestine who did not belong to the imperial family or Roman client-kings. What is the evidence for others as slaveholders? There are well-known references in both Philo and Josephus that describe the Essenes as not having or not desiring to own slaves. In *Every Good Man is Free* (79), Philo claims that there was not a slave among the Essenes, and in the *Antiquities* (18.21) Josephus states that the Essenes did not desire to keep slaves because owning them tempted one to act unjustly. However, these claims stand in tension with how the Damascus Document 11:12 represents slaveholding. Ben Zion Wacholder translates אל ימרא איש את עבדו ואת אמחו ואת שוכרו בשבת as, "One shall not command his manservant, his maidservant or his hireling (to perform tasks) on the Sabbath day."[56] Was this rule merely theoretical and written simply because there was the biblical text for slavery or was it composed because members of the community did actually possess slaves? Interestingly, a recently discovered ostracon from a cemetery at Qumran (KhQ1) containing a Hebrew inscription seems to indicate that at least one Essene (or member of the Qumran Community) owned a slave named "Hisday," who was bequeathed to the Essene (or Qumran) community.[57] However, judgments on whether or not a person named "Hisday" was actually a slave and whether or not the reference to "community" refers to the Qumran community are not conclusive.[58] It is also unclear from this brief text what kind of work (agricultural, managerial, messenger, household, etc.) this slave carried out for his master. One could also wonder about the likely ethnicity of this slave. Would a Jew who belonged to the Essenes or Qumran community have a non-Jewish slave that they would bequeath to serve within the community? It seems unlikely that the community would trust or be at ease with a non-Jew in their midst as they tried to maintain strict practices to ensure ritual purity. However, if it is the case that Hisday was a slave (whether Jewish or not) who was given upon the death of his master to the community, this is then literary evidence that a Jew who probably did not belong to the ruling class would have been known to have slaves. Unfortunately, not much information can be gleaned from this source that would indicate where exactly Hisday's owner was on the social stratification or his wealth.

L. Y. Rahmani documents an example of what is likely a Jewish slave of an elite person, but not one of the imperial family or ruling class. The ossuary, dated between 20 BCE to 70 CE, is of an enslaved physician. It has the Aramaic

---

[56] Ben Zion Wacholder, *The New Damascus Document: The Midrash on the Eschatological Torah of the Dead Sea Scrolls: Reconstruction, Translation and Commentary*, STDJ 6 (Leiden: Brill, 2007), 332–3.

[57] For the Hebrew text of KhQ1 and its English translation, see Frank Moore Cross and Esther Eshel, "Ostraca from Khirbet Qumrân," *IEJ* 47, no. 1/2 (1997): 17–28.

[58] See Cross and Eshel, "Ostraca from Khirbet Qumran"; and Greg Doudna, "Ostraca KhQ1 and KhQ2 from the Cemetery of Qumran: A New Edition," *Journal of Hebrew Scriptures* 5 (2005): 1–46.

inscription of טרפת הנשבה (*ṭrpt hnšbh*).[59] Rahmani argued that the meaning of *ṭrpṭ*, "lax," does not make sense and that in consideration that the adjective *nšbh* refers to a captive or an oppressed person, the term is likely to be a transliteration of a Greek loanword θεραπευτής which refers to a person who is a general servant, caretaker or worshipper but also one who serves as a type of medical attendant.[60] He, therefore, concludes that the inscription should be translated as "the captive physician." Slaves who had roles as physicians were not uncommon in Roman society.[61] Since the inscription is on an ossuary and is written in Aramaic, it is at least highly suggestive that the entombed person was a Jew. But the inscription gives no clear indication as to the specific ethnicity of the slaveowner. The slave's owner or the family could have been non-Jews who approved the use of the ossuary for their former slave (as in the case with Agrippina) or the slave owners themselves were Jewish.

An insightful reference by Josephus regarding non-imperial, non-Herodian slaveowners in Roman Palestine can be found at *A.J.* 20.179–81. Josephus references, in an effort to delegitimize those who were in control of the Temple prior to its destruction, high priests who sent out their slaves to collect tithes at threshing floors. These tithes should have gone to poorer priests but were taken from them by those in Jerusalem. That leading priests shortly before the Roman destruction of the Temple had slaves is attested much later on by *t. Men.* 13:21. Nahman Avigad has claimed that the Tosefta's reference to corrupt high priests recalls a piece of folklore that chronicled the corruption of priests when they beat their slaves.[62] While the Gospels record that the high priest Caiaphas had slaves,[63] is there any archaeological evidence that suggests other priests also had slaves during the period?

Interestingly, Avigad has described two houses (the "Kathros" or Qathros house and the "mansion" house) in the old city of Jerusalem that he believes were likely owned by wealthy priests and appear to be sizeable enough that they would very likely have utilized slaves in the day-to-day operation of the houses. The "Kathros/Qathros" house is so named because a stone scale weight was discovered in the house with the words בר קטרוס (*br qṭrws*) or "son of Kathros."[64]

---

[59] L. Y. Rahmani et al., *A Catalogue of Jewish Ossuaries in the Collections of the State of Israel* (Jerusalem: Israel Antiquities Authority, The Israel Academy of Sciences and Humanities, 1994), 97. Rahmani also considers the possibility that the loan word translated by the Aramaic was θρεπτός "slave, bred in the house," but discounts this possibility because *nšbh* refers to a person who was taken as a captive or was impressed into slavery.

[60] Ibid., 97.

[61] For illustrations of enslaved physicians throughout the Roman Empire, see Clarence Forbes, "The Education and Training of Slaves in Antiquity," *TAPA* 86 (1955): 321–60 (here 326).

[62] Nahman Avigad, "How the Wealthy Lived in Herodian Jerusalem," *BAR* 2, no. 22 (1976): 1, 23–32, 34–5. See also Hillel Geva, *Jewish Quarterly Excavations in the Old City of Jerusalem conducted by Nahman Avigad, 1969–1982, Volume IV: The Burnt House of Area B and Other Studies* (Jerusalem: Israel Exploration Society, 2010), 62–3. Geva notes that the portion of the house that remained after being burned during the siege on Jerusalem is the storage and service wing of the house.

[63] See n. 47.

[64] There appears to be a possible connection between this "Kathros" family and one that is mentioned as a priestly family in the Talmud's variation on *Tosefta Minot* 13:21. For a defense of this

The remains of the house are only a few rooms (courtyard, kitchen, four other unspecified rooms, and a *mikveh*), but appear to have initially belonged to a much larger house. What is significant about the remains is that they are likely the quarters for the household slaves.[65] According to Avigad, the rooms that were left appeared to be used by the slaves for the production of spices and incense that would end up being used in Temple services.[66] The other house, the "Mansion House" in Jerusalem's Jewish Quarter, was named the "Mansion House" because of its relatively large size (600 square meters).[67] Similar but larger than the Qathros House, it was destroyed by the Romans when they burnt Jerusalem. Several features of the house indicate that its owner was a wealthy Jew, very likely a priest.[68] Comparable houses in the rest of the Empire typically had slaves to undertake household operations. If fetters or chains, which were frequently used to constrain slaves, had also been found, they would have provided an even clearer indication that these households had enslaved workers and not merely employed servants. Despite any evidence of this kind, it is not unreasonable to expect that the houses of these wealthy Jewish (possibly priestly) families would also be managed with the use of slaves.

4. The Significance and Limitations of Literature and *Realia* for Identifying Slaveowners in Matthean Parables

There are two obvious limitations that are important to note before forming any conclusive judgments about the ethnic, social, and political identities of the slaveowners in Matthew's parables as they would have been assumed by Matthew's audience with the material about slaveowners in Palestine presented in this essay. First, the literary, epigraphical, and archaeological evidence referenced and presented here represents only a small fraction of the population in Palestine in the first century BCE and CE. They only illustrate slaveowners who were either members of the imperial family (e.g. Agrippina), Roman client-kings (e.g. Herod the Great, Herod Agrippa) or wealthy families whose households—possibly, though not conclusively, associated with priests—were in Jerusalem (e.g. Qathros and Mansion Houses). Collectively, such individuals could be classified among the "elite ruling class," if it could be assumed that the two houses of wealthy Jews were also politically influential. Only the examples from Damascus Document 11:12 and the ossuary of the enslaved physician probably point to slaveowners who may not have been part of the "ruling class," but it cannot be ruled out completely that they could have been. While it is both possible and likely that

---

connection, see Joshua Schwartz's "Bar Qatros and the Priestly Families of Jerusalem," in Geva's *Jewish Quarterly Excavations*, 311.

[65] Geva, *Jewish Quarterly Excavations*, 62–3.
[66] Ibid., 64.
[67] Nahman Avigad, *Discovering Jerusalem* (Nashville, TN: Thomas Nelson, 1980), 95. This house is located below the Wohl Museum in Jerusalem.
[68] In addition to sizable ornate halls, decorated anterooms, a courtyard stone-tables and glassware that indicates the owner's wealth, the house also contained several ritual baths (*mikvoth*). See ibid., 99, 106–8, 116–17.

slaveholders existed in smaller and poorer households throughout Palestine, evidence for it in the literature and *realia* is not available. Stone ossuaries and wills are more than likely the purview of the wealthy. Unfortunately, ownership of slaves among poorer households than the ones examined here is given no attention in the extant literature and *realia*, and such households do not leave behind items that help to show conclusively that they had slaves. However, it should not be concluded that in the absence of such evidence that it was only the very wealthy and very powerful who were slaveholders.

Second, while the slaveowners in the evidence provided here were primarily connected to the few individuals or families who wielded enormous political and economic power within Palestine (both non-Jewish and Jewish), there is still not enough evidence to conclude that Matthew's audience could only have understood these slaveholders as belonging to such individuals. Slaveowners were plentiful in large Roman cities. If Matthew's audience was situated in one of these, such as Syrian Antioch, they could have also known of people with modest dwellings who still had slaves (as the household instructions in the Pauline corpus attests). While Matthew's audience may have viewed the "family-masters," "kings" and "lords" of Jesus's slave parables as members of a more elite group than themselves, it is possible that since there are warnings in Matthew's Gospel about the pursuit of riches (e.g. Matt 6:19–21, 24; 19:23–24), some in Matthew's audience could have been wealthy enough to own slaves themselves.

If the literature and *realia* highlighted in this essay were pointed out when determining who Matthew's audience would have assumed slaveowners in Jesus's parables represent, two points can be made. First, noting the preponderance of evidence from Palestine that identifies slaveowners most frequently associates them with the political and religious powers operative at the time should allow for the conclusion that Matthew's audience would likely know that such characters are frequently (though not exclusively) people who belonged to the elite ruling class and large estate owners. While that information is not new for the parables of the Unforgiving Slave and Wedding Banquet where the slaveowner is a "king," it may be fresh information for imagining how the slaveowners in the other four parables were seen by Matthew's audience when their social, political, and ethnic identities were not made explicit.

Finally, this evidence can be helpful for the modern hearer of these parables. It allows them to appreciate how different their own experience of hearing the Matthean slave-parables may be from how they were potentially heard by Matthew's (or Jesus') audience. Unfortunately, many English readers of these parables do not even see characters as "slaveowners" because many English translations render δοῦλος as "servant" rather than "slave."[69] The identity of these key characters as slaveowners is obscured. These English translations

---

[69] For example, in the parable of the Wheat and Weeds, ASV, ESV, NIV, and NKJV identify the δοῦλοι as "servants" (Wheat and Weeds); the CEV and NLT have "farmer's workers"; while the NRSV correctly identifies them as "slaves." Also, for the parable of the Unforgiving Slave, the ASV, ESV, NIV, NKJV, and NLT have "servants'; the CEV has "officials'; while the NRSV again correctly identifies those serving the king as "slaves."

have likely considered that most readers of the slave-parables are interacting with them having a developed sensitivity to the immorality of slavery and a perspective that those who owned slaves are immoral by doing so. There is also the added discomfort for some that none of the slaveowners in Jesus's parables are condemned explicitly for any behavior, let alone owning slaves. How can Jesus tell stories where such an unjust practice is accepted without any condemnation? But if readers can see that these "servants" are actually enslaved persons and that Jesus has key characters in the parables who are "slaveowners," and not simply people who receive service from another person, then they can also nuance how different their hearing of the parable is to Matthew's (or Jesus') audience. Readers should not only see that these characters are slaveowners but also see that the preponderance of evidence from Palestine points to slaveowners as those among the powerful and wealthy elites. Matthew's audience could have readily assumed this social and political identification for the slaveholders in all the parables (not only for the king in the Unforgiving Servant and Wedding Banquet), while today's audience are often more left in the dark.

Bibliography

Aharoni, Y., and M. Aharoni, *The Archaeology of the Land of Israel: From the Prehistoric Beginnings to the End of the First Temple Period.* Philadelphia: Westminster Press, 1982.

Aristotle. *Politics.* Translated by B. Jowett. New York: The Modern Library, 1943.

Avigad, N. *Discovering Jerusalem.* Nashville, TN: Thomas Nelson, 1980.

Avigad, N. "How the Wealthy Lived in Herodian Jerusalem." *BAR* 2, no. 22 (1976): 1, 23–32, 34–5.

Beavis, M. A. "Ancient Slavery as an Interpretive Context for the New Testament Servant Parables with Special Reference to the Unjust Steward (Luke 16:1–8)." *JBL* 111, no. 1 (1992): 37–54.

Bietenhard, H. "Lord, Master." *NIDNTT* 2:520.

Blomberg, C. *Interpreting the Parables.* Downers Grove, IL: InterVarsity Press, 1990.

Bradley, K. R. *Slaves and Masters in the Roman Empire.* New York: Oxford University Press, 1987.

Bradley, K. R. "On the Roman Slave Supply and Slavebreeding." In *Classical Slavery*, edited by Moses Finley, 53–81. London: F. Cass, 1987.

Broshi, M. "The Population of Western Palestine in the Roman-Byzantine Period." *BASOR* 236 (1979): 1–10.

Cross, F. M., and E. Eshel, "Ostraca from Khirbet Qumran." *Israel Exploration Journal* 47 (1997): 17–28.

Crossan, J. D. *In Parables: The Challenge of the Historical Jesus.* New York: Harper & Row, 1973.

Crossan, J. D. "The Servant Parables of Jesus." *Semeia* 1 (1974): 17–32.

Doudna, G. "Ostraca KhQ1 and KhQ2 from the Cemetery of Qumran: A New Edition." *Journal of Hebrew Scriptures* 5 (2004): 1–46.

Fiensy, D. "Did Large Estates Exist in Lower Galilee in the First Half of the First Century CE?" *JSHJ* 10 (2012): 133–53.

Forbes, C. A. "The Education and Training of Slaves in Antiquity." *Transactions and Proceedings of the American Philological Association* 86 (1955): 321–60.

Galenus, Claudius. *Claudii Galeni Opera Omnia, Vol. 5*. Edited by Karl Gottlob Kühn. Cambridge: Cambridge University Press, 2011.

Garnsey, P. *Ideas of Slavery from Aristotle to Augustine*. Cambridge: Cambridge University Press, 1996.

Geva, H. *Jewish Quarterly Excavations in the Old City of Jerusalem Conducted by Nahman Avigad, 1969–1982, Volume IV: The Burnt House of Area B and Other Studies*. Jerusalem: Israel Exploration Society, 2010.

Gibbs, J. G., and L. H. Feldman. "Josephus' Vocabulary for Slavery." *JQR* 76, no. 4 (1986): 281–310.

Glancy, J. A. *Slavery in Early Christianity*. Oxford: Oxford University Press, 2002.

Glancy, J. A. "Slaves and Slavery in the Matthean Parables." *JBL* 119, no. 1 (2000): 67–90.

Goede, H. "Constructing Ancient Slavery as Socio-historic Context of the New Testament." *HTS* 69, no. 1 (2013): 1–7.

Hachlili, R. "The Goliath Family in Jericho: Funerary Inscriptions from a First-Century A.D. Jewish Monumental Tomb." *BASOR* 235 (1979): 31–65.

Hagner, D. *Matthew 1–13*. WBC. Dallas, TX: Word Books, 1993.

Hagner, D. *Matthew 14–28*. WBC. Dallas TX: Word Books, 1995.

Hanson, K. C., and D. Oakman, *Palestine in the Time of Jesus*. Minneapolis: Fortress Press, 1998.

Harl, K. *Coinage in the Roman Economy: 300 BC to 700 AD*. Baltimore: The Johns Hopkins University Press, 1996.

Harrill, J. A. *The Manumission of Slaves in Early Christianity*. 2nd ed. Tübingen: Mohr Siebeck, 1998.

Harrill, J. A. *Slaves in the New Testament: Literary, Social and Moral Dimensions*. Minneapolis: Fortress Press, 2006.

Harrill, J. A. "The Psychology of Slaves in the Gospel Parables: A Case Study in Social History." *BZ* 55, no. 1 (2011): 63–74.

Harrington, D. *The Gospel of Matthew*. SP. Collegeville, MN: Liturgical Press, 2007.

Harrison, J. "Matthew's Vision for Jesus' Community of Disciples." In *The New Testament Church: The Challenge of Developing Ecclesiologies*, edited by John Harrison and James Dvorak, 1–21. MacMaster Biblical Studies Series. Eugene, OR: Pickwick Publications, 2012.

Harrison, J. "Weeds: Jesus' Parable and Economic and Political Threats to the Poor in Roman Galilee." *Stone-Campbell Journal* 18 (2015): 73–88.

Hedrick, C. *Many Things in Parables: Jesus and His Modern Critics*. Louisville, KY: John Knox Press, 2004.

Hezser, C. *Jewish Slavery in Antiquity*. Oxford: Oxford University Press, 2005.

Horsley, R. "High Priests and the Politics of the Roman Empire: A Contextual Analysis of the Evidence in Josephus." *JSJ* 17, no. 1 (1986): 23–55.

Jensen, M. H. "Rural Galilee and Rapid Changes: An Investigation of the Socio-Economic Dynamics and Developments in Roman Galilee." *Biblica* 93, no. 1 (2012): 43–67.

Kerr, A. J. "Matthew 13:25: Sowing *Zizania* Among Others' Wheat: Realistic or Artificial?" *JTS* 48, no. 1 (1997): 108–9.

Kloppenborg, J. S. "The Growth and Impact of Agricultural Tenancy in Jewish Palestine (III BCE—I CE)." *Journal of the Economic and Social History of the Orient* 51 (2008): 31–66.

Maier, H. O. *New Testament Christianity in the Roman World*. Oxford: Oxford University Press, 2019.

Martin, D. B. *Slavery as Salvation: The Metaphor of Slavery in Pauline Christianity*. New Haven, CT: Yale University Press, 1990.

Meier, J. P. *A Marginal Jew: Rethinking the Historical Jesus, Volume 5*. New Haven: Yale University Press, 2016.

McIver, R. "The Parables of the Weeds Among the Wheat (Matt 13:24–30, 36–43) and the Relationship between the Kingdom and the Church in the Gospel of Matthew." *JBL* 114, no. 4 (1995): 643–59.

Nolland, J. *The Gospel of Matthew*. NIGTC. Grand Rapids, MI: Eerdmans, 2005.

Neufeld, E. "Vulnerable Bodies and Volunteer Slaves: Slave Parable Violence in the Rest of Matthew." *BBR* 30, no. 1 (2020): 41–63.

Patterson, O. *Slavery and Social Death: A Comparative Study*. 2nd ed. Cambridge, MA: Harvard University Press, 2018.

Philo. Translated by Francis Henry Colson. Cambridge, MA: Harvard University Press, 1961.

Rahmani, L. Y. Rashut Ha-'atikot Israel, and Muze'on Yiśra'el. *A Catalogue of Jewish Ossuaries in the Collections of the State of Israel*. Jerusalem: Israel Antiquities Authority, The Israel Academy of Sciences and Humanities, 1994.

Rollins, W. G. "Slavery in the NT." In *Interpreter's Dictionary of the Bible (Supplement)*, 832. Nashville, TN: Abingdon Press, 1976.

Rosenfeld, B.-Z. "Flavius Josephus and His Portrayal of the Coast (Paralia) of Contemporary Roman Palestine: Geography and Ideology." *JQR* 91, no. 1/2 (2000): 143–83.

Schwartz, J. "Bar Qatros and the Priestly Families of Jerusalem." In *Jewish Quarterly Excavations in the Old City of Jerusalem Conducted by Naham Avigad, 1969–1982, Volume IV: The Burnt House of Area B and Other Studies*, edited by Hillel Geva, 308–19. Jerusalem: Israel Exploration Society, 2010.

Scott, B. B. *Hear Then the Parable: A Commentary on the Parables of Jesus*. Minneapolis, MN: Fortress Press, 1989.

Shveka, A. "'For a Pair of Shoes': A New Light on an Obscure Verse in Amos' Prophecy." *VT* 62 (2012): 95–114.

Snodgrass, K. *Stories with Intent: A Comprehensive Guide to the Parables of Jesus*. 2nd ed. Grand Rapids, MI: Eerdmans, 2018.

Stewart, D. *Hosea–Jonah*. WBC. Waco, TX: Word Books, 1987.

Turner, D. *Matthew*. BECNT. Grand Rapids, MI: Baker, 2008.

Van Eck, E. "Interpreting the Parables of the Galilean Jesus: A Social-Scientific Approach." *HTS* 65, no. 1 (2009): 1–12.

Van Eck, E. "Realism and Method: The Parables of Jesus." *Neotestamentica* 51, no. 2 (2017): 163–84.

Van Eck, E., and J. S. Kloppenborg. "An Unexpected Patron: A Social-scientific and Realistic Reading of the Parable of the Vineyard Labourers (Matthew 20:1–15)." *HTS* 71 (2015): 1–11.

Van Eck, E., and M. M. Mashinini. "The Parables of Jesus as Critique on Food Shortage Systems for Vulnerable Households in Urban Townships." *HTS* 72, no. 3 (2016): 1–9.

Wacholder, B. Z. *The New Damascus Document: The Midrash on the Eschatological Torah of the Dead Sea Scrolls: Reconstruction, Translation and Commentary.* STDJ 56. Leiden: Brill, 2007.
Weiser, A. *Die Knechtsgleichnisse der synoptischen Evangelien.* SANT 29. Munich: Kösel, 1971.
Westermann, W. L. *The Slave Systems of Greek and Roman Antiquity.* Philadelphia: American Philosophical Society, 1955.
Zimmermann, R. "Die Gleichnisse Jesu: Eine Leseanleitung zum Kompendium." In *Kompendium der Gleichnisse Jesu,* 3–46. Gütersloh: Gütersloher Verlagshaus.

Whose Voices Matter?
A Persistent Widow in a Polyphonic Parable (Luke 18:1–8)

Ellen Aasland Reinertsen

During a debate over Jeff Sessions' nomination to become attorney general in February 2019, senator Elizabeth Warren read a letter by Coretta Scott King, the widow of Martin Luther King Jr. In the letter, Scott King opposed Sessions' nomination for a federal judgeship in 1986. Senator Warren was prevented from reading the letter after the Republicans in the Senate invoked an "arcane" rule to stop her from speaking. Warren had previously been warned about violating this rule, but expressed her surprise that Scott King's words were considered "not suitable for debate in the United States Senate." Later, the Republican Majority Leader, Mitch McConnell, defended the actions, saying: "Senator Warren was giving a lengthy speech. She had appeared to violate the rule. She was warned. She was given an explanation. Nevertheless, she persisted."[1]

Who gets to tell a story? The account above has some noteworthy similarities with the parable about the Widow and the Unjust Judge in Luke 18:1–8. In both of these cases, persistence and a widow's message are interpreted in opposing ways. In the US Senate case, Warren claims that it is important to read the letter from Scott King. McConnell says that by doing so, Warren is in violation of a senate rule. In the parable, it is also as if several voices tell contrasting stories about the widow's words and actions. In doing so, they interpret the parable in different ways. Is this a parable about praying and not losing hope? Is it perhaps rather about a persistent person who demands justice? Alternatively, is it about an "enraged bag lady hitting a negligent magistrate over the head and literally 'giving him a black eye'"?[2] Or, is it a parable about God's elect with true pistis?[3]

---

[1] https://www.buzzfeednews.com/article/franciswhittaker/people-are-using-nevertheless-she-persisted-to-share-example (May 2, 2019). "Nevertheless, she persisted," has later become a slogan used by, among others, feminist activists.
[2] Luke Timothy Johnson, *The Gospel of Luke*, Sacra Pagina 3 (Minneapolis: The Liturgical Press, 1991), 273.
[3] In the following, I will apply the Greek word *pistis*, since the translation of πίστις is highly debated. The interpretations and commentaries I have studied mainly use the English term *faith* or the

These different perspectives have puzzled contemporary scholars. According to François Bovon, it is as though there were several individuals, who commented and competed over the meaning of the parable through its pre-gospel transmissions.[4] Stephen Curkpatrick sees dissonance in the parable and claims that "(a)ny attempt to read Luke 18:1–8 together with a single interpretation is folly."[5] In the parable's reception history, though, despite the parable's apparent conflicting perspectives, most recipients I have studied seem to hear the parable as a harmony, with one leading voice, with which the others tune in. Mostly, "Luke's" or the judge's perspectives have set the tune and overpowered the other perspectives.

As an analytical tool, to study these competing "commentaries" or this "dissonance," I suggest that we see the different perspectives as various parable voices. These voices are on different narrative and editorial levels. Nevertheless, from the perspective of a reader or of a listener to the parable, they might appear as voices, which recipients might listen to or miss.

In this recipient-oriented study of the parable, I will first briefly introduce these different parable voices. Secondly, I will give examples of the voices that recipients have often heard and those, which have mostly gone unnoticed. Then, as a contribution to the discussion of what reception should be, I will suggest possible interpretations by recipients who are not present in our attested sources, and who might have emphasized the parable's missing voices. Finally, I will discuss what it does to the interpretation of the parable, if we see its different parable perspectives as polyphonic voices in dialogical opposition.

1. Various Voices about the Widow

If we apply my analytical tool, to distinguish between various voices in the parable, the first parable voice belongs to "Luke," the narrator of the greater gospel narrative. We find Luke's voice in the parable frame, before the parable narrative (v. 1).[6] Luke introduces the parable, and at the same time indicates

---

German *Glauben*. I employ the Greek term to keep more of the "width" in the term. For a thorough discussion of *pistis*, see Teresa Morgan, *Roman Faith and Christian Faith: Pistis and Fides in the Early Roman Empire and Early Churches* (Oxford: Oxford University Press, 2015).

[4] François Bovon, "Apocalyptic Traditions in the Lucan Special Material: Reading Luke 18:1–8," *HTR* 90, no. 4 (1997): 383–91. See the entire article, but especially pp. 389–90.

[5] Stephen Curkpatrick, "Dissonance in Luke 18:1–8," *JBL* 121 (2002): 107–21 (here 114). He mainly focuses on the tensions between the frame and the narrative, such as, for example, that the narrative talks about Jesus, and the frame uses "The Lord." See pp. 107–8 n. 1, for other scholars who have noted such tensions. See also Stephen Curkpatrick, "A Parable Frame-up and its Audacious Reframing," *NTS* 49 (2003): 22–38.

[6] Scholars use various terms for parable narratives and their framing. For example, C. H. Dodd talks about *parable story* and *gospel setting*. In addition, he also describes the narrative as the *parable proper* and the immediate frame after the story as its *application* or *moral*. See C. H. Dodd, *The Parables of the Kingdom* (London: Nisbeth & Co., 1935), 17, 90 and 89. Curkpatrick uses *parable* and *frame*. See Curkpatrick, "Dissonance," 114. Mary Ann Beavis describes the parable *application* as fable *epimythium*; see her "Parable and Fable," *CBQ* 52 (1990): 473–98 (here 482). Justin D. Strong, "How to Interpret Parables in Light of the Ancient Fable: The Promythium and Epimythium," in *Overcoming Dichotomies: Parables, Fables, and Similes in the Graeco-Roman World*, ed. A. Oegema, J. Pater and M. Stoutjesdijk, WUNT (Tübingen: Mohr Siebeck, 2022),

how it should be understood. According to him, the parable and consequently the widow's actions are about constant praying and not being discouraged. Luke speaks aloud, to the reader or listener, from a meta-setting, outside the narrative. He narrates all the other voices in the parable.

The second voice (vv. 2–5) is the protagonist of the greater gospel narrative, Jesus. He tells the parable narrative and thus presents the widow and the judge and their voices and actions. Within the gospel narrative, he addresses both the disciples and possibly the Pharisees (17:22/37 and 20). What Jesus says about the widow and her actions is sparse. She is presented as a widow (χήρα) who is in a city, and she kept coming (imperfect of ἔρχομαι) to the judge and is talking, asking, appealing to, or demanding of him (participle of λέγω, followed by an imperative).

What the widow says, ἐκδίκησόν με ἀπὸ τοῦ ἀντιδίκου μου, is our third voice (v. 3). The widow speaks aloud to the judge. Ἐκδικέω has several translational possibilities. It might be translated as "procure or grant justice for someone," "carry out one's obligations in a worthy manner" or to "inflict appropriate penalty for wrong done."[7] The widow's words can thus be either translated "Grant me justice against my opponent" or "Grant me vengeance against my opponent."

Voice four is that of the judge (vv. 4–5). Jesus has already introduced this character more thoroughly than he did with the widow. Not only is he a judge in a city, Jesus has also described him as "not fearing God nor feeling ashamed before human beings" (v. 2). Later, the judge repeats this about himself (v. 4). The later voice, the Lord, also connects him to injustice (ὁ κριτὴς τῆς ἀδικίας, "the judge of injustice"). The judge is thus the only speaker who is characterized in negative terms.[8] This is done by three different voices.[9] He is also the only character who does not speak aloud, but has an inner dialogue, similar to other unethical characters in Luke.[10] The judge is, thus, "the bad guy" in the story, although some commentators see him as ambiguous.[11] The unjust judge gives his

---

327, writes: "These framing devices that follow Jesus's parables have not gone unnoticed by exegetes.... Parable scholars and form critics have frequently remarked on what they perceived to be various notes, lessons, and applications appended to the end of many of the Gospel parables, Luke's in particular." Strong, himself, sees the "framing devices" as *promythium* and *epimythium*. I use *parable narrative* and *parable frame* to emphasize both that the frame and narrative often are interpreted together in the reception history, but that they also might be heard separately.

[7] Cf. BDAG, s.v. ἐκδικέω.

[8] A concept that I have found helpful is *ethos attribution*, as employed by Liesbeth Korthals Altes. She builds on Aristotle's concept of *ethos* as persuasion through character, in addition to Cicero, who included *prior ethos*, the image an audience already has of the speaker, on the basis of his reputation, previous knowledge, or generally known character traits. Cf. Liesbeth Korthals Altes, *Ethos and Narrative Interpretation: The Negotiation of Values in Fiction*, Frontiers of Narrative (Lincoln: University of Nebraska Press, 2014), 2, 5. Ideas about characters' or authors' sincerity, reliability, authority or irony, are of importance for ethos assessment.

[9] Four voices, if we assume that Luke agrees with Jesus.

[10] ἐν ἑαυτῷ. He speaks *in* himself. There are other such silent speeches in the gospel (Luke 12:17; 15:17; 16:3; 18:4). For a discussion of these inner dialogues or monologues in the Gospel of Luke, see François Bovon, *Das Evangelium nach Lukas Lk 15,1–19,27*, EKK 3/3 (Zurich: Benziger, 2001), 282–3.

[11] Stephen Wright suggests that "not fear God" could mean that he did not follow the law in a detailed way and "not respect human beings" could signify that he did not show bias or partiality.

interpretation of the actions and sayings of the widow. In his view, she bothers him and is potentially violent.[12]

The fifth and last voice of the parable belongs to the Lord. We are now in the frame after the parable narrative. The speaker would probably be heard as the same person as Jesus, the storyteller.[13] To distinguish between these two voices, which are at different narrative levels, I will call this voice "the Lord." The Lord gives two perspectives on the parable narrative. The parable is about God granting justice/vengeance (ποιήσῃ τὴν ἐκδίκησιν) to his elect who cry to him day and night and/or about the *pistis* that the Son of Man might or might not find when he comes.[14]

To sum up, I have divided the parable into five voices, on three different narrative levels. Two of the voices are in the frame: Luke's is before the narrative and the Lord's after the narrative. In the narrative, Jesus, the widow and the judge speak. Luke narrates all the other voices in the parable, while Jesus gives words to both the widow and the judge. See Figure 1 for illustration.

The judge could thus be seen as a split or an ambiguous character. Cf. Stephen I. Wright, *Jesus the Storyteller* (Louisville, KY: Westminster John Knox Press, 2015), 133–4. Amy-Jill Levine and Ben Witherington, *The Gospel of Luke*, NCBC (Cambridge: Cambridge University Press, 2018), 482, believe he could be perceived as "fiercely independent" and exactly the person you would want to have to rule in your case. However, according to them, it is more probable that he would be perceived as a bad judge. (I agree with this latter view.) Most listeners would probably know that to fear God and respect your fellow human beings is what a pious, wise or good person should do—see, for example, Exod 10:16; Pss 14:4 LXX; 21:23; 24:12; 32:18; 67:5; 145:9; Prov 1:7; Sir. 35:14–18, or the later *m. Ketub.* 4:12; 11:1–6; 12:3–4; *m. Git.* 5:3. See also Luke 10:27. The Gospel of Luke also employs the term "God-fearers" for gentiles attracted to Judaism (10:2, 22, 35; 13:15, 26). References for not respecting men or being incapable of shame include: Matt 21:37; Mark 12:6; 1 Cor 4:4; 2 Thess 3:14; Titus 2:8. This double description is also used by Josephus to describe King Jehoiakim (*A.J.* 10.81) and by Dionysius of Halicarnassus (10.10.7) about those who "neither fear divine wrath nor respect human fate" (referred from Levine and Witherington, *Gospel of Luke*, 482). Also, the fact that he at first did not want to help the widow, would convince the audience that he is unethical. This negative understanding would be definitely established by "the Lord," when he connects him to injustice (Luke 18:6). However, for a few seconds, the judge could be heard as virtuous, wise and with good will. Initially, the audience hears that "in a certain city there was a judge" (v. 2). The word "judge," prior to the negative characteristics, could possibly evoke positive associations, especially if the listeners would recall stories from the wisdom traditions about "the just judge" (see, e.g., Sir. 35:14–18). The audience might then have an established view that a judge was (supposed to be) just. Then, when the audience hears that he neither feared God nor had respect (or felt shame) for human beings, the audience's understanding of the judge would probably turn. This judge is the opposite of the "good judge."

[12] ὑπωπιάζῃ με can also mean punish or beat him and possibly also damage his reputation (see, e.g. BDAG, s.v.). See John R. Donahue, *The Gospel in Parable* (Minneapolis, MN: Fortress Press, 1988), 183, and Marianne Bjelland Kartzow, "Rewritten Stereotypes: Scripture and Cultural Echo in Luke's Parable of the Widow and the Judge," in *Luke's Literary Creativity*, ed. Jesper Tang Nielsen and Mogens Müller, LNTS 550 (London: Bloomsbury T&T Clark, 2016), 216–17.

[13] According to Stephen Curkpatrick, though, this is Luke's risen Lord (Curkpatrick, "Dissonance," 113).

[14] I will not go into the much-discussed translation of καὶ μακροθυμεῖ ἐπ' αὐτοῖς here, since it is not relevant to my main argument.

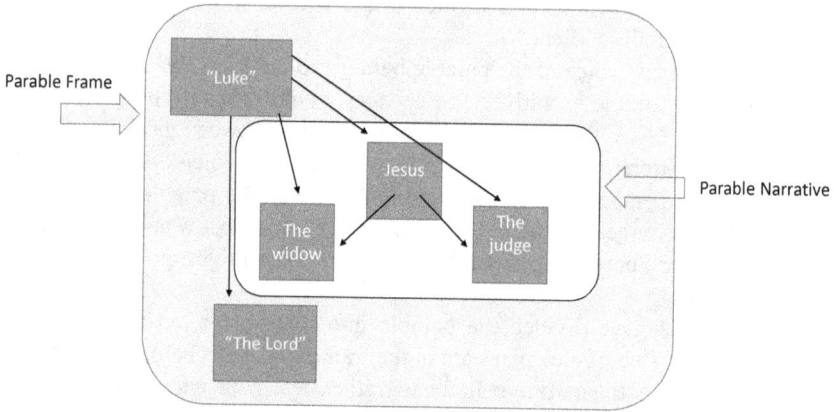

Figure 1. Various voices about the widow.

Four of the voices can be heard by others. The unethical judge speaks to himself. The voices in the frame offer at least three perspectives on the parable: That it is about praying and not giving up (Luke), that it is about the justice/vengeance God will grant to his crying elect and/or about pistis on earth (the Lord). Within the parable narrative, Jesus says that the widow repeatedly came to the judge and talked when she pleaded, begged or commanded. The widow's voice says: "Grant me justice," or possibly "vengeance." The judge claims that what the widow is doing is to bother him and to threaten him with violence.

In this parable's afterlives—or, perhaps we should rather call this its reverberations, the aftersounds, which of these voices have recipients listened to and which have been missed?[15]

2. The Reverberations and their Recorded Reception

I will now present my findings from case studies of the recorded reception of this parable. By recorded reception, I mean written interpretations, which are preserved, and we thus have access to. I see recorded reception as a contrast to all other interpretations of this parables, which have not been kept or were never written down. My case studies are "snap shots" of the reception history. They are examples from different periods I employ to show and discuss some of the tendencies my research has discovered.[16] These examples are from Antiquity,

---

[15] To play with Yvonne Sherwood's term "afterlives"; cf. Yvonne Sherwood, *A Biblical Text and its Afterlives: The Survival of Jonah in Western Culture* (Cambridge: Cambridge University Press, 2000).

[16] For a "snap shot" approach, see Hugo Lundhaug and Liv Ingeborg Lied, "Studying Snapshots: On Manuscript Culture, Textual Fluidity, and New Philology," in *Snapshots of Evolving Traditions*, ed. Lundhaug and Lied (Berlin: de Gruyter, 2017), 1–19 (here 9, 11), as well as my forthcoming Ph.D. dissertation.

from Luther's preserved texts, and from contemporary New Testament research. I have chosen these snapshots because I see these as "power voices"; the texts from antiquity and Luther have been considered so important that they have been preserved, unlike so many other interpretations. In addition, they seem to be influential for later periods, including my own academic and church context. From recent research, I have chosen to study biblical commentaries, as well as explicitly feminist parable research. Biblical commentaries often represent "mainstream" scholarship, which frequently lacks gender analysis. Since "feminist" scholars do include this perspective and mostly have female biblical characters as their main concern, I find it fruitful to study both.[17] Let us move to my findings.

2.1. The Frame Over the Narrative

In the cases I have analyzed, recipients seem to mainly emphasize the frame when they interpret this parable. Most of the time, they listen to Luke's voice, which says that this is a parable about persistent prayer. When this voice has dominated, the parable narrative has usually been seen as an example of this prayer. This is the case with Augustine:

> He [The Lord] said: "We ought always pray and not to faint," and He used the example of a certain widow who wished to be avenged of her adversary, and who petitioned an unjust judge so often that she made him listen to her, not through any motive of justice or compassion, but through weariness of her importunity. In this way we were to be taught how surely the merciful and just God hears us when we pray without ceasing, since the widow, because of her continual petition, could not be treated with contempt even by an unjust and wicked judge....[18]

The same type of interpretation occurs in John Chrysostom, Cyril of Alexandria, Origen, and Martyrius.[19] My study thus suggests that most Antique theologians

---

[17] Amy-Jill Levine is in some sort of "hybrid" position here. She is an explicit feminist, and at the same time the author of a biblical commentary.

[18] Aurelius Augustine, "Letters," in *The Fathers of the Church*, ed. Sister Wilfrid Parsons (Washington, DC: Catholic University of America Press, 1966), 387–8.

[19] *Chrysostom*: "Dost thou wish to learn a third way of repentance? Fervent and diligent prayer, and to do this from the bottom of the heart. Hast thou not seen that widow, how she persuaded the shameless judge? But thou hast a gentle Master, both tender, and kind. She asked, against her adversaries, but thou dost not ask against thine adversaries, but on behalf of thine own salvation." (Johannes Chrysosotomus, "De diabolo tentatore," in *Three Homilies Concerning The Power of Demons* [http://www.ccel.org/ccel/schaff/npnf109.html, 345–407]). *Cyril*: "The present parable assures us God will bend his ear to those who offer him their prayers, not carelessly nor negligently but with earnestness and constancy. The constant coming of the oppressed widow conquered the unjust judge that did not fear God or have any shame. Even against his will, he granted her request. How will not he who loves mercy and hates iniquity, and who always gives his helping hand to those that love him, accept those who draw near to him day and night and avenge them as his elect?" (Cyril, "Commentary on the Gospel of St. Luke," in *Commentary on Luke, Homily 119*, 478). *Origen*: "He prays for those who pray and appeals with those who appeal. He does not, however, pray for servants who do not pray continuously through him. He will not be the Advocate

see this as a parable about prayer.[20] Later receptions do the same. Martin Luther is mainly concerned with the voices of Luke and the Lord, and lets them determine the meaning of the parable.[21] In recent scholarship, I have found that three of the five authors of the mainstream commentaries I have studied[22] also understand this as a parable about prayer. Four of the five see the perspectives in the frame as dominant.[23] An example is Joseph A. Fitzmyer's Anchor Bible commentary on Luke: "If a dishonest judge would yield to the persistence and prayer of a widow, how much more would the upright God and Father of all! If the helpless widow's persistent prayer accomplishes so much with a dishonest judge, how much more will the persistent prayer of Christian disciples!"[24] For Fitzmyer,

---

with God for his own if they are not obedient to his instructions that they always should pray and not lose heart. It says, 'And he told them a parable to the effect that they should always pray and not lose heart. In a certain city there was a judge,'.... Who would hesitate a moment to be persuaded to pray if he believes that the mouth of Jesus cannot lie, when he says, 'Ask, and it will be given you...for everyone who asks, receives'" (Origen, "On Prayer," in *An Exhortation to Martyrdom, Prayer and Selected Writings*, ed. R. H. Greer [New York: Paulist], 101). *Martyrius*: "As our Savior pointed out, even the cruel and wicked judge eventually looked into the poor widow's case because she had wearied him with her insistence. It is quite clear that God does not neglect us. Even if he makes us wait, he will nonetheless answer us and see to our case all of a sudden. When we pray all the time, we should not weary. We should eagerly cry out to him day and night, begging him with a broken heart and a humble spirit. "A humble spirit is a sacrifice to God, and God will not reject a broken heart" (Martyrius, "Book of Perfection," in *Book of Perfection* 75 [Kalamazoo, MI: Cistercian Publications, 1973], 233). An exception is found in Ephrem the Syrian's *Commentary on Tatian's Diatessaron*. In this text, he recognizes more of the voices. For Ephrem, the parable is both about persistence in prayer ("Luke's" voice) and about justice (the voice of the widow/Jesus, and/or of "the Lord'). The following quote shows this: "If we persist in prayer, we should be even more able to prevail on the grace and justice of God to give us fruit that agrees with their nature. Let justice vindicate us, and let grace refresh us. Accordingly, the fruit of justice is the just reward of the oppressed, while the giving of refreshment to the afflicted is the fruit of grace" (Saint Ephrem, "Commentary On Tatian's Diatessaron," in *Saint Ephrem's Commentary on Tatian's Diatessaron: An English Translation of Chester Beatty Syriac MS 709*, ed. C. McCarthy, Journal of Semitic Studies Supplement 2 [Oxford: Oxford University Press, 1993], 250–1).

20 A search on BiblIndex, which includes Biblical Patristica, the most substantial source of biblical quotes in patristic literature and has an even broader collection of references, confirms that antiquity's main focus was on the parable *frame*. Altogether 27 preserved patristic writings comment on verse one: "Luke's" voice. Verses 6–8, "the Lord's" voice, has 68 hits. However, most of these 68 text passages do not connect these verses to the longer parable. In contrast, the *narrative* has 20 hits.

21 I found 23 Luther-texts, which are explicitly about other biblical texts, but where he quotes from this parable or refers to it in various ways. The voices of "Luke" and "the Lord" get the majority of the attention—sometimes separately, sometimes in combination.

22 My criteria for choosing these four commentaries: these are "mainstream" biblical commentaries present in most university libraries. In addition, they encompass four decades and are from North America, the European Continent and Great Britain. One of the commentaries has two authors. See the next footnote for an overview of the commentaries.

23 In addition to the following example by Fitzmyer, Luke Timothy Johnson in his Sacra Pagina commentary understands it as a parable about prayer (Johnson, *Luke*, 268). Bovon sees all the perspectives in the *frame* together, as in harmony, even though he, as described earlier, is aware of the "competition of meaning" within the parable (*Lukas Lk 15,1–19,27*, 189–97). Ben Witherington believes it is primarily about persistent prayer (Levine and Witherington, *The Gospel of Luke*, 489). His co-author, Amy-Jill Levine, is an exception. She only studies the parable *narrative*, where she believes there are many perspectives, and leaves out the *frame*.

24 Joseph A. Fitzmyer, *The Gospel According to Luke (X–XXIV)*, AB 28B (New York: Doubleday, 1986), 1177. He claims that the parable talks about this persistent prayer in a way that moves "from the lesser to the greater" (*a minori ad majus*).

Luke's perspective also seems to be so dominant that it silences the other voices. "Prayer" appears to color all the perspectives in the parable. He even describes the widow as "praying" when she approaches the judge.[25]

2.2. The Judge, But Not the Widow

When the focus is on the voices in the narrative, recipients have mostly given the judge more attention than the widow. From antiquity, we have more texts, which emphasize the judge, rather than the widow.[26] Martin Luther also gives the judge most of his attention. Only once does the widow seem significant in his interpretations.[27] While most contemporary biblical commentaries focus on both the judge and the widow, Fitzmyer focuses on the judge almost exclusively. He names the parable "The Parable of the Dishonest Judge," and thus leaves out the widow from the title. He also claims this is mainly a parable about an unjust judge and not about what he calls "the importunate widow."[28]

2.3. The Widow, Voiced by the Judge

Not surprisingly, the feminist works have mostly focused on the widow. Luise Schottroff claims that the widow's demand for justice should determine the interpretation of the rest of the parable.[29] The widow and her claim to justice is also the interpretational focus in all three commentaries on this parable in Mary Ann Beavis' edited book, *The Lost Coin: Parables of Women, Work and Wisdom*.[30] What is surprising, however, is that even when recipients highlight the widow, it is most often the judge's perception of her that recipients hear. This is the case in all the reception periods I have studied, with antiquity as an exception. Even feminist scholars seem to be influenced by the judge's voice when they describe the widow. We find the most explicit examples in contemporary commentaries. Luke Timothy Johnson claims: "The parable makes its point so forcefully and humorously that little comment is required. Contemporary readers can easily imagine an enraged bag lady hitting the negligent magistrate over the head and literally 'giving him a black eye.'"[31] This portrayal of a hysterical, desperate, and violent woman can only come from the judge's inner dialogue, not from the widow, nor from Jesus's narration about her. To recapitulate, the widow says: "Grant me justice/vengeance against my opponent!," while Jesus says that the widow comes repeatedly or with endurance and talks when she approaches the

---

[25] Fitzmyer, *Luke (X–XXIV)*, 1176.
[26] A search on BibIIndex gives 16 hits on v. 5 (the voice of the judge), but only four on v. 3 (the widow's voice).
[27] The judge is interpreted in at least four texts. The text where the widow is made sense of, is Luther's sermon on Matt 5–7; cf. Martin Luther, *The Sermon on the Mount*, ed. Jaroslav Pelikan, *The Works of Martin Luther*, 55 vols. (Charlottenville: Past Masters, InteLex, 2013), 235–6.
[28] Fitzmyer, *Luke (X–XXIV)*, 1176, 1178, and 1180.
[29] Luise Schottroff, *Lydia's Impatient Sisters: A Feminist Social History of Early Christianity* (London: Westminster John Knox Press, 1994–95), 101, 116.
[30] Mary Ann Beavis, ed., *The Lost Coin: Parables of Women, Work and Wisdom* (New York: Sheffield Academic Press, 2002).
[31] Johnson, *Luke*, 273.

judge. Johnson therefore must be listening to the judge, which also happens in more subtle ways in the interpretation of other scholars. Fitzmyer describes the widow's actions as "continual nagging."[32] François Bovon seems to listen to Jesus and the widow. Yet, the silent voice of the judge comes through when he calls the widow "hartnäckig" (stubborn), says she speaks with "schneidenen Imperative" (cutting imperative), and that she "pocht auf ihr Recht" (she pounds on her rights).[33] This seems to agree with the opinion of the judge and not with Jesus or the widow. Surprisingly, even contemporary scholars with a feminist aim seem to be convinced by the judge. A striking example is Mary W. Matthews. She writes "...this parable must have boggled the minds of its first audience: a mere woman, a widow—by definition in their minds, weak, foolish, silly, impotent, chattering, useless—was not only taking part in a court case, she was browbeating the judge!"[34] Matthews also uses terms like "pestering" to describe the widow and writes that she wishes that Jesus would have said: "When the Messiah comes, Mama will spank."[35] Some of the same applies for Amy-Jill Levine. She lets the judge's opinion color how she understands the widow when she characterizes the widow as "nagging" and writes about the judge that: "By ignoring the woman, he faces physical threat."[36] Levine makes it clear that she will not use stereotypes about widows always being moral persons. Still, nagging and the threat of physical violence—that is the judge speaking. Even Schottroff, who in *Lydia's Impatient Sisters* is very clear that all descriptions of the widow as violent or hysterical are patriarchal slander, writes in her later *The Parables of Jesus*: "The widow also expresses her resistance by violating her social boundaries. She behaves loudly and aggressively in public; she may even scream and shout."[37] Annette Merz also writes that the widow's potential violence is in the head of the judge. Still, Merz briefly lets the judge's voice decide her understanding of the widow and writes that the widow "pesters a powerful man," and does not indicate that this is the judge's perception of the circumstances.[38]

---

[32] Fitzmyer, *Luke*, 1179.
[33] "Hartnäckig" has a range of meanings from persistent to stubborn and could well reflect the voices of Jesus and the widow. However, followed by the next quote, it reflects the judge (Bovon, *Lukas Lk 15,1–19,27*, 191).
[34] Matthews, in Mary W. Matthews, Carter Shelley and Barbara Scheele, "Proclaiming the Parable of the Persistent Widow (Luke 18:2–5)," in *The Lost Coin: Parables of Women, Work and Wisdom*, ed. Mary Ann Beavis (New York: Sheffield Academic Press, 2002), 46–70 Cf. Matthews' part of the article, "'Go Thou and Do Likewise," 50.
[35] Matthews, Shelley and Scheele, "Proclaiming the Parable of the Persistent Widow (Lk 18.2–5)," 52. Barbara Scheele, in the same article, writes: "She finds that justice by elbowing her way through the corrupt political machine" (p. 65). However, this is the only time Scheele seems to listen to how the judge describes the widow. The third contributor to the article, Carter Shelley, seems to hear the voices of Jesus and the widow over the judge's.
[36] Levine and Witherington, *The Gospel of Luke*, 486–7.
[37] Luise Schottroff, *The Parables of Jesus* (Minneapolis, MN: Augsburg Fortress, 2005), 192.
[38] Annette Merz, "How the Woman Who Fought Back and Demanded Her Rights Became an Importunate Widow: The Transformations of a Parable of Jesus," in *Jesus from Judaism to Christianity: Continuum Approaches to the Historical Jesus*, ed. Tom Holmén, LNTS 312 (London: T&T Clark, 2007), 63 and 65.

If we go back through time, Luther also seems to hear the judge's voice, which describes the widow as violent. In his sermon on Matthew 5–7 Luther writes: "Learn from the Widow, who eagerly and persistently would not let go of the judge's throat, and acted so outrageously, that he became convinced and had to help her, in spite of his own will."[39] Recipients in antiquity, however, seem to mainly focus on the widow and her demand. This period is the only exception I have found where recipients seemingly listen to the widow and Jesus more than to the judge.

2.4. The Sound of Silence

For many recipients the voices in the frame determine how they understand the widow. Within the parable narrative, the inside voice, and even more than that, the inner voice, has become the outside voice. The majority of the recipients have trusted this unethical voice. Following the silent views of the judge, recipients have interpreted the widow along gender stereotypes, like the "bag lady" Johnson describes. Even most feminist scholars, who want to focus on the widow, seem to be influenced by this. Why is this dodgy, silent voice so persuasive? Does it have to do with underlying assumptions about gender and authority? A judge seems to be constantly listened to. This is also the case with a bad judge. Are even contemporary feminists so used to listening to a powerful man, no matter what and how he speaks, that his voice persuades them, even when they do not want it to? In addition, do recipients fail to hear the widow's voice because they interpret her stereotypically as poor, marginalized and desperate? The parable provides very little information about the widow. Still, recipients assume quite a bit about her. In almost all the cases I have studied, the recipients "fill in" this sparse information and see her as a marginalized, deprived, despairing victim. The only antique text I have found that emphasizes social factors in its interpretation of the widow sees her as poor.[40] As the quote above shows, Luther's widow is desperate. He also connects her to suffering and deprivation.[41]

In contemporary scholarship, Johnson understands her as "endemically vulnerable." She has lost hope and courage, and therefore has to turn to desperate means.[42] Bovon sees her as the embodiment of vulnerability.[43] Levine and Ben Witherington, in The New Cambridge Bible Commentary, have a dual

---

[39] My own translation of "…leret von der Widwen, die nicht wolt ihrem Richter vom hals lassen mit geilen und anhalten und machtes so unverschampt, das er uberteubt ward und must ihr on seinen danck helffen." Martin Luther, "Wochenpredigten über Matth 5–7," in Martin Luthers Werke. Gesamtausgabe, Vol. 32, ed. Paul Pietsch (Weimar: Hermann Böhlaus Nachfolger, 1906), Sermon 493.

[40] Martyrius describes her as *poor* (Martyrius, "Book of Perfection," 233). Apart from this characteristic, antique receptions mainly focus on her as a symbol of prayer or justice. Social factors seem to be of little importance.

[41] His text compares the need and suffering of Luther's audience to the widow. The widow could thus also be seen as suffering and in need.

[42] Johnson, *Luke*, 273.

[43] Bovon, *Lukas Lk 15,1–19,27*, 191, states that she is "die Verkörperung von Abhängigkeit und Sozialer Zerbrechlichkeit"—"the embodiment of dependence and social vulnerability" (my own translation).

understanding of the widow. Witherington sees the widow as "helpless, marginalized, disenfranchised, and a moral exemplar."[44] In contrast, Levine thinks listeners could construct her as active, subversive, rich and powerful, dangerous, a trickster, wise and demanding, in addition to being in need of help, marginalised or disfranchised.[45] Most other feminists do not share her understanding. As with most "mainstream" research, they interpret the widow as poor, marginalized, and despairing.[46] Schottroff describes her as a victim of injustice.[47] Carter Shelley writes: "The very word widow conjures images of economic insecurity, vulnerability, loneliness, and desperate need on behalf of herself and her children."[48] Is it easier to believe an unjust, but powerful judge than a poor, marginalized, and desperate widow? It seems so. In the following, I ask what might happen to the interpretation of the parable if recipients had a wider, less stereotypical understanding of the widow, and made her the center of their attention, rather than seeing her through the eyes of the judge. As a heuristic tool to do so, I hypothesize about *possible* recipients, who could have focused on the female character and seen her in more nuanced ways.

3. The Reverberations and their Possible Reception

The widow and her voice has often been neglected. When she has been emphasized, the majority of recipients have described her in intersections of marginalization and sexism. Her talking plea has become screaming desperation.

Many contemporary scholars explore parables from the perspective of first audiences or first readers, without specifying which listeners or readers they mean. I find it necessary to discuss and identify the recipients we propose. There is no "natural" or "generic" first reader or hearer. All scholars make conscious or unconscious choices about the audience or readers they assume, about these readers' or listeners' socio-cultural situatedness, as well as about the intertextual stories they might have employed to interpret parables.[49] In the following, I make these choices explicit.

---

[44] Levine and Witherington, *The Gospel of Luke*, 484.
[45] The intertexts she proposes are about the trickster widows (see the definition of intertextual stories in n. 49 below), such as Tamar (Gen 38), Ruth and Naomi (e.g. Ruth 3), Abigail (2 Sam 3:3), the wise woman of Tekoa (2 Sam 14:5), Bathsheba (2 Sam 11) and Judith (the book of Judith). Judith is also both rich and beautiful and an assassin. Compare the demanding widow of Sarepta (1 Kgs 17). Levine also states that the New Testament knows of both rich widows and young widows with their own income, as well as poor widows who were dependent on the church (1 Tim 5). Cf. Levine and Witherington, *The Gospel of Luke*, 484.
[46] Merz is a possible exception. For Merz, "How the Woman," 65, the widow is definitely a victim of injustice. At the same time, she is definitely not helpless and despairing, "but empowered by the knowledge that she has God's law on her side."
[47] Schottroff, *Lydia's Impatient Sisters*, 101.
[48] Shelley, in Matthews, Shelley and Scheele, "Proclaiming the Parable of the Persistent Widow (Lk 18.2–5)," 58.
[49] By *intertextual stories* I mean evoked stories from the Hebrew Bible, LXX, early Christian, Jewish or Greek-Roman worlds recipients have employed or are assumed to have used, to interpret parables.

3.1. Reflecting Recipients Who Hear About Corresponding Characters

As a heuristic tool and a counterbalance to the later recorded reception history, I postulate hypothetical audiences from the first two centuries CE, who could mirror themselves in the widow in the parable. I imagine a variety of listening widows, who, since they were widows themselves, could possibly see themselves represented in the widow character. Such hypothetical listeners are also plausible. It is probable that a variety of widows heard parables read aloud in the first two centuries CE. However, their possible interpretations of this parable are lost. Therefore, we have to imagine them.[50]

Through identification, based on the intersectional similarity of being widows,[51] these listening widows might be seen as reflecting recipients, who hear about a corresponding character in the parable.[52] Through a double-mirroring process, they could not only see themselves in the widow character, but also construe the widow character as themselves. They could thus view themselves as a reflection of the parable character.

Since female parable characters mostly have been narrowly interpreted or overlooked, I think a reading with such reflecting recipients would help us see broader interpretational potential in the widow character, and accordingly also in the parable. In the following, I will explore which of the parable voices such reflecting recipients could possibly have focused on. As part of this, I will ask

---

[50] My project is in line with the shift in many historical, as well as in sociological academic fields, where scholars ask for the missing parts of history and the marginalized groups' participation; cf. Nancy T. Ammerman, "Lived Religion as an Emerging Field: An Assessment of its Contours and Frontiers," *Nordic Journal of Religion and Society* 1, no 2 (2016): 84. In New Testament studies, Dale Martin argues that we must allow room for more *imagination* to think about, for example, how human beings in antiquity experienced families and slavery (Dale B. Martin, "Slave Families and Slaves in Families," in *Early Christian Families in Context: An Interdisciplinary Dialogue*, ed. D. Balch and C. Osiek [Grand Rapids, MI: Eerdmans, 2003], 207–30 [here 230]). Bernadette Brooten creates "historically informed imagined scenarios" from the first century when she imagines scenario of listeners to the Colossian household codes; cf. Bernadette J. Brooten, "Early Christian Enslaved Families (First to Fourth Century)," in *Children and Family in Late Antiquity. Life, Death and Interaction*, ed. Christian Laes, Katarina Mustakallio and Ville Vuolanto (Leuven: Peeters, 2015), 111–34 (here 127–8).

[51] I apply intersectionality in line with Birgitta L. Sjöberg: "Intersectionality can…be regarded as an analytical tool for understanding multiple discriminations created by the intersection of different categories present in the *oikos* including: gender, class, ethnicity, sexuality and age." Cf. Birgitta L. Sjöberg, "More than Just Gender: The Classical Oikos as a Site of Intersectionality," in *Families in the Greco-Roman World*, ed. Ray Laurence and Agneta Strömberg (London: Bloomsbury, 2012), 48–9.

[52] This could be seen as involvement with characters through identification and possibly empathy. The *intersectional similarity* would be the basis of this involvement. As Els Andringa writes: "I would prefer to see involvement as an emotional consequence of the processes of identification and empathy, whereas these processes themselves are defined as the establishment of a relationship between the recipient and the world of fiction. The type of relationship is determined in terms of similarity, desirability, or understanding as a witness" (Els Andringa, "The Interface between Fiction and Life: Patterns of Identification in Reading Autobiographies," *Poetics Today* 25, no. 2 [2004]: 205–40 [here 210]). For various types of "similarity" as important in character involvement, see also Kirsten Marie Hartvigsen, *"Prepare the way of the Lord": Towards a Cognitive Poetic Analysis of Audience Involvement with Characters and Events in the Markan World* (Berlin: de Gruyter, 2012), 70–1, especially n. 184; Suzanne Keen, *Empathy and the Novel* (New York: Oxford University Press, 2007), 68–72, and Keith Oatley, "Meetings of Minds: Dialogue, Sympathy, and Identification, in Reading Fiction," *Poetics* 26, no. 5 (1999): 439–54 (445–6).

how an intersectional variety of listening widows could have construed the widow character. Finally, I will consider what such considerations could mean for the interpretation of the parable.

3.2. The Narrative Over the Frame?

To whom would reflecting recipients have listened? Luke has created a powerful composition, as the parable's reverberations show. If listening widows heard the frame together with the narrative, it is possible that they would also hear the parable as Luke or the Lord says it should be. Still, our listeners could possibly have paid attention to the voices in the parable narrative, and not let them be overpowered by the voices in the frame. They could have been aware that parable narratives might have different frames, and thus know that it could be independent of the frame. They could have heard parable narratives with different frames, from what we call the Synoptic Gospels, or from other early Christian parables in oral form.[53] They could perhaps also know that a rabbinic parable narrative, a *mashal*, could have divergent applications.[54] Alternatively, they could possibly hear this parable as a fable and thus have understood the frame in our parable as *promythium* and/or *epimythium*.[55] It is thus possible that widow listeners, who likely would focus on their corresponding character, might have paid more attention to the voices in the narrative, where the widow appears, than those in the frame.

3.3. The Widow Over the Judge?

Would our listener also have accepted the judge's story about the widow? My reception case studies show that it has been easier to construct a first-century widow in stereotypical, sexist intersections of poor, desperate, and potentially

---

[53] Several of the various parable narratives in the gospels have more and different frames. In addition, Stephen Wright (*Jesus*, 89) suggests that the historical Jesus might have told the same parables with different applications If this is the case, our listeners could be aware of such oral stories with different frames.

[54] See, for example, David Stern, *Parables in Midrash: Narrative and Exegesis in Rabbinic Literature* (Cambridge, MA: Harvard University Press, 1991), 16. The written sources we have of these rabbinic parables are of later dates than our audience. However, the oral traditions could have been known earlier.

[55] Justin Strong ('How to Interpret Parables," 336–9) suggests that this parable is one of the clearest examples of traditional fable genres in the New Testament. Our listeners could have heard 18:1 as a *promythium*, an introduction, which announced the topic or lesson of the fable narrative, addressed its reader or listener or which connected the fable narrative to the broader literary context. Verses 6–8 could have been heard as two or three *epimythia*. An *epimythia* could include more, either complementary, but also unrelated and sometimes even opposing morals. According to Beavis ("Parable and Fable," 497), the synoptic parables are similar to the popular literary genre appealing mainly to children and the uneducated, namely the *gymnasma*. She writes that "with the spread of Greek education in Hellenistic Greco-Roman times, people of many different ethnic and cultural backgrounds, including Jews, and later Christians, would have had direct experience of Aesopic fables through their elementary schooling" (p. 478). Thus, the few educated widows, the few educated widows could have been aware of such distinctions. Widows without education could still be familiar with the widely popular fables and could have heard fable narratives with various types of framing.

violent, than as rich, able, and resourceful, for example. Desperate and violent agree with the voice of the judge, which so often has conquered the other utterings in the parable. I have asked whether this is a reason why recipients have hardly listened to the widow. Would reflecting recipients perhaps invoke other and less stereotypical intersectional knowledge to understand the widow character? Would they thus construe a character, which speaks more easily to them? All listeners or readers employ knowledge they already have, to make sense of a new story or text.[56] From all this knowledge, I focus on what I call intersectional knowledge. This is knowledge about how gender, sexuality, ethnicity, age, economy, and other social factors meet and interact in recipients' socio-historical worlds.

Reflecting recipients could know that a widow does not need to be poor or desperate. Listening widows could, for example, be rich themselves or know of other rich widows. We are aware of such rich widows from, for example, the Babatha archives.[57]

They could also know from their intersectional experience or the life stories of other widows, that it was acknowledged that a widow could ask a magistrate for help. For example, Babatha initiated a case against her son's guardians.[58] The Papyrus P.Oslo II 22 also tells about the woman Sarapous, who petitions the strategus to help her against a man who verbally and physically assaulted her.[59] Listening widows could also know that a widow could bring a plea to a judge more than once. One of the Oxyrhynchus Papyri from the early first century shows the second of two depositions from a widow who pleads to the court about injustices done to her.[60]

They could also know that ethnicity would be in play in such interactions. The Jewish Babatha had to be represented by a guardian in her contact with the authorities. However, another widow in the archives, Julia Crispina, could act in her own right and serve as a guardian herself, probably in her capacity as a Roman citizen.[61]

---

[56] Ralf Schneider, "Toward a Cognitive Theory of Literary Character: The Dynamics of Mental-Model Construction," *Style* 35, no. 4 (2001), 607–39 (607).

[57] See e.g., Emanuel Tov, *The Texts from the Judaean Desert: Indices and an Introduction to the Discoveries in the Judean Desert Series*, DJD 39 (Oxford: Clarendon Press, 2002), 112, and Hannah M. Cotton and Jonas C. Greenfield, "Babatha's Property and the Law of Succession in the Babatha Archive," *ZPE* 104 (1994): 211–24 (here 211–12).

[58] She complained to the governor about her son's guardians because they did not give her son "the tenants" money commensurate with the income from the interest of his money and the rest of his property. Cf. P.Yadin 15 and Hannah Cotton, "The Guardianship of Jesus Son of Babatha: Roman and Local Law in the Province of Arabia," *JRS* 83 (1993): 103.

[59] P.Oslo II 22 (inv. 449)—OPES (uio.no). We do not know whether she is a widow. She does not introduce herself in relation to a husband, but as the "daughter of The...(text missing)." She could, thus, possibly be a woman who lived without a man.

[60] Cited in Schottroff, *Lydia's Impatient Sisters*, 103.

[61] Benjamin Isaac, "The Babtha Archive: A Review Article," *IEJ* 42, no. 1–2 (1992): 62–72 (here 70–1). Cohick also describes several Roman women, some of whom might have been understood as a χήρα who spoke to the senate or in the court. See Lynn H. Cohick, *Women in the World of the Earliest Christians: Illuminating Ancient Ways of Life* (Grand Rapids, MI: Baker Academic, 2009), 286–7.

Hence, to repeatedly petition a judge did not have to be a desperate, potentially violent act, as in the interpretation of the judge.[62] Rather, it could be construed in many possible intersections of power and discrimination.

Thus, through reflecting themselves in their corresponding character, listening widows could conceptualize a wider image of the widow than what has often been the case in the parable's later reception. I propose that they would listen to her. What would such reflecting recipients hear the widow say?

3.4. Intersectional Widow Voice

As noted above, ἐκδίκησόν με has several translational possibilities. It can mean a plea for both justice and vengeance. Most recipients, in all the studied phases of the recorded reception history, seem to have understood the widow as being entitled to what she demands, namely justice.[63] I find it interesting that in the cases where scholars perceive the widow as violent or potentially so, they seem to assume that her actions are justified, since she, as poor and marginalized, has a claim to justice. This is visible both in Luther's "would not let go of the judge's throat" and in Matthews' "When the Messiah comes, Mama will spank." Reflecting recipients would probably have the intersectional knowledge or experience that widows come in all ethical types. In 1 Tim 5:3–16 we hear about widows with a such a variety of morals: widows who, according to the text, are pious or, in contrast, are self-indulgent and live for pleasure. It mentions, in addition, widows who care for their families, or those who do not; widows who do good deeds, show hospitality, wash the feet of the holy, help the suffering, or alternatively, those who do not; widows who are with or without sensual desires, who are idle or not idle, gossip, speak inappropriately and meddle in things they should not, or who do no such things. Thus, to see the widow as immoral and her claim as illegitimate is also a possibility.

In addition to such intersectional knowledge, listening widows could have evoked other intertexts, than those often employed. Most of the recorded recipients employ intertextual stories which group widows together with the poor, orphans and foreigners in need of help.[64] Our listeners could, possibly, have referenced stories about widows who were not deprived, needy or desperate,

---

[62] In addition, they could possibly know of other literary female characters who would argue with public male figures. For example, the *Matrona* in Rabbinic literature, who would ask valid questions to a rabbi and sometimes persuade him. Perhaps they could also know other early Christian stories about women who negotiated with Jesus.

[63] Exceptions are Levine and possibly some theologians in antiquity. For example, according to Augustine ("Letters," 387–8) and Cyril (*Commentary 119*, 478), the widow seeks vengeance/to be avenged. For Levine, the widow in the parable might have a legitimate claim for justice, or she might be an immoral character who wants revenge or claims what is not hers. See her discussion with Witherington, who claims the widow is a moral exemplar; cf. Levine and Witherington, *The Gospel of Luke*, 484.

[64] A main intertext for understanding this parable is Sir. 35:12–29, where God is the just judge who sees the tears and hears the complaints of widows and helps them and other poor and weak people. For more texts, see, for example, Johnson, *Luke*, 269.

but rather smart, capable, bold and sometimes rich, cunning or morally bad.[65] Examples of such widows are Tamar, who, when she did not receive her rights as a widow, worked out a daring plan to get them.[66] Another is Judith, a rich widow, who more or less singlehandedly fooled and overpowered the Assyrian enemies;[67] or possibly the widow from Tekoa, who persuaded King David to intervene in her son's trial,[68] Ruth, who had to be cunning to receive her and her mother-in-law's kinship obligation from Boaz,[69] or the widowed mother of the seven sons, who, in the fourth book of Maccabees, convinced her sons to oppose the tyrant.[70] The text above from 1 Timothy could also have been known to them. Thus, reflecting recipients could have constructed the widow in the parable as capable, resourceful, maybe rich, cunning, sly, revengeful and not only as poor, desperate and potentially hysterical and violent and entitled to the justice she demands. The judge describes a hysterical, violent person. The voice of Jesus, which indicates that the widow's actions are repetitive and/or durative, opens up a wider span of understandings of the widow. I, thus, find it possible, and also plausible, that audiences of widows would listen to the more open description of the words and actions of the widow, over the often-heard limiting definition of the judge.

4. Polyphonic Parable

The different and possibly opposing perspectives in the parable, which have puzzled scholars, have still mostly been interpreted in harmony. In this way, one of the voices has been heard as the leading tune, which has overpowered the others. What this primary voice is has differed. Mostly, the perspectives in the frame, especially Luke's voice, have set the tune. Within the narrative, the judge's silent and unethical voice has overwhelmed the other voices. In the few instances, where the widow's demand has led, she has mostly been heard as the judge constructs her. Whose perspectives matter? To whom do we listen, when Warren and McConnell interpret the reading of Scott King's letter in different ways? Who gets to interpret this parable? Whose perspectives, inside and outside the text, matter? I suggest that imagined reflecting recipients as well as other possible but overlooked intersectional audiences, whose interpretations of the biblical texts we do not have access to, should be considered. Such unnoticed

---

[65] Annette Merz writes: "Despite all the differences in points of detail, these stories of Tamar and Judith, of Ruth, the prudent widow of Tekoa and the mother of the seven sons embody a narrative type in which a widow—traditionally the embodiment of a powerless woman who is dependent on help from others—becomes active and enforces God's will against opposition within Judaism or from external foes." Cf. Annette Merz, "How the Woman Who Fought Back and Demanded Her Rights Became an Importunate Widow: The Transformations of a Parable of Jesus," in *Jesus from Judaism to Christianity: Continuum Approaches to the Historical Jesus*, ed. Tom Holmén, LNTS 352 (London: T&T Clark, 2007), 69.
[66] Gen 38.
[67] The book of Judith.
[68] 2 Sam 14.
[69] Ruth 2–4.
[70] 4 Macc. 14:11–17:6.

understandings may help us see what the later reception has neglected and what might be missing today.

As such, it might be helpful to see both the parable and the various parable voices as polyphonic, in line with Mikhail Bakhtin's understanding. Bakhtin claims that in his source material, Dostoevsky's novels, there is a polyphony of independent and unfused voices or consciousnesses in dialogical opposition. These voices or consciousnesses have opposing points of views, worldviews and values. Still, they all have the same quality and right to exist. In Dostoevsky's novels, the voices are dialogic. They are in conversations or argumentations where the different voices dominate alternately.[71] Our parable's different voices, which seem to go in different directions, could be understood as in dialogue with each other. Like Dostoevsky's consciousnesses, the parable perspectives are also at different narratological levels.[72] However, the parable voices might not have the same quality or right to exist. The judge's voice is characterized as more dubious than the others are. Still, I believe polyphony is a helpful term. For Bakhtin, truth is always dialogical. It cannot rise only from the mind of an author, but also when multiple opinions are allowed through numerous opposing voices within the same text.[73] Might we be able to find, if not "truth," then maybe new interpretational potential in this parable, if we see the many voices as being in a multivalent dialogue? Could this, simultaneously, be a parable about praying, about *pistis* in eschatological times, about a widow's petition, or about a powerful judge who becomes afraid of a widow? Furthermore, could we not only see the different voices as polyphonic, but also study the polyphonic potential within the voices? I have tried to make this visible for the widow's voice, which is often lost. This might be a parable about a poor, desperate and marginal widow with a legitimate claim to justice. It might also be about a rich, resourceful, shrewd

---

[71] Mikhail Bakhtin, *Problems of Dostoevsky's Poetics*, ed. and trans. Caryl Emerson (Minneapolis: The University of Minnesota Press, 1984), 6, 16. Bakhtin mainly found *polyphony* in Dostoevsky's novels. However, already in the antique genre, Bakhtin discerned *menippea*—Bakhtin's own term—which he thinks might have influenced the gospel authors, as witnessed by more and independent voices and elements of dialogism (for a thorough discussion of this term, see C. Cobb, *Slavery, Gender, Truth, and Power in Luke-Acts and Other Ancient Narratives* [Wingate: Palgrave Macmillan, 2019], 42–9). I will not speculate whether "Luke" thought the different voices were polyphonic and dialogic or not, but rather use this modern theory to explore the interpretational potential of the text. Bakhtin's literary theories are already employed in New Testament Lukan studies by Raj Nadella to study the many, and often seemingly contradictory, perspectives in Luke's gospel as a *multivalent literary dialogism*. Nadella claims that the gospel "offers a new, creative, and dialogical version of the truth"; cf. Raj Nadella, *Dialogue Not Dogma: Many Voices in the Gospel of Luke*, LNTS 431 (London: T&T Clark, 2011), 5. Bakhtin, and Nadella's understanding of him, is also recently employed by Cobb, *Slavery, Gender, Truth, and Power*. As she does, I also engage *polyphony* to analyze opposing voices, as well as a tool to focus on often-ignored voices.

[72] Luke narrates all the other voices, Jesus those of the widow and the judge. In Dostoevsky's novels, some are characters, some are narrators, sometimes even the voice of the author is heard (Cobb, *Slavery, Gender, Truth, and Power*, 1, 64).

[73] According to Bakhtin, *Problems*, 110, "truth is not born, nor is it found inside the head of an individual person; it is born between people collectively searching for truth, in the process of their dialogic interactions."

elite widow, who demands more than her share. Or, many things in between. Nevertheless, she persisted.

Bibliography

Altes, L. K. *Ethos and Narrative Interpretation: The Negotiation of Values in Fiction.* Frontiers of Narrative. Lincoln: University of Nebraska Press, 2014.
Ammerman, N. T. "Lived Religion as an Emerging Field: An Assessment of Its Contours and Frontiers." *Nordic Journal of Religion and Society* 1, no. 2 (2016): 83–99.
Andringa, E. "The Interface between Fiction and Life: Patterns of Identification in Reading Autobiographies." *Poetics Today* 25, no. 2 (2004): 205–40.
Augustine. "Letters." In *The Fathers of the Church*, vol. 401. Edited by Sister Wilfrid Parsons. Washington: Catholic University of America Press, 1966.
Bakhtin, M. *Problems of Dostoevsky's Poetics.* Edited and translated by Caryl Emerson. Minneapolis: The University of Minnesota Press, 1984.
Beavis, M. A., ed. *The Lost Coin: Parables of Women, Work and Wisdom.* New York: Sheffield Academic Press, 2002.
Beavis, M. A. "Parable and Fable." *CBQ* 52 (1990): 473–98.
Bovon, F. "Apocalyptic Traditions in the Lucan Special Material: Reading Luke 18:1–8." *HTR* 90, no. 4 (1997): 383–91.
Bovon, F. *Das Evangelium Nach Lukas Lk 15,1–19,27.* EKK 3.3. Zurich: Benziger, 2001.
Brooten, B. J. "Early Christian Enslaved Families (First to Fourth Century)." In *Children and Family in Late Antiquity: Life, Death and Interaction*, edited by Christian Laes, Katarina Mustakallio and Ville Vuolanto, 111–34. Leuven-Walpole, MA: Peeters, 2015.
Chrysosotomus, J. "De Diabolo Tentatore." In *Three Homilies Concerning the Power of Demons.* http://www.ccel.org/ccel/schaff/npnf109.html, 345–407.
Cobb, C. *Slavery, Gender, Truth, and Power in Luke-Acts and Other Ancient Narratives.* Wingate: Palgrave Macmillan, 2019.
Cohick, L. H. *Women in the World of the Earliest Christians: Illuminating Ancient Ways of Life.* Grand Rapids, MI: Baker Academic, 2009.
Cotton, H. "The Guardianship of Jesus Son of Babatha: Roman and Local Law in the Province of Arabia." *JRS* 83 (1993): 94–108.
Cotton, H. M., and J. C. Greenfield. "Babatha's Property and the Law of Succession in the Babatha Archive." *ZPE* 104 (1994): 211–24.
Curkpatrick, S. "Dissonance in Luke 18:1–8." *JBL* 121 (2002): 107–21.
Curkpatrick, S. "A Parable Frame-up and Its Audacious Reframing." *NTS* 49 (2003): 22–38.
Cyril. "Commentary on the Gospel of St. Luke" in *Commentary on Luke. Homily 119.* Studion Publishers, n.d.
Dodd, C. H. *The Parables of the Kingdom.* London: Nisbeth & Co., 1935.
Donahue, J. R. *The Gospel in Parable.* Minneapolis, MN: Fortress Press, 1988.
Ephrem. "Commentary on Tatian's Diatessaron." In *Saint Ephrem's Commentary on Tatian's Diatessaron: An English Translation of Chester Beatty Syriac MS 709*, edited by C. McCarthy. Journal of Semitic Studies Supplement 2. Oxford: Oxford University Press, 1993.
Fitzmyer, J. A. *The Gospel According to Luke (X–XXIV).* AB 28B. New York: Doubleday & Co., 1986.

Hartvigsen, K. M. *"Prepare the Way of the Lord": Towards a Cognitive Poetic Analysis of Audience Involvement with Characters and Events in the Markan World.* Berlin: de Gruyter, 2012.

Isaac, B. "The Babtha Archive: A Review Article." *IEJ* 42, no. 1–2 (1992): 62–75.

Johnson, L. T. *The Gospel of Luke.* Sacra Pagina 3. Minneapolis: The Liturgical Press, 1991.

Kartzow, M. B. "Rewritten Stereotypes: Scripture and Cultural Echo in Luke's Parable of the Widow and the Judge." In *Luke's Literary Creativity*, edited by Jesper Tang Nielsen and Mogens Müller, 208–24. LNTS 550. London: Bloomsbury T&T Clark, 2016.

Keen, S. *Empathy and the Novel.* New York: Oxford University Press, 2007.

Levine, A.-J., and B. Witherington. *The Gospel of Luke.* NCBC. Cambridge: Cambridge University Press, 2018.

Lundhaug, H., and L. I. Lied. "Studying Snapshots: On Manuscript Culture, Textual Fluidity, and New Philology," edited by H. Lundhaug and L. I. Lied, 1–19. Berlin: de Gruyter, 2017.

Luther, M. *The Sermon on the Mount.* The Works of Martin Luther. Edited by Jaroslav Pelikan. 55 vols. Charlottenville: Past Masters, InteLex, 2013.

Luther, M. "Wochenpredigten über Matth 5–7." In *D. Martin Luthers Werke. Gesamtausgabe, 32. Band*, edited by Paul Pietsch. Weimar: Hermann Böhlaus Nachfolger, 1906.

Martin, D. B. "Slave Families and Slave in Families." In *Early Christian Families in Context*, edited by David Balch, 207–30. Grand Rapids, MI: Eerdmans, 2003.

Martyrius. "Book of Perfection 75." In *Book of Perfection.* Kalamazoo, MI: Cistercian Publications, 1973.

Matthews, M. W., C. Shelley, and B. Scheele, "Proclaiming the Parable of the Persistent Widow (Lk 18.2–5)." In *The Lost Coin: Parables of Women, Work and Wisdom*, edited by Mary Ann Beavis, 46–70. New York: Sheffield Academic Press, 2002.

Merz, A. "How the Woman Who Fought Back and Demanded Her Rights Became an Importunate Widow: The Transformations of a Parable of Jesus." In *Jesus from Judaism to Christianity: Continuum Approaches to the Historical Jesus*, edited by Tom Holmén, 47–86. LNTS 352. London: T&T Clark, 2007.

Morgan, T. *Roman Faith and Christian Faith: Pistis and Fides in the Early Roman Empire and Early Churches.* Oxford: Oxford University Press, 2015.

Nadella, R. *Dialogue Not Dogma: Many Voices in the Gospel of Luke.* LNTS 431. London: T&T Clark, 2011.

Oatley, K. "Meetings of Minds: Dialogue, Sympathy, and Identification, in Reading Fiction." *Poetics* 26, no. 5 (1999): 439–54.

Origen. "On Prayer." In *An Exhortation to Martyrdom, Prayer and Selected Writings*, edited by R. A. Greer. New York: Paulist.

Schneider, R. "Toward a Cognitive Theory of Literary Character: The Dynamics of Mental-Model Construction." *Style* 35, no. 4 (2001): 607–39.

Schottroff, L. *Lydia's Impatient Sisters: A Feminist Social History of Early Christianity.* London: Westminster John Knox Press, 1994/5.

Schottroff, L. *The Parables of Jesus.* Minneapolis, MN: Augsburg Fortress, 2005.

Sherwood, Y. *A Biblical Text and Its Afterlives: The Survival of Jonah in Western Culture.* Cambridge: Cambridge University Press, 2000.

Sjöberg, Birgitta L. "More than Just Gender: The Classical Oikos as a Site of Intersectionality." In *Families in the Greco-Roman World*, edited by Ray Laurence and Agneta Strömberg, 48–59. London: Bloomsbury, 2012.

Stern, D. *Parables in Midrash: Narrative and Exegesis in Rabbinic Literature.* Cambridge, MA: Harvard University Press, 1991.

Strong, J. D. "How to Interpret Parables in Light of the Ancient Fable: The Promythium and Epimythium." In *Overcoming Dichotomies: Parables, Fables, and Similes in the Graeco-Roman World*, edited by A. Oegema, J. Pater and M. Stoutjesdijk. WUNT. Mohr Siebeck, 2022.

Tov, E. *The Texts from the Judaean Desert: Indices and an Introduction to the Discoveries in the Judean Desert Series.* DJDS 39. Oxford: Clarendon Press, 2002.

Wright, S. I. *Jesus the Storyteller.* Louisville, KY: Westminster John Knox Press, 2015.

Mirroring and Echoing:
Realism and Figuration in Jesus's Parables

Stephen I. Wright

1. Introduction

The so-called material turn in parables research has highlighted the importance of the economic, social and political context of first-century Palestine for grasping the possible meanings and effects of Jesus's parables. Scholars whose work is represented in this volume have made significant contributions to uncovering the material realia reflected in the parables' imagery and exploring the effect that knowledge of those realia might have on understanding the parables' original thrust. However, detecting a probable material context does not in itself decide the question of what Jesus might originally have "meant" or what his hearers might have "heard." The way in which, and the purpose for which, the material world is reflected are crucial. For example, both Kenneth E. Bailey and Ernest van Eck present a wealth of cultural material to illuminate the parables, but the thrust of their interpretations differs fundamentally: for Bailey these realistic scenes point to theological truths,[1] whereas for van Eck they convey a message related to the economic and social conditions themselves.[2]

Picking up the theme of this collection on "seeing and hearing," I suggest that we must regard the parables as both "mirroring" and "echoing." In their reflection of the realities of life in the ancient Near East, and Palestine in particular, they act as a mirror, inviting their hearers to see themselves, their society, their environment, their relationships. But they always do more than this. They invite hearers to see those realities *in a certain way*. They focus vision, they select episodes (whether typical or atypical), they enlist memories, they evoke traditions. This means that they also act as an echo-chamber within which a hearer's experience can resonate, such that a message or mood is *heard*. They do this through linguistic clues.

---

[1] Kenneth E. Bailey, *Poet and Peasant and Through Peasant Eyes: A Literary-Cultural Approach to the Parables in Luke*, combined ed. (Grand Rapids, MI: Eerdmans, 1983); idem, *Jesus through Middle Eastern Eyes: Cultural Studies in the Gospels* (London: SPCK, 2008).
[2] Ernest van Eck, *The Parables of Jesus the Galilean: Stories of a Social Prophet* (Eugene, OR: Cascade Books, 2016).

The history of parable interpretation might be written as, to a great extent, a story of how parables' mirroring and echoing functions have been respectively emphasized, de-emphasized or held together. Inevitably one risks generalization here, but the centuries prior to Adolf Jülicher in the late nineteenth century can be seen as promoting the "echoing" to the near-exclusion of the "mirroring." The resonance of the parables' imagery with wider biblical and theological themes captured the attention of interpreters, such that the relationship of those images to the daily life of Jesus and his hearers—or indeed that of an evangelist and his audience—was hardly a concern. The fluid dynamic of an echo chamber, in which significant sounds reverberate without respect to time or origin, had become the mesmerizing arena for readers' immersion in the parables.

The tendency of some modern parable scholarship is towards the opposite of this. Historical and social-scientific interest sometimes all but eclipses the interest in echoes and turns our gaze on to the parables' mirroring function: what does their realism, confirmed by an expanding wealth of data and plausible social-scientific studies, suggest about the nature of Jesus's task and aims?[3] Sometimes an interest in "echoes" becomes confined to the task of distinguishing between the Evangelists' texts and the putative function of the parables on Jesus's lips: a simple binary opposition is drawn between the biblical and theological resonances that are evident in the Gospel renderings of many parables and the more everyday, even "secular" quality that the parables would have possessed when spoken by Jesus.

It is notable that Ruben Zimmermann, editor of one of the most comprehensive works on the parables in the twenty-first century so far, firmly resists this polarization of approach. He includes metaphorical quality alongside realism in his definition of a parable: "In [the parable's] appeal structure…it challenges the reader to carry out a metaphoric transfer of meaning that is steered by co-text and context information."[4] In this chapter I will try to elucidate the essential connection between these characteristics in three stages.

First, taking the realism of the parables as given, I will argue that underlying any adequate proposal about their original thrust in their social context must be a plausible account of their referentiality, the semantic force of that realism. Such an account was hinted at but undeveloped in C. H. Dodd's labelling of a parable as a "metaphor or simile drawn from common life."[5] I will explore this with

---

[3] The "mirror" notion was used by Jülicher himself in relation to Jesus's similitudes, which he regarded as so plain in meaning as to need no interpretation: "If one…holds a mirror before someone so that he sees his ugliness or the dirt that disfigures him, no explanatory words are needed. The mirror interprets better than it in truth could be achieved with the longest descriptions": Adolf Jülicher, *Die Gleichnisreden Jesu*, 2nd ed., 2 vols. (Tübingen: J. C. B. Mohr, 1910), 1:114; English translation in Ruben Zimmermann, "How to Understand the Parables of Jesus: A Paradigm Shift in Parable Exegesis," *Acta Theologica* 29, no. 1 (2009): 157–82 (here 160). This article introduces the principles behind the major volume he edited, *Kompendium der Gleichnisse Jesu* (Gutersloh: Gutersloher Verlagshaus, 2007). A second edition of this volume appeared in 2015; my references in this chapter are to the first edition.

[4] Zimmermann, "How to Understand," 170; on the realism of the parables, see pp. 170, 172; see also his section "Die Gleichnisse," in *Kompendium*, 3–46 (here 27).

[5] C. H. Dodd, *The Parables of the Kingdom* (London: Nisbet & Co., 1935), 16.

reference to how certain parable scholars since Dodd have used, and/or tried to resist, the figure of metaphor as a key to unlock this semantic function. Second, building on my own previous work, I will argue that parable studies will benefit from widening attention beyond metaphor to other figures of speech and to narratological categories in grasping the referential force of the parables. Finally, I will discuss the implications of understanding the semantic function of the parable of The Sower (Mark 4:3–9 and par.) as a synecdochic narrative. Engaging with some other recent studies of the parable, I will suggest that this allows us simultaneously to respect the realism of the story, seeing something of what its first hearers would have seen as it was told, while also doing justice to the echoes they would have heard which would enable them to interpret it—echoes of Jesus's wider ministry and the Jewish texts and traditions with which they would have been familiar.

2. Metaphorical Reference in Modern Parable Scholarship

How does the realism of the parables "work"? In what way—if any—do their vivid pictures refer to some sphere beyond the material world denoted by the literal meaning of individual words and sentences? How do these "mirrors" awaken "echoes"? It is reasonable to assume that Jesus and his hearers would have brought to their communication the network of beliefs, worldviews and expectations that they had absorbed from the traditions of their society and culture.[6] This would have formed the framework within which utterances would have been understood, a network particularly important when such utterances were to any degree unclear. It would have included familiar stories and sayings of Scripture and the oral traditions in which they were handed down. This network, in addition to their wider impression of Jesus's words and actions, would have formed the echo-chamber within which his pictures and stories could make sense.[7] If this is the case, the future of parables research cannot depend simply on the accumulation of more data about the social, economic or political situations that may lie behind them, but also (*inter alia*) on continued fertile interaction between such data and working hypotheses about (a) Jesus's broader understanding and demonstration of God's kingdom and (b) the influence of Jewish tradition on his thought-world. Granted that a degree of polyvalence is inherent to the parable genre, as Zimmermann has stressed,[8] the interaction between the data and such hypotheses will enable us to approach with more precision to a plausible view not only of what Jesus's hearers might have "seen," but also what they might have "heard" through what they saw.

---

[6] As underlined in the approach of Zimmermann, *Kompendium*, 32–45.
[7] The way in which Jewish oral tradition—including Scripture, orally transmitted—would have shaped the thinking of Jesus and his hearers is helpfully presented by Richard A. Horsley, *Jesus in Context: Power, People and Performance* (Minneapolis, MN: Fortress Press, 2008), 89–95; see also his *The Prophet Jesus and the Renewal of Israel: Moving beyond a Diversionary Debate* (Grand Rapids, MI: Eerdmans, 2012), 87–8.
[8] Zimmermann, "How to Understand," 173–6; Zimmermann, "Die Gleichnisse Jesus," in Zimmermann, ed., *Kompendium*, 3–46 (here 12–14).

Dodd's conception of a parable as "a metaphor or simile drawn from nature or common life"[9]—together with the brief but highly suggestive treatment of the parables offered in his book as a whole—forms a convenient starting-point for a reflection on modern understandings of the parables' referentiality. This conception was broader than that of his predecessor Jülicher, who assumed that all Jesus's parables had the structure of a simile: "this is like that." This reflected Jülicher's anxiety to escape from what he saw as the obfuscating readings of the past; a metaphor, by replacing one term with another, could be seen as the beginnings of an allegory.[10] By allowing for metaphor, Dodd did justice to the compressed form of many parables, and the fact that they leave unstated the reality(ies) to which their imagery or narrative might be supposed to refer. But he left the nature and working of Jesus's language as "metaphorical" undeveloped, a gap that would be filled through extensive exploration in scholarship since the mid-twentieth century.[11]

Collectively this scholarship constitutes a major challenge to Jülicher's argument that the parables are straightforward illustrations, similes that illuminate some aspect of God's character, operation or requirements through familiar human phenomena. Central to the approaches of these scholars is the insight from modern linguistics that metaphor, through juxtaposing two unlike realities *without* the term "like," frequently serves not merely to illustrate a known concept but fundamentally to reshape aspects of a hearer's understanding or even worldview. Through the juxtaposition of two apparently clashing pictures or terms, metaphors have cognitive value: they do not merely add ornament to clarify known truth, they invite us to see known truth afresh in the light of the alternative image or concept. Metaphor, in other words, can surprise or shock people into new insight, and the hypothesis that Jesus's parables work as metaphors enables us to move beyond the picture of the ideal teacher of universal truth

---

[9] Dodd, *Parables*, 16.

[10] On Jülicher's approach, see Stephen I. Wright, *The Voice of Jesus: Studies in the Interpretation of Six Gospel Parables* (Carlisle: Paternoster Press, 2000; repr. Eugene, OR: Wipf & Stock, 2007), 115–18.

[11] See especially Robert W. Funk, *Language, Hermeneutic and Word of God: The Problem of Language in the New Testament and Contemporary Theology* (New York: Harper & Row, 1966); Madeleine Boucher, *The Mysterious Parable*, CBQMS 6 (Washington, DC: The Catholic Biblical Association of America, 1977); John Dominic Crossan, *In Parables: The Challenge of the Historical Jesus* (San Francisco: Harper & Row, 1973); Ruth Etchells, *A Reading of the Parables of Jesus* (London: Darton, Longman & Todd, 1998); Bernhard Heininger, *Metaphorik, Erzählstruktur und szenisch-dramatische Gestaltung in der Sondergutgleichnissen bei Lukas* (Munster: Aschendorff, 1991); Mogens Stiller Kjærgaard, *Metaphor and Parable: A Systematic Analysis of the Specific Structure and Cognitive Function of the Synoptic Similes and Parables qua Metaphors* (Leiden: Brill, 1986); Paul Ricoeur, "Biblical Hermeneutics," *Semeia* 4 (1975): 29–145; Bernard Brandon Scott, *Hear then the Parable: A Commentary on the Parables of Jesus* (Minneapolis, MN: Fortress Press, 1989); Hans Weder, *Die Gleichnisse Jesu als Metaphern: Traditions- und redaktionsgeschichtliche Analysen und Interpretationen*, 4th ed. (Gottingen: Vandenhoeck & Ruprecht, 1990 [1980]); Claus Westermann, *The Parables of Jesus in the Light of the Old Testament*, trans. and ed. by Friedemann W. Golka and Alastair H. B. Logan (Edinburgh: T. & T. Clark, 1990 [originally published as *Vergleiche und Gleichnisse in Alten und Neuen Testament* [Stuttgart: Calver Verlag 1984]). To ask such questions about semantic function does not, of course, imply that either Jesus or his hearers—any more than most people—were conscious of the niceties of linguistic theory.

painted by Jülicher to a much sharper—and to many eyes, more credible—picture of a provocative prophet. Yet metaphor has not gone unchallenged as a hermeneutical key to the parables.

One reason why some have been reluctant to accept it has been the suspicion that it will re-open the door to allegorical readings—since many of the parables are narrative in form, and allegorical reading takes the surface elements of narrative as a sequence of metaphors. Through such a lens, characters and events are taken as ciphers for God, human persons, events in salvation history, and so on, in need of "decoding"—and had not Jülicher conclusively demonstrated that this approach, normal in premodern commentators, was untenable as a historically sensitive understanding of the texts? A crucial argument that addresses this concern was that of Paul Ricoeur, who explored how narrative functions metaphorically as a "redescription" of reality.[12] By showing that a narrative in its wholeness has metaphorical force, Ricoeur provided a vital insight which can lay to rest the fear that "metaphor" is a slippery slope to "allegory." Ricoeur's work was an important influence on one of the most sophisticated explorations of how attention to the nature of metaphor sheds light on the parables, that of Bernard Brandon Scott.[13] Drawing on philosophical, literary and linguistic theory, Scott argues that metaphor "redescribes" rather than simply reinforcing or illuminating reality,[14] an insight which he exploits throughout his detailed parable readings.

Scott argues that the parables refer in a metaphorical way to the kingdom of God and thus reveal a new perspective on it, whether as short images or longer narratives. He supports his case through the proposal that for Jesus's hearers, "kingdom of God" functioned as a "symbol" that was partly "open": that is, there was no single fixed meaning or content attached to it.[15] It could be understood in a specifically apocalyptic sense, of God re-establishing his rule over his people and defeating their enemies, or in the less-defined sense attested in the Kaddish and Targumim, or as the equivalent of "the yoke of the law," as in the rabbinic literature.[16] This openness meant that the parables could function as an invitation to imagine the kingdom in fresh and specific ways. For instance, whereas Jülicher had seen in the parable of The Prodigal Son a reassuring comparison between the natural welcome given by a father to his contrite son and the openness of God as Father to welcome the most rotten sinner,[17] Scott sees the story as a metaphor which subverts the hearers' notion that "the kingdom of God" is something which divides between the chosen and rejected: the father, at risk to his own honor, goes out to welcome both sons, and thus the parable indicates that "Jesus rejects any apocalyptic notion of some group's being rejected at the expense of another."[18]

---

[12] Ricoeur, "Biblical Hermeneutics," 29–145.
[13] Scott, *Hear*. His key discussion of how the parables work linguistically is on 42–62.
[14] Ibid., 47–9.
[15] Ibid., 56–62.
[16] Ibid., 59–61.
[17] Jülicher, *Gleichnisreden*, 2:362.
[18] Scott, *Hear*, 125.

Such essentially metaphorical reshaping of perceptions may take place even when the surface form of the saying is a simile. Thus, for instance, Scott argues that when Jesus says that God's kingdom is "like" leaven, or a mustard seed, he is subverting the assumption that God's kingdom is to be associated with the pure and lawful. The argument is that these images would have been heard and interpreted according to the normally negative associations of leaven (traditionally a symbol for moral corruption) or a mustard seed sown in a garden (which was illegal according to Rabbinic tradition).[19] For Scott, it is axiomatic that the parables work in this subversively metaphorical way. The comparison between the kingdom of God and some mundane phenomenon does not merely illustrate or reinforce one known concept (God's kingdom) through juxtaposition with another, through familiar and uncontroversial associations of the latter (in these cases, the potential of leaven or seed to generate remarkable growth). Rather, the metaphoric force of the parables is to challenge the standard association of the kingdom with purity through the provocative use of an image that jars with that association.[20]

Scott's approach and his individual parable readings are open to debate at many points. For instance, one might ask why it should be assumed that the parables *always* worked in the "strong" sense of aiming to reshape hearers' thinking? The fact that metaphor *can* create a new view of the world does not imply that it always *does*. After all, we are familiar with plenty of "dead" metaphors, phrases that once may have been vivid but have passed into everyday speech as "literal" language: "what planet is he on?"[21] Why should the associations of Jesus's stories and images always have been the most shocking ones from among the range of possibilities, when juxtaposed with the kingdom of God? Might he not, at least sometimes, have used less controversial language, even "dead" metaphors? The title of Amos Wilder's book *Jesus' Parables and the War of Myths* epitomizes the sense that the parables are the spearhead of an epic struggle: but what if, at least to some degree, they were more ordinary and conventional than that?[22] And if they are shocking, why should one assume that it is always the "apocalyptic" view of the kingdom that they subvert? For my purposes here, however, Scott's argument simply illustrates the need for mounting *some* hypothesis about how Jesus's parable language worked in the context of traditions and expectations concerning God's kingdom, and the resonances of the realistic imagery. If it was not "metaphorical," what was it?

In addition to the suspicion of allegory, a second important reason why the suitability of calling the parables "metaphorical" has been questioned is that since, at its simplest, metaphor entails the use of one thing to signify another, it

---

[19] Ibid., 321–9, on Matt 13:33/Luke 13:20–21/*Gos.Thom.* 96, and 373–87 on Matt 13:31–32/Mark 4:30–32/Luke 13:18–19/*Gos. Thom.* 20. Scott regards the word "garden" in Luke 13:19 as an indication that Luke's version is to be preferred to Matthew's (Matt 13:31): it is the more difficult reading, and more subversive than Matthew's "field."

[20] Scott explicates this in terms of the distinction between "epiphoric" and "diaphoric" metaphors (ibid., 61).

[21] For a discussion of different levels of "liveness" in metaphor, see Kjärgaard, *Metaphor*, 101–5.

[22] Amos Wilder, *Jesus' Parables and the War of Myths* (London: SPCK, 1982).

inexorably predisposes us to see the very this-worldly imagery of the parables as denoting *another* world—invisible, spiritual, "religious"—thus drawing readers' attention away from the full significance of their mirroring of *this* world. Such a predisposition is exemplified, for instance, in John Dominic Crossan's assertion that "the world for which and to which Jesus is speaking is the world of religious experience."[23] More recently Zimmermann, while fully recognizing the parables' realism, writes: "The intended comprehension of a parable succeeds, however, only when the action, sometimes something very trivial like the placement of a lamp, is transferred to a religious dimension."[24] Let us then turn to two proposals which resist calling the parables "metaphorical," in the quest to do justice to their portrayal of this-worldly scenes.

Charles Hedrick proposed that we read the parables as "poetic fictions"—their "poetic" quality being that which gave them their provocative force.[25] He draws a clear distinction between this assumption and the idea that they "point beyond" themselves to another reality: "A reader is not authorized to go outside the world of the story or to use non-story 'referential' language in 'interpreting' the story, unless it is mandated by particular semantic markers in the story itself."[26] He notes that nineteen of Jesus's stories have come down to us without any introductory frames,[27] an indication that even the early Christians did not think they called for a comparison with a broader reality. Thus, he distances himself from Scott's assumption that the stories "reference the kingdom of God or some other transcendent reality."[28] Rather, like poetry, they invite hearers into the world as the poem constructs it: "A poem is a mimetic fiction, a product of the poet's imagination and keen observation of world [*sic*].... What we have in the realistic *mimesis* of the stories of Jesus is, in short, a marriage of common reality and imagination that has the potential of igniting the imaginations of those who consent to enter his fictional world."[29] Hedrick presents this interpretative stance as one that respects the nature of the stories as stories: "Any attempt to *force* meaning out of the story, whether figurative, moral, or referential, in its own way consumes and dispenses with the story.... An emphasis on a 'referential world' is simply another way of taking a reader out of the story."[30]

In order to counter this, Hedrick encourages us to see the "meaning" of the stories as that which emerges from their fictional plots[31] and other features of their internal poetic structure.[32] He recognizes, however, that this does not entail reading them as timeless creations isolated from their setting: on the contrary,

---

[23] Crossan, *In Parables*, 18.
[24] Zimmermann, "How to Understand," 174.
[25] Charles W. Hedrick, *Parables as Poetic Fictions: The Creative Voice of Jesus* (Peabody, MA: Hendrickson, 1994).
[26] Ibid., 3.
[27] Ibid., 16.
[28] Ibid., 31.
[29] Ibid.
[30] Ibid., 35.
[31] Ibid., 46–50.
[32] Ibid., 57–72.

these fictions can be heard as resonating, or clashing, with other stories familiar in first-century Judaism,[33] as expressing "essentially different mental constructs,"[34] "different ways of viewing a given reality."[35] But the fact that he hears the parables participating in this "clash of fictions" (reminiscent of Wilder's "war of myths") shows that Hedrick does, in fact, want us to hear them as referring more widely than themselves: and that being the case, their possible *metaphorical* reference to wider networks of meaning cannot be ignored.

Appearing in the same year as Hedrick's work, William R. Herzog's *Parables as Subversive Speech* similarly eschewed the category of metaphor to analyze the parables. Herzog criticized the approach of scholars such as Funk, Crossan and Scott, with their emphasis on the world-shattering metaphorical quality of Jesus's stories, as equally "idealist" and insufficiently "materialist" as that of their predecessors Jülicher, Dodd and Jeremias.[36] For Herzog, an emphasis on the parables' metaphorical quality inevitably led to the details of the parable being "left behind."[37] Herzog drew deeply on social-scientific studies of Jesus's world to offer a "thicker" description of dynamics at play in the situations Jesus portrays than that offered by previous scholars. He understands the parables' communicative power by analogy to Paolo Freire's "pedagogy of the oppressed," in terms of their capacity to "conscientize" their hearers. That is, they alert them to the false consciousness of the economic situation engendered by the dominant ideology, give them language to name their oppression, and thus enable them to take first steps towards controlling their destiny.[38] While acknowledging the obvious differences between Jesus and Freire, Herzog proposes this suggestive definition which takes seriously the parables' realism and social force: "The parable, then, was not primarily a vehicle to communicate theology or ethics but a codification designed to stimulate social analysis and to expose the contradictions between the actual situations of its hearers and the Torah of God's justice."[39]

Thus, for example, apparent difficulties in the parable narratives, such as the unfairness of the master in The Laborers in the Vineyard (Matt 20:1–16)[40] or the master's praise of the "unjust" steward (Luke 16:1–8),[41] become for Herzog windows onto the phenomena of economic oppression. Instead of pointing to the character of God and the ordering of his kingdom, such stories enable their hearers to see their own circumstances as people caught in a predatory system in which the authority-figures are no more morally exemplary than anyone else.

The key fresh insight which Herzog brings to the analysis of the parables' language is his strengthened emphasis on the *social* force of narrative itself. He cites Frederic Jameson's account of narrative as "a socially symbolic act," and

---

[33] Ibid., 73–89.
[34] Ibid., 88.
[35] Ibid., 89.
[36] William R. Herzog, *Parables as Subversive Speech: Jesus as Pedagogue of the Oppressed* (Louisville, KY: Westminster John Knox Press, 1994), 13.
[37] Ibid.
[38] Ibid., 16–24.
[39] Ibid., 28.
[40] Ibid., 79–97.
[41] Ibid., 233–58.

individual narratives as episodes in "'a single vast unfinished plot,' which tells the uninterrupted story of the struggle between oppressor and oppressed." This requires the interpreter, in Jameson's words, to restore "to the surface of the text this repressed and buried history."[42] But this very insight reveals that Herzog, too, makes a judgment about the parables' semantic referentiality beyond themselves. They are narratives whose snapshots of social situations are intended to reflect their hearers' own plight, enabling them to see it as it is and begin to take positive steps to remedy it. There is a wider plot to which readers are invited, implicitly, to connect the specific story, and a hidden history to be brought to the surface.

Thus despite his comments on the inadequacies of "literary-critical readings of the parables" that focused on their "narrativity and metaphoricity,"[43] Herzog's conception may be seen as a fresh angle on the argument that the parables as narratives function metaphorically as reframing devices, as presented by Scott, building on Ricoeur.

In a later volume representing the "material turn," Ernest van Eck also offers a characterization of the parables' linguistic structure. For him, they are "atypical stories" which function as "comparisons" of one world with another—"the kingdom of the *pax Romana* and the kingdom of the temple with the kingdom of God."[44] This is essentially similar to Herzog's statement cited above, that the parable was designed "to expose the contradictions between the actual situations of its hearers and the Torah of God's justice."[45] In reintroducing the language of "comparison," van Eck awakens the ghost of Jülicher and his argument that the default structure of the parables was that of simile. To be sure, for Herzog and van Eck, the implied statement of the parables is not "This is like that" but "This is *not* like that": in that sense, the parables contrast rather than compare. The weakness of this analysis, however, is the same as the weakness in Jülicher which has led many scholars to think "metaphor" a better default label for the parables than simile: frequently the second term of the implied comparison (e.g. "the kingdom of God") is not expressed, and even when it is, the basis of the comparison—the point of similarity, or contrast, the *tertium comparationis*—is usually not expressed either. "Metaphor" captures this sense of their indirectness or incompleteness, of the work the hearer has to do to match up the spoken words with an unspoken reality, and therefore of their power, in Dodd's words, to tease the mind into active thought.[46]

How, though, can we avoid the potentially misleading effects of calling the parables metaphors, discussed above? How can we do justice both to the depth of their realism and to their genuine power to provoke new ways of seeing that reality through awakening echoes? It is the narrative parables, especially the longer ones, which pose this question most acutely.

---

[42] Herzog, *Parables*, 3, citing Frederic Jameson, *The Political Unconscious: Narrative as a Socially Symbolic Act* (Ithaca, NY: Cornell University Press, 1981), 19–20.
[43] Herzog, *Parables*, 13.
[44] Van Eck, *Parables*, 36–9, quotation on 39.
[45] Herzog, *Parables*, 28.
[46] Dodd, *Parables*, 16.

The British literary scholar and theologian Ruth Etchells made a creative and under-noticed proposal for taking seriously both the parables' realism and the instinct of most interpreters (even Hedrick!) that they do, somehow, refer beyond themselves. She argued that the language of the parables entails a *crossing* of metaphor with metonymy.[47] The fundamental distinction between these two tropes as features of discourse was influentially articulated by Roman Jakobson in 1956.[48] While metaphor works paradigmatically, by the substitution of one entity by another from a different sphere (thus, to take simple examples, in Matt 5:13 "salt" is proposed as a substitution for the disciples, and in Luke 13:32 "fox" is assumed to be a substitute for Herod), metonymy works syntagmatically, by the association of one entity with another in the same sphere. Thus in Ps 89:29, "I will establish his line forever, and his throne as long as the heavens endure," and v. 39, "You have renounced the covenant with your servant; you have defiled his crown in the dust," "throne" and "crown" are well-known objects metonymically associated with kingship, helping to carry that theme forward in the psalm. The literary critic David Lodge applied this distinction to twentieth-century fiction by analyzing the metonymic character of realistic narrative, which weaves together a multitude of details that are designed not for substitution by other entities (as an allegorical chain of metaphors) but for building a coherent picture of the world.[49] Building on Lodge, Etchells argues that in their realism the parables, similarly, function metonymically: that is, the interactions of slaves and masters, a woman and her neighbors, a father and his sons, make up miniature tapestries of coherent, recognizable scenes; on this metonymic axis, the characters represent no one other than the kind of real slaves, masters, women, neighbors, fathers and sons with whom the hearers will be familiar. At the same time, she sees elements of the outrageous or extraordinary in the parables—the size of a debt, the shock of unlooked-for generosity and so on—as well as allusions to traditional tropes (such as the harvest for judgment) as clues to their metaphorical quality, signs that although they are rooted in the real world, they point to another, the extraordinary world of God's kingdom.

This crossing of metonymy and metaphor seems to me closer to the mark as a characterization of how the parables, notwithstanding their realism, nonetheless refer beyond themselves, than simply describing them as metaphorical. However, I have tried to take such analysis a stage further, as I shall outline in the next section.

3. Parables as Synecdochic Narratives

Highly suggestive though Etchells' reading is, one may still question whether it over-emphasizes extraordinary elements or traditional tropes (such as harvest) in the stories, directing attention away from their hard materiality. To some

---

[47] Etchells, *Parables*.
[48] Roman Jakobson, "Aphasia as a Linguistic Problem," in Roman Jakobson and Moris Halle, *Fundamentals of Language*, 2nd ed. (The Hague: Mouton, 1980), 69–96.
[49] David Lodge, *The Models of Modern Writing* (Leeds: Arnold, 1977).

extent, one might seek an answer to this by asking whether, in view of relevant material data and plausible socio-economic models, elements she identifies as extraordinary are in fact quite realistic, and whether traditional tropes are either incidental or imported by Christian transmission. But while this might shed light on particular texts, the more general issue of what kind of wider reference we should anticipate from these realistic stories would remain unaddressed.

I have advanced two complementary approaches to the question of the parables' semantic function. First, as part of a study of how the periods of parable interpretation may be illuminated by the awareness of literary tropes, I argued (with reference to six longer Lucan parables) that rather than metaphor or metonymy, *synecdoche* might be the trope best suited to characterize Jesus's own use of narrative.[50] Zimmermann has since noted that while designating a parable as a whole as "metaphoric," it is possible "for individual parables to contain additional word metaphors in the sense of metonymy or synecdoche or symbolic elements."[51] In distinction from this, I continue to speculate whether it may be helpful to see a narrative parable *as a whole* as synecdochic, rather than metaphoric. Second, I have explored how using the standard tools of narrative criticism may enable us to elucidate a parable's semantic function in more detail.[52]

Synecdoche is traditionally understood as the trope in which a part of something stands for the whole or *vice versa*. Thus, the use of body parts to refer to the whole person is often labelled synecdoche. Mark Forsyth illustrates this both with colloquial examples (e.g. "bums on seats" for "people in the audience") and poetic ones, such as these lines from William Blake's "Jerusalem":

And did those feet in ancient time
Walk upon England's mountains green?...
And did the countenance divine
Shine forth upon those clouded hills?[53]

Forsyth suggests that the power of such synecdoches lies in their character as glimpses: we see, for a moment, the feet or the face of Christ, but are left to imagine the whole person. "Blake works in fragments; when you read his synecdoches you have to see the world in a grain of sand."[54]

It is the power of synecdoche to evoke a wider whole, its invitation to "see the world in a grain of sand," which makes the trope attractive to me as a way of conceiving Jesus's parabolic language. It assumes that this language is thoroughly rooted in the *realia* of his society, while engendering through its sharp

---

[50] Wright, *Voice*, 193–212.
[51] Zimmermann, "How to Understand," 172. Zimmermann does, however, offer "figurativeness" as an alternative to "metaphoricity," which would allow for the possibility that in the parable as a whole, another trope or tropes, such as synecdoche, are in operation; cf. p. 174.
[52] Stephen I. Wright, *Jesus the Storyteller* (Louisville, KY: Westminster John Knox Press, 2015): see the summary of this approach on 53–7, and detailed parable readings on 89–172.
[53] Mark Forsyth, *The Elements of Eloquence: How to Turn the Perfect English Phrase* (London: Icon Books, 2013), 150–1.
[54] Ibid., 151.

focus a fresh perspective on that society. Herzog himself, without naming synecdoche, clearly points in this direction: "If parables offer glimpses into the world of first-century Palestine, they also infer the larger whole of which those glimpses are a part.... Even the characters found in the parables are not individuals but socially recognizable types who stand in for larger social groups."[55] To see the parables as synecdoches is to recognize that through their account of a particular event, they evoke the "story" of a whole society—in Jameson's words, cited (via Herzog) above, "a single vast unfinished plot."[56] Synecdoche does not suggest (as metaphor may) that the scenes and events presented point to a different world altogether. Rather, it entails that the narrative world represents the material world as it is. But like all live tropes, it does not just mirror that world: it invites a new perspective on it. In the terms of our argument here, it enables us to "hear" it in a certain way.[57]

In the study of rhetorical tropes since classical times, synecdoche has been closely related to metonymy, and sometimes subsumed within it.[58] Both involve the use of one term to stand for, or suggest, other associated terms or ideas, rather than terms or ideas from another sphere as in metaphor. Metonymy is classically exemplified in relationships such as that between container and contained, as in "the kettle is boiling," where the kettle stands for the water, or an abstract property and the person possessing it, as when we call someone a "beauty." Whether the part–whole relationship should be classed as metonymy or synecdoche is disputed. Ken-Ichi Seto[59] and Brigitte Nerlich and David Clarke[60] prefer to class it as metonymy, and reserve synecdoche more strictly for the relationship between more and less comprehensive members of the same category (that is, between genus and species): this would fit nicely the basic biblical examples of synecdoche I used in my earlier work, "many" for "all" (Mark 10:45—less comprehensive standing for more comprehensive) and John's use of "the Jews" to mean only the Jewish leaders (more comprehensive for less comprehensive).[61] Elżbieta Chrzanowska-Kluczewska, however, continues to accept the part–whole relationship more broadly as synecdochic, and explores several literary examples of its common manifestation in the use of body parts to evoke corporeality, whether human or animal.[62]

---

[55] Herzog, *Parables*, 53, 54.
[56] Ibid., 3, citing Jameson, *Political Unconscious*, 19–20.
[57] For my fuller original exploration of synecdoche related to six narrative parables, see Wright, *Voice*, 193–212.
[58] See Ken-Ichi Seto, "Distinguishing Metonymy and Synecdoche," in *Metonymy in Language and Thought*, ed. Klaus-Uwe Panther and Günter Radden (Amsterdam: John Benjamins Publishing, 1999), 91–120. Cf., in addition, F. Elżbieta Chrzanowska-Kluczewska, "Synecdoche—an Underestimated Macrofigure?," *Language and Literature* 22, no. 3 (2013): 233–47, especially 234–7, and Brigitte Nerlich and David D. Clarke, "Synecdoche as a Cognitive and Communicative Strategy," in *Historical Semantics and Cognition*, ed. Andreas Blank and Peter Koch, Cognitive Linguistics Research 13 (Berlin: Mouton de Gruyter, 1999), 197–213, especially 197–203. I am grateful to Dr. David Reimer, examiner of my doctoral student Jonathan Squirrell, for drawing my attention to these articles.
[59] Seto, "Distinguishing," passim.
[60] Nerlich and Clarke, "Synecdoche," esp. 197–203.
[61] Wright, *Voice*, 7.
[62] Chrzanowska-Kluczewska, "Synecdoche," esp. 237–45.

It is not germane to my argument whether some linguists or literary critics might prefer to label the parables' referentiality "metonymic" rather than "synecdochic." The key point is that in either case, their main *reference* will be to this world rather than some other world. This would support the contention of scholars such as Herzog and van Eck and give it a more robust linguistic foundation. Conversely, it would argue against the implication of Bailey that the parables, notwithstanding their vivid realism, ultimately refer to a nexus of theological truths. Of course, this might not be the case with all the parables; there is no *a priori* reason to suppose that they all "worked" the same way. Or it might be that the this-worldly reference is interrupted at certain points by metaphorical "crossings," as proposed by Etchells. Again, I am proposing a line of enquiry, not claiming that these narratives functioned as pure synecdoches all the time.

Nonetheless, elements of Chrzanowska-Kluczewska's characterization of synecdoche do strengthen my sense of the applicability of this trope to the parables. She notes the way in which, in the thought of Giambattista Vico (1688–1744), the "*synecdochical pattern*" of thinking "oscillates around a conspicuous feature of an entity, thus starting the process of *generalization* and *integration* around what we would call nowadays *salient qualities*."[63] We can see the parables as foregrounding "conspicuous features" or "salient qualities" of Jesus's social world, through which its characteristics, and his perspective on them, could then be generalized and integrated by his hearers. She also cites Kenneth Burke's labelling of synecdoche as the trope of "representation," which underlines its appropriateness as a label for realistic narrative.[64] For Hayden White, similarly, "synecdoche restores a 'conceptual unity' of objects through the 'elevation' of particulars into universals";[65] this resembles the way that the parables evoke whole patterns of events and behavior through sharply focused individual scenes. Most persuasively of all, this quotation from White speaks of the gathering power of synecdoche in relation to narrative: "[N]arrative can be characterized as a kind of discourse in which synecdoche functions as the dominant trope for "grasping together" (Greek *synecdoche*, Latin *subintellectio*) the parts of a totality apprehended as being dispersed across a temporal series into a whole...."[66] Through terse narratives, I suggest that the parables draw together the dynamics of the real world as perceived and reconceived by the storyteller.

The second approach I have advanced to understanding the referential import of the narrative parables is to employ the standard tools of narrative criticism.[67] It is through the selecting and framing operation of narrative, the devices through which the specific "part" is made to stand for the generic "whole," that the fresh

---

[63] Ibid., 235, her italics.
[64] Ibid., 235, citing Kenneth Burke, *A Grammar of Motives* (Berkeley, CA: University of California Press, 1962 [1945]).
[65] Ibid., 236, citing Hayden White, "The Tropics of History: The Deep Structure of the *New Science*," in *Tropics of Discourse: Essays in Cultural Criticism*, reprint ed. (Baltimore: The Johns Hopkins University Press, 1985 [1978]), 197–217 (here 207).
[66] Hayden White, "Literary Theory and Historical Writing," in *Figural Realism: Studies in the Mimesis Effect* (Baltimore: The Johns Hopkins University Press, 1999), 1–26, (here 21), cited in Chrzanowska-Kluczewska, "Synecdoche," 239.
[67] See Wright, *Jesus*, 53–7, 89–172.

perspective offered by the parables on people's lives and circumstances may be seen. This is how they "help the readers to see themselves and their concrete lives in a new light," in Zimmermann's words.[68] Short as they are, it seems to me that attending to these parables' configurations of setting, character, point of view and plot—not to mention other rhetorical features—can give us a sense of the stories as complex wholes, without reducing their significance to one (or several) "points." This can preserve a focus on the material realities they mirror, while illuminating the storyteller's unique twist on those realities. Narrative is always more than bare description; it shapes a hearer's view of the world.

Thus, to identify the *setting* of a story of Jesus is both to imagine as fully and realistically as possible the wider material context of which it offers us a snapshot (what the hearers "see") *and* the network of traditions and beliefs of teller and hearers (what they "hear"). To study the *characters* is to find reflections of familiar types within society who may sometimes behave in unfamiliar ways, and on whose actions the narrator may pass some implied judgment according to their own framework of belief. That framework of belief may be glimpsed in the *point of view* from which the story is told, to which clues may be found in phraseology and the implied positioning of the narrator in relation to the events and characters. Finally, attention to *plot* awakens us to the connections between one event and another and the nature of their resolution. This is indispensable to grasping the nature of the stories' realism. To what extent is a story reflecting not only the people and material objects of the real world, but the motives which drive events in that world, and the outcome of those events? In other words, how surprising or normal are these stories within the realistic world they depict? This in turn fixes a spotlight on the question of the sources of the storyteller's imagination, the attitudes and beliefs which cause him to picture the world in this way.

While I have characterized the operation of the narratives as wholes by the term synecdoche, parables, like any stories, may employ a range of tropes and other rhetorical devices on the level of words or phrases, as techniques to shape the narrative.[69] Here I would draw attention especially to the trope of metalepsis, by which a speaker or writer alludes to an earlier trope and thereby evokes its context also.[70] I would argue that such "echoes" should not be assumed *a priori* to break the realism of the stories. Rather, they are one of the storyteller's means of showing where his realistic tale is pointing, of encouraging a way of "hearing" the visual scene.

I will now illustrate the working of these hypotheses about the parables in a discussion of the parable of the Sower (Mark 4:3–9 and par.) which takes its realism as a given. This will draw on my earlier brief reading of the parable[71] while engaging with others.

---

[68] Zimmermann, "How to Understand," 175.
[69] As also asserted by Zimmermann: see "How to Understand," 175 and n. 51.
[70] Many New Testament scholars may have been introduced to the workings of this trope through Richard Hays' work, *Echoes of Scripture in the Letters of Paul* (New Haven: Yale University Press, 1989).
[71] Wright, *Voice*, 90–7.

4. The Sower as Synecdochic Narrative?

The parable of the Sower (Mark 4:3–9 and par.) forms an interesting case study of the relationship between realism and figurative reference in the parables. Not only does its placement in Mark, together with the following saying to the disciples ("Do you not understand this parable? How then will you understand all the parables?," Mark 4:13), suggest that this is somehow the archetypal parable. The fact that an interpretation is appended (Mark 4:14–20 and par.) in which the fate of the various seeds is linked to the hearing of "the word" has been pregnant with significance for readers. Through much of Christian history, the presence of the interpretation was a sign that for *every* parable, deeper, spiritual meanings were to be sought beneath the everyday language. By contrast, in modern scholarship since Jülicher, largely suspicious of such allegorical understandings, the interpretation was a sign that the evangelists themselves were already under the spell of this misapprehension and therefore felt impelled to insert it.

On the one hand, at least on a superficial level, the parable itself seems one of the most realistic. Even the size of the crop, although presented in the stylized threefold manner (thirty-, sixty-, a hundredfold) is often not considered extravagant by modern scholars.[72] On the other hand, the parable itself is so compressed that even those interpreters who suspect the interpretation as secondary are compelled to seek a meaning that places the story plausibly in the ministry of Jesus by identifying some kind of metaphorical freight in its language and imagery. To what else—if anything!—does this vignette refer?

Dodd interpreted the parable by means of the traditional metaphorical association of the harvest with the eschaton.[73] For him, Jesus was pointing to the fact that the time has come to reap the harvest. Similarly, Joachim Jeremias, although rejecting the authenticity of the Gospel interpretation of the parable,[74] accepted—like Dodd—its basic premise, that the parable concerns not literal seed but human beings. He relates it to the lack of responsiveness to Jesus reflected in passages such as Mark 3:6 and 6:5–6.[75] Crossan's existential understanding also relates the everyday scene of the parable to a wider reality, "the gift-like nature, the graciousness and surprise of the ordinary"; it is a parable of the Kingdom in its advent.[76]

Scott recognizes that "the proverbial structure of sowing and reaping has a wide and extensive set of metaphorical possibilities" from the tradition.[77] It is interesting then that he resists the idea that those metaphorical possibilities should play a significant role in its reading. In particular he rejects the possibility that it should be heard in the apocalyptic frame of reference of passages such as 2 Bar. 70:2 or 2 Esd. (= *4 Ezra*) 8:38–41, 43–44. These passages speak of human beings

---

[72] Those considering it normal include Hedrick, *Parables*, 172–3, and Scott, *Hear*, 357.
[73] Dodd, *Parables*, 181–3.
[74] Joachim Jeremias, *The Parables of Jesus*, rev. ed., trans. S. H. Hooke (London: SCM Press, 1963), 77–9.
[75] Ibid., 151.
[76] Crossan, *In Parables*, 50.
[77] Scott, *Hear*, 361.

as seed sown by God, and of human responsibility for not bearing fruit as God expects. A key plank in Scott's argument is that the yield of the fruitful seed is not to be understood as "superabundant," as Jeremias thought.[78] In other words, for Scott, a sharper sense of the parable's realism allows him to keep at arm's length a sense of its traditional theological resonances. Yet for him—as for Crossan—it still has a wider reference: the kingdom of God understood in broadly existential terms. The hearer of the parable is left with "a kingdom in which failure, miracle and normality are co-ordinates."[79]

A more radical resistance to discovering traditional metaphorical associations in the parable is advanced by Hedrick, who foregrounds its realism. For him, it is a story about farming, and any wider meanings attached to it have been imported by readers anxious to find a message that connects with their understanding of Jesus's ministry.[80] He sees both the harvest from the good soil and the hindrances to growth elsewhere as realistic portrayals of ancient farming.[81] Although he regards the stark contrast between different types of soil (completely unfruitful vs. completely fruitful) as threatening this realism, he plausibly recognizes this as natural stylization by the storyteller.[82] He is more struck by the failure to mention plowing in light of the description of farming practices in classical authors, and sees this as highlighting the effectiveness of natural processes without either divine or human intervention. Hence this is "a completely secular story of the natural processes" which subverts "a view that looks to God as the source of the blessings and the curses of nature, a view that sacramentalises the cosmos."[83] While recognizing the scriptural connections made between the blessing of God, the obedience of the people and the fruitfulness of the land,[84] he reads the parable as challenging these rather than being informed by them, citing its "tacit failure to acknowledge God's sovereignty over nature."[85] Hedrick forces us to focus on the literal reference of the story and ask exactly on what basis it may be taken to refer beyond that.

We turn now to two more recent treatments in which "seeing" and "hearing," the realistic and figurative character of the parable, are held in tension. The *Kompendium* edited by Zimmermann uses a common structure for its treatment of each parable. Two central sections deal with "socio-historical analysis"—that is, the real-world scene presented by the parable—and the "analysis of background significance" or "tradition of semantic/metaphorical field"—that is, the metaphorical network which provides the clue to the parable's meaning.[86] The

---

[78] Ibid., *Hear*, 356–8, contra Jeremias, *Parables*, 150.
[79] Scott, *Hear*, 356–8.
[80] Hedrick, *Parables*, 166.
[81] Ibid., 173.
[82] Ibid.
[83] Ibid., 177; cf. 184–6.
[84] Ibid., 178.
[85] Ibid., 185.
[86] "Sozialgeschichtliche Analyse (Bildspendender Bereich)" and "Analyse des Bedeutungshintergrunds" (Bildfeldtradition)." The compressed German terms are difficult to translate exactly into English. See the introductory explanations of these categories in Zimmermann, ed., *Kompendium*, 36–41.

scholar's interpretation of the parable then follows in another section which draws the threads together without attempting to close down meaning.[87] This pattern maintains the balance we have been discussing, between the mirroring and echoing functions of the parables. In her chapter on The Sower in that volume, Kristina Dronsch notes in the socio-historical analysis the importance of agriculture to the economy of the ancient world, and states that the story reflects the everyday experience of those who worked the land.[88] That experience was shaped by the cultural perception of "limited goods," whereby—unlike in modern capitalist thinking—economic expansion is never boundless and the prosperity of the individual can never be separated from the needs of the group. In that setting, the failure of some seed is never unimportant but always a reminder of the precariousness of existence. But by contrast with Hedrick, she stresses that in the first-century Jewish setting, the productiveness of the land would never be separated out in people's minds from God's loving care.[89] For Dronsch, therefore, the theological significance of agricultural fruitfulness is a part of the realistic picture the parable paints: the visual scene resounds with meaningful echoes.

In her section on the metaphorical background, Dronsch argues that the parable draws on the familiar Scriptural concept of God as the "sower" of humans, and particularly of Israel.[90] This concept is extended in Philo and *4 Ezra* to the sowing of something *within* humans, such as goodness, insight, or the Law itself.[91] The threats to the seed—birds, wilting, withering, thorns—are also in Scripture threats to humans.[92] She thus sees the tenor of the parable as being much closer to that of the Gospel interpretation (Mark 4:13–20) than modern scholarship has generally done. Although it is only in the interpretation that the metaphorical meaning becomes explicit—a double meaning, in which the seed is identified with both word and people[93]—the clues are already there, she thinks, in the parable itself, especially in the (strange) absence of the word "seed" and the non-agrarian use of the word "sower."[94] This reading of parable and interpretation in close conjunction reflects the ethos of the volume, which refuses the quest in much modern scholarship for precise differentiation between "authentic" and "inauthentic" sayings of Jesus.[95] It leads, in Dronsch's summarizing section, to the proposal that the parable announces God's eschatological renewing

---

[87] "Zusammenfassende Auslegung (Deutungshorizonte)," explained in ibid., 41–3. Zimmermann emphasizes that it is in the nature of parables that they draw in the reader and invite each individual to complete their meaning; it is thus not the scholar's task to dictate meaning but to enable this process by sketching out possibilities and boundaries for meaning.
[88] Kristina Dronsch, "Vom Fruchtbringen (Sämann mit Deutung)," in Zimmermann, ed., *Kompendium*, 297–312 (here 302–4).
[89] Ibid., 303.
[90] Ibid., 305–7.
[91] Ibid., 305.
[92] Ibid., 306.
[93] Ibid., 307.
[94] Ibid., 305.
[95] As outlined in Zimmermann, "How to Understand," 162.

(re-sowing) of his people through his word, with the corollary that they must take responsibility for receiving it.[96]

Hedrick and Dronsch thus represent opposite poles of the debate: Hedrick arguing that the realism of the story forbids theological/metaphorical freight, Dronsch arguing that notwithstanding its realism, the metaphorical history of the imagery's semantic field, combined with clues internal to the parable, propel us towards a metaphorical reading along the lines of the Gospel interpretation.

A second recent treatment is that of van Eck.[97] For him it is awareness of the socio-political context rather than the nature of agricultural practices *per se* which enables us to see the parable as a realistic mirror of its world.[98] It reflects the phenomenon of a peasantry heavily indebted to the elites who extracted rents and taxes, increasingly deprived of their ancestral land and sometimes driven off it altogether. This situation will have been evoked from the start of the story, and reinforced by its details. Roads, like that on which some seed fell, were the means of the elite "siphoning wealth out of the hands of peasant farmers."[99] The birds which came and ate this seed were reminders of the Roman imperial power and ideology, focused in its symbol of the eagle. The rocky places where other seed fell were like those which peasants tried to cultivate, compelled by shortage of land. Thorns traditionally represented the godless and here, van Eck suggests, might represent for Jesus's hearers the temple elite who contributed to their impoverishment through tithes and offerings. The abundant crop yielded from the good soil, he argues, signals not the literal size of a harvest but the well-being which results when people share generously as Jesus taught them (cf. Luke 6:30–31, 35–36).[100] Thus van Eck sums up: "The parable describes the kingdoms of Rome and the temple elite, but also the kingdom of God. In a world with little choice, the parable gives a vision on how to cope in an exploitative world."[101]

Van Eck also takes account of the traditional background of the story, but by contrast to the other scholars just discussed, he sees the story as foregrounding a contrast between the ideals of the promised land and the harsh realities of life under imperial rule. The land was regarded as Yahweh's gift to his people, whose obedience was the key to its prosperity, while the parable, by implication, highlights the present reality that the land was mostly in the possession of outsiders, and according to imperial propaganda was seen as Caesar's, not God's.[102] However, he sees the political allusions in the story working via figures of speech: "The seed that falls on the road *symbolizes* that part of the harvest where tax, tribute and rents were paid in kind.... This *metaphorical* understanding of the part of the harvest that will go to the elite.... What is a possible *metaphoric* reference for the thorns in Mk 4:7?"[103] Thus his emphasis on realism,

---

[96] Dronsch, "Von Fruchtbringen," 307–8.
[97] Van Eck, *Parables*, 44–63.
[98] Ibid., 54–61.
[99] Ibid., 59.
[100] Ibid., 59–61.
[101] Ibid., 61.
[102] Ibid., 57.
[103] Ibid., 58, 59, 60 (emphasis added).

on the image of a literal scene unfolded before the hearers' eyes, does not exclude the "something beyond" indicated by connotative language, through which those hearers find significance in the picture. Indeed, for van Eck, as for the majority of interpreters, the parable points to the nature of God's kingdom. The key difference between his reading and Dronsch's is that for van Eck, the material world depicted in the realistic scene is also central to the kingdom it intends to portray, a kingdom found through the possibility of generosity in the midst of adverse conditions on the land. For Dronsch, the scene opens straightaway through its metaphorical resonances on to the work of God in "re-sowing" his people with his word.

How then might the trope of synecdoche and the tools of narrative criticism help us capture the insights of these scholars and grasp the force of this story more clearly? Van Eck's reading can be taken as a persuasive example of the use of synecdoche as a heuristic key. Jesus gives us a "slice of life"—the hearers' "world in some grains of seed," we might say. In this picture of a single farmer, Jesus does not describe the whole reality of his society, but he implies it—provoking thought, as Dodd put it.[104] This is not bare description, as the urgent injunction to "hear," bracketing the story, emphasizes. Nor can its "realism" be seen as proof against any kind of wider resonance, as Hedrick implies. Rather, it is precisely in its realism that the wider resonances are triggered. The phenomena of first-century Palestinian farming, as briefly outlined by Dronsch and placed in wider political context by van Eck, are brought before the hearers' eyes, not through extended description but through the compact narrative of an individual farmer's activity. When Jesus spoke, his hearers would have "seen" their own surroundings (mirroring perhaps quite literally what they might have "seen" if they had turned around from watching the speaker in the boat on the lake to looking at the hillside behind them). These surroundings, including situations in which much seed went to waste because the ground on which it fell was not fit to nourish it to fruition, were invested with heavy emotional freight. For faithful Jews, the misery of deprivation stood in painful tension with the hope of a sufficient harvest.[105] And the material condition of the hearers is not only the source of the parable's imagery (in Jülicher's terminology, its *Bild*) but also the subject of its message (its *Sache*).

"Synecdoche" is an appropriate label for such a story, insofar as this farmer and his activity represent primarily farmers and their activity—that is, members of the same category—rather than entities from another sphere, such as God and his word. The story depicts a tiny part of the whole world of the hearer, through which that world is seen. Similarly, the road, birds, rocks, thorns and grain itself,

---

[104] Dodd, *Parables*, 16.
[105] Further helpful treatments of the condition of the land in Jesus's time are found in V. George Shillington, "Engaging with the Parables," in *Jesus and his Parables: Interpreting the Parables of Jesus Today*, ed. V. George Shillington (Edinburgh: T. & T. Clark, 1997), 1–20 (here 9–11); Herzog, *Parables*, 53–73; Ched Myers, *Binding the Strong Man: A Political Reading of Mark's Story of Jesus*, 20th anniversary ed (Maryknoll, NY: Orbis Books, 2008 [1988]), 176: Luise Schottroff, *The Parables of Jesus* (Minneapolis, MN: Augsburg, 2006), 72–3.

from this perspective, represent real roads, birds, rocks, thorns and grains. But since this trope, like others, operates not only as a decoration or substitution, but also a generator of new insight, the parable is not a mere pleasing miniature or mirror. It invites a certain "hearing" of the world it synecdochically encapsulates.

It does this through the way the narrative is framed, and narrative-critical categories offer a useful tool of analysis here.[106] The *setting* of a story encompasses the social realities of the time and place. These are both evoked by words and phrases in the story, and form an interpretative backcloth, a fund of knowledge shared by speaker and hearer. Although the extreme brevity of a story such as The Sower allows little space for developing setting, the significance of the unspoken and the power of evocation (as in all aspects of narrative—"showing" rather than "telling") is crucial, and is one reason why I find Hedrick's "secular" reading of The Sower unpersuasive: lack of "religious" language should not be taken to imply an absence of theological assumptions from its setting. Thus the promises and commands of God associated with the land may be taken as fundamental to the story's background, as Dronsch asserts.[107] *Characters* invite a hearer's or reader's identification, and the single character of this story, in his undefined, typical nature, invites a wide range of hearers to self-identify with him.[108]

The *point of view* implied is closely linked to the *plot*. Simple as it is, the story builds to a climax, drawing attention to the great yield of seed on the good soil. This movement is achieved through careful indicators. Dronsch shows how, with each type of unfruitful soil, the seed makes a little more headway.[109] The seeds sown on the unfruitful soils are also contrasted with that sown on the good soil, as noted by various scholars: in Mark, the various "seeds" on the unfavorable soils are all singular, whereas those on the good soil are "seeds," plural.[110] Thus this is not simply a reflective story; it is a reshaping story, in the sense that it gives prominence to the fact of continuing harvests despite adverse conditions on the land. It expresses the hopeful point of view of one who, by implication, claims some authority to give it. Although it is not explicit about the source of that hope, the default assumption of Jewish hearers would be that it was rooted in faith in the creativity, sovereignty and grace of God.[111]

As noted above, to conceive of a narrative as functioning in its entirety as synecdoche (or any other trope, such as metaphor) is not to preclude the identification of various individual tropes within it. Indeed, in oral cultures speech is alive with all kinds of figurative language.[112] The road, birds, rocks, thorns and grains can be seen as individual synecdoches, evoking the same physical

---

[106] For my own summary of these as they may be applied to The Sower, see Wright, *Jesus*, 90–7.
[107] Dronsch, "Vom Fruchtbringen," 303.
[108] See, further, Wright, *Jesus*, 94.
[109] Dronsch "Vom Fruchtbringen," 298.
[110] Matthew and Luke tidy this up, but in the process seem to flatten something of the original oral storytelling dynamic—Matthew has all plurals, Luke all singulars.
[111] See, further, Wright, *Jesus*, 94–5.
[112] See Walter J. Ong, *Ramus, Method and the Decay of Dialogue* (Cambridge, MA: Harvard University Press, 1958), 212, cited in Terence Hawkes, *Metaphor*, The Critical Idiom 25 (London: Methuen & Co., 1972), 27.

realities—a different perspective from van Eck's, though not necessarily in conflict with it, since such a story is open to multiple resonances. The difference is highlighted in my italicization of his words: for him, the road (and the seed falling on it) "*symbolize* pressure and exploitation, silos and vaults, trade and markets";[113] the parable offers a "*metaphorical* understanding of the part of the harvest that will go to the elite" through the birds, which served as "the primary *symbol* of Roman divine favour and election," as well as being "harbingers of evil" in 1 Kgs 16:3–4;[114] the thorns have a "*metaphoric*" reference to the wicked in the Old Testament and thus may represent the oppressors of the poor.[115] His reading of the birds and thorns in particular, which moves beyond seeing them as evoking the actual birds and thorns which threatened the crops, is more metaphoric than synecdochic.

Metalepsis, the echoing of an earlier trope or network of tropes, is surely also at work here. In analyzing how individual cases of metalepsis operate, it is important to identify the nature of the original trope. The difference between Dronsch's and van Eck's readings, in this respect, is that Dronsch sees the parable metaleptically evoking the *metaphorical* network of God's "sowing" of his people. She lists the relevant biblical and postbiblical texts, as well as those in which the threats to this work of God are metaphorically depicted as birds or thorns, wilting or withering.[116] Van Eck (if one may extrapolate a little from his brief treatment of this aspect) sees the parable as metaleptically evoking the *synecdochic* network in which individual promises such as that of eating bread without scarcity (Deut 8:9–10)—and one might add, images such as a land flowing with milk and honey, or sitting under one's own vine and fig tree—stand for a whole realm of literal prosperity.[117] One may augment van Eck's presentation of the allusions to the synecdochic network of seed/fruit/land language by noting how the promised land reverberates as a theme with the garden of Eden, epitomizing the environment given by the creator to all humans (Gen 1–3). These echoes are reinforced by the synecdochic biblical use of some of the terms used in the parable. "Birds (of the air)" and "thorns" both appear as (literal) instruments and signs of God's judgment, synecdoches for whole scenes of desolation.[118]

Such echoes set off my individual words form an auditory backdrop for the visual scene. Whether one thinks of the synecdochic echoes as being heard prior to, more loudly than, or instead of the metaphoric ones will depend partly on how

---

[113] Van Eck, *Parables*, 59.
[114] Ibid.
[115] Ibid., 60. Van Eck's identification of the thorns with the temple elite specifically seems arbitrary.
[116] Dronsch, "Vom Fruchtbringen," 305–6.
[117] Van Eck, *Parables*, 57.
[118] Ibid., 91–2. Birds: Gen 40:16–19; 1 Kgs 14:11; 16:4; 21:24; Ps 79:2. Thorns: Gen 3:18; Isa 5:6–7; 7:23–25; Hos 10:8. A detailed analysis of the texts cited by Dronsch (see n. 116) would probably show that several of them actually belong to the synecdochic Old Testament network rather than, or in addition to, the metaphoric one. For example, when Deut 28:26 warns, "your dead body shall be food for all birds of the air," this would, no doubt, be a literal element of the catastrophic defeat envisaged, one which summed up its horror in concentrated form.

close an attempt is being made to hear the parable as Jesus's hearers might have heard it. It is significant that van Eck, who "explicitly focuses on the parables as sayings of the historical Jesus,"[119] should concentrate on the synecdochic echoes as those which shape the hearing of the parable, while Dronsch, whose essay is part of a volume which explicitly distances itself from attempts to sift out "authentic" from "inauthentic" parable material,[120] should link the parable more closely with its Gospel interpretation, highlighting the echoes of the metaphorical network in which seed represents people. There is a logic in positing that at first hearing, it is the material resonances of the story which would have sounded most loudly. In my own earlier reading (without using the trope terminology) I noted the story's metaleptic allusions to both synecdochic and metaphoric Scriptural networks.[121] In either case, these echoes give moral freight to the story. Perhaps van Eck's supposition that the abundant yield represents the consequence of Jesus-inspired generosity may be a little far-fetched,[122] but he is not wrong to see an implied invitation and challenge hovering around the story's hopefulness.

5. Conclusion

In this chapter I have affirmed the importance of the "material turn" in parables research. I have also shown how an emphasis on the realism of the parables by no means predetermines our interpretation of them. Visual scenes are "heard" via channels of worldview, expectation and tradition. Even the most radically material readings work within a matrix of other assumptions, notably concerning the overall character of Jesus's message, and the traditions which informed his perspective. Many scholars explicitly describe the parables as having a metaphorical referential thrust, while others imply something similar even while resisting certain implications of calling them metaphorical. I have argued that greater clarity and precision in identifying the linguistic tropes and narrative techniques that operate within the parables promise fresh insight and integration in our quest both to "see" what is portrayed in the parables' scenes and to "hear" the accents which helped hearers to make sense of them.

In particular, I have argued that such an approach can clarify how the realism of The Sower functions. This leads to the suggestion that Jesus was not merely using the agricultural vicissitudes faced by local peasant farmers as a convenient

---

[119] Van Eck, *Parables*, xxi.
[120] Zimmermann, "How to Understand," 162.
[121] Wright, *Jesus*, 91–3. Maybe the synecdochic echo, rooted in the realistic impression of a physical scene, would have been heard first—followed only on reflection by the metaphoric one. But as I argued, there is a fundamental connection between the "material" (synecdochic) and "spiritual" (metaphoric) resonances. It is the same word of God that makes the earth fruitful (Isa 55:10) which promises the renewal of his people through their return from exile (Isa 55:11–12); conversely, that return will be accompanied by the regeneration of the land itself: "instead of the thorn shall come up the cypress; instead of the brier shall come up the myrtle" (Isa 55:13).
[122] Van Eck, *Parables*, 60–1. Van Eck here builds on Douglas Oakman's suggestion that abundance at the end of the parable concerns the untaxed seed available for gleaning: *The Political Aims of Jesus* (Minneapolis, MN: Fortress Press, 2012), 140.

sermon illustration for the "spiritual" realities of the kingdom. In line with van Eck's reading of the story, this implies that hearers would have received the story as an expression of concern—on some level—with the plight that underlay those vicissitudes. In bringing before his hearers their own world, and in reflecting it back to them, Jesus was inviting them to see its true contours more sharply, as the impoverishing policies of the imperial power are juxtaposed with the creative generosity of God. The trope of synecdoche, in which the specific stands for the general or *vice versa*, well describes such meaningful realism. The simply painted miniature scene evokes an entire set of socio-economic circumstances: not as a purely aesthetic act, but as an indirect message of hope and challenge. That hope and challenge are mediated through narrative techniques, especially a setting that is pregnant with traditional allusion, a dramatized plot, in which the three unfruitful sowings are contrasted with the one fruitful one, and the metaleptic echoes of biblical images, both those synecdochic images which express the literal promise of fruitfulness, and those metaphoric ones through which seeds stand for people.

Such a reading addresses the reasonable question of how the story resonates with Jesus's wider message and activity, but concludes that the parable form itself refuses precision and closure on this.[123] The parables by their very nature stand as better evidence for a posture rather than a "message," while by no means precluding the notion that Jesus proclaimed such a message more clearly in other ways.[124] The task of relating the specific data to the wider picture goes on. In its hopefulness this parable obviously echoes the words and actions through which Jesus proclaims God's kingdom, but that does not mean that it acts as a "metaphor" for the kingdom as a concept in a straightforward way. Moreover, its understatedness subverts the urge to co-opt it for an "apocalyptic" or "non-apocalyptic" view of Jesus, however those terms are understood. In its ordinariness, it may lend itself to a non-apocalyptic view of Jesus as a teasing wisdom teacher, or to the kind of "apocalyptic" view taken by Horsley, one in which the advent of God's powerful reign is an encouragement to a (non-violent) resistance movement. In its hopeful point of view, it lends itself to a more traditional apocalyptic perspective that confidently announces the salvation of God coming from beyond all human socio-political manoeuvrings. Notably, even the parable's interpretation in Mark 4:14–20 leaves a good deal unexplained.[125] This includes what the story might or might not say on the old question of Jesus's view of the kingdom's timing: here both parable and interpretation remain "open signs" that give no sure indication at all. The dynamics of synecdoche, in which a wider whole is suggested without being defined, and of the allusive quality of narrative itself, preclude any confidence on this point, but they seem to encapsulate that combination of realism and resonance which allow the parable to go on speaking.

---

[123] On this I am in full agreement with the emphasis on the parables' essential openness in Zimmermann, "How to Understand," 173–6, and *Kompendium*, 12–14.
[124] For my own wider conclusions about Jesus as a storyteller and how these fit into our wider picture of his message and ministry, see Wright, *Jesus*, 175–88.
[125] As stressed also by Dronsch, "Vom Fruchtbringen," 301.

Bibliography

Bailey, K. E. *Jesus through Middle Eastern Eyes: Cultural Studies in the Gospels*. London: SPCK, 2008.
Bailey, K. E. *Poet and Peasant* and *Through Peasant Eyes: A Literary-Cultural Approach to the Parables in Luke*. Combined ed. Grand Rapids, MI: Eerdmans, 1983.
Boucher, M. *The Mysterious Parable: A Literary Study*. CBQMS 6. Washington, DC: The Catholic Biblical Association of America, 1977.
Burke, K. *A Grammar of Motives*. Berkeley, CA: University of California Press, 1962 [1945].
Chrzanowska-Kluczewska, F. E., "Synecdoche—an Underestimated Macrofigure?" *Language and Literature* 22, no. 3 (2013): 233–47.
Crossan, J. D. *In Parables: The Challenge of the Historical Jesus*. San Francisco: Harper & Row, 1973.
Dodd, C. H. *The Parables of the Kingdom*. London: Nisbet & Co., 1935.
Dronsch, K. "Vom Fruchtbringen (Sämann mit Deutung)." In *Kompendium der Gleichnisse Jesu*, ed. R. Zimmermann, 297–312. Gutersloh: Gutersloher Verlagshaus, 2007.
Etchells, R. *A Reading of the Parables of Jesus*. London: Darton, Longman & Todd, 1998.
Forsyth, M. *The Elements of Eloquence: How to Turn the Perfect English Phrase*. London: Icon Books, 2013.
Funk, R. W. *Language, Hermeneutic and Word of God: The Problem of Language in the New Testament and Contemporary Theology*. New York: Harper & Row, 1966.
Hawkes, T. *Metaphor*. The Critical Idiom 25. London: Methuen & Co., 1972.
Hays, R. *Echoes of Scripture in the Letters of Paul*. New Haven: Yale University Press, 1989.
Hedrick, C. W. *Parables as Poetic Fictions: The Creative Voice of Jesus*. Peabody, MA: Hendrickson, 1994.
Heininger, B. *Metaphorik, Erzählstruktur und szenisch-dramatische Gestaltung in der Sondergutgleichnissen bei Lukas*. Munster: Aschendorff, 1991.
Herzog, W. R. *Parables as Subversive Speech: Jesus as Pedagogue of the Oppressed*. Louisville, KY: Westminster John Knox Press, 1994.
Horsley, R. A. *Jesus in Context: Power, People and Performance*. Minneapolis, MN: Fortress Press, 2008.
Horsley, R. A. *The Prophet Jesus and the Renewal of Israel: Moving beyond a Diversionary Debate*. Grand Rapids, MI: Eerdmans, 2012.
Jakobson, R. "Aphasia as a Linguistic Problem." In *Fundamentals of Language*, by Roman Jakobson and Moris Halle, 69–96. 2nd ed. The Hague: Mouton, 1980.
Jameson, F. *The Political Unconscious: Narrative as a Socially Symbolic Act*. Ithaca, NY: Cornell University Press, 1981.
Jeremias, J. *The Parables of Jesus*. Rev. ed. Translated by S. H. Hooke. London: SCM Press, 1963.
Jülicher, A. *Die Gleichnisreden Jesu*. 2nd ed. 2 vols. Tübingen: J. C. B. Mohr, 1910.
Kjärgaard, M. S. *Metaphor and Parable: A Systematic Analysis of the Specific Structure and Cognitive Function of the Synoptic Similes and Parables qua Metaphors*. Leiden: Brill, 1986.
Lodge, D. *The Models of Modern Writing*. Leeds: Arnold, 1977.
Myers, C. *Binding the Strong Man: A Political Reading of Mark's Story of Jesus*. 20th anniversary ed. Maryknoll, NY: Orbis Books, 2008 [1988].

Nerlich, B., and D. Clarke. "Synecdoche as a Cognitive and Communicative Strategy." In *Historical Semantics and Cognition*, edited by Andreas Blank and Peter Koch, 197–213. Cognitive Linguistics Research 13. Berlin: Mouton de Gruyter, 1999.

Oakman, D. *The Political Aims of Jesus*. Minneapolis, MN: Fortress Press, 2012.

Ong, W. J. *Ramus, Method and the Decay of Dialogue*. Cambridge, MA: Harvard University Press, 1958.

Ricoeur, P. "Biblical Hermeneutics." *Semeia* 4 (1975): 29–145.

Schottroff, L. *The Parables of Jesus*. Minneapolis, MN: Augsburg, 2006.

Scott, B. B. *Hear then the Parable: A Commentary on the Parables of Jesus*. Minneapolis, MN: Fortress Press, 1989.

Seto, K. "Distinguishing Metonymy and Synecdoche." In *Metonymy in Language and Thought*, edited by Klaus-Uwe Panther and Günter Radden, 91–120. Amsterdam: John Benjamins, 1999.

Shillington, V. G. "Engaging with the Parables." In *Jesus and his Parables: Interpreting the Parables of Jesus Today*, edited by V. George Shillington, 1–20. Edinburgh: T. & T. Clark, 1997.

Van Eck, E. *The Parables of Jesus the Galilean: Stories of a Social Prophet*. Eugene, OR: Cascade Books, 2016.

Weder, H. *Die Gleichnisse Jesu als Metaphern: Traditions- und redaktionsgeschichtliche Analysen und Interpretationen*. 4th ed. Gottingen: Vandenhoeck & Ruprecht, 1990.

Westermann, C. *The Parables of Jesus in the Light of the Old Testament*. Trans. and ed. by Friedemann W. Golka and Alastair H. B. Logan. Edinburgh: T. & T. Clark, 1990. Originally published as *Vergleiche und Gleichnisse in Alten und Neuen Testament* (Stuttgart: Calver Verlag 1984).

White, H. "Literary Theory and Historical Writing." In *Figural Realism: Studies in the Mimesis Effect*, 1–26. Baltimore/London: The Johns Hopkins University Press, 1999.

White, H. "The Tropics of History: The Deep Structure of the *New Science*." In *Tropics of Discourse: Essays in Cultural Criticism*, 197–217. Reprint ed. Baltimore: The Johns Hopkins University Press, 1985 [1978].

Wilder, A. *Jesus' Parables and the War of Myths*. London: SPCK, 1982.

Wright, S. I. *Jesus the Storyteller*. Louisville, KY: Westminster John Knox Press, 2015.

Wright, S. I. *The Voice of Jesus: Studies in the Interpretation of Six Gospel Parables*. Carlisle: Paternoster Press, 2000. Repr. Eugene, OR: Wipf & Stock, 2007.

Zimmermann, R. "How to Understand the Parables of Jesus: A Paradigm Shift in Parable Exegesis." *Acta Theologica* 29, no. 1 (2009): 157–82.

Zimmermann, R., ed. *Kompendium der Gleichnisse Jesu*. Gutersloh: Gutersloher Verlagshaus, 2007.

Matthew 20:1–15:
The Parable of the Workers in the Vineyard or of a Manager-Disciple?

Deborah R. Storie

Growing up white in middle-class Melbourne, the parable of the Laborers in the Vineyard (Matt 20:1–15) always left me with an abiding sense of injustice. No matter how hard preachers tried to expound the parable as a story that demonstrated the grace of God, they never quite succeeded. I identified with the workers who sweated all day beneath the scorching sun. I was no slouch. I got up early. I studied hard. I did well and felt entitled to success. It was unfair that those who'd expended a fraction of my effort received the same reward. I deserved more. I did not want to be equal.

My early reception of this parable was profoundly shaped by the individualistic lens of the culture to which I belonged. I did not distinguish between expositions of the parable and the parable itself. Never hearing the parable taught in relation to the scene to which it belonged, I overlooked its narrative context and did not recognize the need to hear it as part of Matthew's larger story of Jesus. How did the parable intersect with the historical situation of early first-century Palestine and the life experiences of those to whom Jesus told it? How did the world presented by the parable and the world in which I lived compare? It never occurred to me to ask.

Things changed when I moved from Australia to live in rural Afghanistan. Watching land and labor relations play out around me, my inherited reading gradually unravelled and an alternative reading began to evolve. This happened without any conscious decision to read differently and without any exposure to biblical scholarship other than the footnotes provided by an NRSV Study Bible. How I heard the parable changed with the context in which I heard it, the company I kept, and the commitments that shaped my life and work.

This chapter offers a reading of Matt 20:1–15 that takes seriously the parable's historical, narrative and canonical contexts, calls the socio-economic and political structures it depicts into question, and invites readers to practice transformative resistance in contemporary contexts characterized by similarly exploitative structures and practices. The chapter proceeds as follows. First, I introduce William Herzog's conception of parables as Freirean "codes" in relation to my own experience of community development in rural Afghanistan and how that transformed my understanding of Jesus's ministry. Second, I share a reading of Matt 20:1–15 in which the manager of v. 8 plays a pivotal if ambiguous role. Third, I describe the major contours of the dominant tradition of interpreting Matt 20:1–15, identify underlying interpretive predicates, challenge problematic conventions and conclusions, and review the work of interpreters who test the limits of that tradition while still holding the householder to be a positive character, if not a figure for God. Fourth, I explore an alternative interpretive tradition that interrogates the parable's social, political and economic dimensions and does not assume that the vineyard owner represents God. Fifth, I assess the parable's realism and discuss the interpretive implications of two realia that are often overlooked. In conclusion, I suggest that the parable may be read simultaneously as a "codification" of exploitative structures *and* as an allegorical story that speaks of the grace of God.

1. Parables as Codes: A Personal Journey

I am not the only reader troubled by the parable of Matt 20:1–15 as commonly understood. The overwhelming sense of injustice with which it left him, prompted Herzog to search for another way to interpret it and other parables.[1] He realized that what a person believes about the purpose of Jesus's overall ministry determines how they understand Jesus's ministry and, therefore, how they interpret his parables.[2] Apparent similarities between the contexts, purposes, methods and strategies of Paulo Freire and Jesus of Nazareth prompted Herzog to ask:

> What if the parables of Jesus were neither theological nor moral stories but political and economic ones? What if the concern of the parables was not the reign of God but the reigning systems of oppression that dominated Palestine in the time of Jesus? What if the scenes they presented were not stories about how God works in the world but codifications about how exploitation worked in Palestine?… What if Jesus' parables were more like Paulo Freire's "codifications" than like sermon illustrations?[3]

In my case, rural Afghanistan provided many of the "jigsaw pieces" that Herzog collected and collated through careful research. Living and working in Afghanistan for much of the 1990s, perceived similarities between rural Afghanistan and biblical lands brought the worlds of the Bible and daily life

---

[1] William R. Herzog, *Parables as Subversive Speech: Jesus as Pedagogue of the Oppressed* (Louisville, KY: Westminster John Knox Press, 1994), 1–2.
[2] Ibid., 2–3, 14–16, 46–51.
[3] Ibid., 7. See pp. 16–28 for Herzog's comparison of the contexts and pedagogies of Jesus and Freire.

closer together; boundaries began to blur.[4] Our community development team used appreciative questioning techniques—including Freirean codifications—to encourage our neighbors to identify the issues most important to them, and to explore the implications and ramifications of addressing those issues in various ways.[5] We drew pictures, told stories and asked open-ended questions. We listened for "generative themes" (topics that arouse strong emotions), avoided answering questions in didactic or prescriptive ways, and resisted the temptation to transfer information through "banking education."[6] We knew that non-dialogical approaches would implicitly denigrate the knowledge, skills and wisdom of local people and encourage them to accommodate the present order rather than transform it. We learned to watch the play of power and attended to who said what to whom and in what context; we "listened between the lines." When members of the urban elite destroyed a school village people had built for their children—"Why do peasants need to read?"—we learnt how much those in power fear changes to the *status quo*. As our neighbors said, "Keep a man in the dark and act like a king." When we asked why no-one had opposed the vandals, we learnt how much those who live in the shadow of power have to fear. As our neighbors said, "While life and limb remain, we can build another school. Without life and limb and children, what use a school?"[7]

Noticing that the Gospels portray Jesus as a storyteller who rarely gave straight answers, I began to suspect that Jesus was not given to "banking education" any more than we were. I fancied that Jesus, like our community development team, called people to look at their world, analyze the situation and participate in transformative action. Inadvertently, I began to read some of Jesus's parables as codes.

Codes are stories, pictures, songs or other communicative devices that present slices of everyday life in stylized fictitious form that groups can look at, describe and analyze, and to which they may choose to respond.[8] Codes are designed to help people identify, expose and articulate how things are, as opposed to how they are said to be. Effective codes do not spell everything out but require people to enter into the situation imaginatively and assess and analyze it themselves.

---

[4] For a fuller account of how rural Afghanistan transformed my Bible reading, see Deborah Storie, "Reading between Places: Participatory Interpretive Praxis," *Pacifica* 18 (2005): 281–301.

[5] Introductory texts which informed our work include Robert Chambers, *Whose Reality Counts? Putting the First Last* (London: Intermediate Technology Publications, 1997), and Anne Hope and Sally Timmel, *Training for Transformation: A Handbook for Community Workers*, 4 vols. (Gweru, Zimbabwe: Mambo Press, 1984, 1999). I also read James C. Scott's early work at this time, *The Moral Economy of the Peasant: Rebellion and Subsistence in Southeast Asia* (New Haven, CT: Yale University Press, 1976), and *Weapons of the Weak: Everyday Forms of Peasant Resistance* (New Haven: Yale University Press, 1985).

[6] On "banking education," see Paulo Freire, *Pedagogy of the Oppressed* (London: Penguin Books, 1996 [1970]), 52–60. Freire condemns educational approaches that "turn the students into 'containers,' into 'receptacles' to be 'filled' by the teacher."

[7] For a fuller account of this incident, see Deborah Storie, "Voiceless and Silent," *Target: Development News and Insight* 3 (1996): 2–6.

[8] On codifications and conscientization, see Freire, *Pedagogy of the Oppressed*, 86–105. Cf. David Archer and Sara Cottingham, *Reflect Mother Manual: Regenerated Freirean Literacy Through Empowering Community Techniques* (London: International Reflect Network, 2012), 8–18.

Well-constructed codes invite communities to draw connections with analogous situations in their own contexts, identify problems, imagine alternatives and envisage and work toward possible futures.

Hearing some of Jesus's parables as codes enabled me to appreciate and exploit the subversive potential of their realism and the transformative potential of their imaginative appeal. As realistic yet stylized pictures of everyday life, parables unveil the dissonance between "public transcripts" of social and economic relations, how such relations actually function, and whose purposes they serve. They present systems that engender, depend on and perpetuate violence as problems that hearers can identify, question, resist and transform. They are, in Herzog's terms, "earthy stories with heavy meanings."[9]

2. Hearing the Parable Differently

The parable of Matt 20:1–15 sounded different when heard in rural Afghanistan. The world presented by the parable was the world in which I lived. Well before dawn, men arrived at the bazaar and squatted, their tools of trade before them, waiting, hoping to be hired.[10] When there was little work, men waited until nightfall and returned home empty handed. These were seasons of acute hunger. During peak agricultural and construction seasons, the strongest, most skilful men were hired first. The infirm, the elderly, the not-quite-able were hired last, if at all. Hiring these last workers delivered them from the indignity of begging and saved their families from hunger—if only for a day. Maybe the parable does speak of the generosity and grace of God?

But that is not the whole story. Sitting with extended families during lamp-lit winter evenings, I listened to folktales, legends, and even quite recent memories of how things used to be, of how they belonged to the land, God's land, sat beneath their own vines and fig trees, ate the fruit of their own labor, built houses and lived in them, and were not afraid. *Enshallah* (God willing), those days would come again. One day, maybe soon, cash crops that produce luxuries for the rich will give way to barley fields, vegetables and grazing lands, families will till their fields with joy, the land will flow with milk and honey. *Enshallah!*

Yes, the workers are grateful to be hired. Yes, they are grateful to be paid. And, yes, they are angry! The householder's defence, "Is it not lawful for me to do what I will with what belongs to me?" (20:15), awakens ancient memories of dispossession, rekindles the desperate rage of peasant-farmers driven off ancestral lands, and exacerbates the humiliation of begging for work on lands that were once their own.[11]

---

[9] Herzog, *Subversive Speech*, 3.
[10] The Afghan dayworkers were all men; the parabolic ἐργάται may have included women.
[11] Most commentators consider it obvious that the householder/lord of the vineyard (ἄνθρωπος οἰκοδεσπότης/ὁ κύριος τοῦ ἀμπελῶνος) is entitled to do as he wishes with what he owns and that the disgruntled workers and the parable's audiences recognize the validity of his claims. So, for example, Siegfried Goebel, *The Parables of Jesus: A Methodological Exposition* (Edinburgh: T. & T. Clark, 1883), 309. Luise Schottroff, "Human Solidarity and the Goodness of God: The Parable

But neither is that the whole story. The parable tracks the play of power in the hiring process.[12] The householder contracts the first workers for a denarius (20:2). He tells subsequent groups, "You also go into the vineyard, and I will give you whatever is just" (20:4), thus seizing the prerogative to determine what is just.[13] He sends the last workers to the vineyard without promising any payment at all (20:6–7).

But that is still not the whole the story. A *manager*, not the householder, pays the workers (20:8).[14] As far as we know, the householder-now-lord of the vineyard gives the manager only one explicit direction, "Call the workers and give them their hire, beginning with the last and then to the first" (20:8). Most landowners expect their managers to follow the usual rules of business: pay as little as possible to get as much as you can. Did this householder, while offstage, direct his manager to give each worker a denarius?[15] We are not told. We don't know, but I suspect not. Had the lord of the vineyard expected all workers to receive a denarius, he would have been unlikely to direct his manager to pay the

---

of the Workers in the Vineyard," in *God of the Lowly: Socio-Historical Interpretations of the Bible*, ed. Willy Schottroff and Wolfgang Stegemann (Maryknoll, NY: Orbis Books, 1984), 129–47 (here 132); Barbara E. Reid, *Parables for Preachers: The Gospel of Matthew* (Collegeville, MN: Liturgical Press, 2001), 148; Ulrich Luz, *Matthew 21–28* (Minneapolis, MN: Fortress Press, 2005), 533 n. 70, notes that "[t]he owner's absolute power not only to use his possessions, but even to destroy them, corresponds also to the view of Roman law," but neglects to mention that Roman and Mosaic law were antithetical in this and multiple other respects.

[12] Kenneth E. Bailey, *Jesus Through Middle Eastern Eyes: Cultural Studies in the Gospels* (London: SPCK, 2008), 360, glosses over these power-dynamics with the rhetoric of trust and respect: "The men trust [the householder] and accept his terms.... Clearly, the vineyard owner is respected in the community and trusted by the day laborers.... The last group...did not merely trust what the owner said (or didn't say), they trusted the man himself." For a critique of Bailey's tendency to overlook the effect of power disparities on social relationships, see Deborah Storie, "Kenneth E. Bailey, *Jesus through Middle Eastern Eyes: Cultural Studies in the Gospels*," *Pacifica* 22 (2009): 96–109.

[13] The use of direct speech when the householder hires the second and third groups of workers distances "whatever is just" from the creator and narrator of the parable: the householder undertakes to pay what *he* considers to be just. Most commentators take the householder's perspective as normative so that the payments received (20:9–10) resolve the question of "what is just" (20:4). Luz, *Matthew 21–28*, 531, however, notes: "What is just" (20:4) "leaves everything wide open and raises the suspicion of possible conflict."

[14] Most scholars attribute the equal payments to the decision of the "lord of the vineyard" without noticing the "gap" between the instructions given to the manager (ἐπίτροπος) and the payments the workers receive. They are quite dismissive of the ἐπίτροπος. So Craig Blomberg, *Interpreting the Parables* (Nottingham: IVP Academic, 2012), 287: "the steward...merely executes his master's will"; John Nolland, *The Gospel of Matthew* (Grand Rapids, MI: Eerdmans, 2005), 806 n. 141 remarks: he "seems to be superfluous to the fundamental dramatic development of the story... no more than a secondary effect of the introduction of the landowner." Similarly, Klyne R. Snodgrass, *Stories with Intent: A Comprehensive Guide to the Parables of Jesus* (Grand Rapids, MI: Eerdmans, 2008), 367. Leon Morris, *The Gospel According to Matthew* (Grand Rapids, MI: Eerdmans, 1992), 501 n. 11, provides a note on the meaning of ἐπίτροπος, yet overlooks the character when interpreting the parable.

[15] Snodgrass, *Stories with Intent*, 29, prohibits questions of this ilk: "Interpret what is given, not what is omitted. Any attempt to interpret a parable based on what is not there is almost certainly wrong.... The more attention one gives to what is not there without evidence that the author intended some conclusion to be drawn the more one is almost certainly wrong."

first last, a strategy guaranteed to provoke complaint.[16] Might it be the manager who practiced a different ethic? Within his limited sphere of influence, did he put the last first? Did the householder/lord of the vineyard know what his manager was doing *before* the first-hired complained? We are not told. We don't know, but I suspect not.

But the parable alone does not tell the whole story. It concludes one conversation and looks back on another.[17] Attending to who said what to whom and in what context, I imagine hearing the parable as if among those who witnessed the encounter between the young man and Jesus (19:16–22) and overheard or participated in the subsequent conversation between Jesus, Peter and the other disciples (19:17–30). I wonder whether Jesus tells the parable to illustrate his statement of 19:30 or in response to the questions of the disciples (19:25, 27) or the young man (19:16, 20) or the entire preceding encounter and dialogue (19:16–30). These possibilities are not mutually exclusive. Jesus, I notice, did not ask the young man to do the impossible. The question was not one of ability but of will: "If you wish to enter life..." "If you wish to be perfect..." (19:17, 21). The rich can repent, sometimes they do, but did Jesus tell the parable to endorse other, less dramatic forms of discipleship, discipleship possible for those who are not rich and may even be enslaved, discipleship that works best unnoticed— yeast, light and salt? Might it be the manager and the manager's (possible) actions to whom and to which Jesus invites those listening to attend?

The scene in which the parable is told (19:16–20:16) is still only part of the story. It belongs to Matthew's Gospel which continues the story of Israel as interpreted in the scriptures. Listening as if among the crowd, I recall the tragic history of Naboth (1 Kgs 21) and hear again the word with which the prophet Elijah was sent to confront Ahab: "Thus says the LORD: Have you indeed killed and taken possession?" (v. 19). How, I wonder, did the parabolic householder acquire his vineyard? I remember a parable the prophet Isaiah spoke against the rulers and elites of his day: "Woe to you who join house to house and field to field..." (Isa 5:8), and how Isaiah's vineyard imagery gave way to woes against "heroes at drinking wine" (Isa 5:22), at least some of whom were 'lords' of actual vineyards.

No prophet appears in the parable of Matt 20:1–15. The lord of the vineyard has the last word: "Mate, I do you no injustice; did you not agree with me for a denarius?[18] Take what is yours and go; I wish to give to this last the same as

---

[16] Adolf Jülicher, *Die Gleichnisreden Jesu*, 2 vols. (Tübingen: Mohr Siebeck, 1888, 1899), 2:462, and Joachim Jeremias, *The Parables of Jesus* (London: SCM Press, 1970), 35, declare the order of payment as an "unimportant detail." Goebel, *Parables*, 306, believes that the householder intentionally provokes discontent in order "to vindicate the justice of his conduct." Similarly, Bailey, *Middle Eastern Eyes*, 360 asks, "Why cause unnecessary trouble? Obviously the master wants those who had worked all day to observe the grace that he extends to others." Cf. Bernard B. Scott, *Hear Then the Parable: A Commentary on the Parables of Jesus* (Minneapolis, MN: Fortress Press, 1989), 294: "to affront those hired first…was not the owner's intent."
[17] Matt 19:16–20:16 in a single scene in the Gospel.
[18] Translating Ἑταῖρε as "Friend" is misleading. I have rendered it as "Mate," a colloquial Australian address, the connotations of which vary enormously with relational context, tone of voice, and body language. Amy-Jill Levine, *Short Stories by Jesus: The Enigmatic Parables of a Controversial*

you. Is it not lawful for me to do what I wish with what belongs to me? Or is your eye evil, because I am good?" (20:13–15).[19] Whether or not the householder initiated the equal payments, he now claims that decision as his own. His honor and power depend on maintaining the illusion of absolute control. Listening *as if* among the crowd, I hear arrogance, condescension, impatience and, possibly, fear. The lord of the vineyard frames the dispute in terms of his goodness and our evil, his power and our dependence, flaunting his ability to do as he wishes with what he claims to own, the vineyard, employment, denarii and even we workers.[20] His threat of an evil eye accusation is designed to intimidate and calculated to discredit any challenge to elite privilege and power. His blasphemous claim to be "good" is more presumptuous than the young man's claim to have kept the commandments (19:20).[21] The householder might have the last word, but the manager silently testifies that his word neither defines nor determines the story.

3. Traditions of Interpretation

Matthew 20:1–15 is most frequently expounded as a parable that depicts the grace and generosity of God, with the "first" and the "last" serving as allegories for Jews and Gentiles, the rich and the poor, the twelve and later disciples, or those who enter faith earlier and later in life.[22] Associated contrasts between faith and works, grace and merit, or gospel and law are often also drawn.[23] The interpretive

---

Rabbi (New York: HarperCollins, 2014), 214–15, observes that the use of ἑταῖρε elsewhere in Matthew (22:12; 26:50) and some of the word's occurrences in the LXX suggest that it is neither particularly friendly nor particularly courteous. In contrast, Blomberg, *Interpreting*, 287, fancies "a tender address." For further discussion, see K. H. Rengstorf, "Ἑταῖρε," *TDNT* 2:699–701.

[19] Most commentators accept the householder/lord of the vineyard's words despite the parable providing no evaluation of his veracity or reliability. Warren Carter, "Parable of the Householder in Matthew 20:1–16," in *Matthew's Parables: Audience-Oriented Perspectives*, ed. Warren Carter and John Paul Heil (Washington, DC: The Catholic Biblical Association of America, 1998), 124–46 (here 142), argues that the householder's speech (20:13–15) addresses the audience and anticipates assent without exploring how such rhetoric functions in power-laden conflictual contexts. In a later publication, Carter, *Matthew and the Margins: A Sociopolitical and Religious Reading* (Maryknoll, NY: Orbis Books, 2000), 398, identifies "an elitist privilege and strategy." Herzog, *Subversive Speech*, 93–4, observes that the landowner frames the transactions in terms of charity ("the gift of the landowner") rather than payment for services rendered (v. 14b), and that his rhetorical question (v. 15a) articulates "the ideology of his class which has arrogated to itself the prerogatives of Yahweh" and "rubs salt into the wounds" of dispossessed peasants. According to Richard Q. Ford, *The Parables of Jesus: Recovering the Art of Listening* (Minneapolis, MN: Fortress Press, 1997), 117, the householder's claim that the first workers "agreed" to a denarius (v. 13) "represents either self-deception or a deliberate insult."

[20] For Luz, *Matthew 21–28*, 533 n. 81, and most other scholars the connection between ἀγαθός in 19:17 and 20:14 "underscore[s] the allegorical understanding of the house master as God." Senji Takagi, "'The Rich Young Man,' and the Boundary of Distributive Justice: An Economic Reading of Matthew 20:1–209," *BTB* 50 (2020): 207–15 (here 209), rightly observes that it is "the landowner's *self-characterization* as ἀγαθός" (v. 15) rather than the parable's characterisation of the landowner that is often used to identify him as God.

[21] Note the emphatic ἐγὼ ἀγαθός εἰμι (20:15b).

[22] Allegorical and typological readings of the parable flourished between the second and sixth centuries CE. For details, discussion and bibliography, see J. M. Tevel, "The Labourers in the Vineyard: The Exegesis of Matthew 20,1–7 in the Early Church," *VC* 46 (1992): 356–80.

[23] See Luz, *Matthew 21–28*, 526–30.

predicate that the householder (v. 1)/lord of the vineyard (v. 8) represents God has a decisive influence on how other characters and their actions are judged, the parable understood, and connections between the parable and its narrative context explained. If the dominant protagonist is *a priori* good and just, then his wealth and power cannot be interrogated, the goodness and the justice of his actions doubted, nor the veracity of his words impugned. As a result, the householder/ lord of the vineyard is vindicated, the disgruntled laborers put in their place, the late-hired laborers grateful, and the manager overlooked or reduced to an extension of his master's will. Interpreting the householder/lord of the vineyard allegorically requires the parable's other social realia to be reduced to allegories, thereby shielding the power-laden situation and interactions the parable depicts from analysis and critique.

An alternative tradition of interpretation approaches the parable as a realistic picture of exploitative economic and political structures which facilitated the growth of large estates, forced peasant families off ancestral lands, and reoriented agriculture toward profit and trade rather than the sustenance of local populations. Interpreters who approach the parable without assuming that its dominant protagonist represents God or is otherwise good, are free to question the householder's perspective and probity, attend to the fraught history and power dynamics of interactions between the household and the workers, and critique the structures that render the workers so vulnerable—and the householder so rich.

I discuss the interpretive predicates and interpretive choices of the dominant tradition before reviewing intermediate and alternative traditions of interpretation in more detail. In the following section, I argue that the parable gives a realistic, if somewhat unusual, glimpse of land and labor relations, and explore the significance of two of the parable's often-overlooked realia: the presence and agency of the manager, and the use of denarii (imperial currency) to pay the workers.

3.1. Interpretive Predicates of the Dominant Tradition

The interpretive predicate that the householder/lord of the vineyard is a figure for God rests on several mutually reinforcing assumptions about parables and two rarely questioned interpretive choices about parables that feature vineyards or refer to "the kingdom of the heavens" (Matthew) or "of God" (Mark and Luke). These assumptions are that unless Jesus or the Gospel writer explicitly states otherwise: (1) dominant protagonists are good and may represent God or Jesus; (2) things with concrete significance in the worlds behind the text are metaphors or allegories for other things; and (3) parables endorse the situations they depict. I will discuss the first two predicates and related interpretive choices before considering the third.

Are dominant protagonists in Jesus's parables positive? Do they represent God? Should parables be read allegorically? Birger Gerhardsson's passionate defence of these predicates warrants quoting at length:

The figure who plays God's role in a narrative *mashal* is always above opposition and blame. His action is constantly presented so as to receive assent. The king, the owner of the vineyard, the landlord, the magnate, the master of the house, the lord, the father—his action is always treated as blameless. Normally it is just depicted in an unproblematic way. In a few cases, however, it is focused, illuminated and made concrete...to justify God's action.... Never is the possibility suggested that the action could reasonably be criticized. It is axiomatic to the *mashal* narrator that God stands for the good and right, and that therefore he must be met with obedience and love, not with criticism, opposition or strivings for independence. If our texts were secular texts, they would argue for a blind obedience to all authorities. But they move in the religious domain and their message means that human beings shall not be disobedient and independent toward God.[24]

Gerhardsson not only asserts that the actions of dominant figures in parables *cannot* and *must not* be questioned, he also insists that parables *must* be read allegorically and *must not* be read as realistic stories. Snodgrass, equally insistent, declares that to deny that parabolic fathers, masters or kings reference God is to "misunderstand how parables function, fail to do justice to the Old Testament and Jewish context in which the parables were told, and render Jesus' parables lame and ineffective."[25] I differ on all counts.

The interpretive predicate that parables endorse and affirm the situations they depict is often taken-for-granted rather than stated. It surfaces briefly in Takagi's consideration of Matt 20:1–15 where he takes the characters' disparate socio-economic status ("standards of living") as evidence that the parable normalizes these hierarchies.[26] Van Eck is confident that this and other parables could not have critiqued "systemic justice and injustice (present in the economy)" because "the conceptual frameworks to support such critiques were yet to be invented."[27] His confidence is misplaced. There is no reason to suppose that ancient peoples lacked the intellectual and conceptual capacity to analyze and critique systemic injustice. Both Testaments reflect sophisticated, nuanced awareness and analyses of structural injustice expressed through narrative, legislation, poetry, oracle and prayer.

---

[24] Birger Gerhardsson, "If We Do Not Cut the Parables out of Their Frames," *NTS* 37 (1991): 321–35 (here 334). Similarly, Arland Hultgren, *The Parables of Jesus: A Commentary* (Grand Rapids, MI: Eerdmans, 2000), 36.

[25] Snodgrass, *Stories with Intent*, 20. Snodgrass was more moderate in "Reading and Overreading the Parables in Jesus and the Victory of God," in *Jesus and the Restoration of Israel: A Critical Assessment of N. T. Wright's Jesus and the Victory of God*, ed. Carey C. Newman (Carlisle: Paternoster Press, 1999), 61–76 (here 74): "That some parables with a king associate that king with God does not mean that all parables do."

[26] Takagi, "The Rich Young Man," 212.

[27] Ernest van Eck, *The Parables of Jesus the Galilean: Stories of a Social Prophet* (Eugene, OR: Cascade Books, 2016), 142–3.

Scholars' construal of intertextual connections and the interpretive frameworks they retrospectively impose upon the text sometimes foreclose the possibility that parables might critique the situations depicted. Snodgrass's contention that parables should be interpreted with reference only to things explicitly mentioned by the text is a case in point.[28] He fails to appreciate that the power of "high context" communication rests precisely in the "gaps," those things that, left unsaid, "invite readers to participate imaginatively in the production of meaning."[29] Interpreting parables with reference only to what is explicitly stated has a range of unfortunate consequences. It prevents hearers from engaging the presupposition pool shared by Jesus and his contemporaries; trains readers to habitually bridge gaps as convention dictates and so, eventually, forget that the gaps exist; and reinforces inattentive listening habits that miss "how much, not being said, is carefully committed to the listener's imagination."[30] It also precludes the possibility of hearers engaging parables as codes or discerning their "hidden transcripts."[31]

Luise Schottroff mounts a comprehensive and, to my mind, comprehensively convincing, critique of these and related interpretive predicates.[32] Explaining that a range of culturally conditioned conventions exert a subtle yet powerful hold over contemporary interpreters, she identifies three further factors that prevent readers from recognizing the practical ethical implications of Jesus's parables. (1) Those of us habituated to power instinctively empathize with masters rather than slaves and tend to identify the interests of the Gospel with the interests of landowners and slaveholders rather than with those of landless laborers, tenant farmers and slaves. (2) Modern Western readers rarely appreciate the numerous connections between Jesus's parables and the Hebrew Bible. (3) Individualistic and spiritualizing theologies obscure the corporate and communal, political and economic, and historical and institutional dimensions of sin, guilt, forgiveness and salvation. Schottroff urges interpreters to abandon the notion of "fixed metaphors" and interpret possible metaphors within their historical and literary contexts.

Personally, I find the interpretive predicates upon which the dominant tradition rests difficult to maintain in the light of Hebrew Bible traditions such as Ezekiel's parabolic oracle against the "shepherds of Israel" (Ezek 34:2–10) and the parable through which Nathan induced David to pronounce judgment on its dominant

---

[28] See n. 15 (above).
[29] Joel B. Green, "The Challenge of Hearing the New Testament," in *Hearing the New Testament: Strategies for Interpretation*, ed. Joel B. Green (Grand Rapids, MI: Eerdmans, 1995), 1–9 (here 6). On "gaps" and "spaces," see Wolfgang Iser, *The Act of Reading: A Theory of Aesthetic Response* (Baltimore, MD: John Hopkins University Press, 1978); James L. Resseguie, "A Glossary of New Testament Narrative Criticism with Illustrations," *Religions* 10, no. 3 (2019): 35–26 (https://www.mdpi.com/2077-1444/10/3/217/pdf); Meir Sternberg, *The Poetics of Biblical Narrative* (Bloomington, IN: Indiana University Press, 1985), 36.
[30] Ford, *Listening*, 7.
[31] On public and hidden transcripts, see James C. Scott, *Domination and the Arts of Resistance: Hidden Transcripts* (New Haven, CT: Yale University Press, 1990), 1–16.
[32] Here and following, Luise Schottroff, *The Parables of Jesus* (Minneapolis, MN: Fortress Press, 2006), 88–114.

protagonist and, thereby, indict himself (2 Sam 12:1–7). These predicates are impossible to maintain when reading Lukan parables in which the situation portrayed and/or the dominant protagonist is explicitly judged by God or the narrator within the parable itself (see Luke 12:13–21; 16:19–31; 18:1–8).

Rarely questioned interpretive decisions about parables that refer to "the kingdom of the heavens" or "of God" or that feature vineyards further bolster the driving predicate of the dominant tradition. The parable's opening phrase, "For the kingdom of the heavens is like" (20:1a), its vineyard setting, and description of the householder as "the lord of the vineyard" (20:8a), are often taken as irrefutable evidence that *this* householder represents God. Opinion about how to interpret 20:1a is mixed. Form critics evade the question by excising 20:1a from the parable.[33] For most others, the phrase indicates that the householder demonstrates how God rules.[34] Others, myself included, locate the point of analogy with the entire parable, some aspect of which speaks of the reign of God.[35]

The prevalence of Old Testament traditions that deploy vineyards and vineyard imagery as symbols for Israel are commonly thought to *require* allegorical interpretations of New Testament vineyard parables.[36] So Culbertson remarks that "Jewish associations with the figure of the vineyard are so strong in Hebrew Scripture that it is virtually impossible to imagine that Jesus, as a Jew, could have used that figure in any way other than as a representation for the People Israel, the House of Israel."[37] For France, "the familiar Old Testament imagery of Israel as 'God's vineyard'" rules out any possibility that this parable might pertain to the economics and practice of viticulture.[38]

Yet, as commentators universally concede, real vineyards existed in Palestine at the time of Jesus, as they did in ancient Israel. We know quite a lot about how land for vineyards large enough to require a manager and multiple workers was acquired and by whom, and about how vineyards of that scale functioned. The tragic history of Naboth and his vineyard (1 Kgs 21), endlessly repeated, haunts the imagery of vines and vineyards in both Testaments: God stands *with* those whose lands are appropriated and *against* their dispossessors. Isaiah's vineyard parable (Isa 5:1–7) powerfully deploys vineyard imagery *both* to condemn a system/structure that dispossessed many to enrich a few *and* indict the owners of actual vineyards who "add[ed] field to field and house to house" (5:8). Given these prophetic precedents, why would Jesus *not* use vineyard parables and metaphors to unveil and critique unjust power structures and elites and amplify the "bloodshed" and "cries" (Isa 5:7) that accompanied largescale viticulture in his day?

---

[33] So, for example, Herzog, *Subversive Speech*, 83.
[34] So, for example, Luz, *Matthew 21–28*, 525.
[35] So, for example, Schottroff, *Parables*, 209–17; Ben Witherington, *Matthew* (Macon, GA: Smyth & Helwys, 2006), 21.
[36] Isa 5:1–7 is most frequently cited; also Isa 3:14; 27:2–6; Jer 12:10.
[37] Philip L. Culbertson, "Reclaiming the Matthean Vineyard Parables," *Encounter* 49, no. 4 (1988): 257–83 (here 263). Similarly, Snodgrass, *Stories with Intent*, 372.
[38] Richard T. France, *The Gospel of Matthew* (Grand Rapids, MI: Eerdmans, 2007), 749.

3.2. Testing the Limits of the Dominant Tradition

The strong hold of the dominant tradition is evident in the lengths to which interpreters go to defend the householder's justice. A growing number of scholars wrestle with the parable's realia and practical implications and are troubled by the "apparent" injustice of the householder's actions. Having attributed the metaphorical identification of the householder with God to the parable, rather than to its later interpreters, they are obliged to reduce the concept of justice to procedural justice (the fulfillment of contractual obligations) and charitable justice (the provision of work and subsistence wages for all workers) and/or limit its application to the establishment of solidarity and equitable relationships *among* the hired workers. The following review illustrates the problem and highlights significant contributions.

Christine Amjad-Ali and Surekha Nelavala interpret the parable in the light of the precarious lives and livelihoods of dayworkers in rural Pakistan and dalit agricultural workers in India respectively.[39] Amjad-Ali suppresses her instinctive discomfort with a parable that, she wrongly assumes, "equat[es] the kingdom of God with a landowner hiring casual labour for his estate" to conclude that the parable seems unjust only because our imaginations are not yet transformed.[40]

Nelavala, an Indian dalit feminist scholar and person of color living in the United States, is acutely aware that biblical "kingdom" and "king" imagery "provides avenues for perpetrating imperialistic ideology."[41] As a Lutheran scholar who respects the authority of scripture, she seeks to "critically engage the text to reinterpret the kingdom of God as an alternative realm that ensures fairness, equality, liberation and justice for all." Her reading is "loaded with paradox":

> On the one hand, it is liberating for the laborers who experienced invisibility, denial, and lack of opportunities to experience [momentary] liberation through the landlord's initiative for reconciliation. On the other hand, an alternative model that is promised in the parable leaves the laborers in a vulnerable condition, since their lives and livelihood are at the disposal of the "landlord".... While a dalit feminist reading affirms the act of reconciliation of the "landlord," and thus finds the story liberating, a postcolonial stance cautions about the inherent oppressive nature hidden in its structure.[42]

Karen Lebacqz, V. George Shillington, Herman Waetjen and Shinji Takagi attempt to resolve the apparent injustice of the parable through appeal to various

---

[39] Christine Amjad-Ali, "Whose Justice: The Parable of the Laborers in the Vineyard," *Al-Mushir* 30 (1988): 136–40; Surekha Nelavala, "God as 'the King' and His Act of Reconciliation: Hope! Despair! A Postcolonial Dalit Feminist Re-Interpretation of 'the Vineyard and the Laborers'," *Currents in Theology and Mission* 43, no. 3 (2016): 8–11.
[40] Amjad–Ali, "Whose Justice," 137–9.
[41] Here and following, Nelavala, "Re–Interpretation," 8–9.
[42] Ibid., 11.

conceptions of justice.⁴³ Lebacqz and Waetjen speak of Jubilee, Shillington of enabling Sabbath rest for all, and Takagi of a (limited) "distributive justice."

Lebacqz, an ethicist, is wary of suppressing "our natural sense of justice" yet asserts that the parable "thwarts our expectations about justice only because these are not formed with the Jubilee year in mind."⁴⁴ She suggests that Jesus used this parable to evoke "the very depths of the Jewish covenant and law" and call his listeners to embrace "the full (biblical) meaning of justice." Lebacqz understands that Jubilee requires the renewal and realignment of social and economic structures. Unfortunately, her refusal to interrogate the wealth and power of the householder (whom she holds to be God) or the social and economic structures on which they depend, prevents her reading from engaging "the full (biblical) meaning of justice."

Shillington interprets the parable as a critique of "the stratified social situation in agrarian Palestine" that denied Sabbath rest to the most vulnerable members of Israelite society, thus violating "the equalising intent of the Sabbath law."⁴⁵ On his reading, the householder *becomes* an exemplary (wealthy) disciple. Alerted to "gross inequality" by his eleventh-hour excursion, the householder "inverts the *status quo*, reverses the expected order of things, reduces his profits, distributes the means of livelihood, equalizes life in the Jewish marketplace."⁴⁶ Shillington exaggerates the householder's Sabbath-enabling actions and avoids the wider implications of Sabbath and Jubilee legislation.

Waetjen identifies the householder as "an untypical landlord who refuses to increase his own profit at the expense of his workers," a "just vineyard owner" whose "economic practice mirrors the material reality that is divinely intended to be actualised in the world."⁴⁷ He contends that the first-hired workers set the wage to which the landlord agreed and must, therefore, have considered a denarius a sustainable (non-exploitative) wage.⁴⁸ Waetjen focuses on the landlord's small and allegedly atypical generosity without mentioning the history of latifundization or the redemption, restoration and redistribution of land central to the vision and legislation of Jubilee. His reading is not persuasive.

Takagi rightly diagnoses the dominant tradition's interpretive difficulties as "the inevitable consequence of the identification of the landowner with God."⁴⁹ On

---

⁴³ Karen Lebacqz, "Justice, Economics, and the Uncomfortable Kingdom: Reflections on Matthew 20:1–16," *Annual of the Society of Christian Ethics* (1983): 27–53; V. George Shillington, "Saving Life and Keeping Sabbath (Matthew 20:1b–15)," in *Jesus and His Parables: Interpreting the Parables of Jesus Today*, ed. V. George Shillington (Edinburgh: T. & T. Clark, 1997), 87–101; Takagi, "The Rich Young Man"; Herman Waetjen, "Imitation of the Year of Jubilee in the Parable of the Workers in the Vineyard," in *Liberating Biblical Study: Scholarship, Art and Action in Honor of the Center and Library for the Bible and Social Justice*, ed. Laurel Dykstra and Ched Myers (Eugene, OR: Cascade Books, 2011), 93–104.
⁴⁴ Lebacqz, "Uncomfortable Kingdom," citations here and following from pp. 40–4.
⁴⁵ Shillington, "Saving Life," 100.
⁴⁶ Ibid., 100–101.
⁴⁷ Waetjen, "Imitation of the Year of Jubilee," 102–3, 109.
⁴⁸ Ibid., 97. Waetjen's argument hinges on the question of who agreed with whom at 20:2 and a textual point at 20:13b.
⁴⁹ Takagi, "The Rich Young Man," 209.

his reading, the landowner is "a (rich) follower of God who practices economic justice with his 'possessions'…a model for the rich young man to emulate" and "a steward of earthly resources."[50] Takagi cites Deut 15:4 ("no one in need among you") to epitomize Israel's understanding of "collective welfare…a concept of justice concomitant with charity."[51] He neglects to mention that Deuteronomy frames the obligation "to give generously" (15:7–8) as resulting from a prior and ongoing collective failure to observe the entire commandment (15:4–5). With this intertextual sleight of hand, Takagi limits the parable's challenge to a type of alms-giving (charitable employment creation) that leaves exploitative structures and systems untouched.

Warren Carter hears the parable call its audiences to embrace "an egalitarian way of life," resist prevailing "hierarchical, patriarchal structures" and create "a community or household of equals…constituted by 'doing the will of your Father in heaven' (12:50)."[52] Carter identifies a range of "intertextual clues" that mitigate against identifying the householder with God: the householder's "large accumulation of land," failure to redress "the inequality of his own wealth" and "inconsistent" generosity.[53] For Carter, the householder serves as "a cartoon figure with exaggerated and ironic characteristics" and "is certainly not God!"[54]

According to Amy-Jill Levine, the householder is *both* a model of discipleship *and* a figure for God.[55] She contends that Jesus told the parable to encourage landowners to "enact the graciousness of God by employing as many as possible and paying "what is right" to all.[56] Levine supports her argument with a tendentious reading of Deuteronomy, citing 15:11 without mentioning the assurance of 15:4–5 or Sabbatical and Jubilee traditions designed to curtail and redress extremes of wealth and poverty.[57] Although the householder is *not* a model disciple, Levine successfully demonstrates that this parable can be read *both* as a realistic story *and* as an allegorical story about God and God's vineyard ("the ideal community that God intended and that Jesus attempted to call into being in anticipation of the messianic age").[58]

4. An Alternative Tradition

A select group of scholars interpret the parable as a realistic picture of land and labor relations without assuming that the householder/lord of the vineyard is a positive figure. Although each makes a valuable contribution, none notices the

---

[50] Ibid., 210, 214.
[51] Ibid., 213.
[52] Carter, *Households*, 146–60 (here 158); Carter, *Matthew and the Margins*, 394–9; Carter, "Parable of the Householder," 132–3, 143.
[53] Carter, *Matthew and the Margins*, 395, 398.
[54] Ibid., 397–8.
[55] Levine, *Short Stories*, 197–219.
[56] Ibid., 218.
[57] Ibid.
[58] Ibid., 199.

gap between the householder's direction (20:8) and the payments the last-hired workers receive (20:9) or consider the possibility that the equal payments might not have been quite what the householder intended.

Herzog reads the parable of Matt 20:1b–15 as a codification of "the incongruity between the coming reign of heaven and the earthly systems of oppression."[59] On his reading, Jesus introduced the elite householder and his steward in order to "depict the collusion between retainers and elites" and stage "a confrontation between two social groups who might never have encountered each other, the elites and expendables."[60] Herzog's explanation of the multiple and interrelated strategies the householder deploys to reinforce his "unilateral power" and further his strategy of "keeping the oppressed under control" is astute.[61] Unfortunately, his unwarranted assumption that retainers inevitably collude with and invariably obey their masters, leads Herzog to erase the steward's human subjectivity and potential agency and, thereby, collaborate with the exploitative system he purports to expose and oppose.[62] Even so, Herzog's comprehensive rejection of the dominant tradition of interpretation, together with his unflinching focus on the social and economic dimensions of the parable and its worlds, enabled subsequent hearers to take seriously the parable's social realia and hear its critique of exploitative structures and practices.

Richard Ford, a psychologist, interprets the parable as a product of conflicting notions of justice: Greco-Roman justice in which elite interests determined what was right; and Hebraic notions of divine justice in which the land belongs to God and all people are accountable to God.[63] Listening to what characters say and what they don't say, Ford "push[es] back into the story" to recall the violent histories of the relationships depicted.[64] The landowner, Ford suspects, is motivated by inherently incompatible desires: the desire to increase his power and wealth (in line with Greco-Roman norms of justice); and the desire to see himself and be honored by others as just (according to Hebraic norms of divine justice). As Ford explains, "the landowner…cannot realize his ambition to "pay what is just" out of what "belongs" to him until much more of what belongs to his landowning class belongs to the day-laborer class…. At issue…may not be a decision about the worth of twelve hours of labor but rather a judgment about hundreds of years of land-grabbing."[65] History matters.

In her more recent work, Luise Schottroff interprets the parable as a stylized fictional yet entirely realistic picture of the behavior of wealthy landowners and the experience of daily laborers.[66] From a Roman perspective, the landowner's

---

[59] Herzog, *Subversive Speech*, 79–97.
[60] Ibid., 87.
[61] Ibid., 86, 91–2.
[62] Ibid., 85, 87, 89–2.
[63] Ford, *Listening*, 15–21, 107–10.
[64] Ibid., 1–9 (esp. 9).
[65] Ibid., 117–18.
[66] Schottroff, *Parables*, 209 17.

conduct is just and good and his rhetorical questions (vv. 15a, 16b) self-evidently true. From a Jewish perspective, the owner's rhetorical questions are blasphemous and his self-proclaimed justice and goodness cannot conceal the expropriation and exploitation from which he profits. For most of those listening to Jesus, Schottroff reminds us, the loss of ancestral lands "was an open wound" and "the planting of vineyards on land that previously was the source of life for families made visible the economic changes wrought by Rome's expanding world commerce."[67]

Jean-Pierre Ruiz and Ada Maria Isasi-Díaz invite the realities of Latino and Latina dayworkers in the United States to inform their readings.[68] Ruiz demonstrates that the lived experience of immigrant dayworkers equips them to recognize the tactics the parabolic vineyard owner deploys.[69] Why does the owner reverse the usual order of payment? To teach the workers "a lesson about his own power and about their dependence on him, and about the insignificance of their own toil." Why "single out" one of the disgruntled workers "and take him to task in front of the others"? "Making an example" of one worker warns all workers to submit. Isasi-Díaz explains that Latinas know that identifying the *patrón* with God is "inconsistent with a theologically sound image of God" and contradicts central aspects of the biblical message and the wider story and teaching of Jesus.[70] "It makes absolutely no sense…to say that the *patrón* is right and the dayworkers are wrong." Better, as Ruiz suggests, to "see the face of Christ in the faces of today's immigrant day laborers" and, presumably, in their parabolic counterparts.[71]

Gerald West, Sithembiso Zwane and their colleagues with Ujamaa Centre's Theology and Economic Justice Programme drew inspiration from the parable's recognition of "the reality of day laborers" and "the equitable payment of each according to need."[72] At the same time, they were troubled by the landowner's "class identity," "autocratic manner," payment of a minimum wage, and "capitalist sounding rhetorical question" (v. 15a), and frustrated by the paucity of scholarly engagement with the parable's existential and economic dimensions. Studying Matt 20:1–15 "contextually" with casual workers in Pietermaritzburg, they observed that dayworkers who initially struggled to adopt a hermeneutic of suspicion became more critical of the householder as they discovered more about the world behind the text.[73]

---

[67] Ibid., 210.
[68] Jean-Pierre Ruiz, "The Bible and People on the Move: Another Look at Matthew's Parable of the Day Laborers," *New Theology Review* 20, no. 3 (2007): 15–23; cf. William R. Herzog, "A Mujerista Hermeneutics of Justice and Human Flourishing," in *The Bible and the Hermeneutics of Liberation*, ed. Alejandro F. Botta and Pablo R. Andriñach (Atlanta, GA: Society of Biblical Literature, 2009), 181–95.
[69] Here and following Ruiz, "The Bible and People on the Move," 20–1.
[70] Here and following Isasi-Díaz, "A Mujerista Hermeneutics," 181–5.
[71] Ruiz, "The Bible and People on the Move," 22.
[72] Here and following, Gerald West and Sithembiso Zwane, "'Why Are You Sitting There?' Reading Matthew 20:1–16 in the Context of Casual Workers in Pietermaritzburg, South Africa," in *Matthew*, ed. Nicole Wilkinson Duran and James P Grimshaw (Minneapolis, MN: Fortress Press, 2013), 175–88 (here 181–3).
[73] Ibid., 186.

5. Questioning Realism

The parable's realia include dynamics of landownership, tenure and management; vineyards and viticulture; landowners, managers and day laborers; marketplaces, employment, unemployment and underemployment; and denarii, the coins with which the workers are paid. Most interpreters locate the parable's central message in features which they consider unrealistic or surprising. These include, the householder's presence and active participation, repeated visits to the agora, recruitment of eleventh-hour workers, order of payment, and equal payment of first and last-hired workers. Schottroff, Ruiz and Isasi-Díaz accept the realism of the entire parable, as do I.

The following discussion defends the realism of the householder/lord of the vineyard's presence and conduct before exploring two realia that, so far as I know, have not previously been investigated: the agency of the manager and the denarii.

Vearncombe collates evidence from documented inscriptions and papyri to sketch a broad picture of viticulture in Roman Palestine which demonstrates that several features of the parable usually deemed "unrealistic" are neither unrealistic nor particularly unusual.[74] It was not unusual for landowners to take an active interest in their properties, hire workers themselves, or hire additional workers during the day.[75] For Vearncombe, the equal payment of first and last-hired workers (vv. 9, 10) is the parable's one unrealistic feature. She assumes that the payments accorded with the householder's directions, although neither the fact nor the content of those directions are revealed. Besides which, as Schottroff reminds us, occasional largess was one of many mechanisms through which elites exerted power, pursued political interests, and reinforced the dependency of subordinates.[76]

It may be true that absentee landlords and other wealthy landowners did not *usually* or *regularly* visit their estates or participate in their operational management, but *unusual* or *occasional* events and behavior are not necessarily unrealistic. A brief letter from Pliny the Younger (*Epistulae* IX, 20.2) offers a memorable vignette of an elite householder's visit to his estate:

> As for me, at this very moment I am gathering in the grape harvest, which is poor, but better than I had expected; if you can call it "gathering" to pick an occasional grape, look at the press, taste the fermenting wine in the vat, and pay a surprise visit to the servants I brought from the city—who are now standing over the peasants at work and have abandoned me to my secretaries and readers.[77]

---

[74] Erin K. Vearncombe, "Redistribution and Reciprocity: A Socio-Economic Interpretation of the Parable of the Labourers in the Vineyard (Matthew 20:1-15)," *JSHJ* 8 (2010): 199–236 (here 206-31).

[75] Ibid., 209-14.

[76] Schottroff, *Parables*, 210–11, 16, relinquished the metaphorical identification of the householder with God only after learning that occasional lavish generosity and forgiveness of debts "were entirely within the compass of the cool political calculations of Roman elites," and realising that the landowner's conduct epitomized the self-serving benefaction that Jesus condemned.

[77] Pliny the Younger, *Letters, Volume II: Books 8–10. Panegyricus*, trans. Betty Radice, LCL (Cambridge, MA: Harvard University Press, 1969), 119.

My incidental observation of somewhat analogous contexts indicates that absentee landowners are inclined to visit their properties at pleasant times of year (springtime or harvest) and when significant developments such as the construction or planting of vineyards are underway. Visiting "lords" often play at farming, making decisions, negotiating purchases or hiring and directing workers, and frequently visit local agora. When visiting "lords" override their managers' decisions, settled routines are disrupted, confusion spreads and conflicts erupt.

Fragmentary evidence and *ad hoc* observations of somewhat analogous contexts cannot be extrapolated to make generalized claims. Pliny is unlikely to have been a typical landowner; the "lords" whose visits I witnessed may not have been representative of their class. The evidence is insufficient to conclude that most householders/lords of vineyards visited their properties upon occasion, nor to characterize their conduct on such occasions. It is, however, sufficient to demonstrate that the parabolic householder's presence and behavior, while possibly unusual, is not unrealistic.

5.1. Respecting the Manager

The character of the manager appears only in v. 8: "When evening came, the lord of the vineyard said to his manager (ἐπίτροπος), "Call the workers and give them their hire, beginning with the last and then to the first." Before the rise of historical criticism, some commentators followed Irenaeus (*Haer.* 4.36.7) in seeing the manager as a figure for the Holy Spirit or for Christ.[78] For more recent interpreters, the manager serves only to emphasize the householder's wealth and/ or to execute his will.[79]

Matthew 20:1–15 does not disclose who initiated the equal payment of first and last-hired workers. Jeremias and Kenneth Bailey erase this ambiguity. Jeremias writes the missing details into the text: "[T]he issuing of a special order suggests some definite purpose in the mind of the owner. This special intention was certainly not…that the last should be the first to receive their wages, but that all, without exception, should receive the full day's wages. Ἀπόδος τὸν μισθόν therefore means, 'Pay the (full day's) wages'."[80] Bailey appeals to Arabic versions and to the "precise language" of the Greek text to insist that "the steward is instructed to pay 'the wage' which is a full day's pay!"[81] Most others who notice the gap assume that the equal payments ensued from the householder's command. Nolland, for example, maintains that the payments received reveal "important details of the directives given to the steward."[82] Van Eck cannot conceive of the possibility of a steward deviating from his "fiduciary responsibility" to "his employer (or owner)."[83] Of all the scholars surveyed, only

---

[78] E.g., Goebel, *Parables*, 305–6.
[79] See n. 14 (above).
[80] Jeremias, *Parables*, 137.
[81] Bailey, *Middle Eastern Eyes*, 360.
[82] Nolland, *Matthew*, 809; similarly, France, *Matthew*, 750.
[83] Van Eck, *Parables*, 152.

Loba-Mkole raises the possibility that the views of the manager and those of his boss might not align.[84]

The noun ἐπίτροπος denotes a person who gives orders or into whose care something is entrusted.[85] Ἐπίτροπος occurs twice elsewhere in the New Testament: Luke 8:3 introduces Joanna as the wife of the ἐπίτροπος of Herod; Gal 4:2 uses the term in association with οἰκονόμος. In Roman administration, ἐπίτροπος designated specific legal roles or positions, sometimes a person responsible for household, organizational or state administration, most often one responsible for the care and instruction of children as a guardian (where the father is dead) or a tutor (where the father is alive).[86] Its usage in rabbinic literature is similar.[87]

The scholarly consensus that the ἐπίτροπος of Matt 20:8 is incapable of independent action is odd when the noun clearly designates someone with significant decision-making responsibilities.[88] Matthew's decision to have Jesus use a term that occurs in no other parable should at least give us pause. Might it be the ἐπίτροπος and his undisclosed actions to whom and to which Jesus invites us to attend?

5.2. Reading the Denarius

Matthew 20:1–15 mentions a δηνάριον four times (20:2, 9, 10, 13).[89] Earlier in Matthew, one hundred δηνάρια feature in the parable of the two indebted slaves (18:23–34). A δηνάριον next appears in the Jerusalem Temple (22:15–22).

Most scholarly interpreters of Matt 20:1–15 note that a denarius was "the usual daily wage" and ponder the adequacy or inadequacy of that wage. Bailey assure us that it was "a living wage."[90] Levine aligns "the denarius of the day" with rabbinic instruction requiring employers to abide by custom, claiming that, in Jewish contexts at least, "custom itself…creates a fair system."[91] France doubts that the denarius featured in the parable told by Jesus, yet is confident that Matthew's audience would consider it "a fair wage for one day's work by a

---

[84] Jean-Claude Loba-Mkole, "Beyond Just Wages: An Intercultural Analysis of Matthew 20:1–16," *Journal of Early Christian History* 4, no. 1 (2014): 112–34 (here 125–7).

[85] Joseph H. Thayer, *A Greek–English Lexicon of the New Testament, Being Grimm's Wilke's Clavis Novi Testamenti. Translated, Revised and Enlarged by Joseph Henry Thayer* (New York: American Book Company, 1889), 245.

[86] For references and discussion, see R. Menahem, "*Epitropos/Paqid* in the Parable of the Laborers in the Vineyard," *Immanuel* 24, no. 25 (1990): 118–31 (here 122–3).

[87] Ibid., 119–21.

[88] A survey of New Testament uses of the cognate verb reinforces this impression. Ἐπιτρέπω has two senses, "to instruct, order, permit" and "to turn to, transfer, commit, intrust"; cf. Thayer, *A Greek–English Lexicon*, 245. In the New Testament, ἐπιτρέπω invariably conveys the sense of giving permission (Matt 8:21; 19:8; Mark 5:13; 10:4; Luke 8:32; 9:59, 61; John 19:38; Acts 21:39, 40; 26:1; 27:31; 28:16; 1 Cor 14:34; 16:7; Heb 6:3; 1 Tim 2:12), as it does at Job 32:14, its only appearance in the LXX.

[89] Some English versions erase the denarius from the parable: "the usual daily wage" (NRSV); "a penny" (KJV); "the normal daily wage" (NLV); "a silver coin" (GNB).

[90] Bailey, *Middle Eastern Eyes*, 355.

[91] Levine, *Short Stories*, 207.

laborer."⁹² Takagi describes it as a "just" wage "that enables a worker to live a dignified life...sufficient to support a family for three to six days," not a wage that would "leave the worker destitute."⁹³ Waetjen insists that a denarius *must* have been a non-exploitative wage because, on his reading, the first-hired workers set the wage to which the landlord agreed.⁹⁴ Others admit the inadequacy of the payment. Given sporadic employment, it was "a subsistence or lower-than-subsistence wage," "not enough to sustain a dayworker" let alone "support a family."⁹⁵

Scholars' lack of interest in the symbolic, economic and political-theological significance of the denarius is surprising. In Palestine, as elsewhere in the Greco-Roman world, the imposition of tribute, changing patterns of land ownership and tenure, and the commercialization of agriculture were interdependent phenomena.⁹⁶ Roman tribute, together with the requirement to pay certain dues with specific denominations, contributed to the monetization of the economy and, indirectly, promoted changes in landownership and control.⁹⁷ Subjugated peoples were obliged to participate in the cash economy sufficiently to acquire the coinage with which to render rents and tributes. Although there is little archaeological evidence to indicate how monetized the Palestinian economy had become by the time of Jesus, coins recovered from Palestinian sites include the denominations with which various taxes were paid.⁹⁸

The census (κῆνσος) or imperial head tax (*tributum capitis*) was paid with a denarius.⁹⁹ The obverse of the Tiberian denarius bore an image of the head of Tiberius (14–37 CE) crowned with a laurel wreath, a symbol of divinity and victory. Its inscription proclaimed the divinity of Augustus and Tiberius his son. The reverse bore an image of the emperor's mother seated on the throne of the

---

⁹² France, *Matthew*, 749–50.
⁹³ Takagi, "The Rich Young Man," 212, 214.
⁹⁴ Waetjen, "Imitation of the Year of Jubilee," 97.
⁹⁵ Citations from Herzog, *Subversive Speech*, 90; Reid, *Matthew*, 147 n. 9.
⁹⁶ With reference to the Roman Empire, see Peter A. Brunt, "The Army and the Land in the Roman Revolution," *JRS* 52 (1962): 69–86 (here 64–82); Paul Erdkamp, "Agriculture, Underemployment and the Cost of Rural Labor in the Roman World," *CQ* 49, no. 2 (1999): 556–72; Peter Garnsey and Richard Saller, *The Roman Empire: Economy, Society and Culture* (London: Duckworth, 1987), 64–82; Peter Temin, "A Market Economy in the Early Roman Empire," *JRS* 91 (2001): 169–81. With reference to Palestine in the first centuries BCE and CE, see: David A. Fiensy, *The Social History of Palestine in the Herodian Period: The Land is Mine* (Lewiston, NY: Edwin Mellen Press, 1991), 93–5; Gildas Hamel, *Poverty and Charity in Roman Palestine: First Three Centuries C.E.* (Berkeley, CA: University of California Press, 1990), 121–63; Richard A. Horsley, *Galilee: History, Politics, People* (Valley Forge, PA: Trinity Press International, 1995), 220–1; John S. Kloppenborg, *The Tenants in the Vineyard: Ideology, Economics and Agrarian Conflict in Jewish Palestine* (Tübingen: Mohr Siebeck, 2006), 78–349, 555–83; Ze'ev Safrai, *The Economy of Roman Palestine* (London: Routledge, 1994), 357–60.
⁹⁷ See Dominic W. Rathbone, "The Ancient Economy and Graeco-Roman Egypt," in *Egitto e Storia Antica Dall'ellenismo All'età Araba: Bilancio di un Confronto*, ed. L. Criscuolo and G. Geraci (Bologna: CLUEB, 1989), 159–76 (here 170–1).
⁹⁸ Emil Schürer, *The History of the Jewish People in the Age of Jesus Christ (175 BC–AD 135)*, 3 vols. (Edinburgh: T. & T. Clark, 1973–87 [1893]), 2:62–6.
⁹⁹ H. Hart, "The Coin of 'Render Unto Caesar...' (a Note on Some Aspects of Mark 12.13–17; Matt 22.15–22; Luke 20.20–26)," in *Jesus and the Politics of His Day*, ed. Ernst Bammel and C. F. D. Moule (Cambridge: Cambridge University Press, 1984), 241–8. Cf. David A. Fiensy, *Jesus the Galilean* (Piscataway, NJ: Gorgias Press, 2007), 35–6.

gods bearing a sceptre in her right hand and an olive branch in her left, symbols of sovereign divinity and peace. The "denarius was a piece of political propaganda that staked Rome's claim to rule the cosmos."[100]

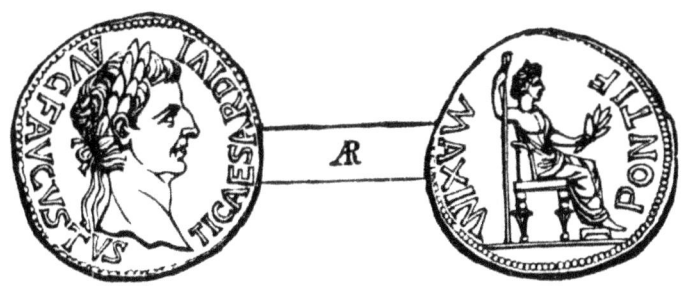

Figure 2. Tracing of a Tiberian denarius.[101]

The head tax was particularly resented, as indicated by the revolts provoked by Quirinius's census (*B.J.* 2.117–18, 433; *A.J.* 18.1–10) and widespread disturbances following the death of Herod the Great (*A.J.* 17.204–18, 271–72, 288–95; *B.J.* 2.4–13, 56, 68–75). From the perspective of those who paid it, the κῆνσος and the δηνάριον with which it was paid were perennial reminders of Jewish humiliation by and subjugation to Rome.

Matthew most often refers to money in the context of taxation (17:24, 27; 22:14–22) or debt (5:26; 18:23–25) or to its extraction or use for nefarious or ambiguous purposes (6:24; 21:12; 25:14–30; 26:14; 27:3–10; 28:12–15). Matthew also refers to money's potential use to give alms (6:2–4; 26:7–9) or purchase bread (14:15) or sparrows (10:29), the price of sparrows being his only reference to the use of money to purchase "everyday" goods or services in an "everyday" situation. As Oakman concludes of the Gospels more generally, Matthew's portrayal of monetary transactions reveals "the reality of power behind money and the political significance of money…an elite political tool, not a universal economic medium."[102]

The use of δηνάρια to pay the workers is integral to the parable's critique of large-scale landownership, profit-oriented viticulture, and the structures and ideologies that enabled both. When telling the parable, Jesus does not explicitly draw attention to the image and inscription on the denarius, nor mention the κῆνσος tax—he doesn't need to; everyone knows! As the narrative unfolds, the

---

[100] Herzog, "Onstage and Offstage," 54.
[101] Image from Educational Technology Clearing House, University of South Florida, http://etc.usf.edu/clipart/6100/6194/denarius_1_sm.gif.
[102] Douglas E. Oakman, "Money in the Moral Universe of the New Testament," in *The Social Setting of Jesus and the Gospels*, ed. Wolfgang Stegemann et al. (Minneapolis, MN: Fortress Press, 2002), 335–48 (here 341–3). Cf. Seán Freyne, "Herodian Economics in Galilee: Searching for a Suitable Model," in *Modelling Early Christianity: Social–Scientific Studies of the New Testament in Its Context*, ed. Philip Esler (London: Routledge, 1995), 23–46. On p. 41, he offers an opposing view.

δηνάριον, its image and inscription, never described but palpably present, take center stage in the Jerusalem Temple (22:15–22). Jesus's opponents ambush him with a question: "Is it lawful to give κῆνσος to Caesar or not?" (22:17b); Jesus demands: "Show me the coin of the census (ἐπιδείξατέ μοι τὸ νόμισμα τοῦ κήνσου)" (22:19). If the loss of ancestral land was "an open wound" for the Jewish people, and vineyard-estates "made visible the economic changes wrought by Rome's expanding world commerce,'[103] the denarius symbolised the entire imperial system, its human consequences and idolatrous claims.

6. Conclusion: Having it Both Ways

Many of Jesus's parables present social, political and economic systems that engender, depend on and perpetuate violence as problems that audiences can identify, question, resist and—potentially—transform. Matthew 20:1-15 is one such parable. Jesus, as the Gospels portray him, affirms both socio-economic/ materialistic and allegorical interpretive approaches. He explains the parable of the sower (Matt 13:3–9 and parallels) allegorically (13:18–23) and the parable of the good Samaritan (Luke 10:30–35) politically: "Which of these three was a neighbor to the man who fell into the hands of the bandits?" "Go and do likewise" (Luke 10:36, 37). But, like much well-crafted communication, Jesus's parables function on more than one level.

Parables that function as "codes" need not *only* function as codes. Allegorising "the vineyard" and its "lord" too absolutely or too hastily prevents us from interrogating the injustices the parable depicts and, therefore, from interpreting the parable in ways that challenge analogous injustices in our worlds. But, *if* we take the parable's social and economic dimensions seriously *and* if we hold potential allegories lightly, we need not abandon the allegorical reading altogether. Many of the parable's so-called difficulties are resolved when its hearers: (1) respect the narrative context provided by Matthew; (2) attend to the historical material and cultural significance of the parable's realia; (3) permit the ἐπίτροπος a degree of agency and influence; (4) sit with the discomfort the parable induces; and (5) locate ourselves within analogous systems of power and privilege. We can hear the parable simultaneously as *both* a realistic fictitious story that critiques exploitative systems and structures *and* as an allegorical story that speaks of the reign of God.

When read allegorically *and* in narrative and canonical context, the parable counters the desire for pre-eminence evident among the disciples, implicit in Peter's question (19:27) and explicit in the request of the mother of the sons of Zebedee (20:21). Such ambitions are ill-aligned with a discipleship ethic; there are no hierarchies in the kingdom of the heavens (19:30; 20:16). Jesus assures the twelve that they will be rewarded (19:28)—as will all his followers (19:29; 20:9). *If* the parabolic lord of the vineyard represents God, God is indeed gracious

---

[103] Schottroff, *Parables*, 210.

and God is indeed good. God is indeed entitled to do what God likes with what belongs to God: "The earth is the Lord's and everything in it; the world and all who live in it" (Ps 24:1).

When read as a fictional yet realistic story *and* in narrative and canonical context, we hear Jesus tell the parable in response to the questions of the young man (19:16, 20), and the disciples (19:25, 27) and the entire preceding encounter and dialogue (19:16–30). The parable reminds the disciples, the crowds and, possibly, the young man listening from a distance, that having many possessions has a history; it doesn't just happen. The parable portrays the power dynamics embedded in land and labor relations. The householder/lord of the vineyard's sense of entitlement (20:14a) and self-assessment (20:15b) preclude any possibility of him being an exemplary disciple. And, no, it is *not* lawful for him to do as he wishes with what he so blasphemously claims to own! The rich can repent and sometimes they do, but the kingdom neither depends on nor waits for the rich. Repentance, as another Gospel reminds us, has practical economic implications: "Whoever has two coats shares with those with none; whoever has food does likewise" (Luke 3:3–14). This type of repentance applies across economic spectrums. It continues until all have enough and none have too much; that is, until we are equal.

And this, I suspect, is where I and those with whom I read so often stumble. Like the young man, we are blind to the structures that enrich us and dispossess others; we have an inflated view of our own achievements: "I have kept all these. What do I still lack?" Like Peter, we focus on personal sacrifice and anticipated reward: "Look, we left everything to follow you. What then shall we have?" Like the vineyard owner, we claim entitlements and attributes that belong only to God, "Mate, I do you no injustice.... Is it not lawful for me to do what I will with what belongs to me? Or is your eye evil because I am good." Like the first-hired workers, we do not want to be equal.

We might not want to be equal, but neither do we want inequality to happen. Few of us *consciously* take more than our share. Inequality increases, despite and against our wishes. The world's structures are systematically biased to favor the strong; the logic of acquisition and accumulation reigns: "To those who have much, more will be given, and from those who have nothing, even what they have will be taken away" (Matt 25:29).

But that is not the whole story. The control of "the powers that be" is not as absolute as they would have us believe. The parable challenges us to push back into the history of global economic relations: present hierarchies of wealth and power didn't just happen; they have a history. For I and others who read on the lands now called Australia, that history involves stolen land, stolen wages and stolen generations. For most of us, it involves complex legacies of appropriation and dispossession and global networks of ongoing exploitation. The parable is a horror-story but the ἐπίτροπος and his (offstage) actions speak of the kingdom. It is possible to work within the system—yeast, light, and salt—to reverse the usual "balance of trade."

Since leaving Afghanistan, the parable still leaves me protesting—at the unjust loss of lands and livelihoods, at the injustice of businesses who choose to be generous to some while paying inhumane wages to all, at the brutal social and economic systems that the parable exposed and at equally brutal systems operational today. But now, with anger comes hope. Those of us who hear the parable as disciples of Jesus are ἐπίτροποι in a different vineyard and serve a different "lord." What influence do we have? How will we use it?

Bibliography

Amjad-Ali, C. "Whose Justice: The Parable of the Laborers in the Vineyard." *Al-Mushir* 30 (1988): 136–40.

Archer, D., and S. Cottingham. *Reflect Mother Manual: Regenerated Freirean Literacy Through Empowering Community Techniques*. London: International Reflect Network, 2012.

Bailey, K. E. *Jesus Through Middle Eastern Eyes: Cultural Studies in the Gospels*. London: SPCK, 2008.

Blomberg, C. *Interpreting the Parables*. Nottingham: IVP Academic, 2012.

Brunt, P. A. "The Army and the Land in the Roman Revolution." *JRS* 52 (1962): 69–86.

Carter, W. *Households and Discipleship: A Study of Matthew 19–20*. Sheffield: Sheffield Academic Press, 1994.

Carter, W. *Matthew and the Margins: A Sociopolitical and Religious Reading*. Maryknoll, NY: Orbis Books, 2000.

Carter, W. "Parable of the Householder in Matthew 20:1–16." In *Matthew's Parables: Audience-Oriented Perspectives*, edited by Warren Carter and John Paul Heil, 124–46. Washington, DC: The Catholic Biblical Association of America, 1998.

Chambers, R. *Whose Reality Counts? Putting the First Last*. London: Intermediate Technology Publications, 1997.

Culbertson, P. L. "Reclaiming the Matthean Vineyard Parables." *Encounter* 49, no. 4 (1988): 257–83.

Erdkamp, P. "Agriculture, Underemployment and the Cost of Rural Labor in the Roman World." *CQ* 49, no. 2 (1999): 556–72.

Fiensy, D. A. *Jesus the Galilean*. Piscataway, NJ: Gorgias Press, 2007.

Fiensy, D. A. *The Social History of Palestine in the Herodian Period: The Land Is Mine*. Lewiston, NY: Edwin Mellen Press, 1991.

Ford, R. Q. *The Parables of Jesus: Recovering the Art of Listening*. Minneapolis, MN: Fortress Press, 1997.

France, R. T. *The Gospel of Matthew*. Grand Rapids, MI: Eerdmans, 2007.

Freire, P. *Pedagogy of the Oppressed*. London: Penguin Books, 1996 [1970].

Freyne, S. "Herodian Economics in Galilee: Searching for a Suitable Model." In *Modelling Early Christianity: Social–Scientific Studies of the New Testament in Its Context*, edited by Philip Esler, 23–46. London: Routledge, 1995.

Garnsey, P., and R. Saller. *The Roman Empire: Economy, Society and Culture*. London: Duckworth, 1987.

Gerhardsson, B. "If We Do Not Cut the Parables out of Their Frames." *NTS* 37 (1991): 321–35.

Goebel, S. *The Parables of Jesus: A Methodological Exposition*. Edinburgh: T. & T. Clark, 1883.
Green, J. B. "The Challenge of Hearing the New Testament." In *Hearing the New Testament: Strategies for Interpretation*, edited by Joel B. Green, 1–9. Grand Rapids, MI: Eerdmans, 1995.
Hamel, G. *Poverty and Charity in Roman Palestine: First Three Centuries C.E.* Berkeley, CA: University of California Press, 1990.
Hart, H. "The Coin of 'Render Unto Caesar...' (a Note on Some Aspects of Mark 12.13–17; Matt 22.15–22; Luke 20.20–26)." In *Jesus and the Politics of His Day*, edited by Ernst Bammel and C. F. D. Moule, 241–8. Cambridge: Cambridge University Press, 1984.
Herzog, W. R. "Onstage and Offstage with Jesus of Nazareth: Public Transcripts, Hidden Transcripts and Gospel Texts." In *Hidden Transcripts and the Arts of Resistance: Applying the Work of James C. Scott to Jesus and Paul*, edited by Richard A. Horsley, 41–60. Atlanta, GA: Society of Biblical Literature, 2004.
Herzog, W. R. *Parables as Subversive Speech: Jesus as Pedagogue of the Oppressed*. Louisville, KY: Westminster John Knox Press, 1994.
Hope, A., and S. Timmel. *Training for Transformation: A Handbook for Community Workers*. 4 vols. Gweru, Zimbabwe: Mambo Press, 1984, 1999.
Horsley, R. A. *Galilee: History, Politics, People*. Valley Forge, PA: Trinity Press International, 1995.
Hultgren, A. *The Parables of Jesus: A Commentary*. Grand Rapids, MI: Eerdmans, 2000.
Isasi-Díaz, A. M. "A Mujerista Hermeneutics of Justice and Human Flourishing." In *The Bible and the Hermeneutics of Liberation*, edited by Alejandro F. Botta and Pablo R. Andriñach, 181–95. Atlanta, GA: Society of Biblical Literature, 2009.
Iser, W. *The Act of Reading: A Theory of Aesthetic Response*. Baltimore, MD: The Johns Hopkins University Press, 1978.
Jeremias, J. *The Parables of Jesus*. London: SCM Press, 1970 [1954].
Jülicher, A. *Die Gleichnisreden Jesu*. 2 vols. Tübingen: Mohr Siebeck, 1888, 1899.
Kloppenborg, J. S. *The Tenants in the Vineyard: Ideology, Economics and Agrarian Conflict in Jewish Palestine*. Tübingen: Mohr Siebeck, 2006.
Lebacqz, K. "Justice, Economics, and the Uncomfortable Kingdom: Reflections on Matthew 20:1–16." *Annual of the Society of Christian Ethics* (1983): 27–53.
Levine, A.-J. *Short Stories by Jesus: The Enigmatic Parables of a Controversial Rabbi*. New York: HarperCollins, 2014.
Loba-Mkole, J.-C. "Beyond Just Wages: An Intercultural Analysis of Matthew 20:1–16." *Journal of Early Christian History* 4, no. 1 (2014): 112–34.
Luz, U. *Matthew 21–28*. Minneapolis, MN: Fortress Press, 2005.
Menahem, R. "*Epitropos/Paqid* in the Parable of the Laborers in the Vineyard." *Immanuel* 24, no. 25 (1990): 118–31.
Morris, L. *The Gospel According to Matthew*. Grand Rapids, MI: Eerdmans, 1992.
Nelavala, S. "God as 'the King' and His Act of Reconciliation: Hope! Despair! A Postcolonial Dalit Feminist Re-Interpretation of 'the Vineyard and the Laborers'." *Currents in Theology and Mission* 43, no. 3 (2016): 8–11.
Nolland, J. *The Gospel of Matthew*. Grand Rapids, MI: Eerdmans, 2005.
Oakman, D. E. "Money in the Moral Universe of the New Testament." In *The Social Setting of Jesus and the Gospels*, edited by Wolfgang Stegemann et al., 335–48. Minneapolis, MN: Fortress Press, 2002.

Pliny the Younger. *Letters, Volume II: Books 8–10. Panegyricus.* Translated by Betty Radice. LCL. Cambridge, MA: Harvard University Press, 1969.

Rathbone, D. W. "The Ancient Economy and Graeco-Roman Egypt." In *Egitto e Storia Antica dall'ellenismo all'età Araba: Bilancio di un Confronto*, edited by L. Criscuolo and G. Geraci, 159–76. Bologna: CLUEB, 1989.

Reid, B. E. *Parables for Preachers: The Gospel of Matthew.* Collegeville, MN: Liturgical Press, 2001.

Rengstorf, K. H. "'Ἑταῖρε.'" *TDNT* 2:699–701.

Resseguie, J. L. "A Glossary of New Testament Narrative Criticism with Illustrations." *Religions* 10, no. 3 (2019). https://www.mdpi.com/2077-1444/10/3/217/pdf.

Ruiz, J.-P. "The Bible and People on the Move: Another Look at Matthew's Parable of the Day Laborers." *New Theology Review* 20.3 (2007): 15–23.

Safrai, Z. *The Economy of Roman Palestine.* London: Routledge, 1994.

Schottroff, L. "Human Solidarity and the Goodness of God: The Parable of the Workers in the Vineyard." In *God of the Lowly: Socio-Historical Interpretations of the Bible*, edited by Willy Schottroff and Wolfgang Stegemann, 129–47 Maryknoll, NY: Orbis Books, 1984.

Schottroff, L. *The Parables of Jesus.* Minneapolis, MN: Fortress Press, 2006.

Schürer, E. *The History of the Jewish People in the Age of Jesus Christ (175 BC–AD 135).* 3 vols. Edinburgh: T. & T. Clark, 1973–87 (1893).

Scott, B. B. *Hear Then the Parable: A Commentary on the Parables of Jesus.* Minneapolis, MN: Fortress Press, 1989.

Scott, J. C. *Domination and the Arts of Resistance: Hidden Transcripts.* New Haven, CT: Yale University Press, 1990.

Scott, J. C. *The Moral Economy of the Peasant: Rebellion and Subsistence in Southeast Asia.* New Haven, CT: Yale University Press, 1976.

Scott, J. C. *Weapons of the Weak: Everyday Forms of Peasant Resistance.* New Haven, CT: Yale University Press, 1985.

Shillington, V. G. "Saving Life and Keeping Sabbath (Matthew 20:1b–15)." In *Jesus and His Parables: Interpreting the Parables of Jesus Today*, edited by V. George Shillington, 87–101. Edinburgh: T. & T. Clark, 1997.

Snodgrass, K. R. "Reading and Overreading the Parables in Jesus and the Victory of God." In *Jesus and the Restoration of Israel: A Critical Assessment of N. T. Wright's Jesus and the Victory of God*, edited by Carey C. Newman, 61–76. Carlisle: Paternoster Press, 1999.

Snodgrass, K. R. *Stories with Intent: A Comprehensive Guide to the Parables of Jesus.* Grand Rapids, MI: Eerdmans, 2008.

Sternberg, M. *The Poetics of Biblical Narrative.* Bloomington, IN: Indiana University Press, 1985.

Storie, D. "Kenneth E. Bailey, *Jesus through Middle Eastern Eyes: Cultural Studies in the Gospels.*" *Pacifica* 22 (2009): 96–109.

Storie, D. "Reading between Places: Participatory Interpretive Praxis." *Pacifica* 18 (2005): 281–301.

Storie, D. "Voiceless and Silent." *Target: Development News and Insight* 3 (1996): 2–6.

Takagi, S. "The Rich Young Man and the Boundary of Distributive Justice: An Economic Reading of Matthew 20:1–16." *BTB* 50 (2020): 207–15.

Temin, P. "A Market Economy in the Early Roman Empire." *JRS* 91 (2001): 169–81.

Tevel, J. M. "The Labourers in the Vineyard: The Exegesis of Matthew 20,1–7 in the Early Church." *VC* 46 (1992): 356–80.

Thayer, J. H. *A Greek–English Lexicon of the New Testament, Being Grimm's Wilke's Clavis Novi Testamenti. Translated, Revised and Enlarged by Joseph Henry Thayer*. New York: American Book Company, 1889.

Van Eck, E. *The Parables of Jesus the Galilean: Stories of a Social Prophet*. Eugene, OR: Cascade, 2016.

Vearncombe, E. K. "Redistribution and Reciprocity: A Socio-Economic Interpretation of the Parable of the Labourers in the Vineyard (Matthew 20:1–15)." *JSHJ* 8 (2010): 199–236.

Waetjen, H. "Imitation of the Year of Jubilee in the Parable of the Workers in the Vineyard." In *Liberating Biblical Study: Scholarship, Art and Action in Honor of the Center and Library for the Bible and Social Justice*, edited by Laurel Dykstra and Ched Myers, 93–104. Eugene, OR: Cascade Books, 2011.

West, G., and S. Zwane. "'Why Are You Sitting There?' Reading Matthew 20:1–16 in the Context of Casual Workers in Pietermaritzburg, South Africa." In *Matthew*, edited by Nicole Wilkinson Duran and James P. Grimshaw, 175–88. Minneapolis, MN: Fortress Press, 2013.

Witherington, B. *Matthew*. Macon, GA: Smyth & Helwys, 2006.

Twenty Years of Experiencing the Parables in Africa

Glenna S. Jackson

1. Thesis

Bob Funk[1] was yelling at the top of his lungs and pounding on the dashboard of the pickup truck he was driving as we were on our way to Sonoma State University in California to give a lecture: "It's obvious from your take on the story of the Hemorrhaging Woman that you've never been to Israel and probably don't even know any Jews!" I could dismiss the second part of his accusation because it wasn't true, but the first was—and served as a dramatic reminder of the need for the real thing, the experiential! This was 1997 and my first sabbatical leave at Otterbein University. I had elected to spend my time at Westar Institute at the feet of the master. I drove back from Sonoma State that day so that Bob could yell without the distraction of driving safely. But I took his criticism about my lack of experience in the Middle East seriously and journeyed through Israel and the Palestinian Territories a year after that episode in California and then eventually through Kashmir, Egypt and Sinai, Jordan, Lebanon, Qatar, and the United Arab Emirates. But the most profound travel I have done is on the continent of Africa, in sixteen different countries seeing innumerable and diverse cultures and listening to countless stories, narratives, and songs in myriad mother tongues. It has now been more than twenty years since I began those nearly thirty journeys (thus far), and it was during my very first time in Zimbabwe where I learned quickly that agrarian cultures know more than any of us in the West could possibly comprehend or even imagine—I have not changed my mind. *Listen up and behold...*

---

[1] Robert F. Funk was President of the Society of Biblical Literature (SBL) in 1975 and founded the Westar Institute/Jesus Seminar with John Dominic Crossan in 1985. The Seminar was the result of working together on parables in the SBL.

2. Background

New Testament parables have intriguing and unique contexts in Africa and the Middle East because they often resonate differently from the Western world. We will not find this kind of knowledge in books. Indeed, my basic argument is that we in the Western world know very little about first-century rural Galilee. We have no way of relating to that kind of poverty, for example—i.e., the absence of technology, electricity, clean water, the ability to get warm or to get cool, a week's worth of groceries, a monthly wage, brilliance without formal educations.

And so, first-hand experiences of the remote villages in Africa give me an altogether different appreciation and understanding of the first-century life and teachings of Jesus. When I became a Fellow in the Jesus Seminar in 1996, three years after completing a Ph.D. in religious studies at Marquette University (at the age of 48), my interests were primarily in the Gospel stories where women were major characters: the women in Matthew's genealogy, Mark's and Matthew's Syrophoenician/Canaanite woman along with Jairus's daughter and the hemorrhaging woman, John's Samaritan woman, and the anointing woman found in all four canonical Gospels. And while being at the table with Bob Funk and Dom Crossan[2] made me acutely aware of the parables in ways that had not interested me previously, it seemed that something was missing from the discussion. Pedal forward four years to my first trip to Africa and I found the answer to my nagging question—the developed world has far less experience with subsistence living. I was so impacted by this realization that the African experience that I had intended to cross off my to-do list, became a once-or-twice-a-year necessity. Indeed, after that first trip, one of my daughters made me a T-shirt with a picture of an acacia tree and the question, "Did someone say 'Zimbabwe'?" The shirt has gone from being worn daily to the point that I only wear it as a nightshirt, but I refuse to give it up. My unexpected and immediate obsession with all things African has dominated my life for more than twenty years—ever since I stepped foot on the campus of Africa University in Mutare, Zimbabwe in August 2000. And, it is the wholistic experience of Jesus's teachings (music and art, economics and daily life, politics and relationships, justice and the law, status and roles of women and children, languages and oral communication, religious and spiritual traditions, history and sociology, botany and the environment, life and death) that help us historians or people of faith understand life as it may have been more than two thousand years ago.

Many people, including family members, wonder aloud why African cultures resonate so deeply with me—why do I choose to spend a few weeks out of every year without running water and seemingly haphazard load-shedding of electricity? My best answer is that, believe it or not, it is like going home. My favorite place to be when I was growing up in southwest Wisconsin was at my maternal grandparents' home in the unincorporated village of Fayette, seven

---

[2] Crossan was President of the Society of Biblical Literature in 2012 and ranks as one of the foremost scholars of parables.

miles from the county seat of Darlington where we lived. They did not have running water and the electricity was a bit shaky (literally), but that was the fun of it—we cousins not only enjoyed waking up in the middle of the night and scaring each other to death on the way to the outhouse where corncobs and the Sears & Roebuck Catalog were "toilet paper," but also argued over who got to pump the water outside near the kitchen door and on Saturday nights *really* fought over who got to take the first bath in the water that was first pumped, then heated over the wood cook stove, and then poured into the huge portable steel tub that hung on the wall during the week and dragged to the middle of the kitchen floor on bath night. I remember having to wash our feet separately and before getting into the tub so as not to contaminate the water for the next bather any more than necessary. We thought it was a funny notion to bathe our feet before we bathed our bodies! We did not know our grandparents were poor. Indeed, there were always nickels in a special teacup in the cupboard to run across the street every afternoon to the country store and get ice cream cones or, my favorite, a Cho-Cho (chocolate malted ice cream in a paper cup with a stick). When my grandparents operated the store, Grandpa would give the brightly-colored flour sacks to my mother to wash and make skirts for my two sisters and me. It, frankly, was the bulk of our wardrobe. Sunday dinners in Fayette were the best—Grandma cooked the freshly killed and plucked chicken (and, yes, chickens do run around with their heads cut off) or, if lucky, a freshly shot pheasant and occasionally squirrel.

So it goes with my favorite places on the continent of Africa. At Justice and Nyathipa's home in Nkhoma, Malawi, supper will be a guinea fowl that the people we visit at Mpalale Village (a remote Muslim village) give us as we leave a day of singing, dancing, and storytelling. The next night, it might be roadkill that someone has left on the doorstep or a goat who has mistakenly wandered into the yard. Other evenings, it will be pigeons that Nyathipa raises—I grew up eating rabbit at least once a week, so that idea was not new to me. And with that note, I must digress a moment:

The second time I traveled in Malawi was the summer of 2003. Along with Africa University students Justice Khimbi and Mike Mwale, a young Japanese volunteer in Zimbabwe flew with us from Harare to Blantyre, Malawi. One day I was driving and Akari was riding shot gun while Justice and Mike sat in the back, laughing uproariously at my inability to stay on the left-hand side of the road and turning on the windshield wipers instead of the indicator lights (directional signals). Several times we had passed very young boys shaking sticks at us and I finally asked what they were doing. Answer: trying to sell us roasted mice. The next time I saw them, I screeched to a halt to see for myself. Sure enough: there were the roasted mice, heads and tails intact. Akari wanted to try one and Justice, always the gentleman and in spite of the fact that he does not personally like roasted mice, ate the head and tail and left the body for her.

Nothing goes to waste in Malawi! We got back in the car and I was feeling a little guilty for not being a good sport by eating a mouse and had decided to stop the next time I saw boys shaking sticks at us when I realized that Akari had drunk nearly a liter of water in less than half an hour. "Are you alright, Akari?" I asked. She responded in a very high-pitched voice, "Prof, I can't get the hairs out of my throat." And that ended my guilt trip and any thought of trying a mouse for lunch. But, and this is the point, Mike, who prefers mice over all meat products and was in mouse heaven when we stopped, could not believe that I would eat a rabbit. And, I have eaten fried locusts in Uganda and fried mopani worms in Namibia—if you did not know better, you might think they were onion rings—plus they are very high in protein.

Back to the thesis: "Listen up and behold," says Jesus and then creates a parable. He did not say, "Read the 'primary sources' and all of the secondary literature and then articulate your own expert scholarly conclusion." In other words, experience the here and now. And, as stated above, my first experience was that I did not know what I was talking about in the context of Jesus's parables and my African students did! During my first time in Africa, I taught at Africa University and had the luxury of teaching a course on the parables of Jesus for an entire semester. On the first day of class, I told the eight fourth-year students (most of whom were already serving as pastors) that I would be learning far more than they would be. At the end of the semester, one of the students admitted that they were wondering what the heck I was doing there if I did not have all the answers! They were accustomed to the traditional method of teaching which consisted of lecture, questions followed by all-knowing answers and conclusions. Several students told me that I was the first professor who had ever asked of their opinions or experiences or cared what they thought in any way—i.e., *colonialism* in the classroom. In this case, students had incredible insights and thoughts about the original intended meaning of the parables based on their own village experience. It is the students from the three classes I taught that very first semester who convinced me to return to Africa so many times and in so many places; they invited me to their home villages over the years where, again, I am the student and they are the teachers. They say to me, "Listen up and behold!"

Two quick anecdotes will serve as illustrations:

2.1. Saltless Salt

I went to Tafadzwa Mabamba's[3] home village in Zimbabwe, he opened his Bible and randomly landed on Matt 5:13–16. He read it in Shona to his friends and relatives who had gathered in the village center and then in English to me: "You are the salt of the earth. But if salt loses its flavor, how will it be made salty? It then has no further use than to be thrown out and stomped on...." I never understood what Jesus was talking about because one can leave salt on the table for months, if not years, and it still tastes salty. So I asked, with Mabamba translating, where they got their salt. They answered that it comes from a tree. They then asked where I got salt. I answered, "In a box at the grocery store." They thought that was hilarious and I suddenly realized that there might be many sources of

---

[3] The Rev. Dr. Mabambe is currently the Station Chairperson at Education-Maun Senior Secondary School in Botswana.

salt, some of which actually lose their savor. I have done just enough research to find out that there are several African trees that produce salt (real sodium chloride [table salt as we know it]). I researched further and, lo and behold, there is a tree in Israel-Palestine called the Tamarix aphylla or Salt Cedar that excretes sodium chloride. If the salt Jesus used comes from a tree rather than prehistoric oceans from which salt mines derive, maybe the saying makes perfect sense; i.e., maybe tree salt does lose its savor as opposed to the salt to which we are accustomed. Tree salt would be free, as opposed to expensive salt transported on the Silk Road.

2.2. Palm Sunday

Another early experience in Africa took place on one of the holiest days in Christianity when I spent spring break in Zimbabwe. I attended Palm Sunday worship at one of the oldest and poorest parts of the city of Mutare. Worshipers were literally filling the rafters of the church to hear a brilliant student pastor, Samuel Dzobo,[4] who was also a student in the Parables class. His message that day was situated in his congregants' plight; that is, if Jesus were a Mozambican who traveled over the Eastern Highland Mountains[5] into Zimbabwe, he would see his people and know their needs—they needed to be freed of political and economic oppression. The people would be so excited that they would greet him with palm branches, dancing and singing. That sermon on a pre-election Sunday was not just powerful, but probably the only time that Palm Sunday ever made sense to me now that I could associate the procession in Jerusalem with conditions in Zimbabwe. (And I was a church organist for 55 years and probably had not missed a single Palm Sunday during that time.) Sam was arrested shortly afterward for preaching that sermon and spent time in prison without anyone, even his family, knowing what had happened to him. Only because one of the guards was a member of his church was he allowed to go free. This incident was certainly reminiscent of that celebratory Palm Sunday more than two thousand years ago. Listen up, behold, and you'll get it!

It must be acknowledged at this point that not everyone in Africa lives in a village or is poor and it is a fair criticism of me that I do not include African city life (skyscrapers, apartment buildings, supermarkets, cars, highways, cell phones, wealthy, middle-class, and poor people) in my research because I can get that in my own world. My fascination with rural living is not only because of my own background, but my unending admiration, respect, and genuine humility regarding a quality of life that is not dependent on materialism. Poverty is not good for all of the reasons that create poverty, but Jesus was right when he said,

---

[4] The Rev. Dr. Dzobo currently serves two United Methodist Churches in Tennessee and teaches at a community college; he splits his time between Zimbabwe and the United States.
[5] When one of my daughters and I hiked a "smugglers' trail" in the Eastern Highland Mountains to see elephants, giraffes, zebra, and white rhino in the Cecil Kop Nature Reserve, we met up with young men who were smuggling sugar from Mozambique to Zimbabwe—it is not just arms and ammunition that get smuggled. (My parents' generation endured a sugar-rationing system during World War II, but I have never wanted for a cup of sugar!)

"Congratulations to the poor"[6]—it is because they get it. And unless one experiences it, one is not going to get it! This is not colonialism or romanticization, it is empathy, support, and partnership. My students at Africa University, especially those in the parables class, were amazed and thrilled that they were contributing to the world of parables scholarship. Many of them indeed grew up in the worst kind of colonialist environment and were not aware how important their voices really are.

3. Method: The Experiential

"Methods help us to find a track off the beaten path."[7]

Sakari Häkkinen agrees with my method of "experiential," and makes the following parallel challenge: "[We must] think about our individual and societal attitudes toward the poor and often implicit practices and begin to see the gospel text through the eyes of the poor and oppressed. For as long as we see the poor only as subjects for whom to preach the good news, we support the problem of poverty in the world."[8] Häkkinen's argument for interpreting the gospel stories in their social context through inter-contextual scriptural research is based on the premises that Jesus was poor, his message was directed to the poor (or at a rich community saying how they should behave), and the poor understood his message in the context of poverty. He argues that people suffering from hunger, from the lack of potable water or medical help, or living under occupation of enemy forces are living much closer to the social status of Jesus and his original audiences than most biblical scholars. He further understands from his own experience that discussing the gospel stories with the poor opens some critical questions to traditional interpretations of the text. These questions help others to see the differences and similarities in contexts between modern and ancient, poor and rich.[9]

The method of the experiential is paradoxically precisely loose and difficult to define or for which to establish strict criteria. It is not a method to establish final answers for New Testament studies, but rather it is for the purpose of establishing parallel contexts from all of human history, including today's world. The experiential dictates endless understandings, even though not all interpretations

---

[6] I had never understood what was "blessed" about being poor—why did Jesus say that according to Luke 6:24? I was relieved and excited to hear Daryl Schmidt argue in the Jesus Seminar that the Greek term for beatitude embodies more of a sense of *congratulations* than *blessing*. Hence, the Scholars Version reads, "Congratulations, you poor! God's domain belongs to you!" *The Five Gospels: What Did Jesus Really Say?*, trans. and ed. Robert W. Funk et al. (Sonoma, CA: Polebridge Press, 1993), 292–3. So, congratulations to the poor because they know how to handle poverty and/or overcome it with dignity, honor, integrity, and generosity.
[7] Ruben Zimmermann, *Puzzling the Parables of Jesus: Methods and Interpretation* (Minneapolis, MN: Fortress Press, 2015), 298.
[8] Sakari Häkkinen, *The Gospel of the Poor* (Republic of Moldova: Lambert Academic Publishing, 2017), 5.
[9] Ibid., 291.

are valid. As Häkkinen notes, "Every scholar is necessarily tied to his[/her] own context." I fully agree with his not-so-subtle mandate that all scholars get out of their personal contexts, at least occasionally. In Häkkinen's specific parallel contexts of the Palestinian Territories and Tanzania, he interacts with the marginalized poor whose very character beautifully illustrates the wide spectrum of divergent populations in two distinctly different parts of the world: the Middle East and the continent of Africa.

Häkkinen and I both admit that not all biblical scholars embrace our methods even though they correspond and supplement other cross-cultural, contextual, and reader-response ways of reading. At the same time, it must be noted that most of us who implement any of these approaches are careful to do all of the academic homework ahead of our on-the-spot investigation, thus engaging with the hermeneutical circle. That is, how does traditional exegesis inform modern understandings of Jesus's teachings and how do modern understandings inform the results of traditional exegesis?[10]

But a question arises: Who gets to tell the stories when they do not originate from one's own culture and context? I have now been doing parable parallels research for more than twenty years, I have published articles and book chapters on the topic and they have been received in both indigenous populations and in my own worlds where different understandings can be surprising, but nonetheless, appreciated. But, as a white, female feminist Westerner, how can I be an effective ally and proponent of the under-voiced? How do I move forward with the information and insights I have gained without objectifying the very ones from whom I've received the stories, understandings and ideas?[11]

The answers to those questions have come not only from the students and their families and friends, but also from academic insiders to the cultures of which I am not an inhabitant, for example, bell hooks[12] and Fidon Mwombeki. According to hooks, an African American, one must engage in bonding across boundaries, both in the experiential and in writing. She argues that, "while [there are] theories about border crossing, there was/[is] little talk about actual practice, of what makes bonding possible across race, class, gender, and diverse politics.... We write more about theory than we do about practice."[13]

Mwombeki, from Tanzania, categorizes different ways that the Bible is used in Africa. One of his observations is that "there is strong affinity between the religious and cultural context of the Bible and that of contemporary Africa."[14] His examples, mixed in with some of my own, include men going out to fish for that day's breakfast and women grinding maize or cassava for the evening meal;

---

[10] Note Häkkinen's (ibid., 255–66) brilliant take on the Widow (Mark 12:41–44). She is a victim of an unjust system, not a model for yearly church budget drives!
[11] Cf. Glenna Jackson, "Framing Insiders by Outsiders," *HTS* 75, no. 4 (2019): 1–6 (here 3).
[12] bell hooks is the scholar's professional name and not capitalized.
[13] bell hooks, *Writing Beyond Race: Living Theory and Practice* (New York: Routledge, 2013), 143–4.
[14] Fidon Mwombeki, "Reading the Bible in Contemporary Africa," *Word & World* 21, no. 2 (2001): 121–8 (here 123). This piece has been instrumental in my teaching and research in Africa.

sifting and winnowing the grain that might be available; small boys catching mice or birds and roasting them on sticks to eat and sell; beggars and prostitutes in the streets; women carrying babies on their backs and baskets on their heads—and phones in their ears; children carrying tables and chairs back and forth on their heads between their homes and the school classroom; many, many young men singing in the back of a small pickup truck. [The first time I rollerbladed on a country road near Africa University, a young mother almost lost the basket off the top of her head and about 25 young men in the back of a truck stood up and nearly toppled it over as they tried to get a better look—it had not occurred to me that they would not be accustomed to a white woman on wheels.] There is light from oil and paraffin lamps on the roads at night that not only provides heat and illumination, but also constitutes a language unto itself for the truck drivers on the road. (That is, the lights let drivers know when to stop and drop off, stop and pick up, or that trouble lies ahead!) There is pottery being sculpted or baked in the oven; exclusion of women and children in counts and censuses; a wife's complaints about the other wives of her husband; a daughter retelling the story of being used as a scapegoat and beaten by her father's first wife because she was the daughter of the third wife; neighbors going to ask for bread to feed an unexpected guest in the middle of the night. [I have been that unexpected guest on numerous occasions.] There are free "all-you-can-eat" weddings for all relatives and friends; demon-possessed men, women and children [including one of my traveling companion's epileptic teenaged brothers who died within a year after I met him because he lacked the necessary treatment]; a completely bent-over woman who stood up tall and danced the "old-fashioned" way with her feet moving unbelievably fast when the music began in worship. When the music ended, she went back to her head-to-feet posture (cf. Luke 13:10–17). Mwombeki continues by arguing that there is strong affinity in social arrangements between African and biblical cultures such as lineage, age-grouping, the value of royalty, birthrights and inheritance laws, the value of the elderly and emotional attachment to ancestral lands. [In the case of Malawi's ancestral lands, there is an amazing irony: gorgeous beach-front property on Lake Malawi that would be worth millions of dollars in California and it houses the poorest of the poor in Malawi.][15]

Mwombeki offers two challenges: (1) the trained reader or theologian must work through what has been called the "hermeneutic of resonance"—to identify the resonance of the biblical text with the theology of the church as well as with the situation of the readers; (2) face African realities. Unless one is in Africa, in the banana groves and the desert places, the stinking refugee camps, the crowded town neighborhoods without proper sanitation, and the hospitals without medicine, one cannot really appreciate how complicated reading the Bible is in such situations and yet, how real.[16] Indeed, I had a conversation with a colleague at the International Society of Biblical Literature Meeting many years ago.

---

[15] Mwombeki, "Reading the Bible," 123; cf. Jackson, "Insiders," 5.
[16] Mwombeki, "Reading the Bible," 127.

We were discussing our summer plans and when I told him that I was looking forward to fishing in Lake Malawi during the night with many, many fishermen in many, many boats, he looked at me in amazement and said, "Can you believe I just wrote a book on fishing in the first century and didn't even wonder what time of day or night they fished?" We can see and hear parallels in socio-economic and material conditions between the world of Jesus and—the contemporary world if we are willing to listen up and behold.

The first part of this method is to engage cross-culturally and then the question becomes, "How can I articulate as an effective ally and with a hermeneutic of resonance?" And so, contained within the method of the experiential that African students helped me to develop is a technique that I have dubbed "Framing the Experience." Simply put, it is a skill that enables one to look outside the *frame* of a picture, a story, or a performance and experience another's environment, culture, or point of view as an empathetic partner rather than merely as a passive observer in the saga of human history.

If we look at a picture, it is always framed, simply because we cannot see beyond the perimeter of it. But we can look inside that frame and observe, describe, interpret, argue, and, importantly, ask questions whose answers may come from outside the frame.[17] Likewise, when we read the framed pictures that the gospel writers have given us and enlarge that frame with descriptions, interpretations, and arguments presented in the secondary research, we still do not have the complete picture. Consider these examples of pictures:

1. Village of Dzobo, Zimbabwe—a crowd of smiling, colorfully dressed people sitting under the trees beside an elementary school house. What cannot be seen? Many are plagued with and/or dying of schistosomiasis, malaria, or HIV-related illnesses.
2. Kigali, Rwanda—people of all ages working and playing in the hills surrounding the city. What cannot be seen? These are some of the same houses from which some of the same adults fled and same hills to which they ran during the genocide in the early 1990s.
3. Rural area outside of Lilongwe, Malawi—several laughing teen-aged children standing under a baobab tree. What cannot be seen? The tree is literally the home of Emmanuel Mwali, orphaned by both of his parents; Emmanuel had untreated epilepsy and died less than a year after the picture was taken.
4. Dirt road outside of Zomba, Malawi—a young woman with a basket on her head, a baby on her back, and a toddler in tow. What cannot be seen? The woman is a widow and the children are fatherless.

---

[17] This is not much different from the scientific method: observe, question, hypothesize, experiment, predict, iterate. In place of "experiment," I would insert "experiential" and argue that the African experience offers dimensions that deepen understandings. By the way, "experiment" can be a colonizing method, at least on the continent of Africa; "experience" can be an inclusive collaboration.

5. Nkhoma, Malawi—school children sitting under a tree with the teacher standing in the center, lecturing—a charming picture. What cannot be seen? There is no physical classroom, the shade of the tree serves the purpose. During the rainy season, classes are often cancelled.[18]
6. Dirt play ground in Rubirizi, Uganda—children playing with a worn soccer ball and having great fun. What cannot be seen? This is an interesting one because what we cannot see, ironically hidden, is that several of the children were starving. In fact, Otterbein students thought that the children's distended bellies were an indication of having plenty of food, but it is the exact opposite—a sign of kwashiorkor (Ghanaian term) or edematous malnutrition or in plain language, starvation.[19]

We must engage in the experiential. We must listen up and behold in order to get it.

The following parables and interpretations include articulations of insights from African students with an introductory story about one of my students at Otterbein University.

4. Jesus's Parables and African Interpretations

4.1. The Doorkeeper (Mark 13:33–37)

> Be on guard! Stay alert! For you never know what time it is. It's like a person who takes a trip and puts slaves in charge, each with a task, and enjoins the doorkeeper to be alert. Therefore, stay alert! For you never know when the landlord returns, maybe at dusk, or at midnight, or when the rooster crows, or maybe early in the morning. He may return suddenly and find you asleep. What I'm telling you, I say to everyone: Stay alert! [Scholars Version]

The role of a doorkeeper or gatekeeper is to keep outsiders out and safeguard insiders (and their belongings) who are in. For the most part, we do not live in gated communities in the United States nor do we have toll booths to any great extent. In fact, most tolls are collected electronically these days. But in Malawi, there are roadblocks every few miles on the one and only major highway as well as on some of the secondary roads. One doesn't necessarily know where the

---

[18] Otterbein students, over a period of four years, provided the funding and some of the labor when on site for a large two-classroom structure that is the only building on the school grounds provided with electricity. It is also the only building that has desks. Students go there in the evenings to do homework and study for exams since many of them do not have electricity at home. The classrooms sit next to the tree that was the original classroom setting.

[19] Our family's knowledge of this condition is extremely personal: our youngest child arrived from Vietnam as a seven-month-old starving baby. Having come from an orphanage in the war-torn city of Saigon, he had little food at the orphanage, less on the two-day flight to Chicago and was hospitalized for ten days once we picked him up at O'Hare. I did not know until that experience how physically painful starvation is—it shrinks organs and tissues inside the body and bloats the stomach!

guards will set up; it may be in one place one day and down the road a few kilometers the next. In any case, one of my Otterbein students, Corinne, was doing her homestay in the northern region of Malawi, the most poverty-stricken part of the country. Her homestay father owned a small kiosk on the road where persons who were stopped at the guard station or roadblock in the same vicinity, might take the time to buy a treat, Coca-Cola, or some other small miscellaneous item. In the meantime, the police guards at the roadblock had befriended Corinne while she was working the kiosk and one day asked her if she would like to be the one to let people pass—or not pass—through the roadblock. That is, she could control the pulley that lifted the gate for trucks, cars, bikers, and pedestrians to pass through. As it happens, I was on the road with two faculty colleagues, our Malawi host Justice and our driver Dennis, while students were with their homestay families. As the five of us approached this particular roadblock in our coaster [bus], Corinne noticed us from a distance and couldn't wait for our surprise upon seeing that she was the gatekeeper and it would be she who could let us through—or not. She gleefully made us sit for a moment, and as she finally operated the pulley to raise the gate, everyone—she, the five of us, the guards, Corinne's homestay father, his customers—were laughing uproariously at the situation. In the hierarchical world of northern Malawi as well as a U.S. classroom, it was the student who had unexpected and immediate control over her professors and supervisors, not the usual other way around! Dennis exclaimed, "Corinne—that girl is welcome to stay in Malawi!" Everyone who witnessed this comedy truly enjoyed the change in the balance of power! And she, as she related to us later on that evening, enjoyed the status as insider with the Malawians and the gatekeepers, temporary though it was.[20] She had a powerful and fun experience outside of her own culture by listening and beholding.

4.2. The Samaritan (Luke 10:25–37)

Even though the previous examples are from actual pictures, one can articulate what one experiences by putting an imaginary picture frame on the information. The significance of the picture is contingent on the frame because every individual's frame, every culture's frame, and every scholar's frame is unique. The story of the Good Samaritan is a perfect example. It is usually put into a good-neighbor frame–treat people well and inherit the kingdom of God.[21] The front and center of the picture is almost always the "good Samaritan." Jean Ntahoturi,[22] an Africa University student from Burundi, had a very different picture because his frame held personal memories of the genocide in Rwanda and Burundi when he was a child:

---

[20] I first told this story in Jackson, "Insiders," 1.
[21] Cf. Ruben Zimmermann, *Puzzling*, 293–331, for a comprehensive discussion and bibliography of The Good Samaritan.
[22] The Rev. Ntahoturi is now the Legal Representative for the Burundi United Methodist Church Annual Conference.

In 1995,[23] I was shopping in the suburb of Bujumbura [capital city of Burundi] when I heard gun fire nearby. Two soldiers were shot dead. The rebels were around. In a confused situation, I ran away in the hills. I was not alone. When we began to climb the hill, one mother realized that her five-year-old son was not with her. She was so disturbed. She decided to go back to look for him. We tried to persuade her not to go back. She refused. "I have to go to look for my son; even if I am to die today, there is no option," she said. When she was moving around, the child saw his mother very far away. He was in rebels' hands. He started crying. The rebels suddenly saw the mother and called her to come and take the child. First, she was afraid, but she got courage and she approached them, took the child, and ran back into the hills unharmed.

According to Ntahoturi, one should frame this parable with the victim front and center in the picture rather than with the so-called good Samaritan because help comes from the most unexpected source, in this case, a soldier from the enemy tribe.[24] Imagine a framed picture with the mother and small boy running into the Rwandan or Burundian hills for safety and the enemy soldier in the background giving them a thumbs up!

A similar event occurred in Israel-Palestine a few years ago on one of my sabbaticals. This is my journal entry that evening:

> Gary (my husband) and I met Sakari and Kati Häkkinen from Finland in the Old City [of Jerusalem] to go on their tour bus to Beit Jalla for dinner at their group's hotel. The city of Beit Jalla borders the city of Bethlehem; both are constituent parts of the Palestinian Territories. Since it's not easy to get a taxi directly from a Palestinian Territory through Jerusalem and to another Palestinian Territory [East Jerusalem where we live], their Israeli tour guide offered to take us back to St. George's College since being a tour guide gives her some leeway in both Israel and Palestine. So we're headed down a steep hill with her, sharp curve ahead of us and sharp curve behind us, when she hits a very large pothole and we can hear the air going out of the front two tires. Her spare tire is also not inflated, so she now has a total of three flat tires out of five. She pulled off to the side of the road in very busy two-way traffic.
>
> She was a bit flummoxed and since we did not understand all of the cultural mores, we were sparse on suggestions and could not offer any alternatives, although she assured us that our company was valuable! We found out later that she tried to take a shortcut and was on a road she didn't belong and was fearful to call anyone. Anyway, we sat about an hour when a young

---

[23] Uganda and Burundi were also experiencing genocide along with the more infamous Rwanda Genocide of 1994. Similar activity continues in Burundi even though this story is more than twenty-five years old and is rarely reported in international news.
[24] I first published this story in Glenna Jackson, "Rebel Soldiers as Good Samaritans: New Testament Parables in an African Context," *HTS* 60 (2004): 239–47.

man stopped to help. She barely rolls her window down to talk with him because she knows that he is a Palestinian. They speak Arabic (she speaks fluent English, Finnish, Arabic, and Hebrew) and he tells her that he is a policeman with the Palestinian police force and would be happy to help get someone to get Gary and me home plus do something about her car. He even told her that just last week his wife had a similar experience with a flat tire and had waited a lengthy amount of time before someone stopped to help. He was so grateful that someone had finally stopped to help her that he had vowed never to simply pass by someone who was in trouble on the road. But our driver told him she did not want his help. OK. She refuses! Now what? We wait another half hour and the Palestinian bus driver with whom she has been working all week comes down the hill to help. At the same time another young man pulls up to see what's going on and long story short, the Palestinian bus driver tells this Jewish young man who turns out to be an engineer, born and raised in Jerusalem, about these two Americans who need to get to East Jerusalem and so if he could take care of us, he would help the woman with the flat tires.

Agreed. So we get into the car with him—what a delight. He drove us around parts of Jerusalem that we had not seen yet, including Netanyahu's home, and then when he took us to East Jerusalem, we gave him a tour because he had never been there in spite of being a Jerusalemite! I, of course, was reminded of the story of the Good Samaritan—from whom are you willing to take help? Surely the Jewish tour guide was not going to take help from a Palestinian stranger, but the Palestinian bus driver was willing to take help from the Jewish stranger and since we were just along for the ride, we didn't care who helped. Strange world we live in.

These examples of interpretations of the Good Samaritan in Burundi and in Israel-Palestine have much more authenticity with the first-century world of Samaritans and Judeans than my own cultural understanding. And it is almost always the case that when I am anywhere on the continent of Africa or in the Middle East, the narrative from stories, songs, and dance constitutes elements of cultural heritage, contemporary social mores, issues of social [in]justice and often are also reminiscent of the contexts of the New Testament parables.

The frame holding these two very different and uniquely cultural pictures is not focused on the good neighbor, but on the victim taking help from the enemy. (Most Western readers of this Lukan parable have no idea that Samaritans and first-century Judeans did not get along, in fact hated one another.[25]) Funk long argued that this story was about the victim, not the Samaritan because Jesus's audience would have viewed the story through the eyes of the victim in the ditch.[26] Ntahoturi, of course, did not know Bob Funk nor had he ever read anything academic about parables at that time in his life; yet, his instinct was that this was

---

[25] Again, see Zimmermann, *Puzzling*, especially, 309–10, 314–15.
[26] Cf., for example, Funk et al., *The Five Gospels*, 324–5.

a victim's story. And, individuals are not the only ones who need to decide from whom to take or refuse help; nations also reject help from countries ideologically opposed to them.

4.3 The Fig Tree (Luke 13:6–9)

This parable is understood in a variety of theological constructs: repentance, crisis, eschatology, exaggerated hope, blessing or curse and judgment, temple longevity, and so on.[27]

> A man had a fig tree growing in his vineyard; he came looking for fruit on it but didn't find any. So, he said to the vinekeeper, "See here, for three years in a row I have come looking for fruit on this tree, and haven't found any. Cut it down. Why should it suck the nutrients out of the soil?" In response he says to him, "Let it stand, sir, one more year until I get a chance to dig around it and work in some manure. Maybe it will produce next year, but if it doesn't, we can go ahead and cut it down." (Scholars Version)

But it can also be understood through inter-cultural exposure and experience. Ntahoturi understood the parable to be all about a barren womb—and the newly wed husband must either divorce his new bride or take on a second wife:

> The Kudzunga family rejoiced when their elder son got married. Everyone in the family looked forward to the success of this couple (Tatenda and Tendai). After the wedding day the aunts expected their sister-in-law to have conceived. Two months, five months, a year, there were no signs of pregnancy. One of the aunts was bold enough, she went and asked her brother, Tatenda. She said, "Tatenda, what is going on between you and Tendai? It is high time that you should have a child." Tatenda calmly responded, "Auntie, give us one more chance; we will do it, just allow us to look into the issue." The auntie finally said, "If your wife is barren you better divorce her and marry somebody who is productive or you better marry a second wife who will give you children."

Ntahoturi, staying true to parable form, did not reveal the end of this story. Did Tendai get pregnant? Did Tatenda took on another wife? Did the couple ignore the auntie? Do other possibilities exist for having children?[28]

---

[27] For example, John P. Meier, *A Marginal Jew: Rethinking the Historical Jesus, Vol. 2: Mentor, Message, and Miracles* (New York: Doubleday, 1994), 985; cf. Funk et al., *The Five Gospels*, 345; Zimmermann, *Puzzling*, 188.

[28] Adoption is unusual in most African countries for complicated reasons. The topic pulled surprised students into my personal life story because Gary and I decided to give birth, adopt a baby of the opposite gender, give birth again, and adopt another of the opposite gender—our version of family planning! Unfortunately, there are taboos against adoption in Africa. An example includes close Malawian friends who adopted three children because of fertility issues and they have been shunned by some family and friends to this day.

Sophirina Sign,[29] another student in the Parables class at Africa University, has a similar understanding of the parable from her Zimbabwean perspective where the same expectations are present:

> Barrenness in my context is associated with women. Fig trees are wild trees. Farmers do not grow fig trees. The trees just grow by themselves in the bush. If a woman is married she is expected to bear children. There is this concept that those with many children are the richest people. Every woman is greatly honored by the society if she bears fruits. If she fails to do so she is regarded a cursed woman. For that reason there are two options: the in-laws ask their son to divorce and marry another woman whose womb is prepared to bear fruit. Or, if the woman is to remain with her husband's family, her parents will be asked to provide a wife to the husband so that she bears offspring on behalf of the aunt or sister. Barrenness in my society is not tolerated. The main purpose of marriage is to produce children for the family. As soon as the two get married, results have to be shown. Without procreation a woman is regarded as useless within the society.

Both Jean and Sophirina made perfect culturally-contextual sense of the parable–not something I would have thought of in my Western cultural context.

Kongnyuh Emmanuel,[30] a student at the Presbyterian Theological Seminary in Kumba, Cameroon, has the following to say about a tree that was in danger of being cut down for very different reasons:

> If one is to understand the Parable of the Barren Fig Tree in my native community, it will be very fitting to consider why cola nut trees, whether fruitful or barren, should not be cut down. In my community, so much value is attached to the cola nut tree. Every courtyard and surrounding has cola nut trees of various sizes and ages. Some of these are as old as the compound, or as old as members of the family. The story is told of an identification officer who came to our locality to establish identity cards for the inhabitants. When the officer sought to know the age of the family head [who did not know his own birth date], he was shown a cola nut tree that was about the man's age. So he was told that if he could estimate the age of the tree he could guess how old the family head was.[31]

That sounds simple enough—cut down the tree, count the inner rings, determine the age of the village elder. As Emmanuel read his parable in class, I was not sure if I understood what he was saying; I needed further explanation.

---

[29] The Rev. Sign is now the Connectional Ministries Director of the Zimbabwe East Annual Conference.

[30] The Rev. Kongnyuh Emmanuel is now a lecturer at the Presbyterian Theological Seminary in Kumba, Cameroon.

[31] I first told this story in Glenna Jackson, "Parable Parallels from Cameroon," *Voices from Kumba* 4 (2013): 238–9.

As his student colleagues grinned at the opportunity to teach me their culture, Emmanuel pictured several frames that the rest of the class fully understood. To be perfectly honest, the only picture I imagined was an old man standing near an innocuous tree with an innocuous government agent. But, listen up and behold! The first picture I needed to see was of a tree being planted by a new father with the new mother and their baby watching. That tradition in Cameroon, like many African and Middle Eastern countries, include a tree planted in a newborn baby's honor. In some cultures an additional tree is planted for every succeeding birthday. I found out, for example, that in Israel-Palestine, by the time a son becomes of marriageable age, his grove of trees will provide enough wood to build a house.[32]

The second picture was of Identification Officers who are not always looked upon kindly—they are sometimes viewed as interlopers working on behalf of a government that can be regarded as ruthless and/or immoral. To need the exact age of the chief or family head, who did not know the year he was born, seemed unnecessary to the community.

A third picture that we could not possibly see from a Western perspective is that the cola nut trees are considered to be sacred, no one cuts them down without proper rituals from a traditional priest. Since the fruit of the tree "brings life," the tree itself must be conserved for the sustainability of the community. Indeed, if a cola nut tree is cut down for some important reason such as the construction of a house or road, mourning rituals are demanded—as though it were a funeral. And so the family dared the officer to cut down the tree to determine the age of their chief.

The final picture would be up to the listener because, just like the parables of Jesus, we do not know the ending, we cannot see the final frame—did the identification officer cut down the tree to fulfill his obligation and, at the same time, risk the dangers inherent in cutting down a sacred tree? Did the officer walk away, thereby admitting defeat to the community as well as to his boss? Again, in true parabolic style, we do not have answers, plus the pacifist resistance in this parable is especially Jesus-like!

4.4. The Empty Jar (Gospel of Thomas 97)

> The Father's empire is like a woman who was carrying a jar full of meal. While she was walking along a distant road, the handle of the jar broke and the meal spilled behind her along the road. She didn't know it; she hadn't noticed a problem. When she reached her house, she put the jar down and discovered that it was empty. (Scholars Version)

---

[32] Cf. Häkkinen's, *Gospel of the Poor*, 267–7, story of Rasheed Abu Mohammed's loss of a large part of his olive orchard to new Israeli zoning that put a security fence in the middle of it. The physical and emotional violence in this story is, according to Häkkinen, illustrative of what happens daily in Israel–Palestine and provides insights into a Roman-occupied Palestine.

Thomas' parable of the Empty Jar has become my all-time favorite parable, thanks to an African understanding. Prior to my experiencing a woman with a jar on her head, my focus was only on the misogyny of the interpretations!

The imaginary picture of this parable is always framed with an ignorant woman in the center, oblivious to the mealie-meal running down her back and, therefore, responsible for God's empire.[33] But there are several aspects to this woman's task from an African perspective of which we Westerners are clueless. Our framed picture does not include the fact that once an object is on the woman's head, she no longer feels its weight and would not know that the load is getting lighter. The picture is missing the baby or toddler wrapped on her back and the water jars in each hand. It is also missing the other women doing the same household tasks and with whom she is traveling and in conversation. What is not missing is a man carrying anything on his head because, for the most part, men do not engage in that activity. Chances are that neither Jesus nor the author of Thomas did either. My hunch is that the culture of women tending to household chores was assumed and a natural observation of grain falling from a broken vessel on top of a woman's head provided fodder for a parable. The woman should not have to bear the brunt of the lesson here—it will not be her fault if God's kingdom slips away! A children's book from Namibia illustrates this picture perfectly. A little girl begins to walk to her grandmother's home in another village with a full basket of fruit on her head. As she travels, a bird, a monkey, and a snake steal the fruit, leaving the basket empty—but Tutala does not notice! And lucky for her, a ram charges a tree just as she passes under it and her basket is restored with fruit just in time as she arrives at her grandmother's house.[34]

5. Conclusion

The pictures and stories began to develop much differently for me once I had traveled to the Middle East and Africa because I listened and beheld. Africans, especially in the rural areas, understand first-century cultures better than today's Westerners ever will. No one claims to have final answers, but African students intuit that parables are intriguing riddles and puzzles, ingenious at pulling in the listener, and meaningful to the extent of the experience of the community. Those of us who work on the teachings of Jesus must also do all we can to understand how he lived. I have been convinced by African students and their families and friends as well as African scholars that we can better discern the context of Jesus's life and teachings if we engage in hooks' "bonding across boundaries," Mwombeki's "hermeneutic of resonance," Häkkinen's "inter-contextuality," Crossan's, Funk's and Zimmermann's "multi-approach polyvalence," and my "experiential" in addition to the traditional methods of exegesis. If we listen up and behold, we might get it!

---

[33] Cf. Zimmermann, *Puzzling*, for an extensive study and bibliography of "The Empty Jar," 361–92.
[34] Susana Camara and Youngshin Sim, *Tutala's Journey* (Penduka Books, n.d.); cf. Glenna Jackson, "The Woman with The Empty Jar (Thomas 97 and Africa)," *The Fourth R: An Advocate for Religious Literacy* 33, no. 3 (2020): 3, 10.

Bibliography

Camara, S., and Y. Sim. *Tutala's Journey*. Penduka Books, n.d.
Funk, R. W. et al. *The Five Gospels: What Did Jesus Really Say?* Sonoma, CA: Polebridge Press, 1993.
Häkkinen, S. *The Gospel of the Poor*. Republic of Moldova: Lambert Academic Publishing, 2017.
hooks, bell. *Writing Beyond Race: Living Theory and Practice*. New York: Routledge, 2013.
Jackson, G. "Framing Insiders by Outsiders." *HTS* 75, no. 4 (2019): 1–6.
Jackson, G. "Parable Parallels from Cameroon." *Voices from Kumba* 4 (2013): 238–9.
Jackson, G. "Rebel Soldiers as Good Samaritans: New Testament Parables in an African Context." *HTS* 60 (2004): 239–47.
Jackson, G. "The Woman with The Empty Jar (Thomas 97 and Africa)." *The Fourth R: An Advocate for Religious Literacy* 33, no. 3 (2020): 3, 10.
Meier, J. P. *A Marginal Jew: Rethinking the Historical Jesus, Vol. 2: Mentor, Message, and Miracles*. New York: Doubleday, 1994.
Mwombeki, F. "Reading the Bible in Contemporary Africa." *Word & World* 21, no. 2 (2001): 121–8.
Zimmermann, R. *Puzzling the Parables of Jesus: Methods and Interpretation*. Minneapolis, MN: Fortress Press, 2015.

Encountering the Parables:
Appreciation and Critique

Mary Ann Beavis

1. Some Preliminary Remarks

The phrase "contexts old and new" in the title of this collection invokes Matt 13:52, quoted in the editors' introduction as an epigraph along with Mark 4:2–3. The comparison of a householder removing items from his storehouse (θησαυροῦ) to "a scribe trained for the kingdom of heaven" is usually interpreted something like this: "The image is that of a storeroom where the master of the house brings provisions of every kind to meet the needs of the household. Christian scribes (cf. 23:34), as reflected in chapter 13, draw on the old (the scriptural tradition) and the new (Jesus's role in it all) to meet needs just as the master of a household would."[1] It's also a parable, which for some reason is seldom included in academic books on the parables, except in passing. Perhaps this is why the standard—and highly questionable—translation of the verb ἐκβάλλει (Matt 13:52c) as "takes out" (NRSV) has received little comment, except in an article by Peter Phillips, who notes that the semantic domain of the verb does not encompass selection but rather implies disposal or expulsion; the householder/scribe is represented as "casting out" both the new and the old. This, Phillips asserts, is a "startling image" rather than a "rather conservative wisdom saying" that fits in better with the preceding parables that portray characters selling their treasures in exchange for the βασιλεία τῶν οὐρανῶν (13:44, 45).[2] I would add that it contrasts somewhat with the immediately adjacent parable of the fishnet (13:47–48), where the bad fish are cast out (ἔβαλον) and the good ones are retained: "So it will be at the end of the age. The angels will come out and separate the evil from the righteous and throw (βαλοῦσιν) them into the furnace of fire, where there will be weeping and gnashing of teeth" (vv. 49–50). Here, the "casting" is preliminary to the

---

[1] Charles H. Talbert, *Matthew*, Paideia Commentaries on the New Testament (Grand Rapids, MI: Baker Academic, 2010), 172.
[2] Peter Phillips, "Casting Out the Treasure: A New Reading of Matthew 13.52," *JSNT* 31 (2008): 3–24 (here 18, 21).

separation of the good from the bad. However, all three parables involve the disposal of property for the sake of the kingdom—as Gundry put it, "the necessity of economic self-deprivation to the true membership of the kingdom."[3]

The householder parable can be used to illustrate several features of academic parable interpretation. Some parables, like Matt 13:52, get little attention. In the case of the householder parable, this may be because of its brevity, because it is only found in Matthew and so is unlikely to go back to the historical Jesus (at least by the lights of, e.g., the Jesus Seminar),[4] or simply because its meaning has been taken to be self-evident. This raises the question of why parables with a high likelihood of "authenticity" are regarded as more worthy of interpretation (even with the proviso that they were remembered in multiple iterations) than other early Christian parables—especially parables not attributed to Jesus, like the two parables ascribed to John the Baptist and the parable of the centurion in Q (3:9, 17; 7:8),[5] or the Sadducees' parable about the widow with seven husbands (Mark 12:20–23),[6] much less the ten complex and mystical parables of Hermas (*Similitudes*). Long ago, Mary Ann Tolbert asked the question of whether "exaggerated claims of power" for the parables might arise from confusion of the speaker (Jesus) with that which is spoken;[7] this question also applies to the academic preference for some parables ("authentic") relative to others (not "authentic").

The quotation from Mark 4:2–3 in the epigraph to the Introduction reminds us of the vast, and somewhat under-appreciated, role of Mark's Gospel in our apprehension of the parables. Although the Q source contains many well-known parables, it remains hypothetical. Mark is the oldest literary source that portrays Jesus as a teller of parables (4:33–34), and that provides not only an explanation of why he used them (4:11–12), but includes a sample interpretation (4:13–20), which, if it were suddenly discovered today, would be embraced (rightly or wrongly) as the hermeneutical key to the parables. Moreover, it is Mark that closely associates the parables with ἡ βασιλεία τοῦ θεοῦ an association not made outside the synoptic tradition. Whether or not scholars take the Markan theory of parables as a guide to how Jesus used and understood them, the evangelist is the first literary parable interpreter. Without the synoptic tradition of which Mark is the bedrock, the New Testament would contain scant indication that Jesus taught in parables, which leads to the question of how significant the parables were to the earliest believers. That said, the synoptic parables have informed Christian understandings of Jesus for two millennia, and Western culture would be the poorer without them.

---

[3] R. H. Gundry, *Matthew: A Commentary on his Handbook for a Mixed Church under Persecution*, 2nd ed. (Grand Rapids, MI: Eerdmans), 275.
[4] Robert W. Funk et al, *The Five Gospels: The Search for the Authentic Words of Jesus* (New York: Scribner, 1993), 197–8.
[5] See Dieter Roth, *The Parables in Q* (London: Bloomsbury, 2018), 18–21.
[6] Mary Ann Beavis, "Feminist (and other) Reflections on the Woman with Seven Husbands (Mark 12:20–23)," in *Hermeneutik der Gleichnisse Jesu: Methodische Neuansätze zum Verstehen urchristlicher Parabeltexte*, ed. Ruben Zimmermann, WUNT 213 (Tübingen: Mohr Siebeck, 2008), 603–17.
[7] Mary Ann Tolbert, *Perspectives on the Parables: An Approach to Multiple Interpretations* (Philadelphia, PA: Fortress Press, 1979), 91.

After a career that has involved a good deal of parable interpretation, I am honored to be asked to respond to the essays in this book. I offer my comments with the humble proviso that they are filtered through my own experiences, preferences, knowledge, and gaps in that knowledge. My preferred approach to the parables has been feminist, reader-oriented, and contextual. I hope that my remarks will be received in the spirit of the traditional interpretation of Matt 13:52 in terms of appreciation for a carefully curated and arranged collection, rather than of the more radical (and, I think, persuasive) interpretation argued by Phillips, and of Mark's injunction to listen, look, perceive and understand the parables—and their interpreters.

2. Three Lines of Enquiry

The editors identify three lines of enquiry that inform the content of this book: (1) careful consideration of the historical and material world of the first century, and of the conceptual and the metaphorical contexts of the parables, with attention to audience response; (2) the "material turn" focusing on the social, political, economic, and material realia of the first century; (3) reception history—"how the parables have been and continue to be seen and heard." To a greater or lesser extent, all of the contributors to this volume engage with these questions.

The first line of inquiry is well-represented by Ruben Zimmermann's programmatic essay "Many-fold Yields by Polyvalent Interpretation: The Parable of the Mustard Seed in the Synoptic Tradition." This is an impressive example of the scholastic, European, philosophically oriented approach to hermeneutics that offers a comprehensive definition of the parable genre "as reader-oriented, metaphoric, narrative texts that are found in communicative contexts." His book, *Puzzling the Parables*, elaborates further:

> A *parable* is a short narratival (1) fictional (2) text that is related in the narrated world to known reality (3) but, by way of implicit or explicit transfer signals, makes it understood that the meaning of the narration must be differentiated from the literal words of the text (4). In its appeal dimension (5) it challenges the reader to carry out a metaphoric transfer of meaning that is steered by contextual information (6).[8]

While Zimmermann's definition covers an impressive array of *parabolai*, I question whether it can stretch to encompass the array of speech forms in the biblical parable tradition: "aphorisms and stories, proverbs and riddles, dialogues and discourses" (and, I would add, allegories) that are metaphorical or figurative.[9] Do novellas like the Good Samaritan or the Prodigal Son really belong to

---

[8] Ruben Zimmermann, *Puzzling the Parables: Methods and Interpretation* (Minneapolis, MN: Fortress Press, 2015), 137.
[9] John Dominic Crossan, "Parables," in *Harpers Bible Dictionary*, ed. Paul J. Achtemeier (San Francisco: HarperSanFrancisco, 1985), 746–9 (here 746).

the same genre as the Mustard Seed or the Lamp? While the first two are clearly quite elaborate fictional narratives, the latter are illustrations from everyday life. Zimmermann asserts that the parables receive their power "from the transfer of real experiences and concrete, real life contexts into the religious domain." The contrast between concrete human experience and the "religious domain" seems out of place with reference to a society where the secular was not clearly differentiated from the religious. Was the kingdom of God that provides the point of comparison in so many parables an expression about a "religious domain," or a theo-political construct conceived over against the Roman empire—and at the same time inversely modeled on it? Or was it a theopoetic expression of the mysterious working of the divine in the everyday process of germination? Or was it the us-versus-them construct of an emergent cult? Different sermons on a single parable delivered to different audiences based on what the people need in each context provide interpretations that span the range of functions identified by Zimmermann—encouragement, hope and protest—all using the same parable, a compelling example of polyvalence in action.

Zimmermann's chapter mentions, but does not give any sustained attention to, the version of the mustard seed parable in Gospel of Thomas 20. Unlike the synoptic versions, Thomas places a special emphasis on the "tilled" or "prepared" soil the seed falls upon. Here, the growth of the mustard seed is dependent on the quality of the soil it falls upon. The parable appears to be one of revelation, where the here-and-now points to a deepened awareness and expansion of the divine *basileia* to and within those who apprehend it properly—a snapshot of cult formation in process? One of the four steps in Zimmermann's approach is "Mapping the Socio-Historical Background" of the parables. In keeping with this collection's interest in the material realia of the first century, he asks the question of which species of mustard is envisioned in the parable. Zimmermann judiciously opts for black mustard (*brassica negra*), a wild-growing plant whose seed, if not "the smallest of all the seeds of the earth," has the smallest seeds of the other species of mustard native to the region, and grows the largest.

Dieter Roth's essay on "Harvest Imagery in Q Parables" focuses on a subset of tradition in the hypothetical sayings source. Interestingly, two of the parables he exegetes are attributed to John the Baptist (Q 3:9, 17). Although harvesting is a quintessentially commonplace activity, these parables are grounded in what Zimmermann calls "stock metaphors and symbols" drawn principally from the Jewish scriptures relating to divine judgment. The theme of judgment implies a divine judge, but Roth observes that it is "the agent active in the harvest/ judgment imagery that is…often overlooked," with the active agent in 3:9 being envisioned as God, and the "Coming One" of 3:17 as Jesus. Roth then turns to two Q parables of Jesus that use harvest imagery (Q 6:43–44; 10:2), the parables of the Tree Being Known by is Fruit, and of Workers for the Harvest. While the first parable involves a simple observation that extends to the ethical character of a person, the second draws significantly from stock images of the harvest in terms of eschatological judgment reshaped to focus on mission; the success of the harvest lies not in the character of the lord of the harvest (ὁ κύριος τοῦ θερισμοῦ) or in the quality of the crop, but in the availability of harvesters.

Oakman's "Written and Unwritten Obligations: Dependency Relations in Early Roman Galilee" seems to touch only tangentially on parables. However, as the editors observe, "it is complementary in that it concentrates on a particular aspect of socio-economic realities, namely dependency relations in Roman Galilee." Parables, Oakman observes, are among the pre-70 traditions in the Synoptic Gospels that inform his reconstruction. The parables he specifically cites as evidence for dependency relations in Galilee are the parable of the Tenants (Mark 12:1–9; *Gos. Thom.* 65); the parable of the Faithful and Wise Steward (Q 12:42); the parable of the Unforgiving Slave (Matt 18:23–24); the parable of the Rich Fool (Luke 12:16–20); the parable of the Weeds among the Wheat (Matt 13:24–30); the parable of the Laborers in the Vineyard (Matt 20:1–3). These and other evidence point to the "mammon ethic" critiqued by Jesus. Oakman casts new light on the story of the woman with the alabaster jar in Luke 7:36–50 by asking why Jesus tells a parable about two debtors (vv. 40–44) in response to a moral evaluation of the woman as "sinful." He points out that "the Aramaic words *chovah/chovayin* that *hamartia/hamartoloi*, as often noted, can denote the materially indebted," which opens up the possibility that the woman "has been liberated from a sex slavery imposed by her indebted father and now expresses her gratitude to her benefactor Jesus. Or perhaps, the money debt for the nard—loaned by the woman's master—has been annulled." A similar theme of the forgiveness of debts informs the parable of the steward in Luke 16:1–17, where the gratefulness of the debtors is garnered by the unwritten cooking of the written books/accounts. Oakman's interpretation of the Rich Fool (Luke 12:13–21) as depicting a landlord who is attentive to his own security, but in fact "is a thief of what could benefit others" coheres well with my own view of that parable.[10] His use of the parables in reconstructing the social and economic realities of Jesus's time demonstrates how intricately interwoven these stories were with the context in which he lived.

Ernest van Eck's "A Realistic Reading of the Parable of the Lost Coin in Q: Gaining or Losing Even More?" zooms in on a single parable that bears on the economic status of a single character, a woman searching for a lost coin (Luke 15:8–9). In contrast with readings that dwell on the theological or christological resonances of the story (that are certainly present in Luke), here, "the woman is just a (peasant) woman, not looking for a sinner or the lost, but a coin with the value of 1 drachma." This is not as easy as it seems, as the detail of the lighting of the lamp illustrates. Would the cost of the oil used in the search for the coin be worth the expenditure? Van Eck augments Schottroff's oft-cited assertion that the drachma (equivalent to a denarius) was enough to buy two days' worth of food (and two days' wages for a female laborer) using extensive papyrological

---

[10] See Mary Ann Beavis, "The Parable of the Foolish Landowner," in *Jesus and His Parables: Interpreting the Parables of Jesus for Today*, ed. V. George Shillington (Edinburgh: T. & T. Clark, 1997), 55–68.

evidence from early Roman Egypt.[11] This procedure, he asserts, can be used to "help to answer the question if the woman in the parable indeed functions as a symbol or metaphor for God, or simply should be seen as a peasant woman looking for a lost coin"—although, I must observe, realism does not obviate the metaphorical reading of the story.[12] Much of his evidence comes from an extensive realistic reading of the parable by Erin Vearncombe, which indicates that the story elements of the woman's property, the activity of seeking and finding, and the use of the lamp, are well within realistic parameters. Her work draws particular attention to the care with which oil was valued and measured, and the complexities of estimating these matters. Van Eck's contribution to Vearncombe's findings is to read the parable as a Q gender pairing corresponding to the Lost Sheep: "In the Lost Sheep the focus is the actions of a shepherd, and in the Lost Coin the focus is on the actions of a woman. In both parables this is unexpected—a despised shepherd and a female, not a male." In the case of the woman, van Eck concludes that the diligence of her search offsets the cost of the oil used so that less was spent than the value of the drachma. The realistic reading, as suggested by van Eck, has an ethical moral that, nonetheless, extends beyond realism: "Because of the risk she gained, and now everybody has enough. The kingdom is visible in the risky and unexpected action of an unexpected person. A poor woman, by taking a chance to end up with even less that she has, made sure that everybody has enough." This is an epimythium of which Luke, I suspect, would have heartily approved, but how does everybody have enough when the woman has simply retrieved the valuable coin, discounted by cost of the oil used in the search?

In something of the same vein, J. R. C. Cousland's "In Ferment: Is Jesus's Parable of the Leaven Hyperbolic or True to Life?" takes a realistic approach to the story of the woman baking bread in Matthew (13:33; cf. Luke 13:21; *Gos. Thom.* 96). He begins with the question of whether Jesus meant "his audience to understand his parables as realistic accounts of the everyday world, as exaggerated stories that were not meant to be mimetic, or as somewhere in between?" He marshals extensive evidence about breadmaking in antiquity, beginning with Pseudo-Virgil's *Moretum*, and points out that the parable highlights only one aspect of the multi-stage process—grinding, sifting, kneading, forming loaves, baking—the leavening, pointing out that the leavening agent was more akin to a sourdough starter than to modern-day yeast. Somewhat contrary to van Eck's assertion that leaven was "a symbol of moral evil, corruption, and uncleanness,"[13]

---

[11] Luise Schottroff, *The Parables of Jesus*, trans. Linda Maloney (Minneapolis, MN: Fortress Press, 2006), 154.

[12] In fact, Erin Vearncombe, whose work van Eck cites extensively, ultimately concludes that the woman stands for God: "Searching for a Lost Coin: Papyrological Backgrounds for Q 15,8–10," in *Metaphor, Narrative, and Parables in Q*, ed. Dieter Roth, Ruben Zimmermann, and Michael Labahn, WUNT 315 (Tübingen: Mohr Siebeck, 2014) 307–37 (here 322–3).

[13] Following Bernard Brandon Scott, "The Reappearance of Parables," in *Listening to the Parables of Jesus*, ed. E. F. Beutner (Santa Rosa, CA: Polebridge Press, 2007), 95–119. In my opinion, Scott's understanding of the "uncleanness" of leaven is a misunderstanding of the Jewish concept, in that he confuses ritual and moral uncleanness. Far from being blasphemous, the representation

Cousland observes that by the first century, leavened bread came to be more highly prized than unleavened. As Craig Blomberg reminds us, "immediate context must take priority over background...at least in Leviticus 7:13–14 and 23:17, leaven was positive; it did not always have negative connotations."[14] In this parable, the leaven symbolism is unequivocally positive: it symbolizes the reign of God. The fact that the woman in this vignette of Jewish village life was preparing leavened bread suggests that it was a commonplace and uncontroversial activity. In adjudicating the thorny question of how realistic or extravagant the detail of "three measures" of flour mentioned in the parable is, Cousland draws attention to the interesting parallel in Gen 18:6, where Sarah prepares bread from three measures of flour for the angelic visitors, which indicates that there was nothing out of the ordinary about the amount (or, I might add, that the author didn't know much about breadmaking). Cousland, like van Eck, downplays the role of the woman in the parable. To be sure, "the divine efficacy of the leaven" is highlighted in the parable. However, as his essay amply demonstrates, the "human activity" involved in the process of bread-making—or even just of leavening—as time-consuming, skillful and strenuous. Holly Hearon and Antoinette Wire's remarks on the parable are worth quoting here: "The parable is generally identified as 'the parable of the leaven.' This title obscures the presence of the woman in the parable. She remains hidden for many interpreters who focus entirely on the leaven.... But Matt 13:33 reads: 'The Kingdom of heaven is like yeast that *a woman took and mixed* in with three measures of flour until all of it was leavened.' Without the woman there is no parable."[15] Without God, there is no *basileia*.

T. E. Goud's "Telling Stories in a Violent World" shifts the perspective from the domestic and agricultural spheres to the larger socio-political context of Galilee in the first century, where violence was frequent and brutal. The harsh realities of political instability, "murder, armed revolt, beating, crucifixion, beheading, banditry, and mass protest (often turning to violence)" and the everyday occurrences of corporal punishment, slavery, torture and executions formed part of conceptual world of the parables. Goud identifies no fewer than 22 synoptic parables featuring violent language and images; I would suggest that parable of the assassin from the Gospel of Thomas is a prime example of a violent parable

---

of the reign of God by leaven is quite consistent with the notion of the holy as ritually defiling. See, e.g., Timothy Lim, "The Defilement of the Hands as a Principle Determining the Holiness of Scriptures," *JTS* 61, no. 2 (2010): 501–15.

[14] Craig L. Blomberg, *Interpreting the Parables*, 2nd ed. (Downers Grove, IL: InterVarsity Press, 2012), 394–5. The biblical symbolism of leaven is not that it is inherently evil, but that it takes time to rise (Exod 23:39) and that it spreads, like slander (cf. Mark 8:15; 1 Cor 5:8). Although unleavened bread is famously part of the Passover festival, and the shewbread was unleavened, an offering of leavened bread was part of the Peace Offering and at Pentecost (Lev 7:11–14; 23:17; Amos 4:5 mentions a thank-offering of leavened bread).

[15] See, e.g., Holly Hearon and Antoinette Clark Wire, "Women's Work in the Realm of God (Mt. 13.33; Luke 13.20, 21; *Gos. Thom.* 96; Mt 6:28–30; Luke 12.27–28; *Gos. Thom.* 36)," in *The Lost Coin: Parables of Women, Work and Wisdom*, ed. Mary Ann Beavis (London: Sheffield Academic Press, 2002), 136–57 (here 137–8).

with some claim on authenticity.[16] As the Jesus Seminar observed: "The sheer violence and scandal of the image of the assassin suggests that it might well have originated with Jesus. It is unlikely that the early Christian community would have invented and have attributed such a story since its imagery is so contrary to the irenic and honorific images, such as the good shepherd, they customarily used for him."[17] In fact, the assassin, and many of the parables Goud discusses, certainly passes the criterion of embarrassment—sayings that would have "embarrassed or created difficulty for the early church,"[18] although they clearly did not scandalize the evangelists to the point of exclusion. Goud's conclusion is that the violence in Jesus's parables "is entirely at home in the context of first-century Palestine. Even the seemingly extreme instances of burning cities and slaughtering enemies, or handing someone over to torturers are easily paralleled in the world of Jesus." Moreover, Goud observes, Jesus (and his interpreters) did not shy away from portraying violence. Although I agree with Goud that this prominent aspect of Jesus's teaching—and of the Gospels—must not be suppressed, my question is, to what end beyond simple historical accuracy, which, although important, seems to fall short of the challenge it poses. Some examples of interpreting these parables "square on" would have been welcome. Do such parables baptize and perpetuate violence, accept it as a simple fact of life, or do they conceal an inherent critique of violence and its perpetrators?

An aspect of the violence inherent in the parable tradition is slavery, the theme of the next essay by John P. Harrison ("οἰκοδεσπότης, κύριος, and βασιλεύς: Identifying Those with Slaves in Matthean Parables"). I have published several articles in recent years that have tried to reconstruct select "slave parables" from the perspective of the enslaved.[19] Harrison's chapter explores the six Matthean parables in which characters are clearly slaveholders: the Wheat and Weeds (13:24–30); the Unmerciful Slave (18:23–34); the Wicked Tenants (21:33–39); the Wedding Banquet (22:1–14); the Faithful/Wicked Slave (24:45–51), and the Talents (25:14–30). The fact that it takes considerable ingenuity to come to a rough approximation of how the enslaved might have reacted to these parables suggests they were written more from the perspective of slaveholders than of slaves. Harrison's paper sets out to "briefly highlight some of the more significant literature and archaeological *realia* that give an indication as to the type of people who owned slaves in Roman Palestine and then…suggest what this

---

[16] See Funk et al., *The Five Gospels*, 524: "The Father's imperial rule is like a person who wanted to kill someone powerful. While still at home he drew his sword and thrust it into the wall to find out whether his hand would go in. Then he killed the powerful one" (*Gos. Thom.* 98).

[17] Ibid., 524.

[18] John P. Meier, *A Marginal Jew: Rethinking the Historical Jesus*, vol. 1 (New York: Doubleday, 1991), 174–5, 317.

[19] Mary Ann Beavis, "Fables, Parables and Slaves: Epictetus, Aesop and the Gospels in Conversation with North American Slave Narratives," in *Overcoming Dichotomies: Parables, Fables, and Similes in the Graeco-Roman World*, ed. Albertina Oegema, Jonathan Pater, and Martijn Stoutjesdijk, WUNT (Tübingen: Mohr, 2022); idem, "The Parable of the Talents (Matthew 25:14–30): Imagining A Slave's Perspective," *Journal of the Gospels and Acts Research* 2 (October 2018): 7–21; idem, "The Parable of the Slave, Son and Vineyard: A Freedman's Narrative," *CBQ* 80, no 3 (2018): 655–69.

evidence might indicate about how Matthew's audience (if not the audience of the historical Jesus) would have heard these parables and envisioned the slaveowners socially, ethnically and politically." That is, rather than simply observing that the parables depict slaveholders, he asks what kinds of people in Roman Palestine owned slaves, and his review of the evidence suggests that they were mostly from the non-Jewish ruling class and rich landowners with large, commercial estates. Moreover, Matthew's slave parables do not question the status quo of slavery, or the treatment of the enslaved by their owners—even when they are manifestly harsh and even violent. Harrison suggests that Matthew's audience would likely have recognized the slaveholder characters as "the wealthy and powerful in the Roman Empire broadly and in Palestine specifically." I would add that Matthew's audience was expected to align themselves with the slaveholders in the parables rather than the slaves, no matter how arbitrarily or cruelly the slaves are treated by their masters. The audience is expected to agree that the unmerciful slave deserves to be tortured (Matt 18:34); that the landowner is justified in sending his slaves to be abused by the "wicked tenants" (21:34–36); that the maltreatment of the slaves in the parable of the wedding banquet is an affront to the king, not to the people injured and killed (22:6); that the punishment afforded to the "wicked slave" is disproportional to his misbehavior (24:51); that no one questions the master's judgment in handing over a huge sum to a slave whose "ability" is clearly inferior to that of his colleagues (25:15),[20] or in punishing him harshly for preserving the sum (25:30). This suggests that the hearers of the Matthean parables were expected to agree with the self-evaluation of slaveholders; as Jennifer Glancy remarks, "In antiquity, Christian slaveholders thought of themselves as morally upright individuals. Or at least, when a Christian slaveholder held himself up to moral scrutiny and found himself wanting, slaveholding did not factor into that judgment."[21] Moreover, with respect to the violence, including summary execution, inflicted on the enslaved by slaveholders in these stories, there is no critique of the perpetrators if they are the recognized owners of the victims. Matthew has no compunction about aligning the "heavenly father" with the master who hands his errant slave over to the torturers (18:35). Although the earliest audiences of these parables likely comprised free, freed and slave, slaveholder and enslaved, it is difficult to imagine that the latter would have found these narratives appealing.

Situated after Harrison's piece, Ellen Aasland Reinertsen's essay—"Whose Voices Matter? A Persistent Widow in a Polyphonic Parable (Luke 18:1–8)"—raises an interesting question—for Matthew, at any rate, it is the voices of the slaveholders that are expected to "matter" to the audience. The Lukan parable

---

[20] "A talent was one of the largest values of money in the Hellenistic world. A silver coinage, it weighted between fifty-seven and seventy-four pounds. One talent was equal to six thousand denarii. It was, then, a large sum of money"; Bernard Brandon Scott, *Hear Then the Parable: A Commentary on the Parables of Jesus* (Minneapolis, MN: Fortress Press, 1989), 224.
[21] Jennifer Glancy, "Christian Slavery in Late Antiquity," in *Human Bondage in the Cultural Contact Zone: Transdisciplinary Perspectives on Slavery and its Discourses*, ed. Raphael Hörmann and Gisa Mackenthun (Münster: Waxmann, 2010), 63–70 (here 64).

does, indeed, contain several voices: the evangelist, Jesus, the widow, the judge, and a final voice that Aasland Reinertsen calls "the Lord" (vv. 6–7)—probably to be identified with Jesus, who offers two interpretations of the parable. The words of the evangelist and of Jesus/the Lord frame the words uttered by the two characters in the parable proper; but the only one who speaks aloud (as opposed to in an inner dialogue) is the widow. Thus, the parable highlights the voice of a woman, a widow who by her own testimony has been wronged by an opponent and by the legal system (v. 3).

Not surprisingly, traditional interpretations of the parable have preferred the voice of the Lord/Jesus, a tendency that endures in recent, non-feminist commentaries; of the two characters in the story, the judge has received more attention (as he does in the epimythium; cf. 18:6: "listen to what the unjust judge says"). As might be expected, feminist interpreters (Schottroff, Matthews, Shelley, Scheele, Levine, Merz) place more emphasis on the widow. Both the non-feminist commentators and even the feminist scholars, Aasland Reinertsen astutely observes, tend to accept (and amplify) the judge's evaluation of the woman as nagging, browbeating, feisty, pestering and potentially violent (v. 5). In contrast, the text simply describes the woman as persistent in asking the judge for justice (or vengeance) against her opponent (v. 3). Commentators, both feminist and non-feminist, tend to describe the widow not only as aggressive but also, rather contradictorily, in terms of biblical stereotypes of the weakness, marginalization, and poverty of widows. The question arises whether even feminist interpreters are "so used to listening to a powerful man, no matter what and how he speaks, that his voice persuades them, even when they don't want it to? In addition, do recipients fail to hear the widow's voice because they see her as in such stereotypical ways as described above?"

The only period in which Aasland Reinertsen finds that interpreters characteristically "listened" to the widow, as opposed to Jesus/the Lord or the judge, is antiquity, leading her to surmise that it was "early recipients, who could have focused on the female character and seen her in more nuanced ways." That is, perhaps ancient interpreters were more likely to see the widow as a plaintiff in a legal case, rather than as a conventional biblical character. However, I must point out that in the ancient examples she adduces (Augustine, Chrysostom, Origen, Cyril of Alexandria, Martyrius, Ephrem the Syrian), the widow is interpreted as an example of the efficacy of persistent prayer, i.e., her significance is determined by the Lucan frame. In fact, the only character in the parable who speaks aloud, the widow, is hedged about by voices (the evangelist, Jesus/the Lord, the judge) that qualify the meaning of her words: "Grant me justice against my opponent."

Amy-Jill Levine is distinctive among interpreters—especially feminist ones—in expressly not allowing stereotypes about widows as being uniformly moral persons to color her interpretation: "Levine thinks listeners could construct her as active, subversive, rich and powerful, dangerous, a trickster, wise and demanding, in addition to being in need of help, marginalised or disfranchised."[22] Aasland

---

[22] Amy-Jill Levine and Ben Witherington III, *The Gospel of Luke*, NCBC (Cambridge: Cambridge University Press, 2018), 484. I would add that the New Testament stereotypes about widows as

Reinertsen points out that ancient listeners would have known that widows could be rich (or even be rich widows themselves), that widows could ask judges for help, and that ethnicity could play a role in women's interactions with the law, e.g., the Jewish Babatha needed to be accompanied by a male guardian, but the Roman citizen Julia Crispina could act on her own behalf and even serve as a guardian herself.[23] I would add that assuming that the widow of the parable was meant to be Jewish, the lack of any hint of a guardian would mark her as either notably bold or as friendless or both. Even the Roman matron Maesia, who represented herself in a criminal trial and famously won, was notable for her (rather immodest) self-representation.[24] Juvenal satirizes the stereotypical woman who is aggressively engaged in the legal system: "There's rarely a lawsuit brought a woman didn't begin. Manilia will accuse, unless she's maybe the defendant. They'll even compose and construct the brief themselves, ready to dictate Celsus' headings and opening speech."[25] Finally, pseudo-Paul's description of the ideal, enrolled widow as praying "night and day" (1 Tim 5:5) is intriguingly similar to the moral of the parable that the elect, like the widow, should pray "day and night" (Luke 18:7), but her assertive behavior toward the judge is drastically different than the circumspect and virtuous conduct required of widows by the Pastor.

The kinds of hermeneutical questions arising from the widow parable—does the widow's plight stand on its own as an instance of social injustice, or does it point beyond itself to theological truths?—are raised by Stephen I. Wright in "Mirroring and Echoing: Realism and Figuration in Jesus's Parables." Wright uses the metaphors of "mirroring" and "echoing" to approach this question: "In their reflection of the realities of life in the ancient Near East, and Palestine in particular, they act as a mirror, inviting their hearers to see themselves, their society, their environment, their relationships. But they always do more than this. They invite hearers to see those realities *in a certain way*. They focus vision, they select episodes (whether typical or atypical), they enlist memories, they evoke traditions." Along with the standard tools of narrative criticism, Wright proposes the notion of the parables as "synecdochic narratives" in order to understand their semantic function. The literary trope of synecdoche, in which the part stands for the whole, is particularly well-suited to encompassing both the parables' mirroring and echoing functions in that to "see them as synecdoches is to recognize that through their account of a particular event, they evoke the 'story' of a whole society."

Wright uses the parable of the Sower (Mark 4:3–9) to illustrate how the use of synecdoche illumines the narrative. He offers three interpretations, by Hedrick, Dronsch and van Eck, that illustrate three different understandings of the use of

---

idle, gossipy, lustful and greedy (1 Tim 5:3–16) hardly portray them as virtuous.

[23] For evidence concerning Jewish women's legal status in antiquity, see Tal Ilan, *Jewish Women in Greco–Roman Palestine* (Peabody, MA: Hendrickson, 1996), 158–75.

[24] Anthony J. Marshall, "Roman Ladies on Trial: The Case of Maesia of Sentinum," *Phoenix* 44, no. 1 (1990): 46–59.

[25] Juvenal, *Satire* VI, 242–45. Translated by A. S. Kline: (https://www.poetryintranslation.com/PITBR/Latin/JuvenalSatires6.php#anchor_Toc282858861).

metaphor in the parable: (1) a thoroughgoingly realist interpretation, in which metaphor plays no part (Hedrick); (2) a reading that, while acknowledging the realism of the parable, offers a metaphorical interpretation along the lines of Mark 4:14–20 (Dronsch); and (3) an interpretation that sees the parable as mirroring Roman imperial oppression (van Eck). Wright then proceeds to show how the device of synecdoche enables a reading that can, to some extent, accommodate all three:

> In this picture of a single farmer, Jesus does not describe the whole reality of his society, but he implies it.... This is not bare description, as the urgent injunction to 'hear,' bracketing the story, emphasizes. Nor can its "realism" be seen as proof against any kind of wider resonance, as Hedrick implies. Rather, it is precisely in its realism that the wider resonances are triggered. The phenomena of first-century Palestinian farming, as briefly outlined by Dronsch and placed in wider political context by van Eck, are brought before the hearers' eyes, not through extended description but through the compact narrative of an individual farmer's activity.

The story is synecdochic in that the Sower represents the larger socio-political-economic context of farmers and farming, as opposed to the realm of divine activity. However, Wright does admit that "the default assumption of Jewish hearers would be that it was rooted in faith in the creativity, sovereignty and grace of God."

I would surmise that perhaps the absence of the term "seed" in the parable (and its interpretation) in both Mark and Matthew suggests from the beginning that the story was meant to be read metaphorically:[26] the Sower sows the word regarding the *basileia*, as the most ancient interpretation of the parable asserts (Mark 4:14–20; cf. Mark 2:2; 4:33; Luke 5:1, 15); the quality of that which is sown is not at issue: "The power of the earth makes the difference."[27] As many interpreters have pointed out, the soils, rather than the (unmentioned) seeds are highlighted in the parable: "In the Synoptics, the three unfruitful soils are pitted against the unfruitful one, and the sower is the unifying figure or the third main 'character.'"[28] Was the intended audience of the parable not the group of peasant farmers envisioned by academics, or missionaries (some from an agrarian background) who experienced different levels of receptivity to their preaching? This is a *Sitz im Leben* that makes sense of the parable in the context of a Jewish

---

[26] Admittedly, the words *speirōn* and *speirai* imply the use of seed (*sporon*), but Luke adds references to seed (8:5, 11) in order to address its absence in the Marcan parable.

[27] Mary Ann Tolbert, *Sowing the Gospel: Mark's World in Literary-Historical Perspective* (Minneapolis, MN: Fortress Press, 1989), 162.

[28] Blomberg, *Interpreting the Parables*, 289. See also Mark L. Bailey, "The Kingdom in the Parables of Matthew 13. Part 2: The Parable of the Sower and the Soils," *Bibliotheca Sacra* 155 (1998): 172–88; Donald Peters, "Vulnerable Promise from the Land: Mark 4:3b–8: The Parable of the Sower/Soils," in Shillington, ed., *Jesus and His Parables*, 69–84 (here 81, 83); Brad H. Young, *The Parables: Jewish Tradition and Christian Interpretation* (Peabody, MA: Hendrickson, 1998), 251.

sect on its way to becoming a new religious movement. This does not rule out the "authenticity" of the parable—Jesus was, after all, a disciple-gathering preacher who (presumably) trained his disciples to participate in his mission.

The final two chapters, "Matthew 20:1–15: The Parable of the Workers in the Vineyard or of a Manager-Disciple?,'" by Deborah R. Storie, and "Twenty Years of Experiencing the Parables in Africa," by Glenna S. Jackson, are, I will admit, my favorites in this collection. Both use their extensive experiences in rural Afghanistan (Storie) and Africa (Jackson) as windows into the meanings of the parables. This is not an altogether new approach. Kenneth Bailey's readings of the Lucan parables through the lens of Middle Eastern peasant cultures,[29] Del Tarr's *Double Image: Biblical Insights from African Parables*,[30] and William R. Herzog's approach to the parables as pedagogy of the oppressed, all, in different ways, spring to mind.[31]

Storie recounts how her experience with community development in rural Afghanistan brought her to the understanding of Jesus's parables as something more akin to Freirean codes than to illustrative stories—"stories, pictures, songs, or other communicative devices that present slices of everyday life in stylized fictitious form that groups can look at, describe and analyze, and to which they may choose to respond." Such codes can prompt communities to identify similar situations in their own settings, clarify values, identify problems, and imagine and work towards better futures. With respect to Matt 20:1–15 in particular, Storie recalls that the story resembled the setting in which she lived, where hiring the less capable laborers "delivered them from the indignity of begging and saved their families from hunger—if only for a day." Moreover, the villagers she worked with retained memories of better times that they hoped would be restored in the future, God-willing. Thus, the landowner's assertion that he had the right to pay the laborers as he saw fit (20:15), "awakens ancient memories of dispossession, rekindles the desperate rage of peasant-farmers driven off ancestral lands, and exacerbates the humiliation of begging for work on fields that were once their own." Storie draws particular attention to the role of the manager in the parable (20:8), who actually pays the workers, raising the question of whether the manager (who, I would add, might have more sympathy with the day-laborers than the landowner) operates by a different ethic than his employer (cf. Luke 6:1–13).

Storie continues by contrasting her approach with hegemonic interpretations that insist on an allegorical reading of the parable where the landowner *must* represent God, whose decisions and actions *must* not be questioned (e.g., Gerhardsson, Hultgren, Snodgrass, Takagi, Levine, van Eck, Kloppenborg),

---

[29] See Kenneth Bailey, *Poet and Peasant and Through Peasant Eyes: A Literary-Cultural Approach to the Parables in Luke* (Grand Rapids, MI: Eerdmans, 1983).
[30] Del Tarr, *Double Image: Biblical Insights from African Parables* (Mahwah, NJ: Paulist Press, 1994).
[31] William R. Herzog II, *Parables as Subversive Speech: Jesus as Pedagogue of the Oppressed* (Louisville, KY: Westminster/John Knox Press, 1994).

thus foreclosing the possibility that the parables critique rather than endorse the hierarchical social relations they portray. The feminist approach advocated by Luise Schottroff undermines such absolutist views by recognizing that academic readers who are "habituated to power instinctively empathize with masters rather than slaves and tend to identify the interests of the Gospel with the interests of landowners and slaveholders rather than with those of landless labourers, tenant farmers and slaves." Storie asserts that such hegemonic interpretations are difficult to square with the prophetic tradition of the Hebrew Bible. In the famous story of Naboth's vineyard (2 Kgs 21), God is on the side of the one victimized by a powerful king; Isaiah's vineyard parable rails against a system that dispossesses the many to enrich the view (Isa 5:1–8).

Storie's rich survey of scholarship on the Matthean parable is impossible to summarize here: suffice it to say that the many scholars from different social and ethnic contexts (e.g., dalit, rural Pakistani, Latin American) she cites as representing "an alternative tradition" conclude to varying degrees and in different ways that the parable is realistic rather than extravagant. She ends by interrogating the significance of the payment of the laborers with a denarius, a form of currency whose symbolic freight "is integral to the parable's critique of large-scale landownership, profit-oriented viticulture, and the systems, structures and ideologies that enabled them."

As much as I appreciate Storie's approach, I am left wondering what the actual Afghan farmers she worked with would have made of the Matthean parable. Would their distance from the theological frame of the Gospel prompt them to see themselves in the story and deplore the economic system that deprived them of their ancestral lands and reduced them to day-laborers dependent on the whims of a hired steward? My curiosity was somewhat satisfied by Glenna Jackson's contribution, which approaches parables through the lens of her twenty years of experience teaching in Zimbabwe and elsewhere in Africa, where subsistence living approximating conditions in ancient Galilee are much more commonplace than they are in the experience of Western academics: "We have no way of relating to that kind of poverty, for example—i.e., the absence of technology, electricity, clean water, the ability to get warm or to get cool, a week's worth of groceries, a monthly wage, brilliance without formal educations." I would add that they are also more attuned to the effects of imperialism, colonization, and cultural dispossession than white, middle-class interpreters. Jackson speaks of her experience of decolonizing the classroom by asking for the thoughts and opinions of her students instead of teaching them only the standard, academic techniques of parable interpretation, which rendered "incredible insights and thoughts about the original intended meaning of the parables based on their own village experience."

Jackson offers three examples via anecdotes of what I would venture to describe as what decolonized parable interpretation looks like, beginning with the famous *crux interpretum* of Matt 5:13–16: how, academics ask, can salt (NaCl) lose its saltiness? The people in her student's village instantly knew that salt comes from a tree, not from a box bought in the supermarket, and that it can indeed lose its flavor. A little research revealed to Jackson that there is a similar tree, the Salt Cedar, that would have been free in ancient Galilee, as opposed to the expensive imported mineral. In a second vignette, Jackson recalls a Palm Sunday (and pre-election) sermon by one of her students that made a parable of the triumphal entry lection: "if Jesus were a Mozambican who traveled over the Eastern Highland Mountains into Zimbabwe, he would see his people and know their needs—they needed to be freed of political and economic oppression. The people would be so excited that they would greet him with palm branches, dancing and singing." In this instance, the pastor was arrested shortly afterwards, a real-life illustration that parabolic preaching can have political implications. For Jackson, parables are not just ancient narratives that require expert exegesis or even inspired preaching, but the polysemic and polyvalent fruits of everyday experiences. She concludes her chapter with interpretations of well-known parables: the Doorkeeper (Mark 13:33–37); the Samaritan (Luke 10:25–37); and the Fig Tree (Luke 13:6–9); and the Empty Jar (*Gos. Thom.* 97), offered by African interpreters that bring these stories to life in unexpected ways.

3. In Conclusion

The essays in this collection well illustrate the three lines of inquiry discussed above; all of them engage with the conceptual, metaphorical and material contexts of the parables. In terms of reception, the final two chapters, as well as Aasland Reinertsen's piece on the Persistent Widow, are notable, although it can be said that every chapter is a distinctive example of the reception of certain parables. However, there is much to do in this area—as noted at the beginning of this response, motifs from the parables are woven into the warp and weft of Western (and, increasingly, global) culture in extensive and complex ways that are seldom recognized even by biblical scholars.

In view of my stated admiration of the last two chapters, the question arises: Of what relevance are complex literary theories to the kinds of hearers they describe (Afghan farmers, African villagers)—or to their ancient audiences? The question implies the answer; those of us living in Western societies far removed from the "everyday experiences" of Galilean peasants, or even of first-century city-dwellers, need the kinds of methods and approaches illustrated in this volume. This includes the respectful and sensitive use of evidence from contemporary cultures that approximate the conditions of ancient Galilee—with the proviso that Afghan farmers and African villagers are very much part of the modern world, and that cultural appreciation (allyship) needs to guard against appropriation for the sake of new scholarly fodder (issues of which Storie and Jackson are well aware). My hope is that new studies of the parables from a variety of cultures and social locations will be forthcoming in future that highlight the insights of global scholarship.

Bibliography

Bailey, K. *Poet and Peasant and Through Peasant Eyes: A Literary-Cultural Approach to the Parables in Luke*. Grand Rapids, MI: Eerdmans, 1983.

Bailey, M. L. "The Kingdom in the Parables of Matthew 13. Part 2: The Parable of the Sower and the Soils." *Bibliotheca Sacra* 155 (1998): 172–88.

Beavis, M. A. "Fables, Parables and Slaves: Epictetus, Aesop and the Gospels in Conversation with North American Slave Narratives." In *Overcoming Dichotomies: Parables, Fables, and Similes in the Graeco-Roman World*, edited by Albertina Oegema, Jonathan Pater, and Martijn Stoutjesdijk. WUNT. Tübingen: Mohr, 2022.

Beavis, M. A. "Feminist (and Other) Reflections on the Woman with Seven Husbands (Mark 12:20–23)." In *Hermeneutik der Gleichnisse Jesus: Methodische Neuansätze zum Verstehen urchristlicher Parabeltexte*, edited by Ruben Zimmermann, 603–17. WUNT 213. Tübingen: Mohr Siebeck, 2008.

Beavis, M. A. "The Parable of the Foolish Landowner." In *Jesus and His Parables: Interpreting the Parables of Jesus Today*, edited by V. George Shillington, 55–68. Edinburgh: T. & T. Clark, 1997.

Beavis, M. A. "The Parable of the Slave, Son and Vineyard: A Freedman's Narrative." *CBQ* 80, no. 3 (2018): 655–69.

Beavis, M. A. "The Parable of the Talents (Matthew 25:14–30): Imagining A Slave's Perspective." *Journal of the Gospels and Acts Research* 2 (2018): 7–21.

Blomberg, C. L. *Interpreting the Parables*. 2nd ed. Downers Grove, IL: InterVarsity Press, 2012.

Crossan, J. D. "Parables." In *Harpers Bible Dictionary*, edited by Paul J. Achtemeier, 747–9. San Francisco: HarperSanFrancisco, 1985.

Funk, R. W. et al. *The Five Gospels: The Search for the Authentic Words of Jesus*. New York: Scribner, 1993.

Glancy, J. A. "Christian Slavery in Late Antiquity." In *Human Bondage in the Cultural Contact Zone: Transdisciplinary Perspectives on Slavery and its Discourses*, edited by Raphael Hörmann and Gisa Mackenthun, 63–70. Münster: Waxmann, 2010.

Gundry, R. H. *Matthew: A Commentary on his Handbook for a Mixed Church under Persecution*. 2nd ed. Grand Rapids, MI: Eerdmans.

Herzog, W. R. II. *Parables as Subversive Speech: Jesus as Pedagogue of the Oppressed*. Louisville, KY: Westminster John Knox Press, 1994.

Hearon, H., and A. C. Wire. "Women's Work in the Realm of God (Mt. 13.33; Lk. 13.20, 21; Gos. Thom. 96; Mt 6:28–30; Lk. 12.27–28; Gos. Thom. 36)." In *The Lost Coin: Parables of Women, Work and Wisdom*, edited by Mary Ann Beavis, 136–57. London: Sheffield Academic Press, 2002.

Ilan, T. *Jewish Women in Greco-Roman Palestine*. Peabody, MA: Hendrickson, 1996.

Levine, A.-J., and B. Witherington III. *The Gospel of Luke*. NCBC. Cambridge: Cambridge University Press, 2018.

Lim, T. "The Defilement of the Hands as a Principle Determining the Holiness of Scriptures." *JTS* 61, no. 2 (2010): 501–15.

Marshall, A. J. "Roman Ladies on Trial: The Case of Maesia of Sentinum." *Phoenix* 44, no. 1 (1990): 46–59.

Meier, J. P. *A Marginal Jew: Rethinking the Historical Jesus, Volume 1*. New York: Doubleday, 1991.

Peters, D. "Vulnerable Promise from the Land: Mark 4:3b–8: The Parable of the Sower/Soils." In *Jesus and His Parables: Interpreting the Parables of Jesus for Today*, edited by V. George Shillington, 69–84. London: T&T Clark, 1997.

Phillips, P. "Casting Out the Treasure: A New Reading of Matthew 13.52." *JSNT* 31 (2008): 3–24.

Roth, D. *The Parables in Q*. London: Bloomsbury, 2018.

Schottroff, L. *The Parables of Jesus*. Translated by Linda Maloney. Minneapolis, MN: Fortress Press, 2006.

Scott, B. B. "The Reappearance of Parables." In *Listening to the Parables of Jesus*, edited by E. F. Beutner, 95–119. Santa Rosa, CA: Polebridge Press, 2007.

Scott, B. B. *Hear Then the Parable: A Commentary on the Parables of Jesus*. Minneapolis, MN: Fortress Press, 1989.

Talbert, C. H. *Matthew*. Paideia Commentaries on the New Testament. Grand Rapids, MI: Baker Academic, 2010.

Tarr, D. *Double Image: Biblical Insights from African Parables*. Mahwah, NJ: Paulist Press, 1994.

Tolbert, M. A. *Perspectives on the Parables: An Approach to Multiple Interpretations*. Philadelphia, PA: Fortress Press, 1979.

Tolbert, M. A. *Sowing the Gospel: Mark's World in Literary-Historical Perspective*. Minneapolis, MN: Fortress Press, 1989.

Vearncombe, E. "Searching for a Lost Coin: Papyrological Backgrounds for Q 15,8–10." In *Metaphor, Narrative, and Parables in Q*, edited by Dieter Roth, Ruben Zimmermann, and Michael Labahn, 307–37. WUNT 315. Tübingen: Mohr Siebeck, 2014.

Young, B. H. *The Parables: Jewish Tradition and Christian Interpretation*. Peabody, MA: Hendrickson, 1998.

Zimmermann, R. *Puzzling the Parables: Methods and Interpretation*. Minneapolis, MN: Fortress Press, 2015.

CONTRIBUTORS

Mary Ann Beavis is Professor Emerita at St Thomas More College, University of Saskatchewan. She is the author of a number of books and articles on early Christianity and feminist hermeneutics including a commentary on the Gospel of Mark in the Paideia commentary series (2011) and *Christian Goddess Spirituality: Enchanting Christianity* (2016).

J. Robert C. Cousland is Professor of Early Christianity and Greek Religion & Mythology at the University of British Columbia and former co-chair of the Synoptic Gospels section of the international meeting of SBL. He is the author/editor of a number of books including *The Crowds in Matthew* (2002) and *Holy Terror: Jesus in the Infancy Gospel of Thomas* (2018).

Thomas E. Goud is Associate Professor of Classical and Early Christian Studies at the University of New Brunswick in Saint John and co-chair of the Synoptic Gospels section of the international meeting of SBL.

John Harrison is Professor of New Testament and Ministry at Oklahoma Christian University and co-chair of the Synoptic Gospels section of the international meeting of SBL. He is the co-editor with Jim Dvorak of *New Testament Ecclesiologies: The Challenge of Developing Ecclesiologies* (2016).

Glenna S. Jackson is Professor Emerata of Religion and Philosophy at Otterbein University and former co-chair of the Synoptic Gospels section of the international meeting of SBL. She is the author of *Have Mercy on Me: The Story of the Canaanite Woman in Matthew 15:21–28* (2002).

Douglas E. Oakman is Professor of New Testament and Dean of Humanities at Pacific Lutheran University. He is the author of many works including *Jesus and the Peasants* (2008), *The Political Aims of Jesus* (2012) and is co-author of *Palestine in the Time of Jesus* (2008).

Ellen Aasland Reinertsen is a Ph.D. Research Fellow at the Faculty of Theology, University of Oslo. Her doctoral dissertation is entitled "Lost in reception? Paradox and Potential in Text and Reception of Parables with Intersecting Female Characters."

Dieter T. Roth is Associate Professor of New Testament at Boston College. He is the co-editor of *Metaphor, Narrative, and Parables in Q. (2014)*, and author of *The Parables in Q* (2018).

Deborah R. Storie lectures in Biblical Studies at Stirling Theological College and is Honorary Research Associate at Whitley College, University of Divinity, and a Pastor with the Baptist Union of Victoria. She previously worked in community development and disaster mitigation and response in conflict affected regions and served on the boards of development agencies in Australia and internationally.

Ernest van Eck is Professor and Head of the Department of New Testament Studies and Related Literature at the University of Pretoria in South Africa and author of *The Parables of Jesus the Galilean: Stories of a Social Prophet* (2016).

Stephen I. Wright is Vice-Principal and Academic Director at Spurgeon's College. He is the author of *The Voice of Jesus: Studies in the Interpretation of Six Gospel Parables* (2000/2007) and *Jesus the Storyteller* (2014).

Ruben Zimmermann is Professor of New Testament and Ethics at Johannes Gutenberg Universität in Mainz and author/editor of many volumes on the parables, including *Hermeneutik der Gleichnisse Jesu* (2008), *Metaphor, Narrative, and Parables in Q.* (2014), *Kompendium der Gleichnisse Jesu* (2007/2015), and *Puzzling the Parables* (2015).

INDEX OF PARABLES

The following list strives to use traditional or widely recognized titles for the parables of Jesus as found in one or more of the Synoptic Gospels. In addition, two parables of John the Baptist and two parables unique to the Gospel of Thomas which are treated at some length are appended to the list. Throughout this volume the contributors have at times used variants of these titles or even "creative" titles along the lines of those in the *Kompendium der Gleichnisse Jesu*.

Parables of Jesus in the Synoptic Gospels
Barren Fig Tree (Luke 13:6–9) 114, 115, 122–23, 125, 129 n. 2, 235–37, 254
Beware of the Thief (Matt 24:43–44; Luke 12:39–40) 67 n. 24, 68 n. 25, 114, 116, 123, 125
Budding Fig Tree (Matt 24:32–33; Mark 13:28–29; Luke 21:29–31) 24
Children in the Market Place (Matt 11:16–19; Luke 7:31–35) 32 n. 6
Corpse and Vultures (Matt 24:28; Luke 17:37) 114, 115, 122, 125
Doorkeeper (Mark 13:34–37) 231–32, 254
Dragnet (Matt 13:47–50) 114, 115, 118 n. 46, 122, 125, 240–41
Faithful and Unfaithful Slaves (Matt 24:45–51; Luke 12:42–46) 114, 117, 118 n. 46, 124–25, 126, 129, 138, 139, 244, 247–48
Fowl and the Flowers (Matt 6:26–30; Luke 12:24–28) 45
God or Mammon (Matt 6:24; Luke 16:13) 32 n. 6, 57, 59–60, 244
Good Samaritan (Luke 10:25–37) 10, 67–68 n. 24, 114, 116, 118–19, 121, 123, 126, 216, 232–35, 242, 254
Great Banquet (Luke 14:15–24) 114, 116 n. 42, 120

Kingdom Divided (Matt 12:22–28; Mark 3:22–26; Luke 11:14–20) 114, 115–16, 122, 125
Leaven (Matt 13:33; Luke 13:20–21) 3, 21 n. 56, 75, 76, 77, 82–102, 175, 200, 217, 245–46
Lost Coin (Luke 15:8–10) 3, 64–79, 244–45
Lost Sheep (Matt 18:12–14; Luke 15:4–7) 32 n. 6, 34 n. 13, 65, 75–79, 245
Mustard Seed (Matt 13:31–32; Mark 4:30–32; Luke 13:18–19) 2, 11–26, 45, 75, 76, 94, 175, 243
Opponent at Law (Matt 5:25–26; Luke 12:58–59) 58, 114, 115, 123, 125
Pearl of Great Price (Matt 13:45–46) 240–41
Pearls to Swine (Matt 7:6) 114, 115, 122
Persistent Widow (Luke 18:1–8) 3–4, 114, 116, 123, 125, 150–167, 248–50
Pharisee and the Tax Collector (Luke 18:9–14) 114, 115, 122
Plants Rooted Up (Matt 15:13) 114, 115, 122, 124, 125
Pounds / Minas (Luke 19:11–27) 52, 58, 114, 115, 117–18, 123–24, 125, 133 n. 16
Prodigal Son (Luke 15:11–32) 133 n. 16, 174, 242
Rich Fool (Luke 12:16–21) 59, 244

Salt (Matt 5:13; [Mark 9:49–50]; Luke 14:34–35) 24, 45, 114, 115, 122, 125, 179, 200, 217, 225–26, 253–54
Seed Growing Secretly (Mark 4:26–29) 14, 21, 24, 92, 94, 100
Sower (Matt 13:3–23; Mark 4:3–20; Luke 8:5–15) 1, 4, 14, 21, 26, 33 n. 7, 172, 183–91, 216, 250–52
Strong Man (Matt 12:29; Mark 3:27; Luke 11:21–22) 114, 116, 122
Talents (Matt 25:14–30) 52, 58, 114, 115, 117–18, 118 n. 46, 120, 123–24, 125, 129, 133 n. 19, 138–39, 247–48
Treasure in the Field (Matt 13:44) 240–41
Treasure Old and New (Matt 13:52) 1, 4, 240–41
Tree Known by its Fruit (Matt 7:16–20; Luke 6:43–45) 20 n. 52, 39–40, 114, 115, 122, 243
Two Builders (Matt 7:24–27; Luke 6:47–49) 32 n. 6, 114, 115, 122, 125
Two Debtors (Luke 7:41–43) 59, 244
Two Slaves (Luke 12:47–48) 114, 114 n. 38, 117, 119, 122, 125
Two Women Grinding (Matt 24:41; Luke 17:34) 75, 76, 87, 97
Unforgiving Slave (Matt 18:23–35) 58, 114, 116, 122, 124, 125, 126, 129, 135–36, 137, 138, 139, 145, 145 n. 69, 146, 244, 247–48

Unjust Steward (Luke 16:1–13) 55, 111 n. 21, 133 n. 16, 135, 177
Wedding Banquet (Matt 22:1–14) 114, 116, 116 n. 42, 118 n. 46, 120, 124, 125, 129, 137, 139, 145, 146, 247–48
Wheat and the Weeds (Matt 13:24–30, 36–43) 114, 115, 118 n. 46, 123–24, 125, 129, 133 n. 19, 134–35, 136, 139, 145 n. 69, 244, 247–48
Wicked Tenants (Matt 21:33–46; Mark 12:1–12; Luke 20:9–19) 3, 10, 24, 33 n. 7, 51, 55, 114, 116, 120–21, 124, 126, 129, 133 n. 16, 136–37, 139, 244, 247–48
Workers for the Harvest (Matt 9:37–38; Luke 10:2) 32 n. 6, 38, 40–44, 243
Workers in the Vineyard (Matt 20:1–16) 4, 56, 67–8 n. 24, 177, 195–218, 252–53

Parables of John the Baptist
Ax at the Root (Matt 3:10; Luke 3:9) 36–38, 40, 243
Coming One and the Threshing Floor (Matt 3:12; Luke 3:16–17) 36–38, 121 n. 59, 243

Parables from the Gospel of Thomas
Empty Jar (Gos. Thom. 97) 237–38
Assassin (Gos. Thom. 98) 246–47

Index of Sources

Hebrew Bible/Old Testament

Genesis
1–3	190
2:19	15
3:18	190
18	98
18:6	94, 98–99
18:7	98
18:8	99
19:3	98
38	160, 165
40:16–19	190

Exodus
10:16	153
12:15	90
21:1–6	132
21:7–11	111
21:20–21	111
22:2	136
23:15	90
23:39	246

Leviticus
7:11–14	246
7:13–14	246
19:19	16
23:17	246
25	53
25:39	136
25:39–55	132

Deuteronomy
8:9–10	190
15	58
15:4	208
15:4–5	208
15:7–8	208
15:11	208
15:12–18	132
16:3–4	90
22:10	16
28:26	190

Joshua
6:24	120
8:19	120
11:9–13	120
16:10	120

Judges
5:26	121
6:19	98
9:53	121

Ruth
2–4	165
3	160

1 Samuel
1:24	98
8:13	89
12:17	43

2 Samuel
3:3	160
11	160
12:1–7	205
14	165
14:5	160

1 Kings
14:11	190
16:3–4	190
16:4	190
17	160
21	200, 205
21:19	200
21:24	190
28:24	100

2 Kings
4:1	136
7:1	86
7:16	86
21	253

Nehemiah
5:3–5	136

Job
4:8	18
32:14	213

Psalms
14:4 LXX	153
21:23	153
24:1	217
24:12	153
32:18	153
67:5	153
79:2	190
89:29	179
89:39	179
103:12 LXX	15
118:22	121
145:9	153

Proverbs
1:7	153
22:8	18
26:1	43
29:19	111

Isaiah
3:14	205
5:1–7	205
5:1–8	253
5:6–7	190

Isaiah (cont.)		4:14 (Theo)	19	*2 Maccabees*	
5:7	205	4:18 LXX	19	5:12	118
5:8	200, 205	4:18–19 LXX	19, 25	5:24	118
5:22	200	4:21	15	6:9	118
5:24	37	4:21–22 (Theo)	19	8:24	118
6:9	1			10:17	118
7:23–25	190	*Hosea*		10:31	118
10:16–17	36	7:4	89	10:37	118
18:5	43	10:8	190	12:26	118
27:2–6	205				
27:12	43	*Joel*		*2 Esdras*	
34:9–10	37	4:13	43	8:38–41	184
47:14	37			8:43–44	184
50:1	136	*Amos*			
55:10	191	2:6	136	*4 Maccabees*	
55:11–12	191	4:5	246	14:11–17:6	165
55:13	191	5:6	37		
61	59			PSEUDEPIGRAPHA	
66:24	36–37	*Obadiah*		*2 Baruch*	
		18	37	36	19
Jeremiah				39–40	19
4:4	37	*Micah*		70:2	43, 184
7:11	119	4:12	43		
7:18	97			*3 Baruch*	
7:20	37	*Nahum*		16	117
12:10	205	1:6	36		
17:27	37	1:10	37	*1 Enoch*	
21:12	37			10:6	36
31:28	15	*Zephaniah*		54:1–2	36
37:21	89	1:18	36	90:24–25	36
				90:30	23
Ezekiel		*Zechariah*		90:30–33	19
17	19, 25	2:14–15	15	90:33	23
17:1–24	19, 25	8:3	15	90:37	23
17:22–23	19	11:4–6	118	100:9	36
17:22–24	19, 25			102:1	36
17:23	19	*Malachi*			
31	25	3:2–3	37	*4 Ezra*	186
31:1–18	19, 25	3:19	37	4:28–32	43
31:6	15, 19, 25	4:1	36	7:36–38	36
34:2–10	204				
		DEUTEROCANONICAL		*Jubilees*	
Daniel		WORKS		9:15	36
4	25	*Judith*	160, 165	36:10	36
4:1–34	19				
4:7–9 LXX	19, 25	*Sirach*		*Psalms of Solomon*	
4:10–12 (Theo)	19	7:3	18	15:4–5	36
4:11 LXX	19, 25	35:12–29	164	15:6–7	36
4:12	15	35:14–18	153	15:10–15	36

Index of Sources

DEAD SEA SCROLLS AND RELATED TEXTS

CD (Damascus Document)
XI, 12   142, 144

1QH (Hodayot)
III, 29–34   36
XIV, 14–16   19
XIV, 15–17   18
XVI, 4–9   19, 25
XVI, 4–12   18
XVI, 5–6   18
XVI, 9   18
XVI, 10–11   18

1QpHab (Pesher Habakkuk)
X, 5   36
X, 13   36

1QS (Rule of the Community)
II, 8   36

11QT (Temple Scroll)
XXIX, 8–10   15

11Q13 (Melch)   59

KhQ1   142

OTHER ANCIENT JEWISH WORKS

Josephus
Antiquitates judaicae
3.193   67
3.282   59
8.31   117
9.86   95
10.81   153
12.175–177   136
14.203   51
15.5–6   137
15.289   113
16.197   140
17.11.4   136
17.204–218   215
17.206–218   108
17.270–273   108
17.271–272   215
17.271–273   108
17.273–277   108
17.278–285   108
17.288–295   215
17.289   108
17.295   108
17.297   108
17.306   53
18.1–10   215
18.3–6   109
18.6   141
18.21   142
18.55–59   109
18.60–62   109
18.85–87   108
18.274   52–53
18.312   67
19.335–336   54
20.9   113
20.26–28   56
20.102   109
20.108   109
20.118–136   109
20.179–181   143
20.181   112
20.211–212   54
20.251   132

Bellum judaicum
1.88   106
1.97   106
1.131–154   107
1.204   107
1.304–313   107
1.484   140
1.485   113
1.527–529   113
1.584–586   113
1.590–599   113
1.648–655   107
1.659–666   107
2.4–13   108, 215
2.55   108
2.56   108, 215
2.57–59   108
2.60–65   108
2.68   108
2.68–75   215
2.75   108
2.76   108
2.95   51
2.117–18   215
2.118   109
2.152–153   113
2.168   51
2.169–174   109
2.175–177   109
2.224   109
2.232–246   109
2.287   51, 57
2.292   51, 54, 57
2.405   51, 54
2.407   54
2.427   52, 60
2.428   52
2.433   109, 215
2.590–593   72
3.10.10   140
4.508   60
5.427   86
7.54–62   52
7.61   52, 56
7.253   109

Vita
16   56
17   52
17–23   56
28   52
63   51
69   51, 54
71   52
75–76   72
77   56
78   55–56
80   51
99   52, 54
105   56
119   52
143   52, 54
153   54
204   51, 56
206   56
259   51, 56
296   51, 54
346–348   56
375   52, 54

Index of Sources

Philo	13:18–21	21, 75–76	12:50	208
De confusione linguarum	13:20–21	77	13	19, 240
152	18	14:26–27	75	13:3–9	33, 216
	14:27	60	13:18–23	216
Quod omnis probus liber	14:34–35	45	13:24	134
sit	15:4–5a	32	13:24–30	52, 114,
79	142	15:4–10	75–76		129, 134,
	15:6	78		244, 247
ANCIENT NEAR	15:7	32	13:27	134
EASTERN WORKS	15:8	78	13:30	115, 135
Epic of Erra	15:8–10	68, 75	13:31	14, 17,
1:57	90	15:9	78		25, 175
	16:13	32	13:31–32	11–13, 15,
NEW TESTAMENT	17:5–6	22		23, 25,
"Q"	11, 31–36,	17:27	75–76		175
	45	17:34–35	75–76	13:32	15–16
3:7–9	36	17:37	40	13:33	82, 175,
3:9	36, 40,	19:13	52		245–46
	241, 243	19:23	52	13:36–43	114, 135
3:16f.	36			13:42	118
3:17	36–37,	Matthew		13:47–50	114
	241, 243	3:9	37	13:50	115, 118
6:43–44	39–40,	3:12	121	13:52	1, 240–42
	243	5–7	157, 159	13:52c	240
6:43–45	40	5:13	114, 179	13:44	240
6:44	40	5:13–16	225, 253	13:45	240
6:45	40	5:25–26	114–15	13:47–48	240
6:47–49	32	5:26	215	13:49–50	240
7:8	241	6:2–4	215	14:15	215
7:18–23	38	6:19–21	145	15:13	114–15,
7:18–35	36	6:24	145, 215		124
7:31–35	32	6:26	25	17:20	22
7:34	58	6:34	20	17:24	215
9:58	15	7:6	114–15	17:27	51, 215
10:2	32, 38,	7:16–20	114	18:6	22, 87
	40, 42,	7:17–18	135	18:10	22
	243	7:20	115	18:15–16	109
10:3	38, 42	7:24–27	114	18:23–24	51, 244
11:11	58	7:27	115	18:23–25	215
11:31–32	75–76	8	132	18:23–33	64
11:42–43	58	8:9	140	18:23–34	129, 135,
12:6	58	8:12	118		213, 247
12:24	45	8:20	15, 25	18:23–35	114, 122,
12:24–28	75–76	8:21	213		215
12:27–28	45	10:29	215	18:25	122
12:42	51, 244	12:22–28	114	18:28	122
12:51–53	75–76	12:25	116	18:30	122
12:59	58	12:29	114, 116	18:34	122, 136,
13:18–19	21, 45, 77	12:34	40		248

Index of Sources

18:35	248	20:15	198, 201,	24:51	118, 248
19:8	213		252	25:14–30	114, 215,
19:16	200, 217	20:15a	201, 210		247
19:16–22	200	20:15b	201, 217	25:15	248
19:16–30	200, 217	20:16	217	25:24	115
19:16–20:16	200	20:16b	210	25:29	115, 217
19:17	200–201	20:21	216	25:30	118, 248
19:17–30	200	21:12	215	26:7–9	215
19:20	200–201,	21:13	119	26:14	215
	217	21:32	137	26:50	201
19:21	200	21:33–39	129, 136,	26:51	132, 140
19:23–24	145		247	26:55	119
19:25	200, 217	21:33–46	33, 114,	26:69	140
19:27	200,		120	26:69–71	133
	216–17	21:34	137	27:3–10	215
19:28	217	21:34–36	248	27:28	119
19:29	217	21:37	153	27:31	119
19:30	217	21:41	124	27:38	119
20:1	202	21:44	121	27:44	119
20:1–3	52, 244	22:1–14	114, 129,	28:12–15	215
20:1–15	64, 195–		137, 247		
	96, 198,	22:2	137	*Mark*	
	200–201,	22:3	137	1:10	15
	203, 210,	22:4	137	1:15	22
	212–13,	22:6	120, 137,	2:2	251
	216, 252		248	2:14	51
20:1–16	177	22:7	137	2:14–15	54
20:1a	205	22:12	201	2:15–16	58
20:1b–15	209	22:13	118, 120,	3:6	184
20:2	41, 199,		137	3:22–26	114
	207, 213	22:14	115	3:24–26	116
20:4	199	22:14–22	215	3:27	114, 116
20:6–7	199	22:15–22	213, 216	4	1, 19, 21,
20:8	141, 196,	22:17b	216		24
	199, 202,	22:19	216	4:2–3	1, 240–41
	209, 212–	23:34	240	4:3–9	14, 21,
	13, 252	24:14–30	129, 138		33, 172,
20:8a	205	24:15	138		183–84,
20:9	209, 211,	24:19	138		250
	213, 216	24:21	138	4:7	187
20:9–10	199	24:24	139	4:11–12	241
20:10	211, 213	24:28	114–15	4:13	5, 184
20:13	213	24:30	139	4:13–20	21, 26,
20:13–15	201	24:41	87		186, 241
20:13b	207	24:43–44	114, 116	4:14–20	184, 192,
20:14	201	24:45–51	114, 129,		251
20:14a	217		138, 247	4:26–29	14, 21, 92
20:14b	201	24:48	138	4:27	93
		24:49	117	4:28	14

Mark (cont.)		14:3	59	11:21–22	114, 116
4:30	21	14:47	132, 140	12:13–21	59, 205, 244
4:30–32	11–14, 17–18, 21, 23–24, 175	14:48	119		
		14:66–69	133, 140	12:16–20	52, 244
		15:6–7	109	12:17	152
		15:20	119	12:35–38	133
4:30–33	20	15:27	109, 119	12:39–40	114, 116
4:31	13	15:43	22	12:42–46	114, 117
4:32	13–15			12:42–48	133
4:33	251	Luke		12:45	117
4:33–34	241	3:3–14	217	12:47–48	114, 117
5:13	213	3:8	37	12:58–59	114–15
6:5–6	184	3:21	77	12:59	115
6:41	15	4	59	13	19
7:34	15	5:1	251	13:1	109
8:15	246	5:15	251	13:6–9	114, 129, 235, 254
9:1	22	6:1–13	252		
9:42	21–22	6:24	227	13:9	115
9:47	23	6:30–31	187	13:10–17	229
9:49–50	24, 114	6:35–36	187	13:15	153
10:4	213	6:43–45	114	13:18	14
10:14–15	22	6:45	40	13:18–19	11–13, 21, 175
10:23–25	23	6:47–49	114		
10:45	181	6:49	115	13:18–21	21
11:13	24	7	59, 132	13:19	15–16, 175
11:15	52	7:2–10	140		
11:17	119	7:36–50	244	13:20–21	175
11:20–21	24, 26	7:40–44	244	13:21	245
11:25	15	8:3	132, 141, 213	13:26	153
12	24			13:28	118
12:1–8	133	8:5	25, 251	13:32	179
12:1–9	51–52, 244	8:5–8	33	14	120
		8:11	251	14:12–24	114
12:1–11	55	8:32	213	14:16–24	133
12:1–12	10, 24, 33, 114, 120	9:58	15, 25	14:34–35	114
		9:59	213	15:4–6	64
		9:61	213	15:4–7	75
12:6	153	10:2	42, 153	15:8–9	244
12:17	51	10:22	153	15:9	78
12:20–23	241	10:25–37	232, 254	15:11–32	133
12:25	15	10:27	153	15:17	152
12:38	58	10:30	118	15:23	98
12:41–44	228	10:30–35	114, 216	16	55
13:25	15	10:34	119	16:1–7	59
13:27	15	10:35	153	16:1–8	177
13:28	24	10:36	216	16:1–8a	133, 135
13:31	15	10:37	216	16:1–17	244
13:32	15	11:14–20	114	16:3	133, 152
13:33–37	231, 254	11:17	116	16:5–7	52

Index of Sources

16:13	59	*John*		*2 Thessalonians*			
16:19–31	205	4:51	140	3:14	153		
17:5–6	22	10	118				
17:7–10	140	10:1	118–19	*1 Timothy*			
17:20	152	10:8	119	2:12	213		
17:22	152	18:10	140	5	160		
17:35	87	18:10–11	133	5:3–16	164, 250		
17:37	114–15, 152	18:16	140	5:5	250		
		18:16–26	133				
18:1	151, 156, 162	18:18	140	*Titus*			
		18:26	140	2:8	153		
18:1–8	114, 150–51, 205	18:39–40	109				
		18:40	119	*Hebrews*			
18:2	152–53	19:18	109	6:3	213		
18:2–5	152	19:38	213				
18:3	152, 157, 249			RABBINIC WORKS			
		Acts of the Apostles		*m. Baba Batra*			
18:4	152	2:26	15	2:1	88		
18:4–5	152	5:37	109	3:5	88		
18:5	157, 249	7:54–60	113				
18:6	153, 249	12	54	*m. Baba Meṣiʿa*			
18:6–7	249	12:20	52	9	52, 55		
18:6–8	156, 162	14:19	111				
18:7	250	16	119	*m. Demai*			
18:9–14	114	21:39	213	2:4	89		
18:11	115	21:40	213	5:1	89		
18:13	54	26:1	213	5:3–4	89		
19:2	54	27:31	213				
19:12–27	114, 133	28:16	213	*m. Giṭṭin*			
19:21	115			5:3	153		
19:27	118	*Romans*					
19:46	119	14:2	16	*m. Hallah*			
20:9–15	133				86		
20:9–18	33	*1 Corinthians*		1:7	91		
20:9–19	114, 120	3:6	102				
20:18	121	4:4	153	*m. Kelim*			
22:31	87	5:8	246	12:7	67		
22:50	140	9:27	116	15:1	97		
22:51	132	14:34	213	15:2	88, 97		
22:52	119	16:7	213	15:3	87		
22:55	133			24:3	97		
22:56	140	*2 Corinthians*		25:7	97		
23:18–19	109	9:6	18, 20				
23:32	119	11	111, 118	*m. Ketubbot*			
23:32–33	109	11:26	119	4:12	153		
23:33	119			5:5	87		
23:39	119	*Galatians*		5:8	86		
		4:2	213	11:1–6	153		
		6:7	20	12:3–4	153		

m. Kil'ayim		*t. Baba Meṣi'a*		96	88, 93, 96, 175, 245
1:2	16	9:14	55		
3:2	17				
		t. Kil'ayim		97	93, 237, 254
m. Ma'aśer Šeni		2:8	17		
5:2	92			98	247
		t. Menaḥot			
m. Makširin		13:21	112, 143	CHURCH FATHERS	
2:8	89			Augustine	
		t. Niddah		*Letters*	155, 164
m. Menaḥot			97		
7:1	95			Cyril of Alexandria	
		t. Pesaḥim		*Commentary on Luke*	
m. Nazir		2:14	91		155, 164
1:5	17				
		b. Berakot		Ephrem the Syrian	
m. Niddah		31a	17	*Commentary on Tatian's Diatessaron*	156
5:2	17				
		b. Pesaḥim			
m. 'Ohalot		45b11	91	Hermas	
5:4	96			*Similitudes*	241
		y. Berakot			
m. Parah		5:1	17	Irenaeus	
5:9	97	5:8d	17	*Adversus haereses*	
				4.36.7	212
m. Pesaḥim		*y. Ma'aśerot*			
3:3	92	5:2 56a17	92	John Chrysostom	
3:4	92, 97			*De diabolo tentatore*	
3:5	91	*y. Pe'ah*			155
		7:4	17		
m. Sanhedrin		7:20b	17	Martyrius	
6	121			*Book of Perfection*	156, 159
7:2	113	*tg. Ezekiel*			
7:2b	113	17:22–23	19–20		
				Origen	
m. Šebu'ot		*Midrash on Psalms*		*On Prayer*	155–56
5:9	97	104:10	23		
				GRECO-ROMAN LITERATURE	
m. Šeqalim		EARLY CHRISTIAN WRITINGS		Apuleius	
1:3	51			*Metamorphoses*	
		Nag Hammadi Texts		9.11–12	87
m. Soṭah		*Gospel of Philip*			
33	59	45	87		
				Aristophanes	
m. Terumot		*Gospel of Thomas*		*Plutus*	
10:2	91	20	11, 13, 175, 243	436b	70
m. Tohorot		64	120	Aristotle	
7:4	97	65	51–52, 55, 244	*Politica* 1.4	131

Index of Sources

Aristotle
Rhetorica
1406b10   18

Athenaeus
Deipnosophistae
3.108–116   86

Cassius Dio
61.9.3   116

Cato
De agricultura
74   85

Codex Theodosianus
5.10.1   131

Columella
De re rustica
11.3   17

Demetrius
De elocutione
161   83

Digesta
48.18   112

Dionysius of Halicarnassus
Antiquitates romanae
10.10.7   153

Epiphanius
On Weights and Measures
            95

Galen
De alimentorum facultatibus
1.78–79   86

Geoponica
2.33   91

Juvenal
6.242–245   250
6.475–495   111

Petronius
Satyricon
49.6   122

Plato
Phaedrus
260d   18

Pliny the Elder
Naturalis historia
18.27–29   86
18.68   90
18.102   96
18.102–104 91
18.104   91
18.171   16
19.170–171 17
20.236   17
20.237–240 17

Pliny the Younger
Epistulae
9.20.2   211

Plutarch
Lycurgus 53

Moralia
2:182a   18
2:394e   18

Pyrrhus
24   117

Solon   53

Pseudo-Virgil
Moretum
            84, 87–88,
            90, 97,
            99–100,
            245
16–49   84–55

Sallust
Bellum catilinae
21   60

Seneca
Epistulae morales
90.23   85

Tacitus
Annales
2.42   51

Historiae
5.9.2   108

Theophrastus
De causis plantarum
4.13.6   43

Historia plantarum
VII 1:1   17

PAPYRI AND INSCRIPTIONS
BGU
13.2306   73
13.2307   73
13.2309   73
16.2602   41

C.Pap.Gr.
1.9   73
1.13   73
1.24   73

Chr.Wilck.
300.1–4   73

O.Berenike
1.4   73
1.26   73
1.28   73
1.87   73

O.Mich.
1.55   73
2.772   73
2.774   73
2.775   73

P.Bad.
2.35   68
4.48   68

P.Berl.Dem.		
3142	68	

P.Brem.		
63	68	

P.Cair.Zen.		
1.59028	69	
1.59049.3–4	42	
4.59704.30	74	
4.59748	69	

P.Col.		
3.21	71	
4.66	69	

P.Col.Zen.		
1.21.4	71	

P.Corn		
1	69	
48	69	

P.Fay.		
101 v.1.9	72	

P.Flor.		
3.332	68	

P.Lond.		
1.131	69	

P.Mert.		
2.83	68	

P.Mich.		
1.26	69	
1.74	69	
2.121	69	
2.123	74	
2.127	74	
2.128.24	74	

5.321	73	
5.322a	73	
5.355	69	
5.355dupl	74	
8.503	69	
11.618	41	

P.Mil.Vogl.		
2.77	69	

P.Oslo		
2.22	163	

P.Oxy.		
1.114	68	
4.736.15	72	
4.739.11	72	
4.739.16	72	
4.819.15	72	
6.932	68	
10.1272	69	
14.1680	69	

P.Petr.		
3.137	72	
3.137.1.4	72	
3.137.1.9	72	
3.137.1.16	72	
3.137.1.21	72	
3.137.2.10	72	
3.137.2.16	72	

P.Rev.		
40.9–20	71	
40.12	71	
40.13	71	
40.15	71	
40.15–16	71	
44–46	73	
53.15	71	
53.20	71	

P.Ryl.		
2.178	73	

P.Soter.		
4.24–28	37	

P.Strass.		
9.872.7–9	37	

P.Tebt.		
2.389	68	
3.1	69	
3.703.174–12	73	
3.885	72	
3.891	72	

P.Yadin		
15	163	

PSI		
IV 531.8	71	
VI 345	42	

SB		
3.6796	69, 74	
12.11125	69	
16.12326	69	
24.16067	72	

UPZ		
2.158	72	

Index of Authors

Aharoni, Miriam 132, 140
Aharoni, Yohanan 132, 140
Albright, W. F. 38
Allison, Dale C. 37–38, 60
Altes, Liesbeth Korthals 152
Amjad-Ali, Christine 206
Ammerman, Nancy T. 161
Amouretti, Marie-Claire 86
Andrejevs, Olegs 33
Andringa, Els 161
Archer, David 197
Armenti, Joseph 56
Arnal, William E. 75, 77
Aviam, Mordechai 49
Avigad, Nahman 143–44
Avitsur, S. 89

Baadsgaard, Aubrey 97
Bailey, Kenneth E. 78, 170, 182, 199–200, 212–13, 252
Bailey, Mark L. 251
Bakhtin, Mikhail 166
Bakker, Jan Theo 88–89
Baldwin, Barry 122
Bammel, Ernst 36
Barthes, Roland G. 7
Batten, Alicia 42, 75
Bauckham, Richard 120
Bazzana, Giovanni B. 41, 67
Beavis, Mary Ann 111, 129, 134, 151, 157, 162, 241, 244, 247
Bergemann, Thomas 34
Berger, Klaus 95
Bietenhard, H. 134–35
Billerbeck, Paul 16
Bishop, E. F. F. 67
Blomberg, Craig L. 14, 21, 23, 65–66, 133, 138, 199, 201, 246, 251
Blümner, H. 86–88, 96
Bock, Darrell L. 38

Bottéro, J. 87, 89–90
Boucher, Madeleine I. 65–66, 173
Bovon, François 16, 26, 151–52, 156, 158–59
Bradley, Keith R. 112, 131, 141
Brooten, Bernadette J. 161
Broshi, Magen 86, 95, 132
Brown, Peter 54
Brunt, Peter A. 112, 214
Bultmann, Rudolf 75
Buntfuß, Markus 9
Burke, Kenneth 182
Burkitt, F. Crawford 33

Camara, Susana 238
Cameron, Ron 36
Carlston, Charles E. 11
Carter, Warren 25, 106, 201, 208
Catchpole, David R. 41, 76
Chambers, Robert 197
Chancey, Mark 56
Charette, Blaine 38
Chrzanowska–Kluczewska, F. Elżbieta 181–82
Clarke, David D. 181
Cobb, C. 166
Cohen, Shaye J. D. 56
Cohick, Lynn H. 163
Collins, Adela Y. 25–26
Cotter (SJ), Wendy J. 23
Cottingham, Sara 197
Cotton, Hannah M. 163
Cousland, J. Robert C. 3, 124, 245–46
Cross, Frank Moore 142
Crossan, John Dominic 2, 10, 65, 75, 77, 129, 134, 173, 176–77, 184–85, 222–23, 238, 242
Culbertson, Philip L. 205
Curkpatrick, Stephen 151, 153

Dahl, Nils A. 21
Dalman, Gustav 16–17, 87–88, 91, 95–96
Dannhauer, Johann C. 6
Davies, W. D. 38
Dean, James Elmer 95
Derrenbacker, Robert A. 35
Dobbeler, Stephanie von 38
Dodd, C. H. 64–66, 94, 151, 171–73, 177–78, 184, 188
Dolby-Stahl, Sandra K. 31–32
Donahue, John R. 54, 153
Doudna, Greg 142
Drake, Lyndon 58
Draper, Jonathan 41
Dronsch, Kristina 186–92, 250–51
Duncan-Jones, R. P. 95
Dunn, James D. G. 37

Eco, Umberto 7
Eder, Jens 42
Ehrman, Bart 60
Elliott, John H. 50
Erdkamp, Paul 214
Eshel, Esther 142
Etchells, Ruth 173, 179, 182
Evans, Craig A. 33
Eve, Eric 33

Feldman, Louis H. 56, 140
Fiensy, David A. 49–50, 54, 132, 135, 214
Finley, Moses I. 51–52
Fitzgerald, William 84
Fitzmyer, Joseph A. 75, 156–58
Fleddermann, Harry T. 32, 36, 39, 44, 75
Forbes Royle, John 16
Forbes, Clarence A. 143
Ford, Richard Q. 201, 204, 209
Forsyth, Mark 180
France, Richard T. 37, 205, 212–14
Freire, Paolo 4, 177, 196–97, 252
Freyne, Seán 42, 106, 215
Fritz, Gerd 9
Funk, Robert W. 24–25, 98, 173, 177, 222–23, 227, 234–35, 238, 241, 247

Gäbel, Georg 16, 18
Gadamer, Hans-Georg 7
Garnsey, Peter 130, 214
Gathercole, Simon 82, 93

Geeraerts, Dirk 9
Gemünden, Petra von 18
Gerhardsson, Birger 202–203, 252
Geva, Hillel 143–44
Gibbs, John G. 140
Glancy, Jennifer A. 111, 134, 136, 248
Goebel, Siegfried 198, 200, 212
Goede, Hendrick 129–30
Goodacre, Mark 82
Goodman, Martin 49
Goud, Thomas E. 3, 246–47
Goulder, Michael D. 75
Green, Joel B. 38, 117, 204
Greenfield, Jonas C. 163
Grenfell, B. P. 71
Gundry, R. H. 241

Habbe, Joachim 42
Hachlili, Rachel 141
Häfner, Gerd 36
Hagner, Donald 134
Häkkinen, Sakari 227–28, 233, 237–38
Hamel, Gildas 55, 214
Hanson, K. C. 135
Harl, Kenneth 138
Harrill, J. A. 131
Harrington, Daniel 134
Harrison, John P. 3, 129, 133, 247–48
Hart, H. 214
Hartvigsen, Kirsten Marie 161
Hawkes, Terence 189
Hayden, B. 70–73
Hays, Richard 183
Hearon, Holly 246
Hedrick, Charles W. 5, 133, 176–77, 179, 184–89, 250–51
Heininger, Bernhard 173
Heinrich, F. 88, 91
Hepper, Frank N. 16–17
Herzog, William R., II 2, 4, 177–78, 181–82, 188, 196, 198, 201, 205, 209–10, 214–15, 252
Hezser, Catherine 59, 111–12, 141
Hirschfeld, Yizhar 89
Hoffmann, Paul 32, 38, 43, 50
hooks, bell 228, 238
Hope, Anne 197
Horsley, Richard A. 41, 105–106, 132, 172, 192, 214
Hudson, Michael 53, 57, 59

Huffman, Norman A. 83
Hultgren, Arland J. 64–67, 75, 78, 83, 203, 252

Ilan, Tal 250
Isaac, Benjamin 163
Isasi-Díaz, Ada Maria 210–11
Iser, Wolfgang 7, 204

Jackson, Glenna S. 4, 228–29, 232–33, 236, 238, 252–54
Jakobson, Roman 179
Jameson, Frederic 177–78, 181
Janowski, Bernd 15
Jasny, Naum 86–87, 89
Jastrow, M. 90
Jensen, Morten Hørning 132
Jeremias, Joachim 17, 43, 67, 83, 94, 177, 184–85, 200, 212
Johnson, Luke Timothy 150, 156–59, 164
Jones, Ivor H. 11
Jones, Peter R. 23
Jülicher, Adolf 8, 16, 83, 94, 96, 100, 171, 173–74, 177–78, 184, 188, 200

Kartzow, Marianne Bjelland 153
Keen, Suzanne 161
Kellermann, D. 90
Kenney, A. J. 84
Kerr, A. J. 135
Kirk, Alan K. 21, 39, 75
Kistemaker, Simon J. 67
Kjærgaard, Mogens Stiller 173, 175
Kloppenborg, John S. 2, 32, 34, 36–38, 41–42, 50, 55, 58–60, 64–65, 67–68, 75–76, 106, 121, 129, 135, 214, 252
Koester, Helmut 76
Kogler, Franz 11, 16, 95, 100
Krauss, S. 87–88, 90–91, 97
Kuss, Otto 23

Labahn, Michael 40
Lachmann, Renate 34
Lambrecht, Jan 76
Lanier, Gregory R. 121
Lapin, Hayim 58
Laufen, Rudolf 11, 44
Lebacqz, Karen 206–207
Levey, Samson H. 20

Levine, Amy-Jill 26, 66–67, 153, 155–56, 158–60, 164, 200, 208, 213, 249, 252
Liebenberg, Jacobus 25
Lied, Liv Ingeborg 154
Lim, Timothy 246
Lischer, Richard 21
Loba-Mkole, Jean-Claude 213
Lodge, David 179
Loisy, Alfred F. 76
Lührmann, Dieter 44
Lundhaug, Hugo 154
Luther, Martin 155–57, 159, 164
Luther, Susanne 6
Luz, Ulrich 199, 201, 205

Mahaffy, J. P. 71
Maier, Harry O. 131
Malina, Bruce J. 50
Mann, C. S. 38
Manson, Thomas W. 23, 38, 75
Marcus, Joel 23
Maresch, K. 70
Marshall, Anthony J. 250
Marshall, I. Howard 38–39, 41–43
Martin, Dale B. 134, 140, 161
März, Claus-Peter 38
Mashinini, Meshack Mandla 129
Mason, Steve 108–109
Matthews, Mary W. 158, 160, 164, 249
Mattila, Sharon Lea 88
Mau, August 87
McArthur, Harvey K. 11
McIver, Robert 135
Meier, John P. 11, 83, 133, 235, 247
Meijlink, Bernhard 88
Menahem, R. 213
Merz, Annette 66–67, 158, 160, 165, 249
Meyers, Carol 97
Meyers, Eric M. 56
Moessner, David P. 43
Montefiore, C. G. 76
Monteix, Nicolas 88–89
Morgan, Teresa 151
Moritz, L. A. 87
Morris, Leon 199
Mundell, Robert 54
Mwombeki, Fidon 228–29, 238
Myers, Ched 188

Nadella, Raj 166
Nelavala, Surekha 206
Nerlich, Brigitte 181
Neufeld, Edmund 129
Neville, David J. 120
Nolland, John 37, 134, 199, 212
Nun, Mendel 54

Oakman, Douglas E. 2–3, 49–50, 54–55, 59–60, 69, 135, 191, 215, 244
Oatley, Keith 161
Oldenhage, Tania 10
Ong, Walter J. 189
Ostmeyer, Karl-Heinrich 94, 100

Patterson, Orlando 134, 140
Pestman, P. W. 70
Peters, Donald 251
Peters, Kurtis 97
Phillips, Peter 240, 242
Piper, Ronald A. 39, 60
Plisch, Uwe-Karsten 13, 93, 96
Polag, Athanasius 76
Popkes, Enno Edzard 114

Rahmani, L. Y. 141–43
Rathbone, Dominic W. 214
Reid, Barbara E. 92, 199, 214
Reinertsen, Ellen 3–4, 116, 248–50, 254
Reiser, Marius 38
Rengstorf, K. H. 201
Resseguie, James L. 204
Ricoeur, Paul 7, 83, 173–74, 178
Robinson, James M. 32, 50
Rodd, C. S. 33
Rohrbaugh, Richard 2
Rollins, W. G. 133
Rosenfeld, Ben-Zion 139
Roth, Dieter T. 3, 11, 13–14, 21, 31–32, 35–37, 39–40, 42, 44–45, 75, 77, 241, 243
Ruiz, Jean-Pierre 210–11

Safrai, S. 92
Safrai, Ze'ev 214
Saldarini, Anthony J. 58
Saller, Richard P. 50, 112, 122, 214
Sandy, D. B. 70–71
Scheele, Barbara 158, 249
Schellenberg, Ryan S. 18

Schleiermacher, Friedrich D. E. 6–7
Schmid, Joseph 34, 39
Schneider, Ralf 163
Schnider, Franz 34
Schörle, Katia 89
Schottroff, Luise 1–2, 4, 8, 67, 157–58, 160, 163, 188, 198, 204–205, 209–11, 216, 244–45, 249, 253
Schröter, Jens 33, 43, 75
Schulz, Siegfried 39, 43
Schürer, Emil 54, 56, 214
Schwartz, Joshua 144
Scott, Bernard Brandon 2, 24, 67, 77, 134, 173–78, 184–85, 200, 245, 248
Scott, James C. 53, 60, 197, 204
Segrè, Angelo 95
Seto, Ken-Ichi 181
Sevenich-Bax, Elisabeth 38
Shafer-Elliott, Cynthia 87, 98–99
Shaw, Brent D. 118
Shelley, Carter 158, 160, 249
Sherwood, Yvonne 154
Shillington, V. George 10, 188, 206–207
Shveka, Avi 136
Sim, Youngshin 238
Sjöberg, Birgitta L. 161
Smith, W. C. A. 70
Snodgrass, Klyne R. 19–20, 23, 35, 65, 67, 83, 98, 117, 133, 135, 199, 203–205, 252
Sparavigna, Amelia Carolina 54
Sparn, Walter 6
Sperber, Daniel 95–96
Starnitzke, Dierk 39–40
Steier, August 17
Stern, David 162
Stern, M. 92
Sternberg, Meir 204
Stewart, Douglas 136
Storie, Deborah R. 4, 197, 199, 252–54
Strack, Hermann L. 16
Strange, James Riley 49
Straus, Erwin 10
Strong, Justin D. 151–52, 162
Syon, Danny 54, 57

Takagi, Senji 201, 203, 206–208, 214, 252
Talbert, Charles H. 240
Tarr, Del 252

Index of Authors

Temin, Peter 214
Tevel, J. M. 201
Thayer, Joseph H. 213
Thurén, Lauri 8–9
Tilly, Michael 38
Timmel, Sally 197
Tiwald, Markus 43–44
Tolbert, Mary Ann 10, 241, 251
Tov, Emanuel 163
Trumbower, Jeffrey A. 37
Tuckett, Christopher 36, 40, 44
Turner, David 134

Uro, Risto 36

Vaage, Leif E. 60
Valantasis, Richard 37
Van Eck, Ernest 2–4, 20, 24–25, 67–68, 77–78, 126, 129, 133, 170, 178, 182, 187–88, 190–92, 203, 212, 244–46, 250–52
Van Niekerk, R. J. 68
Vearncombe, Erin K. 68–70, 74–76, 78, 211, 245
Venetz, Hermann-Josef 43

Wacholder, Ben Zion 142
Waetjen, Herman 206–207, 214
Weaks, Joseph Allen 33

Weder, Hans 76, 173
Weinrich, Harald 9
Weiser, A. 129
Weissenrieder, Annette 26
West, Gerald 210
Westermann, Claus 173
Westermann, W. L. 131
White, Hayden 182
Wilder, Amos 175, 177
Wilson, Andrew 89
Wire, Antoinette C. 246
Witherington, Ben, III 153, 156, 158–60, 164, 205, 249
Wolter, Michael 32–33, 44
Wright, N. T. 60
Wright, Stephen I. 3–4, 152–53, 162, 173, 180–83, 189, 191–92, 250–51

Yoder Neufeld, Thomas R. 121
Young, Brad H. 251

Zeitlin, Solomon 56
Zimmermann, Ruben 2–3, 5–6, 8–11, 13, 35, 37, 41–43, 64, 114, 133, 171–72, 176, 180, 183, 185–86, 191–92, 227, 232, 234–35, 238, 242–43
Zingg, Paul 23
Zohary, Michael 17
Zwane, Sithembiso 210

Index of Subjects

Abraham and Sarah 98–99
Afghanistan 4, 195–98, 218, 252–54
Africa, 4, 210, 222–38, 252–54
agrarian economy 52
Agrippa I 54, 109, 141, 144
Alexander Jannaeus 106–107
allegory 4, 8, 21, 37, 66, 68, 133, 135, 173–74, 175, 179, 184, 196, 201, 202, 203, 205, 208, 216, 242, 252
ancient coins 57–58, 69, 214
Antiochus IV Epiphanes 106
Antipater 107
Archelaus 107–108
Aristobulus 107
Athrongaeus 108
Augustus 108, 214

Babatha 163, 250
bandits 49, 52, 53, 56, 77, 105, 107–10, 118–19, 123, 126, 216, 246
breadmaking 84–90

Caesaraea Maritima 51, 52, 109
census 214–15
cost of oil in antiquity 69–74
Cumanus 109–10

debt: in antiquity 50–53; and Jesus 57–60; in Roman Galilee 52–60
denarius 213–16
drachma 65–74, 77–78, 244–45

echo–chamber 170–72
"echoing" 4, 170–71, 186, 250
eschatological judgement 18, 20, 36–38, 43, 76, 121, 190; and harvest 43, 179, 243
Essenes 113; and slavery 142
"experiential reading" 4, 225–38

fermentation 90–92
Freirean "codes" 196–98, 252

Gentiles 23, 64, 91, 201

harvest imagery 3, 35, 36, 37–45, 243
heaven 15–16
hermeneutics 2, 5–11, 21, 228
Herod Antipas 54, 55–56
Herod the Great 53, 106, 107, 108, 110, 113, 122, 140–41, 144, 179, 213, 215
historical Jesus 11, 50, 57, 59, 60, 105, 129, 133, 248
hyperbole 82–84, 94, 101
Hyrcanus 107

imperial head tax 214–15
intersectionality 161–65
intertextuality 34–35, 45, 98, 160, 164, 204, 208

Jesus's audience 1–2, 3, 4, 21, 41, 64, 65, 130, 146, 160, 170–72, 174
John the Baptist, 35, 36; parables of, 35, 36–39, 40, 241, 243
Judas the Galilean 108

kingdom of God 13, 93, 100, 102, 176, 243; and Leaven parable 76–77, 100, 102; and Mustard Seed parable 16, 20–25, 76–77; parables as metaphor of 174; and Roman empire 25, 178, 243

leaven 90–92
lord of the harvest 41–44, 244

"Mammon Ethic" 57, 59, 244; Jesus's critique of 59–60, 244
Matthew's audience 130, 133, 138, 139, 145, 146, 248

Index of Subjects

metaphor 2, 3, 4, 8, 9, 10, 16, 17, 18, 20, 23, 24, 25, 26, 35, 36, 64, 65, 68, 115, 117, 121, 171–82, 184–92, 202, 204, 205, 206, 242, 243, 245, 250–51, 254
methodology 7–8, 228
metonymy 4, 179–82
"mirroring" 4, 170–71, 186, 250
mustard seed 13–14, 20, 22
mustard tree 15–18, 20

narrative criticism 182–83
narrative 4, 8, 94–95, 172–73, 182, 188

"Our Father" prayer 59

parables (general): as codes 196, 198, 204, 216, 252; definition of 35, 64, 242; and eschatology 64, 243; genre, 8; history of interpretation 171; interpretation of 6–11; as metaphor 64, 171–80; as metaphor for kingdom of God 174, 176, 184; as metonymy 179–80, 182; as poetic fictions 176–77; as simile 171, 173, 175, 178; as subversive speech 177–78; as synecdoche 179–82; voices of 151–52, 165–66
Passover 90, 91–92, 108, 109
pax Romana 110
Pharisees 58, 152
Pompey 57, 106–107
Pontius Pilate 109
poverty 10, 65–66, 69, 78–79, 94, 112, 143, 145, 159–60, 163–66, 190, 201, 208, 223, 226–29, 232, 242, 245, 249, 253

"Q" 11, 31–36, 45, 75–76; parables in 32–34, 35–41, 45; reconstructions of 32–34
Quirinius 108, 215
Qumran community and slavery 142

realia 82, 84, 93, 99, 101, 126, 142, 145, 180, 196, 206, 211, 216, 243; archeological 130, 139–40, 247; social 64–68, 77, 202, 209; material 2–3, 170, 242, 243

redaction criticism 11
revolts 49, 106–108, 110, 215, 246
Roman Egyptian papyri 67–73
Roman Empire 25, 52, 137; and slavery, 130–31, 140, 248

Sabinus 108
Samaritans 109–10, 234
shepherds 64, 65, 77–78, 204, 245
simile, 64, 171, 173, 175, 178
slaveowners 3, 130, 133–46, 248
slavery 53, 129–40, 247; and Matthean parables 133–39, 144; Qumran community 142; in Roman Empire 130–31, 140, 248; in Roman Palestine 130, 132–35, 139–45, 247; and Torah 132, 136
slaves 111–12, 117, 129–46, 247–48
Son of Man 76, 153
synecdoche 4, 172, 179–92, 250–51

taxation 51, 52, 54, 215
tax collectors 58, 59, 122
tithes 51, 55, 112, 143, 187

Ummidius Quadratus 110
unleavened bread 90

violence: and Jesus 127; in Judaea 106–13; language of 115–18; in parables 105–27

wealth 23, 51, 54, 65, 86, 89, 130–40, 142–46, 163, 165, 187, 198, 200–202, 207–209, 211–12, 217, 226–27, 248–50
widow in Persistent Widow parable 151–53, 157–67
woman in Leaven parable 92–94, 96, 97–99, 245–46
woman in Lost Coin parable 65–69, 74, 78–79

www.ingramcontent.com/pod-product-compliance
Lightning Source LLC
Chambersburg PA
CBHW052216300426
44115CB00011B/1706